AGE.

I.Taylor sculp

MVLSVM

MVREI NVM

CHIVM

PRANIVM

FRIGIDA RIVM

TEPIDA RIVM

CALIDA RIVM

THERMOPOLIVM

CVM MILIARIIS

VASIS

CALE FACIENDI AQVAS

AD VSVM POTVVM

CVM VINO ET FRIGIDA

PALERNV

CECVBVM

Wine
into
Words

A History and Bibliography
of Wine Books
in the English Language

by JAMES M. GABLER

with a foreword by
MAYNARD A. AMERINE

BACCHUS PRESS LTD.

Baltimore

First Edition

Library of Congress Catalog Card Number 84-70446

International Standard Book Number 0-9613525-0-7

Typesetting by Mid-Atlantic Photo Composition, Inc.
2 W. 25th Street, Baltimore, MD 21218

Published and distributed by:

Bacchus Press Ltd.
1421 Jordan Street
Baltimore, MD 21217

Made in the United States of America

TABLE OF CONTENTS

LIST OF ILLUSTRATIONS

FOREWORD

There is far more in print in English about wines than most people, including connoisseurs, realize. To bring this to our attention is the objective of this splendid bibliography. Mr. Gabler has thrown his net far and wide and has found some unexpected treasures. The Alderman Abell entries on a scandal in the Vintners' Company, Cambiare's tirade againt Prohibition, Crahan's bibliography of André Simon (plus on his own, as complete a listing of Simon's publications as we are likely to get), Edmond's 1767 book on making wines from herbs, fruits and flowers, the genesis of Fitzgerald's Rubaiyat of Omar Khayyam, Greig's little-noticed scholarly catalogues, Henderson's 1824 "History" (and his remarks on "blind" tasting), George Husmann's contributions to the Missouri and California wine industries, Jullien's great "The topography . . .", Kohler's contribution to the South African wine industry, Busby's importance to the Australian grape and wine industry, Longworth's contribution to Ohio viticulture, Peeke on American drinking habits, Mendelsohn on Samuel Pepys, Mitchell on Madeira, Ott on monks bathing in vats of crushed grapes, Rafinesque on U.S. grape acreage in 1830, Shand on teetotalism (he was against it), Spooner on the Isabella grape, Thudichum on paleobotany, Tomes on bottle breakage in Champagne in 1746, and Wilson on the absurdity of unfermented wine, to name only a few of the authors. Serendipity indeed.

There are books in English from unexpected places (Italy and Germany) plus, of course, all the English-speaking countries. There are entries about not only brandies, grapes and wines but beer, cordials, corkscrews, bottles, glasses, labels, gauging, distilling, health, taxation, Prohibition, cooking, bibliograpy, etc., etc.

We also owe the author a debt of gratitude for the paragraphs on biographical information on some of the authors. These will orient the reader and increase his interest. Some constitute veritable essays on the author. No bibliography can ever be complete (even one with over 3,200 entries) and I am sure the author knows this better than anyone else. Hopefully, then, there will someday be an addendum on further discoveries and emendations and completions. We should be grateful for such a generous list.

For all those who love wines this is an indispensable source of information on what has been published on the subject of grapes, wines and related subjects in English.

I recommend it wholeheartedly.

Maynard A. Amerine
Professor Emeritus of Enology
University of California
Davis, California

June 25, 1984

INTRODUCTION

As the over 3,200 entries attest, there are many books in English about wine. This bibliography (a book about books about wine and wine related subjects) is the first to attempt a listing of all the titles in the English language. The bibliography is not selective. If a book is primarily about "wine," or adds significantly to wine literature, it has been included. While this is the most comprehensive bibliography of wine titles in English, it does not claim to be complete. A bibliography by its nature can never be complete.

Another important feature of the book is an attempt to convey something of the history of wine literature. There are biographies of most of the more prominent writers, and over 1,000 annotations, reviews and vignettes.

As the reader will soon discover, there is more to wine than the making or drinking of it. Wine has involved the entire human experience, and its literature is almost as rich and varied as the varieties of grapes from which it is made, touching on art, religion, science and many other fields.

The compilation has led where it may and a number of themes emerged. Perhaps the major theme is that throughout the ages the quest for wine has been utilitarian. Today there seems to be a perception that wine books are for the gourmet with special emphasis on what wine goes best with what food, what wine should be served in what glasses, etc. These dilettante concerns are a recent phenomena emerging in the 1920's and 1930's with such British writers as H. Warner Allen and Charles Walter Berry. Books about wine prior to then emphasized viticulture and wine making. They tried to make the best wine from the grapes available, and the exotic aspects of wine were rarely mentioned. This was especially true with respect to early American and Australian wine books.

I was also struck by the many early contributions to wine literature by physicians. As examples, the first book about wine (1478) was by Arnaldus of Villanova, a physician. The first complete book in English on wine (1568) was by William Turner, a physician, and the first (Sir Edward Barry), the second (Robert Shannon) and third (Alexander Henderson) books in English that discuss modern wines were by physicians.

Other interesting themes that emerged are the British passion for making wine from just about anything other than grapes, e.g. fruits, berries, flowers, turnips, rhubarb (nearly all 17th and 18th century books); the many books written in the 19th century on the adulteration of wines and the "chemical making" of wines; the extent of the Protestant Biblical controversy concerning the use of fermented or "unfermented" wine; and the extraordinary but unsuccessful efforts that were made in eastern America throughout the 19th century to grow *Vitis vinifera* grapes.

Besides omissions, any compilation such as this will have errors and duplications despite every editorial effort to eliminate them. I encourage readers who discover errors or omissions to report them to the publisher, Bacchus Press, 1421 Jordan Street, Baltimore, Maryland 21217 so that subsequent editions may benefit.

James Gabler

NOTES ON THE BIBLIOGRAPHY

Entries: An entry consists of the following details when known: author, title, place of publication, publisher, date of publication, pagination and whether illustrated. Every entry in Part I has been given a permanent individual reference number that follows the bibliographical entry. This reference number is preceded by the prefix G.

Arrangement of Entries: Author and title are listed in alphabetical sequence. The listing is always by author, editor, compiler, when known. When not known, the listing is usually by title. In some instances where a wine merchant firm is especially well known, e.g., Harvey's, or where a publication has been issued to commemorate a special event, e.g., the firm's centenary, the listing is under the name of the wine merchant firm. There are no anonymous entries. All entries are first edition unless otherwise noted.

Annotation of Entries: Over 1000 of the entries are annotated. The annotations cover such diverse information as historical information about the author, a review of the book, subsequent editions, etc.

Order of Names: The order of authors, editors, compilers, of the same name is the generally accepted one of initials before surnames, e.g.
    Cooper, G.
    Cooper, G.H.
    Cooper, Gerald
    Cooper, Gerald H.

Hyphenated and Personal Names with Prefixes: Hyphenated names are listed under the first part of the surname, e.g. Croft-Cook, Rupert. Personal names with prefixes: "de", "le", "von", etc. have been indexed without the prefix, e.g., Castella, Hubert de. Exceptions have been made where it was clear that personal usage retained the prefix, e.g., De Groot, Roy Andries.

Articles: "A", "An", "The" are taken into account in alphabetization when they occur within the title. However, "A", "An" and "The" are ignored when they begin a title, e.g., "The art of Wine Making" will appear under "Art" but will be listed "The Art of Wine Making."

Mac, Mc and M': Names beginning with "Mac" and its variations Mc and M' have been arranged in their alphabetical or letter-by-letter order. Although this is a break with the tradition of alphabetizing them all as if they were "Mac", the logic of this arrangement prevailed.

Unable to Verify: In some instances an entry has been obtained from a source considered less than totally reliable, e.g. a book bibliography, a catalog, etc. For every entry, the compiler has attempted to verify the books existence by physically examining the book, or through other reliable bibliographical sources such as the *National Union Catalog*, Library of Congress Card Catalog, etc. However, where verification has failed, the notation "Unable to Verify" has been made. This does not mean that the book does not exist. On the contrary, the book probably does exist.

Spelling: The original spelling has been retained in titles and quotations. For example, titles will include winemaking spelled "wine making", "wine-making," and "winemaking." Old English spelling has been quoted in its original form. Generic names for wines such as burgundy, bordeaux, sherry, madeira, claret have not been capitalized. Wine regions such as Burgundy, Bordeaux, Madeira, Champagne, et al. are proper names and are capitalized. This sometimes resulted, for example, in "Burgundy and burgundy" in the same passage. The mark " . . . " indicates an intentional omission of words within a title or sentence. "C" before a date, e.g. c1694 means "circa 1694".

Short-Title Index: The arrangement of this index (Part III) is strictly alphabetical. If the title and not the author is known, consult the short-title index. Every entry in Part I has been given an individual reference number and the numerical citations in the short-title index and chronological index are to those numbers in Part I.

Chronological Index: Part II is a chronological index of titles through 1900 only.

Books Included: Only those wine books and pamphlets printed totally or partially in the English language are included. Books about wine-making, viticulture, wineries and wine history form the backbone of the book. But the term "wine book" has been interpreted in the broadest sense. Books about wine glasses, wine bottles, decanters and other wine accessories have been listed, for they form an essential part of wine drinking and wine lore. Pamphlets pre-dating 1941 have been included. Advertising pamphlets after 1940, of which thousands exist, are not included except where, in the compiler's opinion, they merit inclusion by contributing a special insight into wine. Examples of those listed are pamphlets published by a particular winery celebrating its centenary, or a similar occasion, and providing a history that often cannot be obtained elsewhere. Some books that are not about wine per se are included because of their historical association with wine and their importance to wine literature. Outstanding examples are Fitzgerald's translation of the *Rubaiyat of Omar Khayyam* and Rabelais' *Gargantua and Pantagruel*. Likewise, novels are included where the plot has a wine industry setting.

Books not Included: Though wine and food are inseparable, cookbooks have not been included unless they contribute in some significant way to the service or use of wine. Likewise, inns and taverns books have not been included since, like cookbooks, they form a separate collecting category of their own. Also, there have been thousands of articles published about wine in magazines, periodicals, beverage journals, newspapers, essays, legislation, agricultural reports and the like. Obviously, it has not been possible to include these articles. Where such articles appeared as compiled in book form and published, they have been included. Temperance books have not been included except where their content includes a discussion of wine, especially the books, pro and con, as to the religious significance of wine. Booksellers or auction catalogs of wine items have not generally been included. Exceptions have been made where the catalogs are, in the compiler's opinion, of exceptional interest or importance to wine literature. Technical bulletins are rarely included except for items judged of significant importance or where exclusion would break up an individual bibliography. There are some excellent bibliographies on the technical aspects of wine such as fermentology, yeast culture, soil conditioning, grafting and the like. These publications are included in this bibliography.

Bibliographical Sources: In writing and compiling this history and bibliography, the author's personal wine book collection of over 1,700 volumes has been consulted as have the wine books, card catalogs and other research facilities at the Library of Congress, Washington; Shields Library, University of California at Davis; New York Public Library, main branch and annex, New York; The Enoch Pratt Library, Baltimore; the Napa Valley Wine Library, St. Helena, California; The British Library, London; The Guildhall Library, London; and the Virginia State Library, Richmond. In addition other major library catalogs have been reviewed including the *National Union Catalog*. Other sources consisted of bibliographies appended to wine books, booksellers' catalogs, and specialized bibliographies such as André Simon's *Bibliotheca Vinaria*. Some students of wine may know of titles that should have been included. Others may feel that some of the titles are not properly books about wine. The compiler can say only that despite the time spent, some titles have escaped, but he has attempted to include all books that contribute to the aura, mystery or interest of wine.

ACKNOWLEDGMENTS

A number of people have assisted in the preparation of this book. I wish to especially thank my brother, Robert Gabler, and my nephew, Eric Gabler, for their help in writing, editing and proofreading the manuscript and for their many ideas, including the title *WINE INTO WORDS*. Without their help this book would not exist in its present form. I also extend special thanks to Dr. Maynard A. Amerine for his many research suggestions and for writing the Foreword; to Dan Longone for permission to reproduce a number of his annotations of early American wine books that first appeared in *American Cookbooks and Wine Books, 1797-1950;* to Rob Erich of TMC Corporation in Baltimore for programming the book for the computer; to Betty Lambert for the hundreds of lonely hours spent typing the manuscript; to Ann Hughes for production; to Michael Dresser for editing and proofreading the manuscript in its final form; to Clement Erhardt for the photography; to Wilma Vinck for the jacket cover and title page graphics; to Edward Fleischer of Mid-Atlantic Photo Composition Inc., in Baltimore for typesetting; to John McConnell at the University of California, Davis, for valuable research assistance; to Sue Sult, and many others.

Part
1

Author Index

AARON, S. Jay. Guide to vintage wine prices: 1979-80. New York: Warner Books, 1979. 319p. Illus. G10020

ABBOTT, J.H.C. British wines. London: Yeatman, 1975. 40p. G10015

ABEL, Dominick. Guide to the wines of the United States. New York: Cornerstone Library, 1979. 160p. Illus. G10030

> Reprinted in 1981.

ALDERMAN ABELL

The following pamphlets and tracts were written in 1641 and 1642 as a result of public outrage over a contract entered into between the Vintners' Company of London and King Charles I. Under the terms of the contract the vintners agreed to pay a forty-shilling tax on every tun of foreign wine, and to buy yearly from English importers not less than 4,000 tuns of Spanish wine and 5,000 tuns of French wine. In return, the vintners were permitted to sell cooked victuals (not included in their charters) and allowed to recoup the tax by charging a penny per quart more than the officially established price. The effect of this contract was to increase revenues for the King and to give the Vintners' Company of London a monopoly on the wine trade. Alderman Abell and Richard Kilvert (members of the Vintners' Company) were the leading characters in this remarkable episode in the history of the English wine trade. This attempt to monopolize the wine trade became known as Alderman Abell's "wine project."

On November 14, 1638, Abell and fourteen other London vintners petitioned the King saying that they had " . . . sent many able vintners to the outports and inland towns, with letters of the Council recommending a conformity in all merchants and retailers of wines to the City of London in their trade, to which most of them have submitted and subscribed, as well to the payment of the 40s. duty as otherwise." The vintners requested the King to issue a proclamation compelling all vintners to honor the forty-shilling tax. The proclamation was issued, making it a crime punishable by imprisonment to refuse payment of the tax. In spite of the proclamation, many of the country merchants refused to comply. This resulted in Abell, on behalf of the Vintners' Company, filing a series of complaints against various merchants summoning them to appear before the dreaded Star Chamber. [See Simon, André L.]

Although the vintners could pass the tax along by charging a penny a quart more for their wine, consumers were outraged. Abell and his principal associate, Richard Kilvert, were lampooned throughout England.

The Vintners' Company of London soon came into conflict with the retailers. In order to fill the agreed purchase, and the necessary resale of the yearly 4,000 tuns of Spanish wine and 5,000 tuns of French wine, the vintners attempted to require retailers to buy what quantities and quality of wine they determined. Petitions to the King's Council protesting the vintners' actions were ignored.

When Parliament reassembled in 1640, (it had not been in session since 1629) among the national grievances enumerated by John Pym were the abuses by the Vintners' Company of London. When the Vintners' Company appeared before the House of Commons, they attempted to lay all the blame on their two most prominent members, Abell and Kilvert, claiming they were responsible for the entire scheme. Kilvert, on the other hand, testified that the sole blame lay with the Vintners' Company.

Parliament concluded that they were all responsible of unjust enrichment and "A bill was brought into the House of Commons concerning the wine business, by which it appeared that Alderman Abell and Mr. Kilvert had in their hands which they deceived the King of 57,000 pounds upon the wine license; the Vintners' of London, 66,000 pounds; the wine merchants of Bristol, 1,051 pounds; all of which monies were ordered to be immediately raised on their lands and estates, and to be employed to the public use."

For a more detailed account, see Simon, André L. *The History of the Wine Trade in England, Vol. III.*

M.ʳ Alderman Abell and Richard Kilvert,
the two maine Projectors for Wine 1641.
From a very rare print in the Collection of R. S. Tighe Esq.ʳ
Pub by W Richardson October 1. 1798 York House N° 31 Strand

ABELL, Alderman. The Copie of a letter sent from the roaring boyes in Elizium; to the two arrant Knights of the Grape, in Limbo, Alderman Abell and M. Kilvert, the two great projectors for wine: and to the rest of the worshipful brotherhood of that patent . . . London: J. Barker, c1641. G10050

One of fifty copies printed [no date] for J. Sturt, No. 40 High Street, St. Giles's, by J. Barker, 19 Great Russell Street, Covent Garden, London. Portraits of Abell and Kilvert appear on the title page.

_____. A dialogue or accidental discourse betwixt Mr. Alderman Abell and Richard Kilvert, the two maine projectors for wine . . . contayning the first manner of their acquaintance, how they contrived the Patent it selfe, how they obtained it, and who drew the Patent. London: 1641. G10060

_____. A discourse betwixt Master Abell and Master Richard Kilvert, interrupted at the first by an antient and angry gentlewoman . . . with a woodcut. London: 1641. G10070

_____. An exact legendary, containing the life of Alderman Abell, the projector and patentee for the raising of wines. London: 1641. G10080

_____. The last discourse betwixt Master Abell and Master Richard Kilvert . . . London: 1641. G10090

_____. Old newes newly revived; or the discovery of all occurrences happened since the beginning of the Parliament . . . the fall of wines . . . and the ruine of Alderman Abell's monopoly as, the conclusion of patents, the deputies death, Canterburies imprisonment . . . the fall of wines . . . and the ruine of Alderman Abell's monopoly. London: 1641. G10100

_____. A pack of patentees opened, shuffled, cut, dealt and played [in verse]. 1641 G10110

_____. The petition of the retailing Vintners of London and their propositions and demands contrived . . . amongst themselves . . . whereby it may appear who projected the penny a quart on wines, etc. London: 1641. G10120

_____. Projectors downfall, or time's changeling, wherein the monopolists and patentees are unmasked. 1642 G10130

_____. A reply to a most untrue relation made, and set forth in print, by certaine vintners, in excuse of their wine project. [By R. Kilvert?] London: 1641. 22p. G10140

_____. A true discovery of the projectors of the wine project, out of the vintner's owne orders . . . whereby it clearly appeares that this project was contrived . . . by the drawing vintners of London . . . to suppress the coopers and monopolize the . . . retailing of wines throughout this kingdom. London: Printed for Thomas Walkley, 1641. 28p. G10150

_____. A true relation of the proposing, threatening, and perswading the vintners to yield to the imposition upon wines . . . London: c1641. 32p. G10160

_____. The vintners answer to some scandalous pamphlets published (as is supposed) by Richard Kilvert; and abetted in some points by his brother, Roger, and Alderman Abell. London: 1642. G10170

ABRAHAM, Neville and ANN-GALE, R. The wine quiz book. London: Mills and Boon, 1979. 63p. Illus. G10180

ACCOUNT of the wine industry of Italy. London: 1889. 103p. G10190

ACCUM, Frederick Christian. A treatise on adulterations of food and culinary poisons, exhibiting the fraudulent sophistications of bread, beer, wine, spirituous liquors, tea, coffee . . . and methods of detecting them. London: Longman, Hurst, Rees, Orme, and Brown, 1820. 372p. Illus. G10200

> In the chapter on the "Adulteration of Wine" we are told that it was common practice to add alum to red wine for the purpose of brightening the color and that Brazil wood or the must of elderberries and bilberries were added to give color to port and that oak

wood sawdust was added to impart astringency to immature red wines. The compounding of artificial port was popular and a crust was created by the addition of super-tartrate of potash that had been colored red by a concoction of Brazil wood "and after this simulation of maturity is perfected they [casks] are filled with the compound called Port wine."

The so-called "doctoring" of wines was defended on the grounds that the deceptions were harmless. The author, however, tells of numerous cases of lead poisoning. Lead was thought by some of these "chemists" to help the rejuvenation of spoiled or "ropy wine."

_____. A treatise on the art of making wines from native fruits . . . London: Longman, Hurst, Rees, Orme, and Brown, 1820. 92p. G10210

ACE, Donald L. and EAKIN, James A. Winemaking as a hobby. University Park, PA: 1977. 76p. Illus. G10220

ACTON, George William Bryan. Making wines like those you buy. Andover, England: Amateur Winemaker, 1967. 80p. Illus. G10230

_____. Recipes for prizewinning wines. Andover, England: Amateur Winemaker, 1971. 132p. Illus. G10240

ADAMS, John Festus. The commonsense book of drinking. New York: David McKay, 1960. 210p. G10250

_____. An essay on brewing, vintage and distillation. Garden City, NY: Doubleday, 1970. 108p. Illus. G10260

LEON D. ADAMS (1905)

Leaving the University of California as a young man and traveling through Europe, Mr. Adams developed his interest in wine. Upon returning to California, he got a job as a journalist with the *San Francisco News,* and just before the repeal of Prohibition, he organized the Grape Growers League of California to promote table wines instead of hard liquor. This group was the nucleus of what later developed into the Wine Institute, and Mr. Adams served as its secretary for twenty years. In 1938 he formed the Wine Advisory Board under the California Department of Agriculture. In 1954 he left the Wine Institute to devote full-time to writing and consulting. His other wine activities include serving as technical adviser to the American Wine Society, executive secretary of the San Francisco Society of Medical Friends of Wine and lecturing extensively on wine. He was the first recipient of *Wines and Vines* "Perpetual Trophy for Excellence in Wine Writing."

ADAMS, Leon D. The commonsense book of wine. New York: David McKay, 1958. 178p. G10280

How to buy, store, serve and enjoy wine. Second revised edition published in 1964 and a revised third edition of 228p. in 1975.

_____. Revitalizing the California wine industry. 1974. 154p. Illus. G10300

See California Wine Oral History Series.

_____. The wines of America. Boston: Houghton Mifflin, 1973. 465p. Illus. G10310

> An important reference on North American vineyards and wines. The author explores every wine of consequence from California to those of the scuppernong grapes in South Carolina. The book covers the history of North American wine making from the 16th century to present. A revised second edition of 623p. was published in 1978 by McGraw-Hill and a revised third edition, 1984 that includes over 450 new wineries since the second edition.

ADAMS, Tate. Diary of a vintage: the workcycle of the year 1979 at Wynns Coonawarra Estate in South Australia. Melbourne: Lyrehbird Press, 1981. 60p. Illus. G10330

> Limited edition of 375 copies signed by the artist-author. Twenty-six wood engravings printed directly from the blocks, bound and slip-covered in wine-red silk.

ADAMS, William H. Confessions of a lil' ole winemaker. n.p., 1975. 182p. Illus. G10340

ADDE, Merum. A booklet which may prove of some interest to wine consumers. London: Reid Brothers and Kerr, 1919. 36p. Illus. G10350

ADDISON, Joseph. The trial of the wine-brewers. An essay. San Francisco: Printed by John Henry Nash, 1930. 18p. Illus. G10360

> A reprint of an essay by Joseph Addison published in *The Tatler* on Thursday, February 9, 1709. The beginning paragraph sums up who the "wine-brewers" were: "There is in this city a certain fraternity of chemical operators, who work underground in holes, caverns, and dark retirements. . . . They can squeeze bordeaux out of the sloe, and draw champagne from an apple." The concoctions sold by these charlatans so concerned Addison that he resolved to be very careful of his wines and to ask a friend to secure "two hogs heads of the best stomach wine in the cellars of Versailles for the good of my lucubrations and the comfort of my old age." There follows: "An Inquiry Into Mr. Addison's Drinking" by Edward F. O'Day in the form of a conversation with Dr. Samuel Johnson, who accuses Addison of drinking too much. Printed in limited edition of 385 copies with marbled boards.

ADKINS, Jan. The craft of making wine. New York: Walker Publishing, 1971. 91p. Illus. G10370

JOHN ADLUM (1759-1836)

John Adlum has often been accorded the title of "father of American viticulture" for his efforts with grape cultivation and wine-making. It was a career arrived at after serving in the Revolutionary War, being wounded, captured and released, followed by years as a successful surveyor. At the age of forty, Adlum took a totally different tack when he began experimenting with winemaking. His vineyards began their stubborn fight for existence in the less-than-ideal soil of Georgetown

[Washington, D.C.], where he purchased 200 acres named "The Vineyard."

President Jefferson, who lived just a short distance away during his presidency (1801-1809), became friendly with him. After his retirement to Monticello, Jefferson wrote: "While I lived in Washington you were so kind as to send me two bottles of wine made by yourself, the one from Currants, the other from a native grape, called by you a foxgrape, discovered by Mr. Penn's gardener. The wine of this was as good as the best Burgundy and resembling it. In 1810 you added the great favor of sending me my cuttings. These were committed to the stage Mar. 13. . . .

"They were received April 19 and immediately planted, but having been six weeks in a dry situation not a single one lives. Disenchanted by this failure and not having anyone skilled in the culture, I never troubled you again on the subject, but I have now an opportunity of renewing the trial under a person brought up to the culture of the vine and making wine from his nativity. Am I too unreasonable in asking once more a few cuttings of the same vine? I am so convinced that our first success will be from a native grape, that I would buy no other. A few cuttings as short as you think will do, put into a light box, and mixed well with light moss."

The wine discovered by Mr. Penn's gardener, and thought by Jefferson to be as good as the best burgundy, was made from Schuylkill muscadel grapes, which were originally found near Philadelphia and the Schuylkill River.

During the early stages of his viticultural efforts, Adlum experimented with native wild grapes and strains of European Vitis vinifera. After failing with the European vines, he concentrated on native grapes.

During President Monroe's administration, Adlum proposed "a lease of a portion of the public ground in the city [Washington] for the purpose of forming a vineyard, and of cultivating an experimental farm. It was my intention, had I been successful, to procure cuttings of the different species of the native vine, to be found in the United States, to ascertain their growth, soil, and produce, and to exhibit to the Nation, a new source of wealth, which has been too long neglected. My application was, however, rejected, and I have been obliged to prosecute the undertaking myself, without assistance and without patronage and this I have done to the full extent of my very limited means. A desire to be useful to my countrymen has animated all my efforts, and given stimulus to all my exertions."

In early 1823, Adlum published the first American book on American grape culture titled *Memoir on the Cultivation of the Vine in America, and the best Mode of Making Wine.* He sent Jefferson a copy with two bottles of his wine. Jefferson thanked him for "the two bottles of wine you were so kind as to send me. The first called Tokay is truly a fine wine of high flavour, and, as you assure me there was not a drop of brandy or other spirit in it. I say it is a wine of good body of its own.

"The 2d bottle, a red wine, I tried when I had good judges at the table. We agreed it was a wine one might always drink with satisfaction, but of no peculiar excellence. Of your book on the culture of the vine, it would be presumption in me to give my opinion, because it is a culture of which I have no knowledge either from practice or reading. Wishing you very sincerely compleat success in this your laudable undertaking, I assure you of my great esteem and respect." The wine that Jefferson called Tokay was made from the native catawba grape, which Adlum thought made the best wine and for which he was chiefly responsible for disseminating in this country.

ADLUM, John. A memoir on the cultivation of the vine in America, and the best mode of making wine. Washington: Printed by Davis and Force, 1823. 142p. G10390

_____. A memoir on the cultivation of the vine in America, and the best mode of making wine. 2nd ed. Washington: William Greer, 1828. 179p. G10400

> A compilation of European sources adapted from Adlum's experience for use in America with correspondence from American growers.

_____. A memoir on the cultivation of the vine in America, and the best mode of making wine. Reprint of 1828 edition. Rachel McMasters Miller Hunt Botanical Library, 1967. G10410

_____. A memoir on the cultivation of the vine in America, and the best mode of making wine. Reprint of 1828 edition. Hopewell, NJ: Booknoll Reprints, 1971. 142p. G10420

_____. Adlum on making wine. Georgetown: James C. Dunn, 1826. 36p. G10430

> In a short introduction Adlum tells us "the following sheets, on making wine, were written . . . for the National Journal . . . I thought it best to publish them in a pamphlet form. . . ."

AFRICA, South. Wines, spirits and vinegar act, 1913, Act no. 5 of 1913, with amendments up to and including 1933 . . . Pretoria: English and Afrikaans, 1935. 25p. G10440

AIKEN, Ednah Robinson. If today be sweet. New York: Dodd, Mead, 1923. 272p. G10450

> A novel with a California wine industry setting.

AKENHEAD, D. Viticulture research. London: H.M. Stationary Office; issued by the Empire Marketing Board, 1929. 70p. G10460

> Covers most aspects of viticulture, including climates, soils, stocks, grafting, cultivation and general management. His data is a compilation of standard works of reputed German, French and Italian authorities plus personal experience with vineyards in Chianti, Romagna, the Médoc, Graves, Sauternes, Burgundy, Alsace, Germany, Champagne and the Midi.

ALDERSON, William A., comp. Here's to you. New York: Dodge Publishing, 1908. 268p. G10470

> Mr. Alderson, "of the Los Angeles Bar," compiled this book of toasts, poems and "pastels in prose" for those "who strew flowers, rather than thorns, along the pathway of others." At least ninety pages are given to "Wine and Song." An irritating aspect of the compilation is that Alderson "[S]olely in the interest of impartial judgment . . ." does not name the authors. A number of the verses are from *The Rubaiyat*, many concern the fleetness of life, the joy of wine and women. There is an unpaged [39] index by subject.

The ALFRED Fromm rare wine books library. San Francisco: Wine Museum of San Francisco, Christian Brothers Collection, 1977. [54p.] G10480

> The books are arranged chronologically and there are about 460 entries.

ALLEN, Eileen, ed. Food, wine and cookery; a universal guide to selecting, preparing, cooking and serving. London: George Newnes, 1964. 575p. Illus. G10490

HERBERT WARNER ALLEN

H. Warner Allen acquired a love for wine while an undergraduate at Oxford. Even in his college days Allen aspired to drink the best and tells of an occasion when he returned to his room and found to his horror several thirsty classmates drinking his 1864 Lafite. What appalled Allen more than the loss of the wine was that they did not appreciate what they were drinking.

Allen was a journalist and professional writer with a scholarly disposition that is reflected in his writing style.

He was a friend of André Simon and Charles W. Berry, a member of the Saintsbury Club and a prolific writer on what the author called his "lasting love," wine.

ALLEN, H. Warner. Claret. London: T. Fisher Unwin, 1924. 44p. Illus. G10510

> The greater part of this essay on claret has been taken from *The Wines of France*, although there are a few amplifications such as the section "Claret and Health" and the sixteen "Don'ts" for the claret drinker.

_____. A contemplation of wine. London: Michael Joseph, 1951. 232p. G10520

_____. Gentlemen, I give you wine. London: Faber and Faber, 1930. 38p. G10530

> The first half of this short monograph describes in loving terms a wine tasting Mr. Allen attended with four other connoisseurs. They were to give their opinion as to whether a certain bottle of pre-phylloxera Chateau Margaux was a vintage of 1869 or 1870. "[S]ome of the greatest wines the world has ever known awaited our attention to compose and guide our thoughts." The second half provides guidance in the art of enjoying wine.

_____. Good wine from Portugal. London: Sylvan Press, 1957. 59p. Illus. G10540

> Revised edition of 75p. published in 1960.

_____. A history of wine: great vintage wines from the Homeric age to the present day. 2nd ed. London: Faber and Faber, 1962. 304p. Illus. G10550

> A scholarly account in three parts: part one covers from the Homeric age to the fall of the Roman Empire; part two from the fall of the Roman Empire to the Methuen Treaty in 1703; and part three modern wines.

_____. Mr. Clerihew, wine merchant. London: Methuen, 1933. 277p. G10560

This is a mystery novel with a famous wine merchant, (probably Charles Walter Berry) named Will Clerihew, as its hero and with vintage wines playing an important part in the story. The plot revolves around the theft, at an elegant dinner party, of the Luck of Lusitania, a celebrated ruby that once was a jewel in the crown of Lusitania (the ancient name for Portugal). Mr. Clerihew falls in love, and the ruby gets mixed up with a case of Mouton Rothschild. The story has a suspenseful ending. To reveal more would spoil an interesting story that shows Mr. Allen as a subtle creator of mystery and suspense.

_____. Natural red wines. London: Constable, 1951. 320p. G10570

Contains a report by Frank Schoonmaker on the red wines of America.

_____. Number three St. James's Street; a history of Berry's, the wine merchants. London: Chatto and Windus, 1950. 269p. Illus. G10580

_____. The romance of wine. London: Ernest Benn, 1931. 264p. Illus. G10590

The first part deals with the aesthetics of wine, and the second part with the making of wine in various countries and times. The two most original chapters are on sherry and cognac. The final chapter might be called the third part. It deals with a subject that was one of the author's favorites - the ancient wines of Greece and Rome.

_____. The Saintsbury oration delivered by H. Warner Allen at the 32nd meeting of the Saintsbury Club, 22 April, 1948. London: Privately printed at the Curwen Press for the Saintsbury Club, 1948. 15p. G10600

_____. Sherry. London: Constable, 1924. 117p. Illus. G10610

Although Allen was a journalist, he was also well schooled in the classics, an original thinker and investigator. This monograph explores much more than the history, making and appreciation of sherry. Mr. Allen explores the derivation of wines from English literature and even crosses swords with his mentor, André Simon, about the wine from Lepe mentioned in Chaucer's *Pardoner's Tale*.

André Simon thought Lepe wine was a sweet wine made from overripe grapes or sweetened with honey and flavored with spices, as were most of the wines imported from southern Spain in medieval days. Allen is skeptical because in the climate of southern Spain, a wine is likely to ferment all its sugar.

_____. Sherry and port. London: Constable, 1952. 215p. G10620

In the chapters on sherry Mr. Allen gives us his interpretation of the mystery of the "flor," or flower, and the origins of sherry and its conquest of the English market in Elizabethan days.

_____. Through the wine glass. London: Michael Joseph, 1954. 244p. G10630

_____. White wines and cognac. London: Constable, 1952. 279p. G10640
Second edition, 1954.

_____. The wines of France. London: T. Fisher Unwin, 1924. 261p. G10650

> Although there are chapters on the wines of Bordeaux ("the highest perfection of all wines that have ever been made"), Burgundy, Champagne and other wines of France, the most interesting chapter is "The Gentle Art of Wine-drinking". In the epilogue Mr. Allen describes a wine tasting put on by Charles W. Berry (see Berry) for a small party of connoisseurs. They began with a very old Amontillado ("more than half a century in the wood"), followed by a 1904 Chablis Moutonne ("its subtlety and completeness seemed to pass the bounds of possibility") and then "the full orchestral music of Montrachet 1889." A saddle of mutton and a pheasant "escorted" an 1865 Lafite whose bouquet expressed "the incomparable harmony of a great Claret." An 1875 Lafite caused Mr. Allen to exclaim "that nothing more artistically perfect could be offered to the human senses." But then this group of mortals "like passing from fine prose to the inspiration of poetry" opened a magnum of 1864 Lafite whose bouquet "was bewildering in its exquisite completeness." The perfect ending for one who had been deprived of this vintage in college.

_____. The wines of Portugal. London: George Rainbird and Michael Joseph, and New York: McGraw-Hill, 1963. 192p. Illus. G10660

ALLEN, John Fisk. The culture of the grape, embracing it history with directions for the treatment of the vine, in the northern states of America, in the open air, and under glass structures, with and without artificial heat. Boston: Dutton and Wentworth, 1847. 55p. Illus. G10670

> Prepared at the suggestion of friends, this book was intended for use in Massachusetts and neighboring states. It is an account of the author's own practice in Salem, Massachusetts.

_____. A practical treatise on the culture and treatment of the grape vine: embracing its history with directions for its treatment, in the United States of America, in the open air, and under glass structures, with and without artificial heat. 2nd ed. Boston: Dutton and Wentworth, 1848. 247p. Illus. G10680

> A detailed guide to cultivating grapes in enclosed structures, it includes an extensive description of European and American grape varieties and a summary of viticultural experiences by contemporary vinegrowers from Massachusetts to Florida. To Allen goes the credit for producing the first named and widely disseminated hybrid between the American Vitis labrusca and the European Vitis vinifera. The result, Allen's Hybrid, was obtained in 1844 by fertilizing the blossoms of the native Isabella with pollen from the

French Chasselas de Fontainbleau. Further editions were published in 1853, 1858 and 1860.

ALLEN, Michael. The long holiday. London: 1974. 108p. G10685

The story of a wine venture in Provence.

ALLEN, Paul W. Industrial fermentations. New York: The Chemical Catalog Company, 1926. 424p. G10690

ALLEN, Percy. Burgundy: the splendid Duchy. London: Frances Griffiths, 1912. 302p. Illus. G10700

ALLIED Liquor Industries, Inc. Beverage distilling industry. Facts and figures 1934-1944. New York: Allied Liquor Industries, 1945. 108p. G10710

ALTON, R.E. and AARON, Sam. The pleasures of the bottle; a few words from St. Edmund Hall in the University of Oxford. Oxford: Alden Press, 1966. 20p. Illus. G10720

AMATEUR, Anne. Home brewed wines and unfermented beverages for all seasons of the year. London: George Newnes, 1921. 28p. G10730

AMBROSI, Hans. Comparison of rootstocks in South Africa: 1966 survey. South Africa: Stellenbosch Wine Institute, 1967. Illus. G10740

_____. Where the great German wines grow. New York: Hastings House, 1976. 240p. Illus. G10750

An informative reference on German wine laws and wine districts. It tells how to read a German wine label, provides a German-English dictionary of wine terms and gives details about some ninety wine estates. Dr. Ambrosi is the director of the German Wine Estates, which are owned by the West German republic.

_____. Wine-atlas and dictionary — Germany. Translated by Bill Gavin. New York: Hastings House, 1976. 114p. G10760

MAYNARD ANDREW AMERINE (1911)

Maynard A. Amerine, author, enologist, viticulturist, bibliophile, wine connoisseur, lecturer and consultant, was educated at the University of California receiving his B.S. in 1932 and his Ph.D. in plant physiology in 1936. He was a member of the faculty of the University of California at Davis from 1935 to 1974 as professor of enology and as chairman of the Department of Viticulture and Enology from 1957-1962. During his long and distinguished career as an enologist, Dr. Amerine has received many awards and honors including that of Guggenheim fellow 1954-55, and the merit award from the American Society of Enologists, 1967. Professor Amerine has authored more books on the technical aspects of wine and wine making than any other author in the English language. He has lectured throughout the world and has served as a wine consultant to a number of countries. He is presently a consultant on technical research with the California Wine Institute. One of his greatest contributions to viticulture and enology was to develop, in 1944, together with Professor A.J. Winkler, the heat summation theory relating climatic conditions to the composition and quality of grapes and wine. No longer a theory but a well accepted practice throughout the world, heat summation is the basis for selecting the proper grape varieties for planting in a particular growing area.

AMERINE, Maynard A. Books and pamphlets on grapes, wines and related subjects in the library of Maynard A. Amerine, July 1, 1971, University of California, Davis. 1971. Unpaged. G10780

_____. California sparkling wines: bulk and bottle fermented. San Francisco: Wines and Vines, California Wines, 1950. 12p. G10790

_____. California. Wines of the world pocket library. Edited by André L. Simon. London: The Wine and Food Society, 1951. 15p. Illus. G10800

_____. A check list of books and pamphlets in English on grapes and wines and related subjects, 1960-1968, with a supplement for 1949-1959. Davis: 1969. 84p. G10810

_____. Current wine making practices in California. Commemorative Lectures. Osaka, Japan: Suntory, 1974. 59p. G10820

_____. The golden ages of wines. Address given The Institute of Masters of Wines, July 30, 1969, London, England, Published and circulated under their auspices. 1970. 25p. G10830

_____. The grapes and wines of Alameda, Santa Clara, and Santa Cruz Counties. 1948 Vintage Tour of the Los Angeles and San Francisco Branches of the Wine and Food Society. San Francisco: The Grabhorn Press, 1948. G10840

_____. Hilgard and California viticulture. Berkeley: University of California, 1962. 23p. G10850

_____. Laboratory procedures for enology. Davis: Divisions of Viticulture, University of California, 1951. 96p. G10860

_____. Laboratory procedures for enology. Davis: Department of Viticulture and Enology, University of California, 1955. 108p. G10870

_____. Laboratory procedures for enology. Davis: Department of Viticulture and Enology, University of California, 1960. 124p. G10880

_____. Lecture. Rehovot: Israel Wine Institute, 1969. 33p. G10890

_____. Refrigerated fermentation; processing and storage of wines. Commodity Storage Manual. Colorado Springs, CO: The Refrigeration Research Foundation, 1957. 6p. G10900

_____. A short check list of books and pamphlets in English on grapes, wines, and related subjects 1949-1959. Davis: 1959. 61p. G10910

_____. Syllabus for wine appreciation, to accompany a televised series of lectures on wine appreciation by Maynard A. Amerine. Prepared by Thomas C. Sparks and Lura S. Middleton. Davis: University of California Extension, 1969. 30p. Illus. G10920

_____. The University of California and the state's wine industry. An interview conducted by Ruth Teiser. With an introd. by Emil M. Mrak. Berkeley: University of California, Bancroft Library, Regional Oral History Office, c1972. 142p. Illus. G10930

See California Wine Industry Oral History Series.

_____. Vermouth: an annotated bibliography. Berkeley: University of California, Division of Agricultural Sciences, 1974. 69p. G10940

_____. Vintage Tour 1959 to selected vineyards in the Napa and Santa Clara Valleys. San Francisco: San Francisco Wine and Food Society, n.d. G10950

_____. The well-tempered wine bibber. 1955 Vintage Tour of Los Angeles and San Francisco Branches of the Wine and Food Society. San Francisco: The Grabhorn Press, 1955. G10960

_____. Wine. Reprinted from "Scientific-American" for August 1964. San Francisco: Freeman, c1964. 12p. Illus. G10970

_____. Wine. Reprinted from *Encyclopedia of Chemical Technology*, Vol. 15. New York: Interscience Encyclopedia, c1956. G10980

AMERINE, Maynard A. and CRUESS, William A. The technology of wine making. Westport, CT: Avi Publishing, 1960. 709p. Illus. G10990

> Under twenty different chapter headings, the subject of winemaking is covered starting with an introduction to wines and wine regions of the world and ending with legal restrictions on winemaking. There are extensive bibliographies at the end of each chapter. This is an important reference for those interested in making wine, and the contents have been kept up to date by subsequent editions: second edition of 799p; third edition of 802p. published in 1972; and fourth edition of 794p. published in 1980.

AMERINE, Maynard A. and JOSLYN, Maynard A. Commercial production of brandies. Berkeley: University of California, Agricultural Experiment Station Bulletin 652, 1941. 80p.

> See Joslyn, Maynard A.

_____. Commercial production of dessert wines. Berkeley: University of California, Agricultural Experiment Station Bulletin 651, 1941. 186p.

> See Joslyn, Maynard A.

_____. Commercial production of table wines. Berkeley: University of California, Agricultural Experiment Station Bulletin 639, 1940. 143p. G11030

> See Joslyn, Maynard A.

_____. Dessert, appetizer and related flavored wines: the technology of their production. Berkeley: University of California, Division of Agricultural Sciences, 433p.

_____. Table wines; the technology of their production in California. Berkeley: University of California Press, 1951. 397p. Illus. G11010

> Second edition of 997p. was published in 1970.

AMERINE, Maynard A. and MARSH, George L. Wine making at home. San Francisco: Wine Publications, 1962. 31p. G11050

> Revised edition of 32p. published in 1969.

AMERINE, Maynard A. and OUGH, C.S. Methods for analysis of musts and wines. New York: John Wiley and Sons, 1980. 341p. G11060

_____. Wine and must analysis. New York: John Wiley and Sons, 1974. 121p. G11070

AMERINE, Maynard A. and ROESSLER, E.B. Sensory evaluation of wines. San Francisco: Wine Institute, 1964. 26p. G11080

_____. Wines, their sensory evaluation. San Francisco: W.H.

Freeman, 1976. 230p. G11090

AMERINE, Maynard A. and SINGLETON, Vernon L., comps. A list of bibliographies and a selected list of publications that contain bibliographies on grapes, wines, and related subjects. Berkeley: University of California, Agricultural Publications, 1971. 39p. G11100

_____. Wine, an introduction for Americans. Berkeley: University of California Press, 1965. 357p. Illus. G11110

> Second revised edition of 373p. published in 1977.

AMERINE, Maynard A. and WHEELER, Louise Bessie, comps. A check list of books and pamphlets on grapes and wine and related subjects, 1938-1948. Berkeley: University of California Press, 1951. 240p. G11120

> Comprises 1,789 entries, alphabetically arranged by author from Europe, North and South America and South Africa.

AMERINE, Maynard A. and WINKLER, A.J. California wine grapes. Composition and quality of their musts and wines. Berkeley: University of California, California Agricultural Experiment Station Bulletin 794, 83p. G11130

_____. Grape varieties for wine production. Berkeley: University of California, Agricultural Experiment Station Circular 356, 1943. 15p. G11140

_____. Grape varieties for wine production. Berkeley: California Agricultural Experiment Station Extension Service Leaflet 154, 1963. Illus. G11150

AMERINE, Maynard A., ed. The book of California wine. See Muscatine, Doris.

_____. Wine production technology in the United States. Washington: American Chemical Society, 1981. 229p. G11160

AMES, Richard. The bacchanalian sessions; or the contention of liquors: with a farewell to wine, by the author of the search after claret etc. To which is added, a satyrical poem on the one who had injur'd his memory, by a friend. London: Hawkins, 1693. 24p. G11170

_____. A dialogue between claret and darby-ale. A poem. Considered in an accidental conversation between two gentlemen. London: E. Richardson, 1692. 10p. G11180

_____. A farther search after claret; or, a second visitation of the vintners. A poem. London: Hawkins, 1691. 19p. G11190

> A copy sold at auction at Sotheby's, London, in May, 1981, for 380 pounds. Rare.

_____. Fatal friendship; or the drunkard's misery, being a satyr against hard drinking, by the author of the search after claret. London: R. Taylor, 1693. 26p. G11200

_____. The last search after claret in Southwark; or a committee of that profession thither fled to avoid the cruel persecution of the unmerciful creditors. A poem dedicated to the most ingenuous author of the search after wit. London: Hawkins, 1691. 11p. G11210

_____. The search after claret; or, a visitation of the vintners. A poem in two cantos. London: Hawkins, 1691. 18p. G11220

> A copy sold at auction at Sotheby Parke Bernet, in May, 1981, for 500 pounds or about $1,000. Richard Ames, a 17th century poet, voices in verse the disgust of all wine lovers at William III's edict prohibiting the importation of French wines. The poems were published anonymously. Rare.

AMIS, Kingsley. Kingsley Amis on drink. New York: Harcourt Brace Jananovich, 1973. 109p. Illus. G11230

ANDERSEN, J.B. A basic guide to appreciating wine. Dorn Books, 1979. 93p. G11240

ANDERSON, Burton. Pocket guide to Italian wines. New York: Simon and Schuster and London: Mitchell Beazley, 1982. 144p. G11250

> A revised edition of 160p. published in 1984.

_____. Vino, the wines and winemakers of Italy. Boston: Little, Brown, 1980. 568p. Illus. G11260

> This is an excellent non-technical work on Italian wines. The author obviously spent a great deal of time visiting the wines districts, meeting the winemakers and drinking their wines. An evaluation of the wines is given on the basis of quality. Mr. Anderson writes in a clear, readable style and his enthusiasm for his subject translates to the printed page. A valuable reference. A second edition was published in 1982.

ANDERSON, Russell. One hundred famous cocktails; the romance of wines and liquors, etc. New York: Kenilworth Press, 1934. 46p. Illus. G11270

ANDERSON, Stanley F. and HULL, Raymond. The advanced winemaker's practical guide. New York: Hawthorn Books, 1975. 120p. Illus. G11280

_____. The art of making wine. 2nd ed. New York: Hawthorn Books, 1970. 181p. Illus. G11290 First edition, 1968.

ANDRAE, E.H. A guide to the cultivation of the grape vine in Texas, and instructions for wine-making. Dallas: Texas Farm and Ranch Pub. Co., 1890. 45p. Illus. G11300

The ANDRÉ L. Simon/Eleanor Lowenstein collection of gastronomic literature. San Francisco: The American Institute of Wine and Food, 1982. 67p. G11310

> The 858 entries include a number of early books on wine and wine-making.

ANDREWS, S.W. Be a wine and beer judge: a guide for the lover of wines and beers, both amateur and commercial. Andover: Amateur Winemaking Publications, 1977. 116p. Illus. G11320

_____. Good Housekeeping home made wine and beer. London: Ebury Press, 1974. 159p. G11330

ANDRIEU, Pierre. Treatment of vintage by diffusion. Translated by Raymond Dubois and W. Percy Wilkinson. Melbourne: Robert S. Brain, 1902. 32p. G11340

ANSTIE, Francis E. On the uses of wines in health and disease. New York: J.S. Redfield, 1870. 84p. G11350

> Published in London by Macmillan, 1887.

ANTCLIFF, A.J. Major wine grape varieties of Australia. Clayton, Victoria: CSIRO, 1980. G11360

_____. Some wine grape varieties for Australia. Clayton, Victoria: CSIRO, 1976. G11370

ANTHONY, Daniel. The gauging inspector and measurers assistant. Providence: Muller and Hutchins, 1817. 76p. G11380

ANTZ, August. Legends of the Rhineland; a journey through the land of the monks, knights and rogues. Bonn, Germany: n.p., 1967. 100p. Illus. G11390

> A few of the legends include stories about wine. Translated by Kathlyn Rutherford, with illustrations by August Leo Thiel and Ernst Paul.

An APPEAL to the landholders concerning the reasonableness and general benefit of an excise upon tobacco and wine. London: Printed for J. Peele, 1733. 32p. G11400

APPLEYARD, Alex. Make your own wine. London: Athene Publishing, 1953. 61p. G11410

APPROVED recipes and directions for making wines . . . from English fruits, flowers . . . 2nd ed. Lancaster, England: 1834. 28p. G11420

ARLOTT, John. Krug: house of champagne. London: Davis-Poynter, 1976. 224p. Illus. G11430

> A history of the five generations of a family that created a grand marque champagne.

ARLOTT, John and FIELDEN, Christopher. Burgundy, vines and wines. London: Davis-Poynter, 1976. 268p. Illus. G11440

>A revised edition was published by Quartet in 1978.

ARLOTT, John, comp. Wine. New York: Oxford University Press, 1984. 112p. Illus. G11435

ARNALDUS de Villanova. The earliest printed book on wine, by Arnald of Villanova . . . now for the first time rendered into English and with a historical essay by Henry E. Sigerist, M.D. With facsimile of the original [German] edition, 1478. New York: Schuman's, 1943. 44p. G11460

>Arnald of Villanova was a physician, surgeon, botanist, alchemist, philosopher, writer, astrologer, lay theologian and counselor to kings and popes. About 1310, Arnald wrote a book on wine. Because the printing press had not yet been invented, his book was handwritten. In 1478 his book was translated into German and printed, making it the first book on wine to use this new invention.

>Among the numerous qualities ascribed to wine by Arnald are its ability to clarify turbid blood, to open the body's passages, to warm cold bodies and to cool hot ones, to prevent the "drying out" of the old and to medicate the young. Some of the wines he describes are: "A marvellous wine useful and good for the melancholics and other diseases; purgative wine; wine for the congestion of the spleen and of the liver and for jaundice; wine for memory; eyebright wine." This reprint edition of Arnald's treatise is the first English language version of this book and was limited to 350 copies. Scarce.

The ART and mystery of vintners and wine-coopers: containing approved directions for the conserving and curing all manner and sorts of wines, whether Spanish, Greek, Italian or French, very necessary for all sorts of people. London: William Whitwood, 1682. 79p. G11470

The ART and mystery of vintners and wine-coopers: containing approved directions for the preserving and curing all manner and all sorts of wines. By E.T., a wine-cooper of long experience. London: Printed for J. Roberts, 1734. 70p. G11480

>Second edition published in 1748.

The ART and mystery of vintners and wine-coopers: containing one hundred and fifty-eight approved recipes for the conserving and curing all sorts of wines, whether Spanish, Greek, Italian, or French. London: 1750. G11490

The ART and mystery of vintners and wine-coopers: or a brief discourse concerning the various sicknesses and corruption of wines . . . London: Printed by W.R., 1703. 69p. G11500

The ART of drinking. London: Matthew Clark and Son, 1933. Illus. G11510

The ART of fine wine drinking. New York: W.A. Taylor, 1903. 23p. G11520

ASBURY, Herbert. The great illusion: an informal history of Prohibition. Garden City, NY: Doubleday, 1950. 344p. G11530

Includes material concerning Prohibition's impact on the wine industry.

ASH, Douglas. How to identify English drinking glasses and decanters, 1680-1830. London: G. Bell, 1962. 200p. Illus. G11540

_____. How to identify English silver drinking vessels 600-1830. London: G. Bell, 1964. 159p. Illus. G11550

ASHER, Gerald. On wine. New York: Random House, 1982. 222p.   G11560

This book is based on thirty articles by the author published in *Gourmet* magazine. They are written with a clarity that allows the reader to understand such convoluted subjects as the sherry solera system and Burgundy vineyard ownership.

ASPLER, Tony. Vintage Canada. Toronto: Prentice-Hall, 1983. 213p. Illus. G11570

A history of winemaking in Canada, as well as tasting notes on virtually every Canadian wine available.

AT home with wine. Adelaide: B. Seppelt and Sons, 1949. G11580

ATKINS, Lee. If this be my harvest. New York: Crown, 1948. 281p. G11600

A novel with a California wine industry setting.

ATKINSON, John. See listings under his pseudonym, John Aye.

AUSTIN Nichols and Co. Imported wines and their care and uses. Brooklyn, NY: n.d. 32p. Illus. G11630

_____. Wine and liquor handbook . . . Brooklyn, NY: Austin Nichols and Co., c1936. 96p. Illus. G11640

AUSTIN, Cedric. The good wines of Europe. Andover, England: Amateur Winemaker, 1972. 155p. Illus. G11650

_____. The science of wine. London: University of London Press and New York: American Elsevier, 1968. 216p. Illus. G11660

_____. Whys and wherefores of winemaking. Andover, England: Amateur Winemaker, 1973. 120p. G11670

The AUSTRALIAN Wine Association of Victoria - rules and regulations together with a list of members and officebearers. Melbourne: William Inglis and Co., Printers, 1885. G11680

AXLER, Bruce H. Practical wine knowledge. Indianapolis: Educational Pub., 1974. 134p. Illus. G11700

AYALA Champagne. Fine drinking. London: Blumenthal, 1950. 26p. Illus. G11710

AYE, John. The humour of drinking. London: Universal Publications, 1934. 282p. G11720

_____. Wine wisdom, a simple and concise guide on what to buy and how to serve. London: Universal Publications, 1934. 114p. G11730

AYLETT, Mary. Country wines. London: Odhams Press, 1953. 192p. Illus. G11740

——————. Encyclopedia of home-made wines. London: Odhams Press, 1957. 192p. G11750

BABO, Carl von. Reports on viticulture in the Cape Colony. Cape Town: Department of Agriculture, 1887. 69p. G11760

BACCHUS and Venus: a collection of near 200 of the most witty and diverting songs . . . London: Printed by R. Montague, 1737. 118p. G11800

BACCHUS and Venus: or, the triumph of love and wine, exhibited in a select collection of such songs, catches and glees as are celebrated for the most refined wit, inimitable mirth, and high-seasoned humour. With a great number of original songs and whimsical burlesques. . . . To which is added a mouth-piece to the glass, or a curious collection of the best toasts, sentiments and hob-nobs. By a Bacchusarian professor and P.R.S. of Venusa. London: S. Smith and T. Lewis, n.d.. 144p. Illus. G11805

BACCHUS. Brewer's guide for the hotel, bar and restaurant. Valletta Series. Hints on the manufacture of beer, wines, spirits and liquors Norwich: n.p., Printed by St. Giles Printing Works, n.d. 185p. G11780

BACCHUS and Cordon Bleu. New guide of the hotel, bar, restaurant, butler and chef. London: c1885. 496p. G11790

A management handbook.

BACH, J.S. Wine and taxes. A letter written by Johann Sebastian Bach in 1748 to his cousin. Facsimile. New York: Pierpont Morgan Library, 1970. Unpaged. G11810

Includes the German text and the English translation.

BACHCHAN, Harivanshrai. The house of wine. London: Fortune Press, 1950. 46p. Illus. G11820

BAGENALL, B.W. The descendants of the pioneer winemakers of South Australia. Adelaide: By the Author, 1946. 27p. G11830

BAGNALL, Gordon A. Wines of South Africa; an account of their history, production and nature. Paarl, South Africa: K.W.V., 1961. 95p. Illus. G11840

Illustrated with wood engravings.

BAILEY, Liberty Hyde. American grape training. An account of the leading forms now in use in training the American grapes. New York: Rural Publishing, 1893. 95p. Illus. G11850

——————. Sketch of the evolution of our native fruits . . . New York: Macmillan, 1898. 472p. Illus. G11860

Contains an excellent survey of the early history of grape growing in the eastern United States with an eight-page bibliography of grape books and pamphlets.

_____. Sketch of the evolution of our native fruits . . . Reprint. Wilmington, DE: Scholarly Resources, 1974. 472p. G11870

BAILEY, Paul Dayton. The gay saint. Hollywood: Murray and Gee, 1944. 310p. G11880

   A novel with a California wine industry setting.

BAIN, George. Champagne is for breakfast. Toronto: Newpress, 1972. 277p. Illus. G11890

BAKER, Charles H. The gentleman's companion. Contents- Vol. 1. being an exotic cookery book. Vol. 2. being an exotic drinking book. Indianapolis: Derrydale Press, 1939. 216p. G11910

_____. South American gentlemen's companion. Contents- Vol. 1. being an exotic cookery book; or, up and down the Andes with knife, fork and spoon. Vol. 2. being an exotic drinking book; or, up and down the Andes with jigger, beaker and flash. New York: Crown, 1951. G11920

BAKER, John V., ed. The paragon of wines and spirits. Vol. 1. London: Heidelberg Press, 1972. 203p. Illus. G11930

   Over seventy wines and spirits from eleven countries are evaluated and rated. The tasting notes are prefaced with articles by well-known wine writers or experts. See Russell, Mark, ed. for reference to Vol. 2.

BAKER, Oliver. Black jacks and leather bottells, being some account of leather drinking vessels in England and incidentally of other ancient vessels. London: E.J. Burrow, 1921. 190p. G11940

BALDWIN'S rancho winery and price list. Arcadia, CA: c1895. G11950

BALDWINSON, John. Plonk and super-plonk. London: Michael Joseph, 1975. 116p. Illus. G11960

   1977 edition of 141p.

ROBERT LAWRENCE BALZER

Mr. Balzer's life with wine and food has involved writing a syndicated wine column for the *Los Angeles Times*, publishing a nationally distributed wine newsletter, teaching courses in wine appreciation and collecting books on wine. He serves as the food and beverage editor for *Holiday Magazine*. An accomplished photographer, Mr. Balzer's photographs appear in many of his books.

BALZER, Robert Lawrence. Adventures in wine. 2nd ed. Los Angeles: Ward Richie Press, 1969. 114p. Illus. G11980

_____. Book of wines and spirits. Los Angeles: Ward Richie Press, 1973. 118p. Illus. G11990

_____. California's best wines. Los Angeles: Ward Richie Press, 1948. 153p. Illus. G12000

Mr. Balzer selects thirteen wineries that he defines as the best in Calilfornia. The wineries reviewed are Almaden Vineyards, Beaulieu Vineyards, Concannon, Fountaingrove, Freemark Abbey, Inglenook Vineyards, Korbel and Bros., Charles Krug, Los Amigos, Louis Martini, Novitiate of Los Gatos, Paul Masson and Wente Bros. Second edition published in 1979.

_____. The Los Angeles Times book of California wines. New York: Abrams, 1984. 169p. Illus. G12005

This is a revised and updated edition of *The Wines of California* and nicely illustrated with about fifty of Balzer's color photographs.

_____. The pleasures of wine. Indianapolis: Bobbs-Merrill, 1964. 319p. Illus. G12010

Introduction by André L. Simon.

_____. This uncommon heritage; the Paul Masson story. Los Angeles: Ward Richie Press, 1970. 118p. Illus. G12020

_____. Wines of California. New York: Harry N. Abrams, 1978. 270p. Illus. G12030

Beautiful color photographs by the author. 128 vineyards are visited and information is given on their histories, their founders, present owners and the wines.

BANIS, Victor J. The earth and all it holds. New York: St. Martins, 1980. 364p. G12040

A novel with a California wine industry setting.

_____. This splendid earth. New York: St. Martins, 1978. 439p. G12050

A novel with a California wine industry setting.

BANK of America. California wine outlook. San Francisco: Bank of America, n.d. 20p. G12060

BANNING, Kendall. The Squire's recipes wines as described in the journal of Thomas Hoggson, Gent., 1765. New York: Charles Edmund Merrill, 1924. 38p. G12070

Limited edition of 1524 copies. This book is a very pleasant hoax that nearly succeeded. See J. Street, *Table Topics* page eighty-nine for full details about the hoax.

BANTHORPE, Guy David. The fundamental approach and processes of making wine at home. Cheltenham, England: By the Author, 1968. 16p. Illus. G12080

BARNES, Linda. Bitter finish. New York: St. Martin's Press, 1983. G12090

A murder mystery novel with a California wine industry setting.

BARNETT and FOSTER. Recipes for the manufacture of aerated waters, cordials . . . London: c1900. 121p. Illus. G12100

Includes recipes for wines.

BARRON, Archibald F. Vines and vine-culture: being a treatise on the cultivation of the grape vine; with descriptions of the principal varieties. London: Journal of Horticulture Office, 1883. 240p. Illus. G12110

> This work was well received in all parts of the world, resulting in a revised second edition in 1887, a revised and enlarged third edition in 1892, a fourth edition in 1900 and a fifth edition in 1912. There are thirty plate illustrations of grapes that were photographed directly onto the wood block and then engraved, plus over fifty other illustrations.

BARRY, Sir Edward. Observations, historical, critical and medical on the wines of the ancients and the analogy between them and modern wines. London: T. Cadell, 1775. 479p. Illus. G12120

> This is the earliest major work in English on the wines of the Ancients, and the first book in English that discusses modern wines. The body of the text concerns Barry's translation of passages from ancient wine writers, and, as such, brought to light their views, which had been previously unavailable in English. Both Alexander Henderson and André L. Simon accuse Barry of having compiled his knowledge of ancient wines from a book by Andreae Bacci, written almost 200 years earlier. In any event, the most interesting part of Barry's book is the fifty-seven page appendix that deals with modern wines. Barry's comments about modern wines give us an insight into the thinking of a distinguished Englishman about wines available in England in the same year that George Washington was commissioned by the Continental Congress as Commander-in-Chief of the Continental Armies. Aside from content, Barry's book will interest the book collector for its sheer physical beauty. It is a large volume and an interesting example of printing and typography, i.e. the arrangement on a page of type, ornaments and illustrations. It was printed in 1775 on much the same kind of wooden press as were Gutenberg's Bibles in the 15th century. [No fundamental change occurred until 1800, when Charles Stanhope invented and produced an iron press.] After more than 200 years the pages are almost as unblemished as the day the book was published. Scarce.

> An attempt to determine through the British Library the number of copies printed was unsuccessful. The question of edition sizes is and was purely a commercial matter, and this information can only be found in the records kept by the publisher. Thomas Cadell was an important publisher and bookseller during the last quarter of the 18th century, but he died in 1802. No records of this publishing firm that predate 1793 have been found.

BARRY-KING, Hugh. A Tradition of English wine. The story of two thousand years of English wine made from English grapes. Oxford: Oxford Illustrated Press, 1977. 250p. Illus. G12130

BARTON, Sir D. Plunket. The story of our Inns of Court. London: G.T. Paulis, 1924. G12140

OBSERVATIONS

HISTORICAL, CRITICAL, and MEDICAL,

ON THE

WINES OF THE ANCIENTS.

AND THE

ANALOGY between them and MODERN WINES.

WITH

General OBSERVATIONS on the PRINCIPLES and QUALITIES
of WATER, and in particular on thofe of BATH.

Indagatio ipfa rerum tum maximarum tum etiam occultiffimarum habet oblectationem. Si
vero aliquid occurret quod verifimile videatur, humaniffima completur animus vo-
luptate. Cic. in Lucullo.

By Sir EDWARD BARRY, Bart.
Fellow of the Royal College of Physicians, and of the Royal Society.

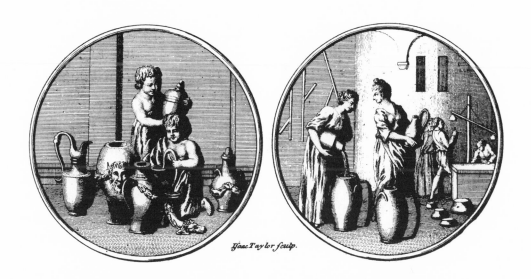

Yaac Taylor fculp.

LONDON,
Printed for T. CADELL, in the Strand. 1775.

Although not a wine book per se, this fascinating account of the English Inns of Court provides for the wine lover a most interesting chapter on Inn life in former days. It centers around the Hall where members met for breakfast, dinner and supper, which they took in common for centuries. "The food was of a simple character; for breakfast and supper it was merely bread and beer. At dinner there was fish in Lent; beef and mutton at other times. . . . You can trace in the Black Books the introduction of Canary and Port, of arrac punch, and in 1775 we have the first mention of champagne."

Some distinguished alumni of the Inns are: William Blackstone, John Austin, Sir Thomas More, Sir Francis Bacon, Thomas Macaulay, William Congreve, James Boswell, William Thackeray.

BATCHELOR, Denzil. For what we are about to receive. London: Herbert Jenkins, 1964. 210p. G12150

_____. Wines great and small. London: Cassell, 1969. 190p. G12160

BATTAM, Anne. Collection of scarce valuable recipes together with directions for making several sorts of wine. London: By the Author, 1750. 198p. G12170

BATTY, R.B. The "medicated wines" fraud as denounced by doctors. Manchester: 1913. 15p. G12180

BAUS, Herbert S. How to wine your way to good health. New York: Mason and Lipscomb, 1973. 230p. G12190

BAYARD, Luke. The complete wine guide. 2nd ed. London: Wine and Spirit Publications, 1973. 381p. Illus. G12200

First published in book form in 1969.

_____. The wine guide. 5 vols. London: Wine and Spirit Publications, Illus. G12210

Reprinted from *Wine Magazine*: Vol. I, 1963; Vol. II, 1964; Vol. III, 1965; Vol. IV, 1966; Vol. V, 1967.

BEACH, Frank Hainer. Grape growing in Ohio. Columbus, OH: Agricultural Extension Service, The Ohio State University, 1944. 47p. Illus. G12230

BEACH, S. New and complete cellar book for homemade wines. London: T. Traveller, 34p. G12240

BEADLE, Leigh P. Brew it yourself; a complete guide to the brewing of beer, ale, mead and wine. New York: Farrar, Straus and Giroux, 1971. 104p. Illus. G12250

_____. Making fine wines and liqueurs at home. New York: Farrar, Straus and Giroux, 1972. 110p. Illus. G12260

BEAR, J.W. The fortication and falsification of wine. Melbourne: Tytherleigh and Bayne, 1895. 30p. G12270

_____. The viticultural resources of Victoria. Melbourne: Melville, Mullen and Slade, 1893. G12280

BEARDSALL, Francis. Treatise on the natural properties and composition of ancient and modern wines. London: By the Author, 1839. 54p. G12290

BEASTALL, William. The grocer and distiller's useful guide, being a complete directory for making and managing all kinds of wines and spirituous liquors . . . 2nd ed. New York: By the Author, 1832. 432p. G12300

_____. A useful guide for grocers, distillers, hotel and tavern-keepers, and wine and spirit dealers . . . New York: By the Author, 1829. 340p. G12310

> Contains recipes for making about everything potable. The author promotes the domestic production of beverages so as not to be at the mercy of foreign powers.

BEATTY-KINGSTON, William. Claret; its production and treatment, with notes on celebrated vineyards and vintages and a description of the Médoc. London: Vinton, 1895. 85p. Illus. G12320

BEAULIEU Vineyard. Beaulieu's family of wines. San Francisco: Beaulieu Vineyard, 1946. 24p. Illus. G12330

BEAVEN, Donald Ward. Wines for dining. Christchurch, England: Whipcoulls Publishers, 1977. 63p. Illus. G12340

BECK, E. James. Wine: its history, culture and making. Sydney: Rhinecastle Wines, 1946. 59p. Illus. G12350

> Covers interesting historical data on Australian viticulture and the making of wines.

BECK, E. James, ed. The aesthetics of wine, the history of wine in Australia, the story of the making of outstanding wines, together with a complete dictionary of wine terms in common usage. Sydney: Rhinecastle Wines, 1946. 56p. Illus. G12360

BECK, Frederick K. The Fred Beck wine book; Fred Beck's gay, clear-cut explanation of the wines of the world, with special recognition of the wines of California. New York: Hill and Wang, 1964. 242p. Illus. G12370

> The wines to buy, judging wines, vineyard tours.

BECK, Hastings. Meet the Cape wines. Cape Town: Purnell and Sons, 1955. 41p. Illus. G12380

> Second edition published in 1966.

BECKER, Peter. Grapes of delight. California rediscovered. St. Helena, CA: Images Unlimited, 1976. G12390

BECKETT, Richard. What wine is that? 2nd ed. Sydney: Ure Smith, 1975. 57p. Illus. G12400

> Australian wine guide by label identification; 398 labels in full color.

BECKETT, Richard and HOGG, Donald. The bulletin book of Australian wineries. Ultimo, N.S.W.: Gregory's Publishing, 1979. 276p. Illus. G12410

A vineyard guide by a journalist and a photographer with some original photographs.

BECKWITH, A.R. The vintner's story. Sydney: Oswald Ziegler, 1959. 35p. Illus. G12420

Republished in 1969.

_____. The vintner's story. Tempe, N.S.W.: Penfolds Wines, c1970. 32p. Illus. G12430

BECKWITH, Edward Lansdale. Practical notes on wines. London: Smith, Elder and Co., 1868. 106p. G12440

Beckwith was a wine merchant and juror and reporter on wines at the Paris exhibition in 1867. He submitted a "report on the Wines and other Fermented Liquors of all Nations" to the Queen's Commissioners, and this small book is a slightly revised version of that report, which treats in a concise manner the wines of every country that exhibited. Beckwith found American wines disappointing and commented: "In the United States of America the show of wines is naturally very small; but I need only, in explanation, quote the terse remark of one of the United States commissioners: 'We do not exhibit for the sake of selling, but with the object of learning.' Such being obviously the case, I shall be absolved from all imputations of unfriendliness in noticing the extreme sparseness of the wine product of North America." The author comments on only one American grape varietal, the catawba. Beckwith's scant mention of Greek wines caused James L. Denman (see Denman) to publish an excoriating attack on the wine opinions expressed by Beckwith in this book.

BEDFORD, J.R. Discovering English vineyards. London: Shire, 1982. 56p. G12450

BEECH, Frederick Walter. Homemade wines, syrups and cordials. London: National Federation of Women's Institutes, 1954. 117p. G12470

Second and third editions published in 1964 and 1970.

BEECH, Frederick and POLLARD, A. Winemaking and brewing. Andover, England: Amateur Winemaker, 1972. 197p. G12480

_____. Wines and juices. London: Hutchinson, 1961. 180p. Illus. G12490

BEEDELL, Suzanne. Winemaking and home brewing, a complete guide. London: Sphere Books, 1969. 189p. Illus. G12500

BEETON, Mrs. M. Isabelle. Jam making . . . and homemade wines. London: Ward, Lock, 1924. 128p. G12510

BEGIN, Emile Auguste Nicolas Jules. Wine in the different forms of anaemia and atonic gout. (Translated from the French.) Paris: J.B. Bailliere, 1877. 24p. G12520

BEILENSON, Peter. French wit and wisdom. [Being sayings of Rochefoucauld and others.] Drawings by Fritz Kredel. Mt. Vernon, NY: Peter Pauper Press, 1956. 61p. Illus. G12530

——————. Peter Pauper's drink book; a guide to drinks and drinking. Illustrated by Ruth McCrea. Mt. Vernon, NY: Peter Pauper Press, 1964. 62p. Illus. G12540

BELL, Bibiane. The wine book. New York: Golden Press, 1969. 310p. Illus. G12560

BELLOC, Hilaire. Advice. London: Harvill Press, 1960. 37p. Illus. G12570

Personal advice on serving, bottling and drinking wines.

——————. The praise of wine, an heroic poem. Privately printed, 1931. 8p. G12580

BELLOWS and Co. Catalog of notes on the selection, care, service and proper uses of wines, together with a chart of vintage years. New York: 1934. 28p. G12590

——————. A catalogue of fine wines and spirits. 3rd ed. New York: 1949. 28p. G12600

BELLOWS, Charles. Madeira. New York: Bonforts Circular, 1896, 1897 and 1900. 43p. Illus. G12610

BELPERROUD, John. The vine; with instructions for its cultivation for a period of six years; the treatment of the soil, and how to make wine from Victorian grapes. Being two essays. Geelong: Heath and Cordell, 1859. 97p. G12620

A facsimile reprint of this text was published by Casuarina Press in 1978 and limited to 1,000 copies.

BELT, Thomas Edwin. Flower, leaf and sap wines. London: Mills and Boon, 1971. 91p. G12630

——————. Plants unsafe for winemaking. Andover, England: Amateur Winemaker, 1972. 84p. G12640

——————. Preserving winemaking ingredients. Andover, England: Amateur Winemaker, 118p. Illus. G12650

——————. Vegetable, herb and cereal wines. London: Mills and Boon, 1971. 96p. G12680

——————. Wild plants for winemaking. Andover, England: Amateur Winemaker, 1974. 87p. G12660

——————. Wines from jams and preserved fruits. London: Mills and Boon, 1971. 93p. G12670

BELTH, George. Household guide to wines and liquors. London: Bellson Syndicate, 1934. 48p. G12690

BEMAN, David, comp. The mysteries of trade, or the great source of wealth: containing receipts and patents in chemistry and manufacturing; with practical observations on the useful arts. Boston: Printed for the author by W. Bellamy, 1825. 152p. G12700

Covers such diverse subjects as fermentation, distillation, brewing, London porter, ale, small beer, cider, mead, and currant, gooseberry, elderberry, quince, peach and birch wines.

BENNETT, R. Bennett's guide to winemakers, brewers, distillers . . . containing tables arranged to specific gravity . . . Cincinnati: By the Author, 1852. 48p. G12710

BENSON, Carl [pseud]. Anacreontics. New York: Privately printed, 1872. Illus. G12720

> Anacreon was a Greek poet of the sixth century B.C. whose odes and epigrams were devoted to the praise of love and wine.

BENSON, Jeffrey and MacKENZIE, Alastair. Sauternes. A study of the great sweet wines of Bordeaux. London: Sotheby Parke Bernet Publications, 1979. 172p. Illus. G12730

> The wines of the Sauternes *cru classé* chateaux are covered in detail with color photographs of the chateaux and their owners. Other chapters list the non-classified chateaux of Sauternes and satellite districts and the chateaux in the neighboring sweet wine appellations of Cerons, Loupiac and St. Croix-du-Mont. Sauternes vintages from 1890 to 1978 are covered with tasting notes. This is the only modern reference book about these wine districts. Also published by The Wine Appreciation Guild in 1981.

_____. The wines of Saint-Émilion and Pomerol. London: Sotheby Publications, 1983. 278p. Illus. G12740

> Although the vineyards of Saint-Émilion and Pomerol have been producing wine since the third and fourth centuries, they were little known in wine circles until comparatively recently. This low recognition is due in part to a lack of literature about these wines. This is the first book in English that chronicles every single property of these two areas, the associated districts of the Lalande de Pomerol and the communes that are entitled to add "Saint-Émilion" to their names. The authors have undertaken (with considerable success) to "describe, with the help of the camera's eye, the geography, soil and climate, the grape varieties and their combination, the methods of viticulture and vinification, the individual properties and, of course, the taste and smell of the wines. . . . " For those who buy, sell or collect the wines of Saint-Émilion or Pomerol, this is an invaluable reference.

BENSON, John. The spirit merchant and licensed victualler's guide. London: n.p., n.d. G12750

BENSON, Robert. Great winemakers of California. Santa Barbara, CA: Capra Press, 1977. 303p. Illus. G12760

> Interviews with twenty-eight winemakers set out in question-and-answer format.

BENSTEAD, C.R. Hic, haec, hock! A low fellow's grammar and guide to drinking; a low fellow being anyone who is not a connoisseur or a teetotaller. London: Frederick Muller, 1934. 212p. Illus. G12770

> This book is far more interesting than the subtitle might indicate. The writing reveals a competent knowledge of both wine and wine literature.

BENTLEY, Iris. Wine with a merry heart. New York: Comet Press Books, 1959. 30p. Illus. G12780

BENWELL, W.S. Coonawarra, a vignoble. Melbourne: Collins, 1973. 43p. G12790

_____. Journey to wine in Victoria. Melbourne: Pitman, 1960. 120p. Illus. G12810

> Second edition of 224p. published in 1976; third edition was published in 1978.

BERG, Harold W. Grape classification by total acidity. San Francisco: Wine Institute, 1960. 53p. G12820

BERGERON, Victor Jules. My selection of California wines. San Francisco: Trader Vic, 1966. 44p. Illus. G12830

BERIDZE, G. Wines and cognacs of Georgia. Moscow: Prodinterg (All-Union Export-Import Association), 1965. G12840

BERKMANN, Joseph and HALL, Allen. Berkmann and Hall's good wine guide, 1978. London: Chantal Wine Publications, 1978. 135p. Illus. G12850

> Was published annually.

BERNARD, Bertram M. Liquor laws of the forty-eight states . . . New York: Oceana Publications, 1949. 87p. G12860

> Intended as a guide for restaurants, hotels, taverns, package stores, clubs and other retail establishments, it covers legal restrictions on the sale of wines and liquors in the various states.

BERNSTEIN, Leonard S. The official guide to wine snobbery. New York: William Morrow, 1982. 159p. Illus. G12880

> A delightful book for the wine lover who doesn't take himself too seriously. In fifty humorous essays the author pokes fun at the wine snob.

BERRY BROS. Tokay. London: Berry Bros., 1933. 29p. Illus. G12890

BERRY, Charles Walter. In search of wine: a tour of the vineyards of France. London: Constable, 1935. 389p. Illus. G12900

> A day-by-day account of the author's eight-week tour of the vineyards of France in 1934. At the end of each chapter, Mr. Berry gives a summary of the vintages. Although the wines discussed are no longer available, there is a great deal of information the wine lover will find of interest.

_____. A miscellany of wine. London: Constable, 1932. 104p. G12910

> The title well describes the contents, i.e. sixteen essays that range from a description of a blind tasting of a rare Chambertin to a discourse on the medicinal uses of wine.

_____. Viniana. London: Constable, 1929. 140p. G12920

> The contents of this book were stated in a review from the *Man-*

chester Guardian: "We are privileged to dine with an anonymous and happy bank of scholars, wits and wine-lovers on three occasions, and at all three, the conversation is deftly guided by the host so that it not only throws light on the quality of different vintages as they are brought to the table, but also gives us glimpses into the character of the diners themselves." The three occasions involve a claret dinner, a burgundy dinner and a champagne dinner. A fourth dinner celebrating hock is discussed in the form of a letter from the author to his host. The text is illustrated with nine prints about wine.

A revised and enlarged edition was published by Constable in 1934 and an American edition was published in 1938 by Knopf.

BERRY, Cyril John James. Amateur Winemaker recipes. Andover, England: Amateur Winemaker, 1968. 132p. Illus. G12930

_____. First steps in winemaking. Andover, England: Amateur Winemaker, 1963. 110p. Illus. G12940

Subsequent editions.

_____. An introduction into winemaking. Andover, England: By the Author, 8p. G12950

_____. 130 new winemaking recipes: a guide to making wines. Andover, England: Amateur Winemaker, 1963. 82p. Illus. G12960

Another edition, 1967.

_____. Winemaking with canned and dried fruit . . . Andover, England: Amateur Winemaker, 1968. 91p. Illus. G12970

BERRY-SMITH, F. Vines under glass. Wellington, New Zealand: New Zealand Department of Agriculture, 1962. 36p. Illus. G12980

_____. Viticulture. Wellington, New Zealand: Ministry of Agriculture and Fisheries, 1973. 98p. Illus. G12990

BESPALOFF, Alexis. The Family Circle guide to wine. New York: Family Circle, 1973. 127p. Illus. G13000

_____. The fireside book of wine. New York: Simon and Schuster, 1977. 445p. Illus. G13010

_____. The first book of wine. New York: World, 1971. 232p. Illus. G13020

_____. Guide to inexpensive wines. New York: Simon and Schuster, 1973. 157p. Illus. G13030

Subsequent revised editions.

_____. The new Signet book of wine. New York: New American Library, 1980. G13040

_____. The Signet book of wine. New York: New American Library, 1971. 272p. G13050

Many subsequent editions.

The BEST of food and wine. New York: American Express, 1984. 240p. Illus. G13055

BETTER Homes and Gardens. Favorite Americans wines and how to enjoy them. Des Moines: Meredith, 1979. G13060

BEVERAGE Research Bureau. A manual on beers, wines and liquors for everybody. Alliance, OH: 1934. 32p. G13070

BEWERUNGE, Wilhelm. German wine on the Danube and Rhine. Berlin: Hauptvereinigung der Deutschen Weinbauwirtschaft, c1935. 55p. G13090

Text in English.

BIANE, Philo. Wine making in southern California and recollections of Fruit Industries, Inc. 1972. 100p. G13100

See California Oral History Series

BICKERTON, L.M. An illustrated guide to eighteenth-century English drinking glasses. South Brunswick, NJ: Great Albion, 1971. Illus. G13120

A revised limited edition of 1,000 copies published in 1984.

BICKHAM, Jack M. The winemakers. Garden City, NY: Doubleday, 1977. 570p. G13130

A novel with a California wine industry setting.

BIDDLE, Anthony Joseph Drexel. The land of the wine; being an account of the Madeira Islands at the beginning of the twentieth century, and from a new point of view. 2 vols. 2nd ed. Philadelphia: Drexel Biddle, 1901. 267/300p. Illus. G13140

_____. The Maderia Islands. 2 Vols. London: Hurst and Blackett and New York and Philadelphia: D. Biddle, 1900. Illus. G13150

BIERMANN, Barrie. Groot Constantia; from wine country. Cape Town: Buren G13160

_____. Red wine in South Africa. Cape Town: Buren, 1971. 156p. Illus. G13170

BIJUR, George. Wines with long noses. London: Hampton Hall Press, 1951. 31p. Illus. G13180

Second edition published in 1977.

BILLINGTON, Ernest A. The handicaps of the wine trade. London: The Wine Trade Club, 1934. G13190

This booklet grew out of an essay competition by the Education Committee of the Wine Trade Club.

BIOLETTI, Frederick T. Bench grafting resistant vines. Berkeley: California Agricultural Experiment Station, 1900. 38p. Illus. G13200

_____. The best wine grapes of California . . . Sacramento: University of California, Bulletin No. 193, 1907. 19p. G13210

_____. Bioletti papers. Bound in San Francisco: 1969. G13220

Volume I. Nine articles and pamphlets/bulletins on enology and viticulture.

_____. Elements of grape growing in California. Berkeley: California Agriculture Extension Service, Circular No. 30, 1929. 37p. Illus. G13230

_____. Grape culture in California. Berkeley: University of California Agriculture Bulletin No. 197, 1908. G13240

_____. Head, cane, and cordon pruning of vines. Berkeley: University of California, 1924. 32p. Illus. G13245

_____. Manufacture of dry wines in hot countries. Sacramento: University of California, Bulletin No. 167, 1905. 66p. Illus. G13250

_____. A new method of making dry red wines. Sacramento: State Print. Off., 1906. 36p. G13260

_____. New wine-cooling machine. Sacramento: State Print. Off., 1906. 27p. Illus. G13265

_____. Oidium or powdery mildew of the vine. Berkeley: University of California, 1915. 12p. Illus. G13262

_____. The phylloxera of the vine. Sacramento: State Print. Off., 1901. 16p. Illus. G13267

_____. Possible uses for wine-grape vineyards. Sacramento: 1919. 18p. G13269

_____. The principles of wine-making. Sacramento: University of California, 1911. G13270

_____. Report on condition of vineyards in portions of Santa Clara valley. Sacramento: State Print. Off., 1901. 11p. Illus. G13280

_____. Resistant vineyards: grafting, planting, cultivation, 1906. Sacramento: State Print. Off., 1906. 144p. Illus. G13290

BIRD, William. French wines; a practical guide for the cellarman, wine-butler and connoisseur. Paris: French Government, 1955. 78p. Illus. G13300

There are prior and subsequent editions.

_____. A practical guide to French wines. Paris: Three Mountains Press, n.d. 80p. G13310

BIRKETT, E. The golden wine of old Britain. London: By the Author, 1952. 122p. Illus. G13320

BIRMINGHAM, F.A., ed. Esquire drink book. New York: Harper and Row, 1956. 310p. G13330

Subsequent edition by Muller, 1962.

BISHOP, Allen. Knowing and selling wines, liquors, liqueurs, cordials. 1934. 56p. G13350

BISHOP, Geoffrey C. Australian winemaking; the Roseworthy influence. Hawthorndene: Investigator Press, 1980. 344p. Illus. G13360

> Details the contribution of Alan Hickinbotham and the Roseworthy Agricultural College to winemaking in Australia.

_____. The vineyards of Adelaide: a history of the grape growers and winemakers of the Adelaide area. Blackwood, S.A.: Linton Publications, 1977. 152p. G13370

BLAKE, Philos. Guide to American corkscrew patents, vol. 1, 1860-1895. New Castle, DE: Bottlescrew Press, 1981. Illus. G13380

_____. Guide to American corkscrew patents, vol. 2, 1896-1920. New Castle, DE: Bottlescrew Press, 1981. 63p. Illus. G13390

BLANDY, Graham. See Simon, André L. *The Bolton Letters.* G13395

BLANKENHORN, Adolph. The participation of the Enological Institute Blankenhornsberg at the International Exhibition in Sydney. 1879. 10p. G13400

> Also published in 1881.

BLEASDALE, John Ignatius. An essay on the wines sent to the Intercolonial Exhibition by the Colonies of Victoria, New South Wales and South Australia, with critical remarks on the present condition and prospects of the wine industry in Australia. Melbourne: F.F. Bailliere, 1876. 35p. G13410

_____. On colonial wines: a paper read before the Royal Society of Victoria, 13th May 1867, by J.J. Bleasdale . . . Melbourne: Privately printed by Stillwell and Knight, 1867. 24p. G13420

> Subsequent edition published in 1873.

_____. On wines. [Melbourne: 1872]. 33p. G13425

_____. Present conditions and prospects of the wine industry in Australia. Melbourne: Bailliere, 1876. G13430

_____. Pure native wine considered as an article of food and luxury. Adelaide: Andrews, Thomas and Clark, 1868. G13440

_____. Two essays drawn up for the official record of the exhibition held in Melbourne in 1872-3: appended, two reports and a paper read before the Royal Society. Melbourne: Mason Firth, 1873. G13460

BLOOMFIELD, William. The servant's companion; or practical housemaid's and footman's guide. London: Blonsell, 1830. G13470

> Bloomfield, who described himself as the headwaiter at the York House Hotel in Bath, gives "Rules for managing wines; to clarify wines; to fine Claret; to restore flat wines; to correct sharp and tart wines; to improve poor wines; to clear foul and ropy wines". He ends by giving recipes for making "Gooseberry wine; British

Champagne; Compound wine; Mulberry wine; Damson wine; Peach and Apricot wine; Grape wine; Turnip wine; Balm wine; Ginger wine; English Port wine; Cherry wine."

BLOUT, Jessie Schilling. A brief economic history of the California wine growing industry. San Francisco: The Wine Institute, 1943. 21p. G13480

Emphasizes the post-Prohibition period.

BLUM, Howard L. The wines and vines of Europe. New York: Benjamin Co., 1974. 175p. Illus. G13490

BLUMBERG, Robert S. and HANNUN, H. California wine. Menlo Park, CA: 1973. 224p. G13500

_____. The fine wines of California. Garden City, NY: 1971. 311p. Illus. G13510

Revised edition of 416p. published in 1973.

BLYTH, James. The commercial development of the French colonies: "The wine production of Algeria." London: c1904. 16p. G13520

BOAKE, A. Specialties for the treatment of wines and spirits. London: Roberts and Co., 193?. 19p. G13530

BOAKE, W.B. The production of wine in Australia. London: Boake, Roberts, 1889. 13p. G13540

BODE, Charles. Wines of Italy. London: Peter Owen, 1956. 135p. Illus. G13550

BODINGTON, C. Wines of the Bible. London: S.P.C.K., 1887. 31p. G13560

BODKIN, Thomas. The Saintsbury oration delivered by Professor Thomas Bodkin at the 31st meeting of The Saintsbury Club, 23 October 1947. London: Privately printed at the Curwen Press for The Saintsbury Club, 1947. 15p. G13570

BOEHM, E.W. and TULLOCH, H.W. Grape varieties of South Australia. Adelaide: Department of Agriculture, South Australia, 1967. 95p. Illus. G13580

A major text for identifying grape varieties of South Australia.

BOHEMIAN Club. Wine List: California and Imported Wines, Brandies, Liqueurs. San Francisco: Bohemian Club, 1940. [32]p. Illus. G13590

BOIREAU, Raimond. Wines, their care and treatment in cellar and store . . . Sacramento: California State Board of Viticultural Commissioners, 1889. 148p. G13600

BOLITHO, Hector. The wine of the Douro. London: Sidgwick and Jackson, 1956. 26p. Illus. G13610

BOLSMANN, Eric H. Bertrams guide to South African wines of origin. c1977. G13620

_____. The South African wine dictionary. Cape Town: Balkema, 1977. 154p. Illus. G13630

BOLTON, Mary. Homemade wines, confectionery and sweets. London: W. Foulsham and Co., 1957. 128p. G13640

BONE, Arthur. "How to" book of choosing and enjoying wine. London: Blandford, 1981. 96p. Illus. G13650

BONETTI, Edward. The wine cellar. 4th ed. New York: The Viking Press, 1977. G13660

> Stories dealing with an Italian immigrant family and wine.

BONNARD, H.E. Report of the executive secretary on the Bordeaux International Exhibition of Wines, 1882. Sydney: 1884. 130p. Illus. G13670

_____. Report of the executive secretary on the Bordeaux International Exhibition of Wines, 1882. Canberra: The Thumb Press, 1982. 150p. Illus. G13680

> A facsimile reprint edition limited to 385 copies, including ten pages of illustrations.

BONNEFONS, Nicolas de. The French gardiner: instructing how to cultivate al sorts of fruit-trees, and herbs for the garden: together with directions to dry, and conserve them in their natural: an accomplished piece, written originally in French. amd now translated into English, by John Evelyn. London: Printed by S.S. for Benji Tooke, 1672. G13690

> The first edition of 294p. was published in 1658 and translated by John Evelyn with editions in 1669 and 1675. Also 1691 edition of 215p.

BONOEIL, John. His majesties gracious letter to the Earle of South-Hampton, treasurer, and to the councell and company of Virginia heere: commanding the present setting up of silke works, and planting of vines in Virginia . . . Together with instructions how to plant and dresse vines, and to make wines . . . Set foorth for the benefit of the two reowned and most hopefull sisters, Virginia, and the Summer-Ilands. By John Bonoeil, Frenchman, servant in these imployments to His most excellent Majesty of Great Brittaine, France, Ireland, Virginia, and the Summer-Ilands. Published by authority. London: Printed by Felix Kyngston, 1622. 88p. G13700

A BOOK of wine and the wholesale prices of wines in the Savory Cellars. London: 1933. 33p. G13710

A BOOKE of secrets: shewing diuers waies to make and prepare all sorts of inke, and colours: as blacke, white, blew, greene, red, yellow and other colours . . . translated out of Dutch into English by W.P. Hereunto. As annexed, a little treatise intituled, instructions for watering of wines: shewing how to make wine . . . written first in Italian, and now newly translated into English, by W.P. London: Printed by Adam Islip for Edward White, 1596. 40p. G13720

BOORDE, Andrew. The breuiarie of health. London: Thomas Este, 1598. G13730

Boorde, a physician, tells us in the beginning of his treatise that "Boorde hates water but likes good Ale and Wine." The wine he drank was Gascon wine, although he would sometimes drink Muscatel or Alicante and approved of the white wines of Anjou and Orleans and red and white Rhenish wines. The doctor goes on to set out some excellent advice, which is quoted in the original spelling. "Chose your wyne after this sorte; it must be fyne, fayre, and clene to the eye; it must be fragraunt and redolent, havynge a good odour and flavour in the nose; it must spryncle [sparkle] in the cup when it is drawne or put out of the pot into the cup; it must be colde and pleasaunt in the mouthe; and it must be and subtyll of substaunce." Such wine "if moderately drunken, doth acuate and quicken a man's wits, comfort the heart, scour the liver; specially if it be white wyne, it doth rejoice all the powers of man and nourish them; it doth engender good blood, comfort and nourish the brain and all the body, and it resolveth flegm; it ingendreth heat, and is good against heaviness and pensifulness; it is full of agility; wherefore it is medicinable, specially white wine, for it doth mundify and cleanse wounds and sores."

Dr. Boorde usually abstained from drinking what he called "hot" dessert wines but gives a list of fourteen then available: Malmsey, Corsican, Greek, Romanysk, Rumney, Sack, Alicant, Bastard, Tyre, Osey, Muscadell, Capryke, Tynt, Roberdany. Of these, he lists as lighter wines Muscadell, Bastard, Osey, Caprique, Alicant and Tyre. These and "other hote wynes be not good to drynke with meate; but after meate, and with oysters, with salades, with fruyte, a draught or two may be suffered.

"Wines high and hot of operation doth comfort old men and women, but there is no wine good for children and maidens. In High Almayne, otherwise Germany, there is no maid shall drink no wine but still she shall drink water until she be married. The usual drink for youth is fountain water."

The doctor recommends that with meals one should drink "meane wynes" as opposed to "hyghe wynes." 'Wynes of Gascony, Frenche wynes, and specially Raynysshe wyne that is fyned, is good with meate, specyally claret wyne. It is not good to drynke nother wyne nor ale before a man doth eat somewhat, althoughe there be old fantastycall sayings to the contrarye."

And as a prescription for sound mental and physical health, he tells us "To comfort and to rejoice these spirits: first, live out of sin, and follow Christ's doctrine, and then use honest mirth and honest company, and use to eat good meat and drink moderately; second, to comfort the stomach, use Ginger and Galingale, use mirth and well to fare; use Pepper in meats and, beware of anger, for it is a shrode heart that maketh all the body fare the worse." Rare.

Earlier editions of this book were published in 1547, 1552, 1557, 1575 and 1587.

_____. Compendyous regyment or a dyetary of helth made in Moutpyllier. London: Robert Wyer for John Gowghe, c1542. G13740

Subsequent editions were published in c1545, 1562, 1567 and 1576.

BOOTH, David. The art of wine-making in all its branches . . . London: F.J. Mason, 1834. 123p. Illus. G13750

BOOTHBY, Josiah. Adelaide almanack, town and country directory and guide to South Australia. Adelaide: 1865. G13760

BORDEAUX wine and liquor dealer's guide. A treatise on the manufacture and adulteration of liquors. By a practical liquor manufacturer. New York: Dick and Fitzgerald, 1858. 163p. G13770

> Was written for a group of "chemists" involved with the adulteration and imitation of wines and liquors. It is prefaced: "In this book *not one* article in the smallest degree approximating to a poison is recommended, yet it teaches how Cognac, Brandy, Scotch and Irish Whiskey, Foreign and Domestic Rum, all kinds of wines from the choicest to the commonest, can be imitated to the perfection that the best judges cannot detect the method of manufacture."

BORELLA. The court and country confectioner . . . distilling, making fine flavoured wines. London: G. Riley and A. Cooke, 1770. 271p. G13780

BORG, P. Report on a tour of inspection in the wine-growing districts of western Europe and Algeria. Malta: Gov't. Print. Off., 1922. 65p. G13790

BORN, Wina. The concise atlas of wines. New York: Scribner, 1974. 160p. Illus. G13800

> Translated from the Dutch with a foreword by George H. Rezek.

BOSDARI, C.de. Wines of the Cape. Cape Town: A.A. Balkema, 1955. 95p. Illus. G13810

> There are subsequent editions.

BOSWELL, Peyton. Wine makers manual. A guide for the home wine maker and the small winery. New York: Orange Judd, 1935. 96p. Illus. G13820

> Reprinted in 1943, 1944 and 1947.

BOUCHE, Paul. Wine, its connection with health, legislation, individual rights, family happiness, the raising of chickens . . . New York: By the Author, 1913. 12p. G13830

BOULESTIN, X.M. What shall we have to drink? London: Heinemann, 1933. 85p. Illus. G13850

BOULESTIN, Xavier Marcel. Having crossed the channel. London: Heinemann, 1934. 188p. Illus. G13840

> An account by a Frenchman living in London of a trip to Bordeaux and on to Burgundy, Touraine, Anjou, Spain, Brussels, Amsterdam, etc., with emphasis on the wines and foods enjoyed along the way.

BOURKE, Arthur. Winecraft; the encyclopedia of wines and spirits. London: Harper, 1935. 182p. Illus. G13860

BOWERS, Warner Fremont. Gourmet cooking with homemade wines. Harrisburg, PA: Stackpole Books, c1975. G13870

BOWNESS, Charles. The Romany way to health. London: Thorsons, 1970. 96p. G13880

BOYDELL, James. The village cask gauger. London: By the Author, 1860. 143p. G13890

BOYLE, Peter. The publican's and spirit dealer's daily companion, or plain and interesting advice to wine vaults and public house keepers, on subjects of the greatest importance to their own welfare, and to the health, comfort, and satisfaction of their customers and society at large, by following the directions and receipts in this work, they will save at least 25 per cent monthly in their own trade. 6th ed. London: By the Author, c1810. 145p. G13900

BRACONI, Frank. The U.S. wine market. New York: Morton Research, 1977. 154p. G13910

BRADFORD, Sarah. The Englishman's wine - the story of port. London: Macmillan, 1969. 208p. Illus. G13920

_____. The story of port. Rev. ed. London: Christie's Wine Publications, 1978. Illus. G13930

> This is a revised and retitled edition of *The Englishman's Wine*. Another edition published in 1983.

BRADLEY, Nellie H. Wine as a medicine; or Abbie's experience. Rockland, ME: Z.P. Vose and Co., 1873. 22p. G13940

BRADLEY, Robin. Australian wine pocket book. 1978. 115p. G13960

> Second edition published in 1983.

_____. Three days of wine. Victoria: Australia International Press and Publications, 1977. 74p. Illus. G13970

BRADT, O.A. The grape in Ontario. Toronto: Ontario Ministry of Agriculture and Food, 1972. 49p. Illus. G13980

BRAGATO, Romeo. Report on the prospects of viticulture in New Zealand. Wellington, New Zealand: Gov't. Print. Off., 1895. 20p. Illus. G13990

_____. Viticulture in New Zealand (with special reference to American vines). Wellington, New Zealand: J. Mackay, 1906. 60p. Illus. G14000

BRAILLIAR, F.B. Suitability of grapes for general culture in the states of the Old South. Nashville: George Peabody College for Teachers, 1922. 35p. G14010

BRANNT, William T. A practical treatise on the raw materials and the distillation and rectification of alcohol, and the preparation of alcoholic liquors, liqueurs, cordials and bitters. Edited chiefly from the German of Dr. K. Stammer, Dr. F. Elsner, and E. Schubert. Philadelphia, PA: H.C. Baird, 1885. 330p. Illus. G14030

——————. A practical treatise on the raw materials and the distillation and rectification of alcohol, and the preparation of alcoholic liquors, liqueurs, cordials and bitters. Edited chiefly from the German of Dr. K. Stammer, Dr. F. Elsner, and E. Schubert. 1900. 555p. Illus. G14040

——————. A practical treatise on the manufacture of . . . cider and fruit wines . . . 3rd ed. Philadelphia: Henry Carey Baird, 1914. 543p. Illus. G14050

BRATHWAITE, Richard. Barnabae Itinerarium: Barnabees journal; to which is added the song of Bessie Bell. London: Penguin Press, 1933. 175p. G14060

——————. The law of drinking. (Solome disputation theoretke and practike briefely shodowing . . .) New Haven: Published by Hooker, 1903. 107p. G14070

Originally published in London, 1617. Edited by W. Brian Hooker.

——————. Drunken Barnaby's four journeys to the north of England. In Latin and English verse. 2nd ed. London: c1716. 151p. G14080

The original edition of Barnaby's travels has no date but the frontispiece is engraved by W. Marshall, whose business flourished from about 1635 to 1650. It was written first in Latin (1636) and later published with an English translation (c1638). Because the book was published under the pseudonym Cothymbaeus, its true authorship was not discovered until 1818. Subsequent editions were published in 1723, 1758, 1778 (has misprinted title page dated 1788), 1805, 1808, 1818, 1820 and 1822.

If Barnaby was a drunkard, he certainly was well-educated, as he was well-acquainted with the history, antiquities and customs of the places he visited. Barnaby tells us that after four journeys to Appleby on Westmoreland he married, turned farmer and bought and sold horses. Brathwaite gives one of the earliest references in English for the saying: a good wine needs no bush.

"Good wine no bush it needs, as I suppose, let Bacchus' bush be Barnabee's rich nose. No bush, no garland need a cypresse greene, Barnabee's nose may for a bush be seene."

The expression, "good wine needs no bush" is an ancient proverb, far antedating Shakespeare's time where, in the epilogue of *As You Like It*, Rosalind says, "If it be true that good wine needs no bush, 'tis true that a good play needs no epilogue. Yet to good wine they do use good bushes, and good plays prove the better by the help of good epilogue."

The proverb means, of course, that good wine needs no advertising and goes back, at least, to Roman days.

In times when only a few could read, a sign told the traveler where certain goods were sold. The most ancient tavern signs were a bush or garland of ivy (wine) or a chequered board (food). A tavern sign is mentioned in Aristophanes, and tavern signs have been found in the ruins of Pompeii and Herculaneum.

From medieval manuscripts we know that the wine signs were in the form of ivy or holly wreaths or a swatch or ball (bush) of evergreen branches.

Just why the bush evolved as the symbol of good wine is not entirely clear, but it probably derived from the wreath of ivy with which Bacchus was crowned and which is often shown twined around his tyrsos [staff]. "As the ivy is evergreen, so is Bacchus ever young . . . as the ivy winds its closely clinging vine around all things, so Bacchus enmeshes the senses of men."*

Given the complexity and confusion of the modern wine trade, perhaps Shakespeare was right, "to good wine they do use good bushes."

*Endell, Fritz. *Old Tavern Signs*. Cambridge: Houghton Mifflin. 1916.

BRAVERY, Harold Edwin. Amateur winemaking. London: Collins, 1964. 160p. Illus. G14090

_____. The complete book of home winemaking. London: MacGibbon and Kee, 1971. 153p. Illus. G14100

_____. The complete book of home winemaking. 2nd ed. New York: Collier Books, 1973. 210p. Illus. G14110

1977 edition of 175p.

_____. Country wines and cordials. London: Marshall Cavendish Editions, 1980. 184p. Illus. G14120

_____. Home booze. London: Macdonald and Jane's, 1976. 205p. Illus. G14130

Another edition, 1978.

_____. Home-made beers, wines and liqueurs. London: Queene Anne Press, 1974. 128p. Illus. G14140

_____. Home wine and beer making. London: MacGibbon and Kee, 1974. 147p. Illus. G14150

_____. Home wine-making. London: Arco, 1968. 112p. Illus. G14160

_____. Home wine-making — all the year round. London: Max Parrish, 1966. 175p. Illus. G14170

Another edition, 1972.

_____. Home wine-making and vine growing. London: Macdonald, 1973. 146p. Illus. G14180

_____. Home wine-making without failures. London: Max Parrish, 1963. 221p. Illus. G14190

Revised edition published in 1974.

_____. The simple science of wine and beer making. London: Macdonald, 1969. 168p. Illus. G14200

_____. Successful modern winemaking. London: Arco, 1961. 151p. G14210

_____. Successful wine making at home. New York: Arco, 1962. 151p. G14220

BREDENBEK, Magnus. What shall we drink? Popular drinks, recipies and toasts. New York: Carlyle House, 1934. 215p. Illus. G14230

BREMAN, Paul. The Penguin guide to cheaper wines. New York: Penguin, 1976. 158p. G14240

BRENNER, Gary. The naked grape. Indianapolis: Bobbs-Merrill, 1975. 154p. Illus. G14250

BRIDGEMAN, Thomas. The fruit cultivator's manual. London: By the Author, 1844. 175p. G14270

> Contains a chapter about grapes. Subsequent editions in 1847 and 1857.

A BRIEF case of the distillers and of the distilling trade in England . . . London: T. Warner, 1726. 52p. G14280

> Unable to verify.

BRIEF discourse on wine. London: J.L. Denman, 1861. 138p. G14290

BRIEF historical description of the cellars at San Lorenzo and Casa Madero, S.A. n.d. 48p. Illus. G14300

BRIGHT, William. Bright's single stem, dwarf and renewal system of grape culture, adapted to the vineyard, the grapery and the fruiting of vines in pots, on trellises, arbors . . . Philadelphia: By the Author, 1860. 121p. G14310

> William Bright was a nurseryman who propagated native and European vines at his Logan Nursery in Philadelphia. His *Grape Culture* includes an advertisement offering nearly one hundred varieties of "the best foreign grapes." A second edition of 155p. was published in 1851.

BRINK, Andre P. Brandy in South Africa. Cape Town: Burden, 1973. 176p. Illus. G14320

_____. Dessert wine in South Africa. Cape Town: Burden, 1974. 136p. Illus. G14330

BRINKLEY, Robert C. Responsible for drinking. New York: Vanguard Press, c1930. G14340

BRISE, Sheelah Maud Emily Ruggles. Sealed bottles. London: Country Life, 1949. 175p. Illus. G14350

BRITISH guide; or, a directory to housekeepers and innkeepers, containing the best directions in making and managing of choice British wines . . . by an experienced gentleman. Newcastle upon Tyne: Watson, 1813. 186p. G14360

MICHAEL BROADBENT (1927)

Michael Broadbent was born in 1927 in Yorkshire. His first employment was as a wine trainee under the tutelage of Thomas A. Layton (See Layton) in 1952. From that modest beginning he has become one of the world's foremost wine experts.

In 1955 he joined Harvey's of Bristol where his mentor was Harry Waugh (See Waugh). He passed the Master of Wine examination in 1960 and wrote a pamphlet for Harvey's that was expanded into *Wine Tasting*. In 1966 he was hired by the prestigious auction house of Christie, Manson and Wood to start and head a wine auction department. His efforts in this regard have been very successful. In 1983, the value of wine auctioned by Christie's exceeded six million pounds. He is a partner in Christie's.

_____. BROADBENT, Michael. The André L. Simon memorial lecture. London: Christie's Wine Publications, 1971. 23p. Illus. G14380

_____. The complete guide to wine tasting. New York: Simon and Schuster, 1984. Illus. G14385

_____. The great vintage wine book. New York: Knopf, 1980. 432p. Illus. G14390

> Mr. Broadbent is an inveterate note maker and has "systematically noted and indexed every wine I have ever tasted and drunk. . . ." The author's positions with Harvey's, and as head of the Wine Department of Christie's, has afforded him the opportunity to taste the world's rarest and finest wines. His personal tasting notes of over 6000 wines spanning a 200-year period recorded over twenty-seven years form the basis for this extraordinary work. It is an important reference for anyone who sells, buys, trades, collects or drinks fine or rare wine.

_____. Guidance in the technique of tasting. Bristol: John Harvey, 1963. 13p. G14400

_____. Michael Broadbent's complete guide to wine tasting and wine cellars. New York: Simon and Schuster, 1984. 272p. G14405

_____. Michael Broadbent's pocket guide to wine tasting. London: Mitchell Beazley, 1982. 114p. Illus. G14410

_____. Wine tasting. London: Wine and Spirit Publications, 1968. 78p. G14420

> An important reference for those wanting to learn how to distinguish between wines on a subjective basis. Describes the subtleties of wines including how to smell, taste and assess wine as you drink it. There have been numerous subsequent editions.

BROADBENT, Michael, ed. Christie's vintage wine price index, 1982 edition. London: Christie's Wine Publications, 1982. 147p. G14430

> Beginning in 1981 the two elements of Christie's Wine Review were split. The wine articles section appeared in 1981 as *Christie's Wine Companion* (see Matthews, Patrick). The auction price section first appeared in a stand-alone format in 1982 enlarged and in pocket size. This price index is published annually.

_____. Christie's wine review. 9 vols. London: Christie's Wine Publications, 1972-1980. Illus. G14440

> Each review contains an indexed guide of recent auction prices, market trends, historical notes and interesting articles for the connoisseur and collector. The articles cover a variety of wine subjects, among which are decanter labels, vintage cognac, collectors' pieces, Schloss Vollrads, the history of the corkscrew. Discontinued after the 1980 edition.

BROCK, R. Barrington. More outdoor grapes. Surrey: Viticultural Research Station, Report No. 2, 1950. 61p. Illus. G14450

_____. Outdoor grapes in cold climates. Surrey: Viticultural Research Station, Report No. 1, 1949. 71p. Illus. G14460

_____. Progress with vines and wines. Kent: Tonbridge Printers, 1961. 64p. Illus. G14470

_____. Starting a vineyard. Surrey: Viticultural Research Station, Report No. 4, 1964. 78p. Illus. G14480

BRODY, Iles. On the tip of my tongue. New York: Greenberg, 1944. 274p. G14490

> Mainly on food, with a chapter on the wines that appeal to the author.

BROWN, Bob. Homemade hilarity. Weston, VT: The Countryman Press, 1938. 16p. Illus. G14500

BROWN, Cora Lovisa, Mrs. The wine cook book, being a selection of incomparable recipes from France, from the Far East, from the South and elsewhere, all of which owe their final excellence to the skillful use of wine in their preparation. Boston: Little, Brown, 1934. 462p. G14510

> Menus with suggestions for wines and recipes using wine, together with notes on wine and other alcoholic beverages. There are numerous subsequent editions, some with slightly different wording following the first part of the title.

_____. The wining and dining quiz; a banquet of questions and answers from soup to nuts. New York: Appleton-Century, 1939. 165p. G14520

> Questions on foods and wines.

BROWN, George Garvin. The holy Bible repudiates "Prohibition". Compilation of all verses containing the words "wine" or "strong drink", proving that the scriptures commend and command the temperate use of alcoholic beverages. Louisville, KY: By the Author, c1910. 103p. G14530

BROWN, Jefferson. Your vines and wines. Whitbourne, Worcester: Temeside Enterprises. G14540

> Unable to verify.

BROWN, John Hull. Early American beverages. Rutland, VT: C.E. Tuttle Co., 1966. 171p. Illus. G14550

> Also published by Prentice-Hall and Bonanza Books in 1967.

BROWN, Michael and BROWN, Sybil. Food and wine of south-west France. London: Batsford, 1980. 240p. Illus. G14560

BROWN, Neil W. Liquor dealer's and bartender's companion. New York: 1865. 44p. G14570

BROWN, Sanborn C. Wines and beers of Old New England: a how-to-do-it history. Hanover, NH: University Press of New England, 1978. 157p. Illus. G14580

BROWN, W.L. An address on inebriety amongst the ancients and how they "cured" it. London: Medical Magazine Co., 1898. 60p. Illus. G14590

> The author, a Scottish physician, explains in the prefatory note that "the plan of the work has been to show the development and extent of drinking customs among ancient nations; how . . . they sought to avoid the evil consequences of vinous and other intoxication; how remedies were applied to restore tone and vigour to the overzealous banqueter; what penalties and punishments over indulgence and habitual inebriety incurred; and, lastly, to consider which such treatment had been beneficial to the individual or to the race." There is much about wine including illustrations of grape picking and the treading of the must in Egypt more than 5,000 years ago.

BROWNE, Charles. The Gun Club drink book. New York: Scribner's, 1939. 190p. Illus. G14600

> An extensive chapter on wines, including wines served at special dinners and the St. Regis wine list.

BRYANT, William Baily. Nineteenth century handbook on the manufacture of liquors, wines and cordials without the aid of distillation. Owensboro, KY: Industrial Publishing, 1885. 310p. G14610

> This is another work that proves "wine" has been made without grapes. There is also an 1899 edition.

BUCHANAN, Robert. The culture of the grape, and wine making. 2nd ed. Cincinnati: Wright, Ferris, 1850. G14620

> In the preface to this edition, the author comments that the first edition of 1,000 copies was exhausted in a few months. This book remained popular through a third edition in 1852, a fourth edition in 1853, a fifth edition in 1855, a sixth edition in 1860, a seventh edition in 1861 and an eighth edition in 1865. These various editions contain a great deal of information about American viticulture and wine making activities in Ohio, Kentucky and Missouri during this fifteen-year period. The treatise was compiled from articles on grape culture published by members of the Cincinnati Horticultural Society and includes in the appendix an article on the "Cultivation of the Strawberry" by Nicolas Longworth. Subsequent editions.

> Buchanan praises the local catawba wines and Nicholas Longworth's Sparkling Catawba, America's first sparkling wine and an enormous commercial success. Unfortunately, the euphoria pervad-

ing Buchanan's book about the success of the Catawba in the Ohio Valley was stilled almost as the words were being written. Fungal diseases, then uncontrollable, attacked the Cincinnati vineyards, and by the start of the Civil War, they had virtually ceased to exist.

BUCK, John. Take a little wine. Christchurch, Australia: Whitcombe and Tombs, 1969. 160p. Illus. G14630

BUCKLEY, Francis. A history of old English glass. London: Ernest Benn, 1925. G14635

Contains several chapters on 18th century English wine glasses.

The BUCK'S bottle companion: being a complete collection of humorous, bottle and hunting songs. Among which are a great variety of originals. With about two hundred toasts and sentiments London: R. Bladon, 1775. 226p. G14640

BUDD, Joseph L. and HANSEN, N.E. American horticultural manual . . . 2 vols. New York: J. Wiley and Sons, 1902-03. Illus. G14650

Chapter XVII of Part I gives a brief history of the development of grape varieties in the United States. Part II has a chapter that provides more detailed information on contemporary varieties. Republished in 1911-14.

BUELL, J.S. The cider makers' manual. A practical work for use with the new labor-saving machines, in part, with many recipes for turning cider into wine, vinegar, champagne . . . 1869. 111p. G14660

BUMSTEAD, George, comp. Specimen of a bibliography of old books and pamphlets illustrative of the mug, glass, bottle, loving cup and social pipe . . . spiced with anecdotes of celebrated topers; compiled by me. London: Printed for the compiler, 1885. 144p. G14670

Divided into three sections: Part I is a bibliography taken from the auction catalog of George Smith, the distiller of the original "Old Tom Gin." Smith was also a great collector of books of distilling, gin, wine, taverns, etc. Section II is a sketch of the history of intoxicating liquors and Section III "The Vine and Wine." Interspersed with anecdotes.

BUNYARD, Edward A. Anatomy of dessert. 2nd ed. London: Chatto and Windus, 1934. 216p. Illus. G14680

Contains a chapter on wines and advises the kind of fruits with which each wine should be served.

BUNYARD, Edward and Lorna, eds. The epicure's companion. London: J.M. Dent, 1937. 539p. Illus. G14690

Consists of the editor's preface, and three parts. Part I, food; part II, drink; and part III, after dinner. The preface is an essay on the word Epicure. Part II includes a discussion by Mr. Bunyard on "The Art of Drinking," and André Simon on "Recent Bordeaux Vintages." Part III covers "Wine and Food Abroad," by various authors, and ends with an article on the Wine and Food Society.

BURDEN, Rosemary. A family tradition in fine winemaking: one hundred and twenty-five years of Thomas Hardy and Sons; 1853-1978. Adelaide: Thomas Hardy and Sons, 1978. 103p. Illus. G14700

_____. Wines and wineries of the Southern Vales. Adelaide: Rigby, 1976. 171p. Illus. G14710

BURGER, Robert E. The jug wine book. New York: Stein and Day, 1980. 153p. Illus. G14720

BURGESS, H.T. The fruit of the vine. Adelaide: South Australian Total Abstinence League and Band of Hope Union, 1878. 138p. G14730

>Although this is essentially a temperance essay, it is devoted exclusively to the subject of wine and colony wine in particular. Scarce.

BURING, Herman Paul Leopold. The art of serving wine. Sydney: Lindeman, 32p. Illus. G14740

_____. Australian wines: 150th anniversary of the wine industry of Australia. Sydney: Federal Viticultural Council of Australia, 1938. 15p. Illus. G14750

BURKA, Fred and MASSEE, William. Pulling corks. Washington: Fred Burka, 1951. 39p. G14760

BURMAN, Jose. Wine of Constantia. Cape Town: Human and Rousseau, 1979. 192p. Illus. G14770

BURROUGHS, David and BEZZANT, Norman. The new wine companion. London: Heinemann, 1980. 207p. Illus. G14780

>*The Wine Companion* was originally written as a student manual for those taking the British Wine Trade examinations. This is a revised, updated and enlarged edition.

_____. The wine trade student's companion. London: Collins, 1975. 208p. Illus. G14790

>Appendix, glossary and pronunciation guide.

_____. Wine regions of the world. London: Heineman for the Wine and Spirit Education Trust, 1979. 313p. Illus. G14800

BURT, Jocelyn. Wineries of the Barossa Valley. Adelaide: Rigby, 1975. 31p. Illus. G14810

BURTON, A. The story of the Swan District 1843-1938. Perth: n.d. 82p. Illus. G14820 Includes a section on the wine industry.

JAMES BUSBY (1801-1871)

The father of Australian viticulture, James Busby was born and raised in Kirkton, Edinburgh. Busby emigrated to Australia at the age of twenty-two when his father, a civil engineer, was assigned the formidable task of developing a water system for the city of Sydney. James Busby was so proud of his father's success in this regard that he acknowledged it in dedicating his third book to his father. But James Busby's contribution to the Colony was at least equal to that of his father—he gave it wine.

As soon as Busby learned that his father would be moving to Sydney he "was induced to spend some months in the best wine districts of France, [Bordeaux] with a view of acquainting myself with the cultivation of the vine for the making of wine, and having the power to ascertain to what extent it might be profitably cultivated in South Wales."

Busby wrote part of his treatise while en route to Australia, and within a year of his arrival, he published *A Treatise on the Culture of the Vine and the Art of Making Wine.*

Three months after his arrival in Sydney, he was given a grant of 2,000 acres in the Hunter River Valley about 130 miles north of Sydney. Between 1828 and 1830 Busby planted three acres of vines. He named it Kirkton after his birthplace.

In 1830 he published *A Manual of Plain Directions for Planting and Cultivating Vineyards, and for Making Wine in New South Wales.* This work was "addressed to that more numerous portion of the community constituting smaller settlers" because it was Busby's "belief that no greater service could be rendered to this Colony than to induce its inhabitants to cultivate the vine."

Realizing the inadequacy of vines available in the Colony, Busby returned to Europe in 1831, touring France and Spain, where he made a collection of several hundred varieties. These cuttings arrived in Australia in 1832 and were planted at the Sydney Botanic Garden but were subsequently neglected and lost. Fortunately, some of these vines were planted at Kirkton and ultimately had a bearing upon wine growing in Australia.

BUSBY, James. Catalogue of vines in the Botanic Garden, Sydney, introduced into the colony of New South Wales in the year 1832. Sydney: Gov't Print. Off., 1842. 11p. G14840

_____. Journal of a tour through some of the vineyards of Spain and France. Sydney: Printed by Stephens and Stokes, 1833. 138p. G14850

Although Busby collected hundreds of vines for shipment to Australia, his travels are of interest to the wine buff for the factual data he uncovered. For example, in Tain he was told that "the greatest part of the finest growth [of Hermitage] is sent to Bordeaux to mix with the first growth of Claret." He gives a detailed account of his visits to Chambertin, Clos Vougeot, Champagne, Rousillon, and the vineyards of Jeres.

Busby's grandson, Hal Williams, a London architect, who had a copy of the diary Busby kept, wrote the following account of his grandfather's vineyard tour to the *The Times* of London: "My grandfather had always been interested in wine and had been greatly struck with the potentialities of the Australian soil and climate in this respect. Before 1831 he had distributed upwards of 10,000 vine cuttings among some fifty individuals and on visiting England in 1831 he brought with him ten gallons of a Burgundy type wine of the 1829-30 vintage made by Mr. Sadleir at the Orphan School, Sydney. This was distributed among persons interested in the Colony of New South Wales and was well thought of. James Busby was particularly interested in raisins and determined to visit Malaga and obtain cuttings of the raisin grape. His tour lasted from September 6 to the end of December, 1831, and took him through Xeres, Malaga, Catalonia, Perpignan, Rousillon, Rivesaltes, Montpelier, Tarascon, Marseilles, Hermitage, Beaune, Dijon, and the Cote d'Or, and Rheims. He collected from the Royal Botanic Gardens at Montpelier and the Royal nursery of the Luxemborg 547 varieties of the vines cultivated in France and some other parts of Europe. Of these, with two or three exceptions, he obtained two cuttings. Independently of these he secured 'a competent quantity of all the most valuable varieties which I found cultivated in the best wine districts of France and Spain, both for wine and raisin.' These numbered some 500-600 cuttings of 100 varieties.

"The cuttings were packed in sand and earth in cases lined with double-oiled paper, a suggestion of M. Urban Andibert, of Tarascon. With the consent and cooperation of Lord Goderich, His Majesty's Principal Secretary of State for the Colonies, they were sent out in a convict ship, and arriving at Sydney in excellent condition, were planted and nurtured by Mr. McLean, of the Botanic Garden. Some of the cuttings from the South of Spain, which did not arrive till later, were planted in open boxes by Mr. Richard Cunningham, of Kew, afterwards the Colonial Botanist of New South Wales. These were sent to Sydney in the convict ship *Canden,* and not ten out of the 500-600 cuttings failed."

Richard Cunningham, of Kew Gardens, who packed the cuttings, was appointed director of the Botanic Gardens in the summer of 1832, but died six months later during a botanical expedition in the Antipodes. Cunningham's successor, John McLean, was so concerned for the vines when they began to bear fruit in 1833 that he "placed a watchman day and night in charge of them." L. Woolf, a gardener at the Botanic Gardens, recalled in 1898 that his first job when he came to the gardens in August, 1857, was to root up the Busby vines due to their neglected condition.

The 1834, 1839 and 1840 London editions, the 1835 New York and Boston editions, and the 1838 Philadelphia editions have slightly varied titles but the text is identical.

_____. A journal of a tour through some of the vineyards of Spain and France. Facsimile reprint. Hunter's Hill, N.S.W.: David Ell Press, 1979. 138p. G14860

Edition limited to 1,000 copies.

_____. A manual of plain directions for planting and cultivating vineyards, and for making wine in New South Wales. Sydney: R. Mansfield for the Executors of R. Howe, 1830. 96p. G14870

In his introduction Busby makes a strong appeal to his new countrymen to plant vineyards and make wine.

_____. A manual of plain directions for planting and cultivating vineyards, and for making wine in New South Wales. Facsimile reprint. Hunter's Hill, N.S.W.: David Ell Press, 1979. 96p. G14880

Edition limited to 1,000 copies.

—————. A treatise on the culture of the vine and the art of making wine; compiled from the works of Chaptal, and other French writers; and from the notes of the compiler during a residence in some of the wine provinces of France. Sydney: Printed by R. Howe, Gov't. Print., 1825. 270p. G14890

> The first book published in Australia about viticulture and wine making.

—————. A treatise on the culture of the vine and the art of making wine; compiled from the works of Chaptal, and other French writers; and from the notes of the compiler during a residence in some of the wine provinces of France. Facsimile reprint. Hunter's Hill, N.S.W.: David Ell Press, 1979. 270p. G14900

BUSH, Isidore and Son. Illustrated descriptive catalogue of grape vines, small fruit, and potatoes. St. Louis: R.P. Studley, 1869. Illus. G14910

> Isidore Bush has been called America's greatest 19th century viticulturist. This catalog describes ninety-seven native hybrids with twenty-three woodcut illustrations. His second catalog in 1875 describes 206 hybrids and his third catalog in 1883 describes 336 varieties and has three full-page color prints. Bush's last catalog was published in 1895 and contains sixty-six illustrations and 353 varieties. These catalogs helped create an interest in wine made from hybrid grapes.

BUSH, Isidore and Son and Meissner. Illustrated descriptive catalogue of American grape vines, with brief directions for their culture. Bushberg Vineyards and Grape Nurseries, Bushberg, Jefferson Co., Missouri. 2nd ed. St. Louis: R.P. Studley, 1875. G14920

—————. Illustrated descriptive catalogue of American grape vines. A grape grower's manual. 3rd ed. St. Louis: R.P. Studley, 1883. 208p. Illus. G14930

> Fourth edition, 1895.

BUSH, John H. Veritas in vino. Grand Blanc, MI: By the Author, 1973. 28p. Illus. G14940

> This folio size book contains ten sequential illustrations of drinking one through ten glasses of wine with the moral that "when wine conquers truth falls." An interesting curiosity. Scarce.

The BUTLER: his duties and how to perform them. . . London: Houlston and Sons, c1877. 111p. G14950

The BUTLER, the wine-dealer, and private brewer; containing the duties of the butler, instruction for the management of wines . . . London: G. Biggs, c1850. 136p. G14960

BUTLER, Frank Hedges. Wine and the wine lands of the world. New York: Brentano's, 1926. 271p. Illus. G14970

> In addition to standard information, this book contains interesting chapters on Kashmir and its wines; sake and the Geisha; the wines of Polynesia and Melanesia; and how the author traveled over the wine regions of France and Germany in a balloon.

BUTLER, Ormon Rourke. Observations on the California vine disease. New York: n.p., 1910. 43p. Illus. G14980

> The introduction contains an historical description of the Anaheim disease epidemic starting in 1886.

BUYING guide to California wines. San Diego: Wine Consultants of California, 1974. 69p. G14990

BYNUM, Lindley Davis. California wines; how to enjoy them. Los Angeles: Homer H. Boelter, 1955. [40]p. Illus. G15000

BYRN, M. LaFayette. The complete practical distiller, comprising the . . . art of distillation and rectification . . . Philadelphia: Henry Carey Baird, 1866. 198p. Illus. G15010

BYRNE, Oliver. Practical, complete and correct gager. London: A.H. Bailey, 1840. 328p. G15020

CABERNET selections. 20 award winning Cabernets with winemakers comments and tasting notes. St. Helena, CA: Colonna, Caldewey, Farrell: designers. Distributed by Vintage Image, 1979. Unpaged. Illus. G15030

CAHALAN, D. American drinking practices; a national study of drinking behavior and attitudes. New Jersey: Publications Division, Rutgers Center of Studies, 1969. 260p. G15040

CAINE, Philip J. The wonderful world of wine. Trenton, NJ: By the Author, 1976. 139p. Illus. G15050

CAINE, William. The glutton's mirror. London: T. Fisher Unwin, 1925. 88p. Illus. G15060

> Contains a chapter on how the glutton views wine.

CALDAWAY, Jeffrey. Wine tour: Napa Valley. A guide-book for the wine traveller with a chapter on restaurants and picnic areas. Bradt Enterprises, 1979. 58p. Illus. G15070

_____. Wine tour: Sonoma-Mendocino. A wine lover's guide to the birthplace of California's wine trade; with chapters on food, lodging, picnic areas and a winery index. Bradt Enterprises, 1979. 70p. Illus. G15080

CALIFORNIA Grape Protective Association. How prohibition would affect California. San Francisco: 1916. G15090

CALIFORNIA. Board of State Viticultural Commissioners. Sacramento: State Printing, 1880-94; 1914-1919. G15100

> The Commission was created by the California Legislature in 1880 to promote the progress of the viticultural industries in the state. By legislative act of 1895, the Commission was discontinued and its property and duties transferred to the University of California. It was again created in 1913 and functioned until 1919. The annual reports and special publications of this commission contain a great deal of valuable information about the early history of California viticulture and its wines. The *First Annual Report,* for the year 1880, includes a fascinating account of the discovery and possible origins of the phylloxera pest, first identified in Sonoma in

1873. By 1880 it had spread to Napa, Solano, Yolo, Placer and El Dorado counties. A folding map of the state contained in the *Report* identifies all viticultural areas and those infested with the pest. In 1891 the board published a directory of grape growers and winemakers of California. Arranged by counties, it lists vineyard owners, acreage, production and grape varieties grown. A partial list of eastern grape growers identifies vineyards in thirty-two additional states.

CALIFORNIA WINE ORAL HISTORY SERIES

The California Wine Industry Interviews series was underwritten by the Wine Advisory Board and administered by The Bancroft Library at the University of California at Berkeley. The interviews were conducted under the direction of Ruth Teiser. Bound, indexed copies of the transcripts are available at cost to libraries open to scholars.

See listings under: Adams, Leon D. *Revitalizing the California Wine Industry;* Amerine, Maynard A. *The University of California and the State's Wine Industry;* Biane, Philo *Wine Making in Southern California and Recollections of Fruit Industries, Inc.;* Critchfield, Burke H., Wente, Carl F. and Frericks, Andrew G. *The California Wine Industry during the Depression;* Cruess, William V. *A Half Century of Food and Wine Technology;* Joslyn, Maynard A. *A Technologist Views the California Wine Industry;* Lanza, Horace O. and Baccigaluppi, Harry *California Grape Products and Other Wine Enterprises;* Martini, Louis M. and Louis P. *Winemakers of the Napa Valley;* Meyer, Otto E. *California Premium Wines and Brandies;* Olmo, Harold P. *Plant Genetics and New Grape Varieties;* Perelli-Minetti, Antonio *A Life of Wine Making;* Petri, Louis A. *The Petri Family in the Wine Industry;* Peyser, Jefferson E. *The Law and the California Wine Industry;* Powers, Lucius *The Fresno Area and the California Wine Industry;* Repetto, Victor and Block, Sydney J. *Perspectives on California Wines;* Rossi, Edmund A. *Italian Swiss Colony and the Wine Industry;* Setrakian, Arpaxat A. *Setrakian, a Leader of the San Joaquin Valley Grape Industry;* Timothy, Brother *The Christian Brothers as Winemakers;* Wente, Ernest A. *Wine Making in the Livermore Valley;* and Winkler, Albert J. *Viticultural Research at University of California.*

CALPIN, G.H. Sherry in South Africa. Cape Town: Tafelberg, 1978. 114p. Illus. G15320

CAMBIAIRE, Celestin Pierre. The black horse of the apocalypse. Wine, alcohol, and civilization. Paris: Librairie Universitaire, J. Gamber, 1932. 486p. G15330

> The author has taken his title from the book of *Revelation;* the opening of the seals and the appearance of the four mysterious horses—white, red, black and pale. Biblical scholars have long regarded the Red Horse as symbolical of the wars and devastations of the time of Adrian, who died A.D. 138, and the Black Horse as symbolical of the famine that followed those wars. The author has given the Black Horse a modern significance, i.e., Prohibition. In the final page of the book, the author concludes his scathing attack on Prohibition by observing: "It is obvious that at least in so far as it forbids the use of unadulterated wine, Prohibition violates the Lord's divine commandment very clearly expressed in the Book of

Revelation (Ch. VI: 6): 'AND SEE THOU HURT NOT . . . THE WINE.' It is time that the black horse of the Apocalypse and his rider should not be allowed under any condition to 'hurt . . . the wine,' in imprudent disregard of God's warning, and thus bring disasters and curses upon the greatest of all nations."

Although the main thesis of the book is that Prohibition can never benefit civilization, the book's scope and significance is much broader. In many respects it is an eulogy on wine as can be seem from some of the chapter headings: "The Psychology of Drinking," "Wine and Medical Science," "Antiquity of Wine Drinking," "France an Ideal Field to Study the Liquor Problem," "Alcoholic Beverages and Industry," "Alcohol and Efficiency," "Wine-Drinking Frenchmen more Efficient than Total-Abstinent Turks," "Wine, Nature's Preventive Against Epidemics," "Failure of Prohibition," "Wine, Progress and Prosperity," "Alcohol and Civilization," "The Debt of Modern Civilization to Wine-Drinking Greece," "Our Debt to Wine-Drinking Romans," etc.

Although there is no indication as to whether this book was first written in English, or is an English translation of a French work, it is well written and is an interesting addition to wine literature.

CAMPBELL, George W. Descriptive list of hardy native grape vines . . . Delaware, OH: O. Lee and Thompson, 1870. 24p. G15340

Campbell, of Delaware, Ohio, established his nursery in 1857. He was one of the leading growers of the area and carefully described the different varieties he offered.

_____. Descriptive list of hardy native grape vines. Delaware, OH: 1878. G15350

This edition contains five full-page engravings of grapes, illustrating the different varieties.

CAMPBELL, Ian Maxwell. Reminiscences of a vintner. London: Chapman and Hall, 1950. 276p. Illus. G15360

_____. Wayward tendrils of the vine. London: Chapman and Hall, 1947. 210p. G15370

CANADIAN wine at your party. Toronto: Canadian Wine Institute, 1966. 20p. Illus. G15380

CARADEUC, H. De. Grape culture and winemaking in the South. Augusta, GA: Aiken Vine Growing Ass'n., 1859. 23p. G15390

CAREY, Mary. Step-by-step winemaking. New York: Golden Press, 1973. 64p. Illus. G15410

CARLING, Thomas Edward. The complete book of drink. London: Practical Press, 1951. 208p. G15420

_____. Wine aristocracy; a guide to the best wines of the world . . . London: Rockliff Publishing, 1957. 136p. G15430

_____. Wine data. London: For the Author by Practical Press, 1959. G15440

_____. Wine drinker's aide-memoire. Canterbury: Practical Press, 1959. 35p. G15450

_____. Wine etiquette . . . Whitstable: By the Author, 1949. 39p. G15460

_____. Wine lore; a critical analysis of wine dogma. London: Practical Press, 1954. 55p. Illus. G15470

_____. Wine: thumbnail sketches of wines of the world from *The Wine and Spirit Trade Review*. London: Barrie and Rockliff, 1960. 56p. G15480

_____. Wine-wise. How to know, choose and serve wine. 2nd ed. Canterbury: By the Author, 1949. 65p. G15490

CARLISLE, Donald Thompson and DUNN, Elizabeth. Wining and dining with rhyme and reason. New York: Minton, Balch, 1933. 128p. Illus. G15500

> Written to remind Americans (who had just gone through "dry" years) of the approved methods of drinking and enjoying wine.

CARNELL, Philip Pery. A treatise on family wine making: calculated for making excellent wines from the various fruits of this United Country; in relation to strength, brilliancy, health, and economy. Explanatory of the whole process, and every other requisite guide after the wine is made and in the cellar; composed from practical knowledge and written expressly and exclusively for domestic use, containing sixty different sorts of wine. To which is also subjoined the description of part of a recent British Vintage inclusive of an interesting experimental lecture. London: Sherwood, Neeley and Jones, 1814. 158p. G15510

CAROSSO, Vincent P. The California wine industry, 1830-1895: a study of the formative years. Berkeley and Los Angeles: University of California Press, 1951. 241p. G15520

> An essential reference for those interested in the years from the first commercial production of wine by Jean Louis Vignes in Los Angeles in the early 1830's to a period when wine production became one of the basic industries of California. It contains chapters on such famous early California wine personalities as Jean Louis Vignes, John Frohling, Charles Kohler and Agoston Haraszthy.
>
> Reissued by the University of California Press as a California Library Reprint Series Edition, 1976. Map, notes, bibliography.

CARR, John Geoffrey. Aroma and flavour in winemaking. London: Mills and Boon, 1974. 88p. Illus. G15530

> Reprinted in 1978.

_____. Biological principles in fermentation. London: Heinemann Educational Books, 1968. 97p. G15540

> Contains chapters on wines.

CARRE, G.F. Drinking in France. London: Harrap, 1974. 16p. G15550

CARRIER, R. Food, wine and friends. London: Sidgwick and Jackson, 1980. 120p. Illus. G15560

CARTER, Everett. Wine and poetry. Davis, CA: University of California and Wine Museum of San Francisco, 1976. 18p. Illus. G15570

CARTER, Youngman. Drinking bordeaux. London and New York: Hamish Hamilton and Hastings House, 1966. 87p. Illus. G15580

_____. Drinking burgundy. London and New York: Hamish Hamilton and Hastings House, 1966. 95p. Illus. G15590

_____. Drinking champagne and brandy. London: Hamish Hamilton, 1968. Illus. G15600

CARVAHLO, Bento de and CORREIA, Lopes. The wines of Portugal. Lisbon: Junto Nacional do Vinno, 1979. 37p. Illus. G15610

> This booklet contains photographs of the wine districts, the growers, the wineries and the people.

CASANAVE, Armand. Practical manual for the culture of the vine in the Gironde. Sacramento: California Viticulture Commission, 1885. 61p. G15630

CASAS, Penelope. The foods and wines of Spain. New York: Knopf, 1984. G15640

The CASE of the Company of Vintners, and other retaylors of wine. London: c1690. G15650

> Unable to verify.

The CASE of the Distillers' Company, and proposals for the better regulating of the trade. London: c1736. G15660

> Unable to verify.

CASE, Suzanne D. Join me in Paradise, the history of Guenoc Valley. Guenoc Valley, CA: Guenoc Winery, 1983. 93p. G15670

CASSAGNAC, Paul de. French wines. London: Chatto and Windus, 1930. 242p. G15680

> The translation by Guy Knowles starts with a discussion of the vineyards of France and the "influences" on wines such as soil, vines, sun, cellar, etc. The author is also an authority on foods and discusses how they should be cooked and what wines should be served with them. There are chapters on Bordeaux, Burgundy and Champagne and the "Maids of Honour" i.e. the wines of the Loire, the Rhone, etc. Scarce.

CASTELLA, Francois de. The grapes of South Australia. Adelaide: The Phylloxera Board of South Australia, 1941-2. G15690

_____. Home wine making. Melbourne: 1921. 24p. G15700

_____. The wine grapes of the Murrumbidgee irrigation areas; a report made by Mr. F. de Castella to the Wine Grapes Marketing Board for the shires of Wade, Willimbong and Carrathool. Griffith, Australia: "Area News", 1944. 34p. G15710

> Recommendations for improving the viticultural practices of this region in Australia.

CASTELLA, Hubert de. John Bull's vineyard. Reprint. ed. Burwood, East Victoria: 1981. 263p. Illus. G15720

_____. Notes of an Australian vine grower by Hubert de Castella; translated with preface and notes by C.B. Thornton-Smith. Melbourne: Mast Gully Press, 1979. 75p. Illus. G15730

> Translated from the French with a preface and notes by C.B. Thornton-Smith. Edition limited to 750 numbered copies. A facsimile reprint of *Notes d'un Vigneron Australien* published in Melbourne in 1882.

_____. Handbook on viticulture for Victoria. Melbourne: Robert S. Brain, Gov't. Print., 1891. G15740

_____. John Bull's vineyard. Australian sketches. Melbourne: Sands and McDougall, 1886. 263p. Illus. G15750

Describes early viticulture in Victoria.

CASTILLO, Jose Del and HALLETT, David R. The wines of Spain. Bilbao, Spain: Proyeccion Editorial, 1972. 255p. Illus. G15760

> Originally published in Spanish, the present English version is a result of the efforts of David R. Hallett. The book is divided into three parts. Part one concerns the history of Spanish wines; part two the types of Spanish wines; and part three the gastronomic regions of Spain and the local wines. The color illustrations are imaginative and beautifully reproduced. The black and white photographs are of poor quality. This is a valuable work for those interested in Spanish wines.

CATALOGUE of books belonging to the Institute of Masters of Wine deposited in Guildhall Library. London: Guildhall Library, 1972. 176p. G15770

> The Institute of Masters of Wine acquired the greater part of this library from the Wine Trade Club when it closed in 1966.

A CATALOGUE of the ancient and other plate, tapestry . . . belonging to the worshipful Company of Vintners, with some particulars of the Company and of its eminent members. London: c1911. 47p. G15780

CATO, Marcus Poricus. On agriculture (De Re Rustica). English translation by William Davis Hooper. London: Heinemann, 1934. G15790

CATTELL, Hudson and MILLER, Stauffer Lee. Pennsylvania wines. Lancaster, PA: L and H Photojournalism, 1976. 24p. Illus. G15800

_____. The wines of the east, native American grapes. Lancaster, PA: L and H Photojournalism, 1980. Illus. G15810

_____. The wines of the east, the hybrids. Lancaster, PA: L and H Photojournalism, 1978. 28p. Illus. G15820

_____. The wines of the east, the vinifera. Lancaster, PA: L and H Photojournalism, 1979. Illus. G15830

CATTS-Patterson Co. Proposed plan for the development of the Australian wine industry. Melbourne: 1929. 12p. G15840

CAVE, Peter L. Best drinking jokes. 3rd ed. London: Wolfe Publishing, 1973. 64p. G15850

CAVETT, Dick, host. The video wine guide. San Francisco: The Wine Appreciation Guild, c1982. G15855

> With only one other exception, a recording of André Simon, all of the items in this bibliography are printed material. However, the enormous increase in the number of VHS and Betamax video tape players is already changing the "books" of the future. The video players accessibility, easy-play features and extended playing time, make it far more feasible as a "book" than the movie projector. This particular tape brings together Alexis Lichine and other experts and, in its ninety-minute running time, covers wine geography of Europe and California, introduces the winemakers, their wines, tasting techniques and pronunciations. Section I covers wine making, history, and wine tour. Section II is the how and why of wine tasting and matching food with wine. Section III is a video appendix on the basics of wine tasting, investing in wine, building a wine cellar and pronunciation of wine terms. As these "books" proliferate, future bibliographies will have to take them into account.

CAZAUBON, D. Treatise and practical guide of the apparatus for the fabrication of gaseous drinks, sparkling wines, etc. Paris: Printed by A. Henninger, 1876. 132p. G15860

CELLAR work at a glance. Instructions to licensed victuallers, barmen, etc., by a retired licensed victualler. London: By the Author, 1896. 24p. G15870

CENTRAL coast wine tour. St. Helena: Vintage Image, 1980. 88p. Illus. G15875

CERLETTI, G.B. Descriptive account of the wine industry of Italy. Rome: Societa Generale dei Viticoltori Italiani, 1888. 107p. G15880

> Translated from the Italian by Guido Rossati.

CHALLONER, F. Port, Oporto and Portugal. London: 1913. 23p. G15890

CHALONER, Len. What the vintners sell. London: Heath Cranton, 1926. 159p. Illus. G15900

> Introduction by André Simon.

CHALONER, W. Chute. A history of 'The Dyne' in Hampshire. Winchester: 1888. G15910

> Unable to verify.

CHAMBERLAIN, Bernard Peyton. A treatise on the making of palatable table wines, recommended to gentlemen, especially in Virginia, for their own use. Charlottesville, VA: By the Author, 1931. 97p. G15930

CHAMBERLAIN, Samuel. Bouquet de France - an epicurean tour of the French Provinces. New York: Gourmet, 1952. 619p. Illus. G15940

> Based on a series of articles that began in *Gourmet* in March, 1949. Much about wine. Several subsequent editions.

CHAMPAGNE - the world situation for Champagne. London: Harper Trade Journals, 1977. 22p. Illus. G15950

CHAMPIN, Aime. Vine grafting. Sacramento: California Viticultural Commissioner's report no. 2, Appendix no. 3, 134p. G15960

CHANCELLOR, Charles Williams. Light wines and table-tea as moral agents. n.p., c1870. 10p. G15970

CHAPPAZ, George and HENRIOT, Alexandre. The champagne vine country and champagne wine. Epernay: Moet and Chandon, 1920. 32p. Illus. G15980

CHAPTAL, Jean A.C. Treatise upon wines. Charleston, SC: J.H. Sargent, 1823. 166p. G15990

CHARDONNAY selections. 20 award winning Chardonnays with winemakers comments and tasting notes. St. Helena, CA: Colonna, Caldewey, Farrell: designer. Distributed by Vintage Images, 1979. Unpaged. Illus. G16000

CHARLETON, Dr. Walter. Two discourses: 1. concerning the different wits of men. 2. of the mysterie of vintners. London: R.W. for William Whitford, 1669. 230p. G16010

> "Mysterie" does not mean "mysterious" but is a corruption of the French "mestier" which means trade. Second edition of 235p. published in 1675.

_____. The vintner's mystery display'd: or the art of the wine trade laid open . . . London: T. Warner, [17-?]. 76p. G16020 There is also an edition of the "Mysterie of Vintners," from a discourse delivered to the Royal Society in 1662 in Gresham College.

CHARTER, constitution and by-laws, of the Cincinnati Horticultural Society: with a report of its transactions for 1843, '44 and '45: list of members. Cincinnati: L'Hommedieu, 1846. 68p. Illus. G16030

> Includes a "communication from the president of the Society [N. Longworth] on the cultivation of the grape, and manufacture of wine; also on the character and habits of the strawberry plant."

CHASE, Edithe Lea. Waes Hael; a collection of toasts. New York: Crafton Press, 1903. 299p. G16040

> Second edition, 1905.

CHAUTAUQUA fruits, grapes and grape products. Chautauqua, NY: Chautauqua Grape and Wine Association, 1901. G16050

> Descriptions of the various vineyards of Chautauqua County, New York, and their owners.

CHATEAU-Tanunda, South Australia. Adelaide: Adelaide Wine Company, 1901. 56p. G16060

CHATTERTON, B.A. Home wine-making. Adelaide: Rigby, 1972. 68p. Illus. G16070

> Reprinted in 1975.

_____. Sunday Mail guide to S.A. wineries. Adelaide: Advertiser-News Weekend Publishing, 1973. 72p. Illus. G16080

CHEERS! . . . 50 years of wine [cartoons] in the New Yorker. New York: The New Yorker, c1977. 28p. Illus. G16090

CHENE, P. Le. Helpful hints for sommeliers and wine waiters. 2nd ed. France: 1973. 28p. Illus. G16100

CHESTERON, Gilbert Keith. Wine, water and song. London: Methuen, 1915. 63p. G16110

> Poems, reprinted from his novel, *The Flying Inn*. The seventeenth edition was published in 1943.

CHEVALLIER, Gabriel. Clochemerle. London: Martin Secker and Warburg, 1936. 373p. G16120

> A novel about the Rabelaisian happenings in the town of Clochemerle in Beaujolais in 1922. Translated from the French by Jocelyn Godefrori.

_____. Clochemerle-Babylon. London: Secker and Warburg, 1955. 304p. G16130

> A novel translated from the French by Edward Hyams.

_____. Clochemerle-les-Bains. New York: Simon and Schuster, 1965. 415p. G16140

> A novel translated from the French by Yan Fielding.

_____. The scandals of Clochemerle. New York: Simon and Schuster, 1937. 317p. Illus. G16150

A novel translated from the French by Jocelyn Godefrori.

_____. The wicked village: a story of Clochemerle. New York: Simon and Schuster, 1956. G16160

> A novel translated from the French by Edward Hyams.

CHIDGEY, Graham. Guide to the wines of Burgundy. London: Pitman, 1977. 123p. Illus. G16170

> Second edition in 1978.

CHIMAY, Jacqueline de. The life and time of Madame Veuve Clicquot Ponsardin. Preface by Evelyn Waugh. Reims: Champagne Veuve Clicquot, 1961. 54p. Illus. G16180

CHIRICH, Nancy. Life with wine. San Francisco: Ed-It Productions, 1984. G16185

CHLEBNIKOWSKI, Nick. European wine vintages. Victoria: Nick's Wine Merchants, 1981. 88p. Illus. G16190

CHODOWSKI, A.T. Wine, its use and abuse: the fermented wines of the Bible. Christ Church, New Zealand: Christ Church Press, 1893. 22p. G16200

_____. Wine, its use and abuse: wines of the Bible. Sydney: Carters Printing Works, 1920. 16p. G16210

CHORLTON, William. The American grape grower's guide. Intended especially for the American climate . . . New York: Orange Judd, c1852. 204p. Illus. G16220

> Chorlton's guides to cultivation of European grapes under glass were based on his experience as gardener to J.C. Green, Esq. of Staten Island. Chorlton gives a long list of European grapes suitable for indoor cultivation and suggests the American varieties isabella, catawba, diana and concord for outdoors. This was a very popular treatise and there were numerous subsequent and revised editions including 1853, 1856, 1858, 1859, 1860, 1865, 1883, 1887, 1899, 1908 and 1911.

_____. The cold grapery, from direct American practice: being a concise and detailed treatise on the cultivation of the exotic grape-vine, under glass, without artificial heat. New York: J.C. Riker, 1853. 95p. Illus. G16230

CHRIST, Edwin A. and FISK, F.R. That book about wine. Columbia, MO: (Privately printed at) Columbia Press, 1955. 31p. G16240

CHRISTODOULOU, Demetris. The evolution of the rural land use pattern in Cyprus. London: Geographical Publications, 1959. 230p. G16250

> Contains material on the grape and wine industry.

CHROMAN, Nathan. The treasury of American wines. New York: Crown Publishers, 1973. 249p. Illus. G16260

> Covers the principal California and New York state vineyards in existence at the time of publication. Also treats wineries in Baja California, Michigan, Missouri, Ohio, Pennsylvania, Oregon, and Washington state. The text is nicely illustrated with both black and white and color photographs.

> Mr. Chroman, an attorney, has made wine his avocation. He writes for several wine publications, teaches a course on wine appreciation and serves as chairman of the wine judging committee at the Los Angeles County Fair.

CHUBB, W.P. Receipt book or oracle of knowledge containing nearly one thousand useful receipts with directions for making British wines. London: J. Smith, 1825. 230p. G16270

CHURCH, Ruth Ellen. The American guide to wines. Introduction by Morrison Wood. New York: Quadrangle Press, 1963. 272p. Illus. G16280

> With recipes for 100 dishes cooked with wine. Subsequent editions.

_____. Entertaining with wine. Chicago: Rand McNally, 1976. 174p. Illus. G16290

_____. Wines of the Midwest. Athens, OH: Swallow Press, Ohio University Press, 252p. G16300

CHURCHILL, Creighton. The great wine rivers. New York: Macmillan, 1971. 222p. Illus. G16310

> "A connoisseur's guide to the vineyards and vintages of the

Moselle, Rhine, Rhone and Loire, of Burgundy and Bordeaux, with expert advice on choosing and savoring the best of the wines - famous or unfamiliar."

_____. A notebook for the wines of France: a wine diary or cellar book listing the nine hundred most important French wines and/or their vineyards, with space for the wine drinker's own records and notations. New York: Knopf, 1961. 386p. Illus. G16320

_____. The world of wines. New York: Macmillan, 1964. 271p. Illus. G16330

Revised editions in 1974 and 1980.

CHURCHILL, S.D. All sorts and conditions of drinks. London: c1893. 67p. G16340

A price list issued by S.D. Churchill, wine merchant of Cardiff, but it provides information about many wines.

CHYMISTRY of wine, The: [extracts from an article which appeared in the *Times,* April 18th 1872, with subjoined comments thereon from the *Lancet* and *Medical Times and Gazette.*] London: Denman, 1872. 8p. G16350

CINZANO glass collection. London: Cinzano, 1978. 264p. Illus. G16360

English introduction with English, Italian, French, German, Spanish and Portuguese text. Text by Peter Lazarus and photographs by Derek Balmer.

CLAIRE, Aileen. The connoisseur's wine book. New York: Award Books, 1973. 237p. G16370

CLARETS and sauternes: classed growths of the Médoc and other famous red and white wines of the Gironde. London: Wine and Spirit Trade Record, 1920. 398p. Illus. G16380

CLARK, Selden. California's wine industry and its financing. New Brunswick, NJ: Rutgers University, 1941. Illus. G16390

CLARKE, Ebenezer. The worship of Bacchus: a great delusion. London: James Clarke, 1877. 86p. Illus. G16400

CLARKE, Frank K. Make your wine at home; a book for beginners. London: Elek Books, 1968. 88p. Illus. G16410

CLARKE, Nick. Bluff your way in wine. London: Wolfe, 1967. 63p. Illus. G16420

_____. The bluffer's guide to wine. New York: Crown, c1971. 63p. G16430

Same book as above but with a different title.

CLARKE, William. Complete cellar manual: the publican and innkeeper's practical guide, and wine and spirit dealer's director and assistant . . . [with] the laws and excise regulations affecting publicans and . . . dealers . . . London: Sherwood, Gilbert and Piper, 1829. 264p. Illus. G16440

CLELAND, Charles. Abstracts of the several laws that are now in force, relating to the importation and exportation of wines. Into and out of Great Britain. London: Printed for the Author, 1737. 172p. G16450

CLELAND, Robert G. California in our time (1900-1940). New York: Knopf, 1947. 320p. Illus. G16460 Includes materials on vineyards and the wine industry.

"CLEMENTS". Homemade wines, liquors and vinegars. London: W.H. Allen, 1888. 35p. G16470

CLOTHO. (Pseud). Prosit: a book of toasts. San Francisco: Paul Elder, 1904. 134p. Illus. G16480

CLUESLANT, F. Disease of the vine and how to cure it. Melbourne: George Robertson, 1886. G16490

COATES, Clive. Claret. London: Century Publishing, 1982. 424p. Illus. G16500
> The author presents the histories of fifty-three chateaux, including historical and technical data and tasting notes for the last twenty or so vintages. These notes should interest the wine collector. The author admits relying mainly on secondary sources for the histories of the chateaux, including material produced by or on behalf of the properties themselves; therefore, the accuracy of these histories should be judged accordingly.
>
> Mr. Coates is a wine merchant and a Master of Wine. He writes regularly for *Decanter* magazine and other wine publications.

COBB, Gerald. Oporto, older and newer; being a tribute to the British community in the north of Portugal in continuation of *Oporto old and new,* by C. Sellers. London: Chichester Press, 1965-66. 110p. Illus. G16510

COCHRANE, G.R. Commercial viticulture in South Australia. Christchurch: 1963. 24p. G16520

COCKBURN, Ernest H. Port wine and Oporto. London: Wine and Spirit Publications, c1950. 132p. Illus. G16530
> Illustrated with nineteen black and white photographs. Detailed account of the Douro region and of port wine.

COCKBURN, Harry A. A centenary retrospect: R. and J. Cockburn 1805. Cockburn and Campbell 1831-1931. London: McCorquodale, c1933. 28p. Illus. G16540

COCKBURN, F.A., et al. Wine and the wine trade. London: Wine Trade Club by Wine and Spirit Publications, 1947. 50p. G16550
> Four lectures delivered to wine trade students at Vintners' Hall, London and at Birmingham, in the Autumn of 1946. "Sherry" by Charles K. Williams; "Red Bordeaux Wines" by Henri Binaud; "Port Wine" by F.A. Cockburn; "Cellar Management" by E.H. Clark. Scarce.

COCKS, Charles. Bordeaux: its wines and the claret country. London: Longman, Brown, Green and Longmans, 1846. 215p. G16560

This was the seminal edition of what we know today as *Bordeaux et ses Vins*. Charles Cocks was English. Only eighty-eight of the 215 pages were devoted to wine.

_____. Bordeaux and its wines, classed by order of merit. 2nd English ed. Improved by Edouard Feret. Paris: Masson, 1883. 616p. Illus. G16570

Translation of fourth French edition and illustrataed by E. Verqez.

_____. Bordeaux and its wines, classed by order of merit. 3rd English ed. Bordeaux: Feret, 1899. 831p. Illus. G16580

Translated from the seventh French edition.

CODMAN, Charles Russell Sturgis. Vintage dinners; a treatise in which some of the oenophilic and gastronomic experiences of Le Club des Arts Gastronomiques are described and other general information offered pertaining to the subject of wines. Boston: Privately printed, 1937. 129p. Illus. G16590

_____. Years and years; some vintage years in French wines. Boston: S.S. Pierce, 1935. 27p. G16600

CODMAN, Mrs. Theodore Larocque. Was it a holiday? Boston: Little, Brown, 1935. 235p. G16610

An account of the author's trip with her husband through the wine districts of Burgundy, Anjou and Bordeaux.

COGAN, Thomas. The Haven of Health chiefly made for the comfort of students, and consequently for all those that have a care of their health amplified upon five words of Hippocrates: Labour, Meat, Drinke, Sleepe, Venus . . . London: Printed by Melch, Bradvvood for John Norton, 1606. G16620

Thomas Cogan, a physician, considered wine the healthiest of all beverages and remarked: "Life and wine for the likeness of nature are most agreeable. And this is the cause I think why men by nature so greedily covet wine; except some *odde Abstemius,* one among a thousand perchance, degenerate and is of a doggish nature; for dogges of nature do abhor wine". This preference for wine as a beverage had at least one modern medical justification. Water purification was not developed until much later, and physicians in the 17th and early 18th centuries cautioned against the indiscriminate use of water. Earlier editions of 1584, 1588, 1589 and 1596. Subsequent editions of 1612 and 1636.

COLBRIDGE, A.M. Wine making. London: Barrie and Jenkins, 1973. 33p. G16630

COLBURN, Frona Eunice. Wines and vines of California; a treatise on the ethics of wine-drinking. Berkeley: Howell-North Books, 1973. 215p. G40480

A facsimile edition of the Bancroft publication of 1889. The introduction is by Maynard A. Amerine.

COLBURN, Frona Eunice Waite. In old vintage days. San Francisco: Printed by John Henry Nash, 1937. 178p. Illus. G16640

> Stories about early wine makers in Northern California. Scarce.

COLE, Emma Aubert. Champagne at the wedding. New York: W.A. Taylor, 1947. 16p. Illus. G16660

COLE, R.L. Sacramental wine: intoxicating, or non-intoxicating? London: C.H. Kelly, 1913. 24p. G16670

COLLIER, Carole. 505 wine questions your friends can't answer. New York: Walker, 1983. 174p. G16680

COLUMELLA, Lucius Junius Moderatus. On agriculture (De Agricultura). English translation by H.B. Ash. London: Heinemann, Loeb Classics Library, 1941. G16690

COMBE, William. A history of Madeira. 1821. 118p. Illus. G16700

> Contains twenty-seven hand-colored aquatint plates.

COMITÉ Interprofessional du Vin de Champagne, Epernay. Champagne wine of France. 2nd ed. Paris: Lallemand Editeur, 1968. 20p. G16710

> Text in English.

COMPANHIA Geral da Agricultura das Vinhas do Alto Douro. Institution of the General company for the culture of the vineyards of Alto Douro. London: Printed by T. Gardner, 1758. 55p. G16720

> An English translation of the petition made in 1756 to the Portuguese king for the formation of a Portuguese company to control the wine production of the Alto Douro area and thus limit the activities of the English factory.

The COMPLEAT planter and cyderist: or, choice collections and observations for the propagating of all manner of fruit trees, and the most approved ways and methods yet known for the making and ordering of cyder, and other English - wines. By a lover of planting. London: Printed for Tho. Basset, 1685. 256p. G16730

The COMPLETE distiller, combining theory and practice, and explaining the mysteries and most recent improvements of distilling and brewing in a most simple, easy, and familiar manner . . . Edinburgh: Printed for Peter Hill, 1793. 151p. G16740

> Includes a chapter on "Of Making and Refining British Wines."

The COMPLETE grocer being a series of very valuable receipts for distilling and mixing cordials of all kinds . . . with a variety of information respecting the making and treatment of both foreign and home made wines . . . New York: John Turney, Printer, 1832. 204p. G16750

CONANT, James Bryant, ed. Pasteur's study of fermentation. Cambridge, MA: Harvard University Press, 1952. 57p. G16760

CONDITIONING wines with Darco. New York: Darco Corporation, 1936. G16770

CONIL, Jean. The Epicurean book. London: George Allen and Unwin, 1962. 250p. G16780

_____. Gastronomic tour de France. New York: E.P. Dutton, 1960. 376p. Illus. G16790

Contains information on French regional wines.

CONN, Donald D. The California vineyard industry; five year report of Donald D. Conn. Submitted to the California Vineyardists Association, and the subscribers thereto, composed of civic and industrial groups and individuals; rendered with recommendations and conclusions. San Francisco: 1932. 60p. G16800

A CONSUMER'S guide to 110 Chardonnays. Los Angeles: Cheshire Booksellers, 1979. G16810

A CONSUMER'S guide to 125 Zinfandels. Los Angeles: Cheshire Booksellers, 1980. G16820

A CONSUMER'S guide to 144 Cabernets. Los Angeles: Cheshire Booksellers, 1981. G16830

A CONSUMER'S guide to 161 jug wines. Los Angeles: Cheshire Booksellers, 1981. G16840

CONSUMERS Union report on wines and liquors. Mt. Vernon, NY: Consumers Union, 1937. 72p. G16850

Subsequent editions.

The CONSUMERS Union reports on wines and spirits; ratings, recommendations and buying guidance covering wines, whiskies, gins, vodkas, rums, brandies, and cordials. Mount Vernon, NY: Consumers Union of United States, 1962. 158p. G16860

Subsequent editions.

CONYERS, G. Vinetum angliae, or a new and easy way to make wine of English grapes and other fruit. London: c1672. G16870

Unable to verify.

COOK, Fred S. The wines and wineries of California. Jackson, CA: Mother Lode Publishing, 1966. 88p. G16880

COOK, Philip. A wine merchant's assessment of burgundy. London: Ridley's Wine and Spirit Trade Circular, 1965. 28p. Illus. G16890

[COOK, Richard.] Oxford night caps being a collection of receipts for making various beverages used in the University. Oxford: H. Slater, 1827. 38p. G16900

COOKE, Matthew. Injurious insects of the orchard, vineyards . . . Sacramento: H.S. Crocker, 1883. 472p. Illus. G16910

Illustrated with 750 woodcuts, and twenty-five pages of classified illustrations.

COOL, R.C. The Scuppernong grape: its growth and care under vineyard conditions. Raleigh: Edwards and Broughton Printing, 1913. 15p. G16920

COOMBE, Bryan G. Phylloxera and its relation to South Australian viticulture; a report to the Phylloxera Board of South Australia on phylloxera in the United States of America and elsewhere and the application of this information to conditions in South Australia. Adelaide: W.L. Hawes, Gov't. Print., 1963. 90p. Illus. G16930

COOPER, Ambrose. The complete distiller, containing: I. The method of performing the various processes of distillation, with description of the several instruments; the whole doctrine of fermentation; the manner of drawing spirits from malt, raisins, molasses, sugar, etc., and of rectifying them; with instructions for imitating to the greatest perfection both the colour and flavour of French brandies. II. The manner of distilling all kinds of simple waters from plants, flowers, etc. III. The method of making all the compound waters and rich cordials so largely imported from France and Italy, as likewise all those now made in Great Britian . . . and instructions for choosing the best of each kind . . . London: P. Vaillant, 1757. 266p. Illus. G16940

> Other editions were published in 1760, 1763, 1800, 1803, 1810 and 1826.

COOPER, Charles. The English table in history and literature. London: Sampson, Low, Marston, 1928. 230p. G16950

> This book not only depicts English table habits and customs from the 14th to the 19th century, but the author also discusses the wines served and makes some interesting observations. Mr. Cooper takes issue with those writers, such as William of Malmesbury, who reported not only the cultivation of the vine in Britain but a quality ". . . more pleasant in flavour. For the wines do not offend the mouth with sharpness since they do not yield to the French in sweetness." Mr. Cooper relies on English literature to support his contention that English wine made in the Middle Ages was ". . . nothing but the thinnest and most acid kind of liquor." "The passion which men have for talking or writing about the liquor they drink is independent of time, age or nationality. Horace sang the praises of Falernian in his odes, and Shakespeare has told us a great deal about Sack in his comedies; there are oceans of hot water and Brandy in Pickwick, and the soundness of the Claret is a constant theme of the Irish novelist at his best. But what writer in prose or verse for the past seven hundred years has ever penned a line that goes to prove that English vintaged wine was ever a common drink of priest or lord, franklin or squire? They, these writer of plays, poems or romances, are the truest historians, for the habits and temper of their times are unconsciously reflected in their works."

COOPER, Derek. The beverage report. London: Routledge, 1970. 222p. Illus. G16960

————. Wine with food. London: Artus Books, 1980. 128p. G16970

COOPER, John Ralph and VAILE, J.E. Response of American grapes to various treatments and vineyard practices. Fayetteville, AK: Arkansas Agricultural Experiment Station, 1939. 74p. Illus. G16980

Influence of fertilizers, pruning, thinning, rootstocks, etc., on the ripening of grapes.

COOPER, Rosalind. The wine book. London: Willow Books, 1982. 96p. Illus. G16990

COPPINGER, Joseph. The American practical brewer and tanner. New York: Van Winkle and Wiley, 1815. 246p. G17000

Includes wine and an interesting description of the French method of handling the various Bordeaux growths.

COPPOLA, Edward J. Edward J. Coppola, Jr.'s Salty Pelican wine specialties. By the Author, 1977. 68p. G17010

CORBAN A.A. and Sons. Father to son tradition in wine making. Henderson, New Zealand: By the Author, n.d. 23p. G17020

COSSART, Noel. Madeira the island vineyard. London: Christie Wine Publications, 1984. 199p. Illus.

COTTEN, C.B. Formula of New York, Philadelphia and Baltimore manufacturers of wines and liquors. Cincinnati: By the Author, 1851. 36p. G17030

COUCHE, Donald Douglas. Modern detection and treatment of wine diseases and defects. London: The Technical Press, 1935. 98p. Illus. G17040

"The articles . . . were published in Ridley's Wine and spirit trade calendar, Harper's Wine and spirit gazette, and The Brewer and wine merchant."

COURTENAY, J.M. de. The Canada vine grower. Toronto: James Campbell, 1866. 58p. G17060

_____. The culture of the vine and emigration. Quebec: Joseph Durveau, 1863. 55p. G17070

COUVESLANT, F. Disease of the vine and how to cure it. 2nd ed. Melbourne: George Robertson and Company, 1886. 20p. G17080

COVER, Doe, ed. The price guide to good wine. Addison Wesley, c1983. 130p. Illus. G17090

[COWNLEY, James E.] Notes for an epicure. A handbook on the traditions and service of wines and other beverages. c1933. 44p. Illus. G17100

COX, Harry. The wines of Australia. London: Hodder and Stoughton, 1967. 192p. Illus. G17110

COXEN, C. Vine disease. 2nd ed. Brisbane: 1848. 20p. G17130

[COZENS, F. W.] Sherryana by F.W.C. London: c1887. 54p. Illus. G17140

COZZENS, Frederic S. Cozzens' wine press. New York: The Wine Press, 1854-1855. 95p. G17150

An early commercial trade paper. This volume consists of twelve periodical articles, dating from June 20, 1854 to May 20, 1855. Each issue is eight pages. Also published in subsequent years.

_____. Sayings, wise and otherwise. New York: American Book Exchange, 1880. 265p. G17160

Cozzens was a New York wine merchant and publisher of Cozzens' Wine Press 1854-1861, an early American wine journal that advocated the production and use of American wines. This is a collection of his essays on various topics, including wine and dining.

CRABTREE, Bill. The best wine recipes. London: Foulsham, 1979. 96p. Illus. G17170

CRADOCK, John [Bon Viveur] (pseud). An A.B.C. of wine drinking. London: Frederick Muller, 1954. 96p. Illus. G17180

_____. Wining and dining in France with Bon Viveur. London: Putnam, 1959. 225p. G17190

CRADOCK, Johnnie. Wine for today. London: Frederick Muller, 1975. 198p. Illus. G17200

CRAHAN, Marcus Esketh. California and its place among the wine nations. Los Angeles: Homer E. Boelter, 1949. 12p. Illus. G17210

Lithographed on Strathmore text by Homer H. Boelter. Limited to 150 copies. This is the transcript of a talk given before the Los Angeles Westerners on August 20, 1948.

_____. Early American inebrietatis. Review of the development of American habits in drink and the national bias and fixations resulting therefrom. Los Angeles: The Plantin Press for the Zamorano Club, 1964. 62p. Illus. G17220

Limited edition of 150 copies. Contains many interesting items on the early wine situation in the United States.

CRAHAN, Marcus Esketh, comp. The Wine and Food Society of Southern California; a history with a bibliography of A.L. Simon. Los Angeles: The Society, 1957. 60p. G17230

Books written and published by A.L. Simon from 1905-1956, pages 52-60.

CRAIG, Elizabeth. Wine in the kitchen. London: Constable, 1934. 136p. G17240

Includes information on the choice of wine for the kitchen, table use and wine service.

[CRAIG, William.] The cooper's craft. London: 1899. G17250

Unable to verify.

CRANE, Frances Kirkwood. The man in gray. New York: Random House, 1958. 206p. G17260

A novel with a California wine industry setting.

CRAWFORD, Anne. A history of the Vintners' Company. London: Constable, 1977. 319p. Illus. G17270

A valuable reference for those interested in the history of the London wine trade. Many fascinating details emerge including the legend of the five kings' feast. The Company employed a future saint (Thomas More) as counsel before the Star Chamber Court (See Simon, André).

CRAWFORD, Iain. Make me a wine connoisseur. London: The Dickens Press, 1969. 64p. Illus. G17280

_____. Wine on a budget. London: Paul Hamlyn, 1964. 96p. G17290

CRAWFURD, Oswald John Frederick. Portgual. Notes on the proposed establishment of a monopoly wine company in the consular districts of Oporto. London: Harrison and Sons, 1889. 5p. G17300

_____. Portugal old and new. London: Kegan Paul and New York: Putnam's, 1880. 386p. Illus. G17320

There is a discussion of port wine on pages 218-67.

CREAMER, Hanna Gardner. The household myth. Boston: Charles H. Whiting, 1885. G17330

A novel with a California wine industry setting.

CRESTA BLANCA WINE CO. Nature smiled . . . and there was Cresta Blanca. Los Angeles: Cresta Blanca Wine Co., 1944. 108p. Illus. G17340

_____. 90 years of Cresta Blanca. San Francisco: Cresta Blanca Winery, 1972. G17350

CRITCHFIELD, Burke H., WENTE, Carl F and Frericks, Andrew G. The California wine industry during the depression. 1972. 79p. Illus. G17355

See California Wine Oral History Series

CROFT, John. A treatise on the wines of Portugal; and what can be gathered on the subject and nature of the wines . . . since the establishment of the English factory at Oporto, Anno 1727: also a dissertation on the nature and use of wines in general, imported into Great Britain, as pertaining to luxury and diet. In two parts. York: Printed by Crask and Lund, 1787. 27p. G17360

A revised edition was published in 1788. Croft (1732-1820) was a member of the Factory at Oporto.

CROFT-COOKE, Rupert. The life for me. New York: St. Martins Press, 1952. 258p. Illus. G17370

With chapters on wine and drink.

_____. Madeira. London: Putnam, 1961. 224p. Illus. G17380

_____. Port. London: Putnam, 1956. 219p. G17390

_____. Sherry. London: Putnam, 1955. 232p. G17400

_____. Wine and other drinks. London: Collins, 1962. 160p. G17410

CROMBIE, Max, ed. And the toast is . . . A miniature anthology of drinking songs seasoned with a little prose. Northwood, Middlesex: Knights Press, n.d. 23p. Illus. G17420

_____. The infidel grape. An anthology in miniature in praise of wine. Northwood, Middlesex: Knights Press, n.d. 23p. Illus. G17430

_____. The wassail bowl. An anthology in miniature of conviviality. Northwood, Middlesex: Knight Press, n.d. 23p. Illus. G17440

CROPSEY, Gilves B. and PETERS, Albert E. Special Federal income tax aspects of vineyard operations. San Francisco: Forbes and Co., 1983. G17450

CROSBY, Everett. The vintage years; the story of High Tor vineyards. New York: Harper and Row, 1973. 227p. Illus. G17460

> The story of a couple who planted a vineyard and built a winery just thirty-five miles from New York City on the Hudson River.

CROSLAND, J. Crosland's wine calculator . . . or, assistant to wine merchants . . . London: T.D. Dewdney, 1881. 27p. G17470

CROSS, Frank Baker. Grapes in Oklahoma. n.p. Stillwater, OK: 1939. 40p. Illus. G17480

CROTCH, W. Walter, ed. The complete year book of French quality wines, spirits and liqueurs, compiled under the editorial and technical direction of Walter Crotch. Paris: Editions M. Ponsot, 1947. 1230p. Illus. G17490

> A compendium of wines from all wine areas of France. Includes maps and lists of major firms.

CROWDY, William Morse. Burgundy and Morvan. London: Christophers, c1925. 200p. Illus. G17500

> An interesting account of the author's travels through Burgundy, and the lesser-known district of Morvan, and provides histories of the ancient towns. In speaking of Auxerre, Mr. Crowdy reported: "It was on the flavor of three vintages, Migraine, Lachainette and Judas that the boast, 'Auxerre est la boisson des rois.' " These wines are so little known today that they are not mentioned in the reference works of Hugh Johnson, Alexis Lichine or Frank Schoonmaker. This book is beautifully illustrated by the Irish artist Percy Francis Gethin and includes sketches of the towns of Autun, Semur, Avallon, Vezelay, Auxerre, Clumny, Dijon and Beaune.

CROZE, Austin de. What to eat and drink in France; a guide to the characteristic recipes and wines of each French province, with a glossary of culinary terms. London: F. Warne, 1931. 332p. G17510

CRUESS, William V. A half century of food and wine technology. 1967. 122p. G17515

> *See California Wine Oral History Series*

_____. Investigations of the flor sherry process. Berkeley: The College of Agriculture, University of California, 1948. 40p. Illus. G17520

> William Vere Cruess (1886-1968) was a biochemist and Professor of Food Technology at the University of California, Berkeley. He became known as the man who invented the fruit cocktail.

_____. The principles and practices of wine making. New York: Avi Publishing, 1934. 212p. Illus. G17530

Second edition of 476p. published in 1947.

CRUESS, William Vere, JOSLYN, Maynard A. and SAYWELL, L.G. Laboratory examination of wines and other fermented fruit products. New York: Avi Publishing, 1934. 111p. Illus. G17540

CSAVAS, Zoltan. The Louis Martini Winery. St. Helena, CA: The Winery, 1983. 96p. Illus. G17550

CUNYNGHAME, Francis. Reminiscenses of an epicure. London: Peter Owen, 1955. 156p. G17560

CUSHNER, Nicholas P. Lords of the land: sugar, wine and Jesuit estates of coastal Peru, 1600-1767. Albany: State University of New York Press, 1980. 225p. Illus. G17570

CUTHILL, James. A treatise on the vine disease . . . London: Groombridge, 1873. 31p. G17580

CYPRUS wine. London: Cyprus Trade Center, 1976. 31p. Illus. G17590

DALEY, Robert. Strong wine red as blood. New York: Harper's Magazine Press, 1975. 400p. G17610

A novel with a Bordeaux wine setting.

DALI, Salvadore; text by ORIZET, Louis. The wines of Gala. New York: Harry N. Abrams, 1978. 296p. Illus. G17620

Over 100 illustrations by Dali, many of which are original for this book. The illustrations are beautifully reproduced by Draeger Freres.

DALLAS, Philip. The great wines of Italy. Garden City, NY: Doubleday, 1974. 399p. G17630

_____. The great wines of Italy. 2nd rev. ed. London: Faber and Faber, 1983. 336p. G17640

DALRYMPLE, J., Sir. On the distillery law. London: n.p., 1786. G17650

Unable to verify.

DANIELS, Dorothy. The wines of Cyprien. New York: Pyramid Books, 1977. 317p. G17660

A novel with a California wine industry setting.

DARAIO, John P. Healthful and therapeutic properties of wine, beer, whiskey, bitters, liquors in general. New York: n.p., 1937. 112p. G17670

D'ARMAND, F. Art of fine wine drinking. 1903. G17680

Unable to verify.

D'ARMAND, F. Jr. Key to the trade. Sacramento: H.S. Crocker, 1865. 70p. G17690

Contains chapters on brandies and wines.

DART, Colin John. Woodwork for winemakers. Andover, England: Amateur Winemaker, 1971. 120p. Illus. G17700

DAVID, H.J., ed. The wine book of South Africa. The western province of the Cape and its wine industry. Stellenbosch: Wine and Spirit, 1936. 224p. Illus. G17710

> This publication covers not only South Africa's vineyards but also its mountains, valleys, homesteads and people. It contains over 200 photographs and illustrations.

DAVIDSON, William Mark. The grape phylloxera in California. Washington: Gov't. Print. Off., 1921. 128p. Illus. G17720

DAVIDSON, William R. The wholesale wine trade in Ohio. Columbus: Ohio State University Press, 1954. 94p. G17730

> Covers the period 1934-1954.

DAVIES, John Brutus. The butler, by an experienced servant. London: Houlston and Stoneman, 1855. 108p. G17740

> There is also an 1880 edition published by Houlston and Sons.

_____. The butler's guide to the making of wines, beers and liquors in a gentleman's cellar. Auckland: Wineglass Publishing, 1977. 96p. G17750

> A reprint of the 1808, ninth edition, of the above book with a reworded title.

_____. The innkeeper's and butler's guide, or, a directory in the making and managing of British wines; together with directions for the managing, colouring and flavouring of foreign wines and spirits. 2nd ed. Leeds: Printed by G. Wilson, 1806. 200p. G17760

> This popular book was issued in many subsequent editions.

DAVIS, Derek C. English bottles and decanters 1650-1900. London: Charles Letts, 1972. 80p. Illus. G17780

DAVIS, Frank. Antique glass and glass collecting. Feltham: Hamlyn, 1973. 96p. Illus. G17790

DAVIS, J. Irving. A beginner's guide to wines and spirits. London: Stanley Nott, 1934. 93p. Illus. G17800

DAVIS, Nathaniel Newnham. Dinners and diners: where and how to dine in London. London: Grant Richards, 1899. 335p. G17810

> A series of essays originally published in the *Pall Mall Gazette*.

DAVIS, S.F. History of the wine trade. London: The Wine and Spirit Ass'n of Great Britain, 1969. 19p. G17820

DAVISON, Almond D. Sanitation guide for wineries. San Francisco: Wine Institute, c1961-1963. 68p. Illus. G17830

De BERNARDI MATEOS, Pedro. Wines from the district of Utiel-Requena. Requena, Spain: 1970. 35p. Illus. G17840

De BLIJ, Harm J. Viticulture. Miami: University of Miami, 1981. G17850

The author is a professor of geography at the University of Miami in Coral Gables, and this monograph was prepared primarily for classroom use. A revised and expanded version was published as *Wine, A Geographic Appreciation.*

_____. Wine, a geographic appreciation. Totowa, NJ: Rowman and Allanheld, 1983. 224p. Illus. G17860

Covers not only the traditional wine regions, but also many less familiar regions such as China and Japan, and countries of the Southern Hemisphere - Australia, New Zealand, South Africia, Chile and Argentina.

De GROOT, Roy Andries. Esquire's handbook for hosts. New York: Grosset and Dunlap, 1973. 476p. Illus. G17880

_____. Feasts for all seasons. New York: Knopf, 1966. 730p. Illus. G17890

_____. The wines of California, the Pacific Northwest, and New York. New York: Summit Books, c1982. 463p. Illus. G17900

De JONGH, S.J. Encyclopedia of South African wine. New York: McGraw Hill, 1976. 130p. Illus. G17910

De SALIS, Mrs. Drinks a la mode. Cups and drinks of every kind for every season. London: Longmans, Green, 1891. 100p. G17920

Subsequent editions.

DEAN, Albert B., ed. The licensed victuallers' official annual, legal text book, diary and almanack for the year 1909. London: Licensed Victuallers' Central Protection Society, 1908. 337p. Illus. G17930

DEANE, Samuel. The New England farmer . . . Worcester, MA: Printed by Isaiah Thomas, 1790. 335p. G17940

Deane's book, the first of its kind in this country, is a "georgical dictionary" based on the practical experience of its author as well as on information from classic English horticulture works, such as Miller's *The Gardener's Dictionary.* Contains numerous entries describing the cultivation, preservation and use of various foodstuffs, including wine and cider. Under "Vine," Deane describes the native vines of Boston and states, "Who can doubt whether the appearance of these indigenous vines indicate, that nature has designed such a country for vineyards?" Then follows a lengthy excerpt from an unidentified source that summarizes wine making practices in the various regions of France. Second edition, 1797 and third edition in 1822.

DEARING, Charles. Home utilization of muscadine grapes. Rev. ed. Washington: Gov't. Print. Off., 1942. 26p. Illus. G17950

_____. Muscadine grapes. Washington: Gov't. Print. Off., 1947. 29p. Illus. G17960

_____. New muscadine grapes. Washington : Gov't. Print. Off., 1948. 28p. Illus. G17970

Describes fifteen new varieties.

DEBUIGNE, Gerard. Larousse dictionary of wines of the world. London: Hamlyn, 1976. 272p. Illus. G17990

DeCHAMBEAU, Andre. Creative winemaking. Rochester, NY: Information Services, 1972. 159p. Illus. G18000

DEGHY, Guy and WATERHOUSE, Keith. Cafe Royal. Ninety years of Bohemia. London: 1956. 211p. Illus. G18010

DEIGHTON, Len, ed. Drinksmanship. Town's album of fine wines and high spirits. London: Haymarket Press, 1964. 133p. Illus. G18020

>Wine information contributed by wine writers such as Cyril Ray and Hugh Johnson. Covers such subjects as London's wine houses; a French wine primer; wines for tomorrow; the making of sherry and port; what to drink with exotic food, etc.

DEJAY, Maries. Victorian cups and punches. London: Cassell, 1974. G18030

DELAFORCE, John. The Factory House of Oporto. London: Christie's Wine Publications, 1979. 108p. Illus. G18040

>Revised edition of 122p. was published in 1983.

DELANY, Laurance. Blood red wine. New York: Dell, 1981. G18050

>A novel with a California wine industry setting.

DELAVAN, Edward C. Letter to the Bishops of the Episcopal Church on the adulteration of liquors. Albany: C. Van Benthuysen, 1859. 36p. G18060

——————. Temperance of wine countries. A letter to the Rev. Dr. E. Nott. Manchester, London: Kingdom Alliance, 1860. 16p. G18070

DELMON, Philip. Making wine once a week. London: Mills and Boon, 1971. 142p. G18080

——————. Ten types of table wine. London: Mills and Boon, 1971. 96p. G18090

——————. The wine maker's reciter: a miscellany of odd odes, interspersed with moral poems, educational ballads and sundry literary bric-a-brac concerning wine makers that we all know (and sometimes wish we didn't). Andover, England: Amateur Winemaker, 1972. 78p. Illus. G18100

DELMON, Philip and TURNER, B.C.A. Quick and easy winemaking from concentrates and fruit juices. New York: Hippocrene Books, 1973. 107p. Illus. G18110

DEMKO, Dr. Charles. Growing grapes in Florida. State of Florida Dept. of Agriculture Bulletin no. 63. Tallahassee: 1957. 26p. Illus. G18120

DENMAN, James L. A brief discussion on wine; embracing an historical and descriptive account of the vine, its culture and produce in all countries, ancient and modern, drawn from the best authorities. London: By the Author, 1861. 138p. G18130

THE

VINE AND ITS FRUIT,

MORE ESPECIALLY IN RELATION TO

THE PRODUCTION OF WINE:

EMBRACING

𝔄n 𝔥istorical and 𝔇escriptive 𝔄ccount of the 𝔊rape,

ITS CULTURE AND TREATMENT IN ALL COUNTRIES,

ANCIENT AND MODERN,

DRAWN FROM THE BEST AUTHORITIES,

AND INCORPORATING

A BRIEF DISCOURSE ON WINE.

BY JAMES L. DENMAN.

SECOND EDITION, REVISED AND ENLARGED.

LONDON:

LONGMANS, GREEN, AND CO.

1875.

_____. Denman's annual wine report. London: 1862. 21p. G18135

_____. Pure wine and how to know it. London: Spottiswoode, 1869. 39p. G18140

_____. The vine and its fruit . . . London: Longmans, Green, Longman, Roberts and Green, 1864. 346p. G18150

_____. The vine and its fruit, more especially in relation to the production of wine: embracing an historical and descriptive account of the grape, its culture and treatment in all countries, ancient and modern, drawn from the best authorities, and incorporating a brief discourse on wine. 2nd ed. rev. and enl. London: Longmans, Green, 1875. 518p. Illus. G18160

> An interesting account that contains a great deal of historical information. We are told that the tiny Rhone estate of Chateau Grillet was expensive even then in England, but unlike the present dry, floral scented wine, the grapes were allowed "to become shrivelled and almost rotten before they were gathered . . . and a sweet *vin-de-dessert*" was made. This is a valuable reference. Scarce.

_____. What is wine? An inquiry suggested by the most recent correspondence in "The Times" on the alleged adulteration of sherry. London: 1874. 47p. G18170

_____. What should we drink? An inquiry suggested by Mr. E. L. Beckwith's "Practical Notes on Wine.". London: 1868. 118p. G18180

> This is a criticism of Mr. Beckwith's book (See Beckwith), where Greek wines had all but been ignored. Mr. Denman, who was an agent for the Greek Archipelago Wine Company, never missed an opportunity to praise Greek wines and claimed Greek wines ". . . the strongest wines which nature produces . . . and possessing a pure flavour and bouquet which no art could possibly impart." In this book he attempts to show that Beckwith made conflicting statements about the quality of certain wines, and gives a long list of press reports in favor of Greek wines. In spite of its genesis, this is an interesting little book.

_____. Wine and its adulterations. London: Spottiswoode, 1867. 34p. Illus. G18190

> Has folding map of the wine districts of Europe, a map showing the 1866 volcanic eruption at Santorin (an island in the Greek Archipelago where most of the best Greek wines were made) and a folding plate illustrating Savatin wine glasses. Rare.

_____. Wine and its counterfeits. London: Briscoe, 1876. 59p. G18220 A small book written in praise of Greek wines and denouncing both sherry and port because of the addition of brandy. Denman never let up on his abhorrence of any type of adulteration of wine.

_____. Wine as it is drunk in England, and as it should be, pure, wholesome and refreshing. London: Chifferial, 1865. 550p. G18200

_____. Wine as it should be, pure, wholesome and refreshing. An address to wine consumers. London: 1866. 50p. G18210

_____. Wine, the advantages of pure and natural wine . . . London: By the Author, 1865. 31p. G18230

DENNISTON, G. Grape culture in Steuben County in New York. Albany: C. Wendell, 1865. 22p. G18240

Six maps showing grape properties on Keuka Lake and a special report on wines with descriptions of local vineyards and wineries.

DENT, Herbert Crowley. Wine, spirit and sauce labels 18th and 19th centuries. Dorwich: H.W. Hunt, 1933. 15p. Illus. G18250

Reviews the evolution and nomenclature of wine decanter and other labels and contains six plates of representative specimens. Limited edition of 250 copies. Scarce.

DERAMOND, J. French wines. n.d. 78p. G18260

DESPEISSIS, J.A. The handbook of horticulture and viticulture of Western Australia. Perth: Gov't. Print. Off., 1895. 338p. Illus. G18280

Second edition of 620p. was published in 1902; subsequent edition in 1921.

_____. The vineyard and the cellar with two chapters on wine fermentation and racking. Sydney: Charles Potter, Gov't. Print. Off., 1894. 61p. G18290

DETTORI, Renato G. Italian wines and liqueurs. Rome: Italian Institute for Foreign Trade, 1953. 158p. Illus. G18300

DEWEY, H.T. and Sons. Fiftieth anniversary 1857-1907. New York: 1907. 32p. G18310

DEWEY, Suzette. Wines for those who have forgotten and those who want to know. Chicago: Lakeside Press, 1934. 97p. Illus. G18320

Edition limited to 1,200 copies.

DeWITT, William A. Drinking and what to do about it. New York: Grosset and Dunlap, 1952. 186p. G18330

DEXTER, Philip. Notes on French wines. Rev. ed. Boston: Privately printed, 1933. 76p. G18340

DICEY, Patricia, comp. Wine in South Africa: a select bibliography. Cape Town: University of Cape Town, 1951. 29p. G18350

DICK, William B., ed. Dick's book of toasts, speeches and responses . . . New York: Dick and Fitzgerald, c1883. 172p. G18360

DICKENS, Cedric. Drinking with Dickens. London: 1980. 127p. Illus. G18370

Cedric Dickens, the great-grandson of Charles Dickens, includes over sixty-five drink recipes and text on drinking with the great novelist. (See Hewlett, Edward.)

DICKENSON, Charles H. The California State Board of Viticultural Commissioners: from creation to dissolution. n.p., 1975. 53p. G18380

DIGBY, Sir Kenelm. The closet of the eminently learned Sir Kenelm Digby, Knight, Opened: whereby is discovered several ways of making . . . cherry-wine . . . Published by his son's consent. London: E.C. for H. Brome, 1669. 312p. G18390

> A third edition, corrected, of 251p. was published in 1677 by H.C. for H. Brome.

DIGBY, Thomas Sir Kenelm. The closet of Sir Kenelm Digby, Knight, Open: newly edited, with introduction, notes, and glossary, by Anne Mac-Donell. [Reprint with facsimile reproduction of original title page of 1669.] London: P.L. Warner, 1910. 291p. G18400

DIGIACOMO, Louis J. The clear and simple wine guide. Harrisburg, PA: Stackpole Books, 1981. 159p. Illus. G18410

DILL, George H. Prohibition and the vineyard. San Francisco: By the Author, c1906. 8p. G18420

DINGMAN, Stanley T. The wine cellar and journal book. Westover Publishing, 1972. 41p. Illus. G18430

DIRECTOR, Anne. The standard wine cook book. Garden City, NY: Doubleday, 1948. 218p. G18440

> Covers such basics: wine names and classifications, wine service guide, wine glassware, wine buying and cellaring, etc.

DIRECTORY of the eastern wine and grape industry. New York: Eastern Grape Growers and Winery News, 105p. Illus. G18450

DISCOVER Oregon wines and wineries. Portland, OR: Oregon Winegrowers Association, c1983. 29p. Illus. G18460

DISCOVERING Italian wines. An authoritative compendium of wines, food, and travel throughout the nineteen producing regions of Italy. Los Angeles: Ward Ritchie Press, 1971. 136p. Illus. G18470

DISHER, M. Willson. Winkles and champagne . . . London: Batsford, c1938. 147p. G18480

> Winkles are large marine snails used for food.

The DISTILLER of London, compiled and set forth by the special license and command of the King for the sole use of the Company of Distillers of London. London: R. Bishop, 1639. 67p. G18490

> Other editions 1668 and 1698.

The DISTILLER of London . . . for the sole use of the Company of Distillers of London. London: 1725. G18500

> Unable to verify.

The DISTILLER of London: with the clavis to unlock the deepest secrets of that mysterious art . . . London: Tho. Huntington and Wil. Nealand, 1652. 167p. G18510

DIX, Irving Wesley and MAGNESS, J.R. American grape varieties. Washington: U.S. Department of Agriculture, 1937. 33p. G18520

DIXON, Campell, comp. Daily Telgraph fourth miscellany. London: Hutchinson, n.d. 343p. G18530

>   Contains an interesting chapter of wine potpourri titled, "The Agreeable Mocker."

DOBLACHE, Guillermo. My first trip to Villa Nueva. Reprinted from Bonfort's Wine and Spirit Gazette. London: 1896. 15p. G18540

DOMECQ, Pedro. European award Mercurio D'Oro. Turin, Italy: Domecq, 1971. Unpaged. Illus. G18550

>   30,000 copies of this promotional monograph were published by Pedro Domecq in five languages. The receipt of the Mercurio D'Oro by Jose Ignacio de Domecq on behalf of Pedro Domecq is recorded in the first three pages. Thereafter the text is devoted to the history of the Domecq family and its wines and brandies. Interestingly illustrated with black and white and color photographs and prints, several of which are tipped in. Large folio.

The DOMESTIC service guide to housekeeping . . . cellarage of wines; home brewing and wine-making . . . London: Lockwood, 1865. 420p. Illus. G18560

DON, Robert S. Wine. London: English Universities Press, 1968. 202p. Illus. G18570

>   Subsequent editions.

DON, Robert S., ed. Wine list decorations, 1961-1963. Bristol: John Harvey and Sons, 1964. 100p. Illus. G18580

>   Illustrations and maps from Harvey's wine lists.

DON, Robin. Off the shelf. London: Brown and Pank, 1967. 128p. Illus. G18590

_____. Wine. London: English Universities Press, 1968. 202p. Illus. G18600

>   A second edition of 197p. was published in 1977 by Hodder and Stoughton.

DONNER, Gail and WAVERMAN, Lucy. The pennypincher's wine guide. Toronto: Peter Martin Associates, 1974. 133p. G18610

DORAN, J. Table traits, with something on them. London: R. Bentley, 1854. 547p. G18620

DORCHESTER, Daniel. The liquor problem in all ages. New York: Phillips and Hunt, 1884. 656p. Illus. G18630

>   The author, a minister, spent twenty-two years gathering data for this book. Although the message is one of temperance, the text contains much information about wine. A number of the illustrations have been taken from the works of Henry Vizetelly.

DORNAT, C.C. The wine and spirit merchant's own book; a manual for the manufacturer, and a guide for the dealer in wines, spirits . . . to which are subjoined more than three hundred valuable receipts on the manufacturing of all liqueurs, and fruits preserved in brandy. London: Raginel, 1855. 136p. G18640

Translated from the French.

DOROZYNSKI, Alexander and BELL, Bibiane. The wine book. New York: Golden Press, 1969. 310p. Illus. G18650

Beautiful and interesting illustrations and well written text.

DOUGHARTY, John. The general gauger: or, the principles and practice of gauging beer, wine and malt . . . London: James Knapton, 1719. 240p. G18660

Numerous subsequent and revised editions.

DOUGHTY, Brian, ed. A guide to good wine. 3rd ed. London: Abbey Library, 1970. 208p. Illus. G18670

DOVAZ, Michael. Encyclopedia of the great wines of Bordeaux. Paris: Juilliard, 1981. 255p. Illus. G18680

A book for the claret buff who loves detailed information. The book concerns itself with only the classed growths of Médoc, Graves, Sauternes and St. Émilion. The author has made one exception for Chateau Petrus which he believes should be in the first growth club. Each chateau is accorded two pages, which includes a general note about the chateau, a colored photograph of the chateau, a reproduction of the label, a map indicating the chateau's relationship to its neighbors, a vintage chart with ratings covering all the important years from 1961 through 1980, over thirty technical details about the wine, the ideal drinking age of the wine, and the wine's ideal accompaniment, which in the case of Chateau Petrus happens to be "roast pheasant a' la perigourdine."

DOW, Michael and ENDEMANN, Carl T., eds. Voices of the wineland: an anthology by twenty-two Napa Valley poets. 3rd ed. Calistoga: Alta Napa Press, 1978. Illus. G18690

DOWLEY, D.M. Nuttall's wine facts. London: Warne, 1979. 48p. G18700

DOWNEY, A.J. Australian grape grower's manual for the use of beginners. Melbourne: Robertson, 1895. 70p. G18710

DOWNMAN, Francis. Not claret. 2nd ed. London: Richards, 1937. 96p. G18720

A debate over the BBC's refusal to accept wine and liquor advertisements.

DOXAT, John. The book of drinking. London: Triune Books, 1973. 144p. Illus. G18730

_____. The world of drinks and drinking; an international distillation. Cookery Book Club, c1971. 256p. G18740

DOXAT, John, ed. The indispensable drinks book. New York: Van Nostrand Reinhold, 1981. 224p. Illus. G18750

The first section of this book, "Wine," was written by Jancis Robinson and covers most of the world's better known wine areas.

DRAKE, Albert. Wine and you. Los Altos, CA: 1970. G18755

DREX, A. ABC of wines, cocktails and liqueurs. New York: Crown Publishing, 1933. 46p. Illus. G18760

DRINKING glasses. London: Victoria and Albert Museum, 1947. 28p. Illus. G18770

> Thirty-six black and white photographs of drinking glasses, decanters and other table glassware.

DRINKWATER, Caleb. How to serve wine and beer. Cleveland: Watkins Publishing, 1933. 80p. Illus. G18780

DRISCOLL, W.P. The beginnings of the wine industry in the Hunter Valley. Newcastle, N.S.W.: 1969. 81p. Illus. G18790

DRIVER, John. Letters from Madeira in 1834. London: Longman, 1836. 85p. G18800

DRIVER, Sydney C. Some principles of the wine trade. London: Upcott Gill, 1909. 65p. G18810

DRUITT, Robert, M.D. Report on cheap wines of France, Italy, Austria, Greece, and Hungary; their quality, wholesomeness, and price, and their use in diet and medicine. With short notes of a lecture to ladies on wine, and remarks on acidity. London: Henry Renshaw, 1865. 179p. G18820

> Wine had become much cheaper in Great Britain after Gladstone, as Chancellor of the Exchequer, lifted the duty on it on April 4, 1862. The author, a member of the Royal College of Physicians, became interested in the subject of intemperance and bought inexpensive wine for his own drinking in order to ascertain what the public could buy for a moderate price. Dr. Druit made notes on his drinking experiences and published them in the *Medical Times and Gazette*. Urged on by his medical brethren, he published those papers in the form of this informative book.
>
> In the words of the author, the object of the book was "to know how far these wines may be useful to the medical practitioner as agents in the restoration of health, and how far they are fit to appear at our tables as part of our ordinary diet." We are told that claret is good for measles, scarlatina and rheumatism. In fact, Dr. Druit thinks so highly of Bordeaux wine as a dinner beverage in place of sherry and port that he remarks: "I say try claret, and you will add ten years to your patient's life and to your own fees."
>
> On burgundy, Dr. Druitt remarks that "its body is aromatic, not alcoholic. Of course, like all great artists, I am drawing from the live model. I write with a bottle before me, which I am sacrificing for my own inspiration and my reader's profit." And for those physicians and others who might want to know the good doctor's opinion as to how much wine one can safely drink with dinner, the answer is on page twenty-eight.

————. Report on cheap wines of France, Italy, Austria, Greece, and Hungary; their quality, wholesomeness, and price, and their use in diet and medicine. With short notes of a lecture to ladies on wine, and remarks on acidity. 2nd ed., rewritten and enlarged. London: H. Renshaw, 1873. 179p. Illus. G18830

Du BREUIL, Alphonse. Vineyard culture, improved and cheapened. Translated by E. and C. Parker of Longworth's wine house. With notes and adaptions to American culture by John A. Warder. Cincinnati: Robert Clarke, 1867. 337p. Illus. G18840

Du BREUIL, M. The Thomery system of grape culture. New York: Geo. E. Woodward, c1876. 60p. Illus. G18850

DU PLESSIS, C.S. A study of wine bouquet precursors in grapes. Stellenbosch, South Africa: University of Stellenbosch, 1970. 142p. Illus. G18860

DU PLESSIS, Stefanus Johannes. Anthracnose of vines and its control in South Africa. Pretoria: Gov't. Print., 1940. 47p. G18870

_____. Bacterial blight of vines (Vlamsiekte) in South Africa caused by *Erwinia Vitivora*. Pretoria: Gov't. Print., 1940. 105p. Illus. G18880

_____. Comparison of the effectiveness of various fungicides and the methods of their application for the control of Botrytis rot of grapes. Pretoria: Gov't. Print., 1939. 31p. G18890

DUBOIS, Raymond. Co-operation in viticulture; lecture delivered at the Working Men's College, on 14th July 1900, by R. Dubois, Director of the Viticultural Station, Rutherglen. Melbourne: R.S. Brain, Gov't. Print., C1900. 46p. Illus. G18900

_____. Trenching and subsoiling for American vines. Melbourne: R.S. Brain, Gov't. Print., 1901. 171p. Illus. G18910

DUBOIS, Raymond and WILKINSON, Percy W. New methods of grafting and budding as applied to reconstitution with American vines. Melbourne: R.S. Brain, Gov't. Print., 1901. 72p. G18920

DUBRUNFAUT, Augustin Pierre. A complete treatise on the art of distillation . . . also the whole art of rectification, in which is particularly treated the nature of essential oils. From the French of Dubrunfaut. By John Sheridan. To which is prefixed, the Distillers' practical guide, by Peter Jonas, with genuine recipes for making rum, brandy, Hollands' gin, and all sorts of compounds, cordials and liqueurs. 4th ed. London: Sherwood, Gilbert and Piper, 1830. 532p. Illus. G18930

DUFOUR, John James. The American vine-dresser's guide, being a treatise on the cultivation of the vine, and the process of wine making adopted to soil . . . of United States . . . Cincinnati: Printed by S.J. Browne, 1826. 314p. Illus. G18940

> By the author's accreditation on the title page, he was "formerly of Swisserland [sic], and now an American citizen, cultivator of the vine from his childhood, and for the last twenty-five years, occupied in the line of business, first in Kentucky, and now on the borders of Ohio, near Vevay, Indiana." This was the first of several viticultural works characterized by a preference for Old World vines and the belief that previous failures to cultivate them in America were due largely to an ignorance of proper (i.e., Euro-

pean) viticultural practices. John Dufour came to America from Switzerland at the age of thirty-three to engage in grape growing and winemaking. Before forming the Kentucky Vineyard Society, Dufour made an inspection tour of all of America's vineyards. What he saw is set out in this book and is the most accurate account of grape growing in the United States at the beginning of the 19th century.

Dufour's attempts to cultivate the *Vitis vinifera* in Kentucky were a failure. Thinking that location was the problem, he settled in Vevay, Indiana and continued his efforts to cultivate Old World grapes. The only variety to succeed was the native Alexander grape, which Dufour stubbornly and incorrectly insisted was from the Cape of Good Hope.

DUFOUR, Perret. The Swiss settlement of Switzerland County, Indiana. Indianapolis: Indiana Historical Commission, 1925. 446p. Illus. G18950

About a grape-growing colony.

DUIJKER, Hubrecht. The good wines of Bordeaux and the great wines of Sauternes. London: Mitchell Beazley, 1983. 200p. Illus. G18960

Covers the lesser known "bourgeois" wines of Médoc, St. Émilion, Pomerol, Graves and the more remote wine areas. Also covers Sauternes and is illustrated with hundreds of labels.

_____. The great wine chateaux of Bordeaux. London: Mitchell Beazley, 1983. 200p. Illus. G18970

_____. The great wines of Burgundy. London: Mitchell Beazley, 1983. 200p. Illus. G18990

_____. The great wines of the Loire, Alsace and Champagne. London: Mitchell Beazley, 1983. 200p. Illus. G19000

DUMBRA, Carl Dominick. Forward American wines, including wine producers' formulae. 2 vols. Sacramento: By the Author, 1948. 518/657p. Illus. G19010

DUMBRELL, Roger. Understanding antique wine bottles. London: Antique Collectors' Club/Christie's Wine Publications, 1983. 340p. Illus. G19020

DUNCAN, Peter Moncrieff. Winemaking with concentrates; a practical guide to good winemaking and the production of enjoyable wine from grape and other popular fruit juice concentrates. Andover, England: Amateur Winemaker, 1974. 92p. G19030

DUNCAN, Peter Moncrieff and ACTON, Bryon. Progressive winemaking, a textbook covering fully the theory and practice of winemaking. Andover, England: Amateur Winemaker, 1967. 445p. Illus. G19040

Second edition published in 1971.

DUNCAN, T.B. Atlantic Islands: Madeira, the Azores and the Cape Verdes in seventeenth-century commerce and navigation. Chicago: Univ. of Chicago Press, 1972. 291p. G19050

DUNLOP, John. On the wine system of Great Britain. Greenock: R.B. Luck, 1831. 57p. G19060

DUNN, James B. Are beer and light wines to be encouraged as against the stronger distilled liquors? n.p., n.d. 11p. G19070

DUPLAIS, W.M. A treatise on the manufacture and distillation of alcoholic liquors . . . Translated by M. McKennie. Philadelphia: Henry Carey Baird, 1871. 754p. G19080

DuPONT de NEMOURS, Alicia. The cultivation of vineyards in southwestern France. New York: Brentano's, 1920. 273p. Illus. G19090

DURAC, Jack. A matter of taste; wine and wine-tasting. New York: Dutton, 1974. 241p. Illus. G19100

> Several subsequent editions. Published by Dutton in 1974 under the title: *Wines and the Art of Tasting.*

DURKAN, Andrew. Vendange; a study of wine and other drinks. New York: Drake Publishers, 1972. 327p. Illus. G19110

DYER, George Bell. The three-cornered wound. Boston: Houghton Mifflin, 1931. G19120

> A novel with a California wine industry setting.

EAKIN, John R. Rudiments of grape culture. Little Rock, AK: 1868. 81p. G19140

EALES, Mary. The compleat confectioner; or the art of candying and preserving in its unmost perfection. By the late Mrs. Eales . . . to which is added, a 2nd part: containing a curious collection of receipts in cookery, pickling, family physicik, with the best . . . methods of brewing all sorts of malt liquors, and preparing sundry kinds of excellent made wines . . . 3rd ed. London: R. Montheu, 1842. 103p. G19150

EASTON, George. The wine of Cana. 3rd ed. Grahamston, England: Printed by T. Paul, 1877. 44p. G19160

EBY, Gordon. Napa Valley. Eby Press, 1972. G19170

EDEN, Dorothy. The vines of Yarrabee. New York: Coward-McCann, 1969. 316p. G19180

> A novel about the wines and vineyards of Australia in 1830.

EDMONDS, George and THOMPSON, Jeremiah. The country brewer's assistant and English vintner's instructor. London: Printed for Iassac Fell, 1769. 134p. G19190

> This book is in two parts: Part one by George Edmonds covers fifty-one pages on the art of brewing beer; Part two is by Jeremiah Thompson and gives the recipes for making wine from grapes, mulberries and more than sixty other fruits, herbs, flowers, etc.

EDMONDS, W. of Hereford. A new and easy way of making wines from herbs, fruits and flowers . . . London: Printed for J. Williams, 1767. 84p. G19200

Although the title is descriptive of its contents, the author devotes the first eight pages of his treatise to improving the planting of vines and ". . . making wine of grapes equal to that of France." After discussing the method of pressing the grapes, we are told that from ". . . your ordinary white grapes you make a good white sort of wine, of the red grapes a Claret, and if want of colour, heighten it with a little Brazeil, boiled in about a quart of it, and strained very clear. The white grapes, not too ripe, give a good Rhenish taste, and are wonderful cooling, and a sort of muscadel grapes growing now in many parts of England, may be brought by the help of a little loaf-sugar to feed on, to produce a curious sweet wine, little different from Canary, and altogether as wholesome and pleasant; so that with some change, labour, and industry, we might well furnish ourselves with what we now are beholding to strangers for at great expense, hazard at seas, and a vast deal more toil and labour than this would require." Rare.

EDWARDS, Walter N. The beverages we drink. London: Ideal Publishing Union, 1898. 220p. Illus. G19210

EHLE, John. The cheeses and wines of England and France. New York: Harper and Row, 1972. 418p. Illus. G19220

EICHLER, Fr. A. A treatise on the manufacture of liquors, syrups, cordials and bitters, including instructions for making vinegars, ciders, wines, punch essences . . . 6th ed. Philadelphia: Ashenbach and Miller, 1884. 94p. Illus. G19230

ELKINGTON, George. The Coopers: Company and craft. London: Sampson Low, Marston, 1933. 310p. Illus. G19240

The history of the Coopers' Company was first written by James Francis Firth in 1848. The book was privately printed and is now rare. Mr. Elkington's book is not a revised edition of Firth's work but an entirely new study on this subject.

After describing the general constitution and government of a London guild, Mr. Elkington presents a scholarly outline of the history of the Coopers' Company. From the earliest history of the trade, the account advances to the Roman period, to the lake dwellers and Saxons, through the Dark Ages to the end of the 17th century, and, finally, to the contemporary status of cask making.

ELLIOTT, C. Distillation in practice. London: Ernest Benn, 1925. 188p. Illus. G19250

ELLIOTT, Franklin Ruben. Elliott's fruit book or, the American fruit-grower's guide . . . 1854. 503p. G19260

Includes grapes.

ELLIOTT, Virginia. Quiet drinking; a book of beer, wines and cocktails and what to serve with them. New York: Harcourt, Brace, 1933. 112p. G19270

ELLIS, Charles. Origin, nature and history of wine: its use as a beverage, lawful and needful to civilized man. 2nd ed. London: F.S. Ellis, 1861. 56p. G19280

ELLIS, John, M.D. The fruit of the vine: unfermented or fermented -which? . . . New York: National Temperance Society and Publication House, 1893. 128p. G19290

_____. Pure wine. Fermented wine . . . in light of the new dispensation. New York: By the Author, 1890. 48p. G19295

_____. Reply to the Academy's review of the wine question in the light of the New Dispensation. New York: By the Author, 1883. 270p. G19300

_____. Reply to "The Holy Super . . ." in which the essential points in the wine question are carefully considered. London: New Church Temperance Society, 1895. 128p. Illus. G19305

_____. The wine question in the light of the New Dispensation. New York: By the Author, 1882. 228p. G19310

Also published in 1886.

ELLWANGER, George H. Meditations on gout with a consideration of its cure through the use of wine. New York: Dodd, Mead, 1897. 208p. G19330

The message of this book is clear - mature wine imbibed in reasonable quantities will not only cure the gout but add to the imbiber's longevity. The author alleges that the disproportionate amount of gout in England when compared to other countries can be traced directly to the Methuen Treaty of 1703, which gave favorable treatment to brandied port.

_____. Meditations on gout with a consideration of its cure through the use of wine. Ridland, VT: Charles E. Tuttle, 1968. 208p. G19340

Reprint of 1897 edition.

_____. The pleasures of the table. An account of gastronomy from ancient days to present times. New York: Doubleday, Page, 1902. 477p. Illus. G19350

ELSHOLTZ, John Sigmund. Curious distillatory . . . written originally in Latin . . . put into English by T. Sherley. London: Printed by J.D. for Robert Boulter, 1677. 111p. Illus. G19360

EMERSON, Edward R. Beverages past and present; an historical sketch of their production, together with a study of the customs connected with their use. 2 vols. New York: Putnam's, 1908. 563/514p. G19370

Covers both intoxicating and non-intoxicating beverages, with much attention given to wine, from its place in mythology to the development of wine production in the United States. An interesting work and significant for the wealth of historical information it contains.

_____. A lay thesis on Bible wines. New York: Merrill and Baker, 1902. 63p. G19380

_____. The story of the vine. New York: Putnam's, 1902. 252p. G19390

> Chronicles ancient, European, United States, African, Chinese and other vinifera wines. The history of the vine in the United States is excellent.

EMMERY, Lena and TAYLOR, Sally. The grape escape. San Francisco: Sally Taylor and Friends, 1978. 32p. Illus. G19410

> Bicycle tours of the California wine country.

The ENGLISH innkeeper's guide containing one hundred eighty receipts to make and manage wines and liquors. Manayunk: S. Murphy, c1879. 120p. G19420

ENSRUD, Barbara. The pocket guide to wine. New York: Putnam, 1980. 131p. Illus. G19430

> A reference describing popular wines alphabetically by country and giving a rating for quality and value for money, with emphasis on bargain buys. Supplementary sections give information and advice on storing and serving wine, investing in wine, visiting vineyards, etc.
>
> A revised edition issued in 1982.

ENTHOLT, Hermann. The Ratskeller in Bremen. Bremen: G. Winters, 1930. 70p. Illus. G19440

ERMITANO. (pseud). Shillingsworth of Sherry. London: Sociedad de Alamencenistas de Vinos Espanoles, 1874. 155p. G19450

ESCRITT, L.B. The small cellar. London: Herbert Jenkins, 1960. 192p. Illus. G19460

_____. The wine cellar. 2nd rev. ed. London: Wine and Spirit Publications, 1972. 75p. G19470

> Contains many innovative suggestions for converting available space into a wine storage area. The author also advises on how to equip and stock the wine cellar.

ESQUIN Imports. Your key to our wine cellar. San Francisco: Esquin Imports, 1968. 60p. Illus. G19480

> A catalog of wines and books on wine, but with much commentary on vintages and vineyards. There have been subsequent yearly editions. Now known as Draper and Esquin, their most recent catalog, "Winter, 1983-1984" contains ninety-six pages of wine prices, commentary on the wines, wine trivia and is nicely illustrated with photographs, copies of wine labels and old prints.

ESSEN, William van. See Serjeant, Richard. G19490

EVANS, Bob. The pocket wine book. Atlanta: Apotheca Press, c1978. 212p. Illus. G19500

EVANS, George G. What shall we drink? Philadelphia: By the Author, 1877. 46p. G19510

EVANS, Len. Australian winebuyers' guide. Sydney: Hamlyn, 1973. 208p. G19520

_____. Cellarmaster says . . . a revised guide to Australian wines. Sydney: The Bulletin, 1968. 142p. G19530

> A revised edition of his *Guide to Australian Wines.*

_____. Good Evans. Sydney: The Bulletin, 1981. 184p. Illus. G19540

Articles from the *Weekend Australian.*

_____. Guide to Australian wines. 3rd ed. Sydney: The Bulletin, 1967. 84p. G19550

> Cover title: *Cellarmaster's Guide to Australian Wines.*

_____. How to make your own wine cellar. Sydney: Hamyln, 1973. 111p. G19560

> An abridged edition of the *Complete Book of Australian and New Zealand Wines.*

_____. Indulgences. Sydney: 1980. 176p. Illus. G19570

_____. Wine. Melbourne: Lothian Publishing, 1973. G19580

EVANS, Len, ed. Australian and New Zealand complete book of wines. Sydney: Hamlyn, 1973. 528p. Illus. G19590

> Although there have been dramatic developments in Australian wines since the publication of this book, it is still the most complete single text on the history, types, and vintners of Australian and New Zealand wines. It is nicely illustrated with color and black and white photographs, maps and wine labels.

_____. Australian complete book of wine. Sydney: Hamlyn, 1976. 500p. G19600

> Revised edition of the Australian section of his *Australian and New Zealand Complete Book of Wines.* Subsequent edition in 1978.

EVANS, Lloyd. Wine. Melbourne: Lothian, 1973. 96p. G19610

EVANS, Tom. The incompleat wine-maker. Wheaton, MD: 1970. 51p. Illus. G19620

EWELL, Raymond. Dining out in San Francisco and the Bay area. 2nd ed. Berkeley: Epicurean Press, 1947. 96p. G19630

> A list of recommended restaurants and California wines.

FABRE, Jean H.C. Analysis of wines and interpretions of analytical results . . . 2nd ed. n.p., 1945. 128p. G19640

FACHURI, Antonio P., ed. Bacchus joins Lucullus. London: McCorquodale, 1934. 61p. Illus. G19650

> A brochure designed to provide a few hints on the art of eating and drinking.

FADIMAN, Clifton and AARON, Sam. Wine buyers guide. New York: Abrams, 1977. 159p. Illus. G19660

>Emphasis on North American and French wines.

_____. The joys of wine. New York: Abrams, 1975. 450p. Illus. G19670

>The information on wine is standard but there are many interesting illustrations.

FADIMAN, Clifton, ed. Dionysus; a case of vintage tales about wine. New York: McGraw-Hill, 1962. 309p. Illus. G19680

>A collection of short fiction stories and some poems about wine. The authors range from the unknown to the famous, e.g., Edgar Allan Poe: "The Cask of Amontillado."

FAIRBRIDGE, Dorothea. Historic farms of South Africa. The wool, the wheat, the wine of the 17th and 18th centuries. London: Humphrey Milford, 1931. 194p. G19690

FAIRBURN, Ann. That man Cartwright. New York: Crown, 1970. G19700

>A novel with a California wine industry setting.

FAIRCHILD, Thomas. The city gardener. London: T. Woodward, 1722. 70p. G19710

FAITH, Nicholas. Chateau Margaux. London: Christie's Wine Publications, 1982. 120p. Illus. G19720

_____. Victorian vineyard: Chateau Loudenne and the Gilbeys. London: Constable, Christie's Wine Publications, 1983. 160p. Illus. G19730

_____. The winemasters. London: Hamish Hamilton, 1978. 328p. Illus. G19740

>Contains the best account in English of "Winegate," the Bordeaux (Cruse) wine scandal, that occurred in 1973, but that is only the concluding part of an interesting history of Bordeaux wines. The author, a journalist and wine lover, details the activities of the Chartronnais—the families of wine merchants who settled in Bordeaux in the early 13th century and proceeded over several centuries to establish the Bordeaux wine market.

FALLON, James Thomas. Handbook of Australian vines and wines. Melbourne: Murray Valley Vineyard, 1874. 49p. G19750

_____. Murray Valley Vineyard, Albury, New South Wales and Australian vines and wines. Melbourne: Azzoppardi, Hildreth, 1874. 49p. G19760

>A collection of articles, republished from Australian journals, on the Murray Valley Vineyard. The vineyard was owned by J.T. Fallon, whose articles on Australian vines an wines forms a large part of the pamphlet. Another edition, 1878.

_____. The wines of Australia. London: Unwin, 1876. 47p. G19770

FALUDY, Andrew. The crisis in the Languedoc wine trade. Brighton: Noyce, 1977. 38p. Illus. G19780

A FAMILIAR treatise on the art of brewing with directions for the selection of malt and hops . . . Instructions for making cider and British wines: also a description of the new and improved brewing saccharometer and slide rule, with full instructions for their use. London: 1857. G19790

>Unable to verify.

FANTE, John. The brotherhood of the grape. Boston: Houghton Mifflin, 1977. 178p. G19800

>A novel with a California wine industry setting.

FARLEY, James. New and complete cellar book or butler's assistant. London: Whittaker, 6p. G19810

FARMAR, Frank C. Guide to Farmar's wine and spirit merchants' rule. The standard for the entire trade. 9th ed. Liverpool: By the Author, 1909. 75p. Illus. G19820

>A tenth edition of 106p. was published in 1911.

FARMER, Winton. Wine making at home. New York: Pyramid Communications, 1973. 159p. Illus. G19830

FARRELL, Kenneth Royden. The California grape industries: economic situation and outlook. Berkeley: 1966. 37p. G19840

_____. The California wine industry: trends and prospects. Berkeley: 1963. 16p. G19850

_____. Potential impacts of tariff reductions for wine and brandy on the California grape and wine industries. Berkeley: 1960. 37p. G19860

_____. World trade and the impacts of tariff adjustments upon the United States wine industry. Berkeley: California Agricultural Experiment Station, 1964. 114p. G19870

FAST, Howard. The immigrants. New York: Houghton Mifflin, 1977. 494p. G19880

>A novel with a California wine industry setting.

_____. The second generation. New York: Houghton Mifflin, 1978. 441p. G19890

>A novel with a California wine industry setting.

FAUBEL, Arthur Louis. Cork and the American cork industry. Rev. ed. New York: Cork Institute of America, c1941. 151p. Illus. G19900

FAUQUEUX, M.C. The men who make wine. Paris: M. Lehmann, 1955. 30p. Illus. G19910

>Profiles twelve famous Burgundian winemakers and lists prices of the 1953 wines. Produced by M. Lehmann, Inc., now Sherry-Lehmann.

_____. Wines and spirits catalogue: 1962. Paris: M. Lehmann, 1962. 70p. Illus. G19920

>Price list of wines and spirits from France, California, Germany, and other countries and regions. Illustrated by the well-known

printer-engraver (especially of children's books) Michael Ciry. Produced by M. Lehmann, Inc. (now Sherry-Lehmann), wine merchants in New York City.

FAUST, Albert B. The German element in the United States. 2 vols. Boston: Houghton Mifflin, 1909. G19930

> Volume two contains information on prominent Germans engaged in California viticulture.

FAVORITE American wines and how to enjoy them. Des Moines: Meredith, c1979. 96p. Illus. G19940

FEGAN, Patrick W. Vineyards and wineries of America, travelers guide. Brattleboro, VT: S. Greene Press, 1982. 314p. Illus. G19950

> This is a tour guide of more than 930 American wineries.

FELDMAN, Herman. Prohibition: its economic and industrial aspects. New York: D. Appleton, 1927. 415p. G19960

FELLMAN, Leonard F. Merchandising by design: developing effective menus and wine lists. New York: Lebhar-Friedman Books, c1981. G19970

FENTON, Ferrar. The Bible and wine. Extracted by Frank Hamilton. New York: Published by Frank Hamilton by L.B. Printing Co., c1938. 31p. G19990

_____. The Bible and wine being an open letter to John Abbey, with new translations of all the texts referring to wine and strong drink, and notes by F.F . . . A reply and an appeal to the Archbishop of Canterbury, by J. Abbey. 2nd ed. London: Partridge, 1907. 125p. G19980

FERET, Edouard. Bordeaux and its wines classed by order of merit. 3rd English ed. Bordeaux: Feret and Fils, 1899. 828p. Illus. G20000

_____. Guide alum de l'amateur des grands vins de Bordeaux. Bordeaux: Feret, 1931. 88p. Illus. G20010

> Text in English, French, German and Spanish. 224 black and white illustrations of chateaux by name, label, cork inscription, capsule inscription, and box or case inscription. Scarce.

FESSLER, Julius H. The art of making wine and wine vinegar. Berkeley: Berkeley Yeast Laboratory, 1941. 8p. G20020

_____. Guidelines to practical winemaking. Oakland: By the Author, 1965. 98p. Illus. G20030

> Second edition, 1968 and third edition, 1983.

FEUCHTWANGER, Lewis. Fermented liquors, a treatise on brewing, distilling, rectifying, and manufacturing of sugars, wines, spirits, and all known liquors . . . New York: By the Author, 1858. 215p. G20050

> The author, a 'practical chemist' from New York, provides information on an amazing variety of alcoholic beverages.

FEUERHEERD, H.L. The gentleman's cellar and butler's guide. London: Chatto and Windus, 1899. 91p. G20060

FIELD, S.S. The American drink book. New York: Farrar, Straus and Young, 1953. 282p. Illus. G20070

> Includes much about wine, including a dictionary of wine, a geography of major American wine-producing areas and a directory of award-winning wineries.

FIELD, Sara Bard. The vintage festival: a play pageant and festivities celebrating the vine, in autumn of each year at St. Helena in the Napa Valley. San Francisco: Printed by John Henry Nash, 1920. 24p. G20080

> Limited edition of 500 copies.

FIELDEN, Christopher. Harvey's pocket guide to wine. 160p. G20085

FILBY, Frederick Arthur. A history of food adulteration and analysis. London: George Allen and Unwin, 1934. 269p. G20090

> Traces the adulteration of foods and wines from ancient to modern times. Adulteration is defined as "the art of debasing a commercial commodity, with the object of passing it off as genuine, for illegitimate profit, or the substitution of an inferior article for a superior one, to the detriment of the purchaser." According to the author, the history of adulteration falls roughly into three periods — from the earliest times to about 1820; from 1820 to 1900; and from 1900 to the present.
>
> The author has divided the book into chapters that deal with the larger English companies, i.e., the Bakers, the Brewers, the Distillers, the Grocers, the Vintners, etc.
>
> Regarding wine we are told: "The beginnings of the adulteration of wines are lost in antiquity. It is at least highly probable that the additions of lime, chalk, gypsum; and even lead for the counteracting of acidity was known to the Greeks and Romans."
>
> In early times it was the responsibility of the guilds to police the purity of their particular products. The author refers to a remark attributed to a past Master of the Vintners' Company that "certain taverners who, convicted of making and selling unsound wines, were punished by being made to drink of them, the rest being poured over their heads." In some countries the penalties were more severe, even punishable by death.
>
> As is evident from a number of books listed in this bibliography, there developed a body of literature describing how to make most any kind of wine without the use of grapes and this became particularly prominent in the mid-19th century.

FINDLATER, Mackie, Todd and Co. About decanter labels and good wines. London: Findlater, Mackie, Todd, 1926. Illus. G20100

> An interesting brochure about decanter labels that reminds us: "There is no occasion so trivial or so noble that it is not ennobled by a glass of wine. Hospitality demands wine as that which in proper use is beyond all else friendly in spirit. Blessed indeed is the man who lays down a cellar for his friends. . . ."

_____. About wine furniture and fine wines. London: Findlater, Mackie, Todd, 1927. Illus. G20110

> The writer, "H.C.S.", tells us that it was not until the late 18th century that the practice of "laying wine down" developed. Before then the purpose of the bottle was to convey the wine to the dining room. The bottle was filled from the cask in the cellar and placed into an open "wine cooler," which stood on the floor near the dinner table. The first receptacles for wine were oval cisterns or wine coolers of metal or marble resting on low feet. "Cisterns or wine coolers of silver, silver gilt, pewter, copper and brass" are often mentioned in old inventories.

> Towards 1730 wine coolers and cellarets began to be made in wood. The great cabinet makers of the time — Chippendale, Hepplewhite, Sheraton — lavished their taste and skill on their construction. With the introduction of the corkscrew came cellarets with regular partitions for the reception of bottles of matured wine of uniform size. About 1780 the sideboard, as we know it, came into fashion. "Its right-hand drawer usually contained a cellaret partitioned and lined with lead to hold ten or a dozen bottles. The last phase in the history of wine furniture is reached in the early years of the 19th century, with the introduction of the sarcophagus-shaped cellaret which found a place under the massive early Victorian mahogany sideboards of our great-grandfather's time."

FINLAY, A.K. The phylloxera - a short treatise on the vine destroyer. Melbourne: George Robertson, 1880. G20120

> Unable to verify.

FIRTH, James Francis. The Coopers' Company, London. Historical memoranda, charters, documents, and extracts from the records of the Corporation and the books of the Company, 1396-1848. London: 1848. 136p. Illus. G20140

> See also Elkington, George for additional reference to the history of the Coopers' Company.

FISHER, Agneta. Baccarat: how to choose and use wine glasses. LaMesa, California: Schuster and Wulf, n.d. 22p. G20150

FISHER, Mary Frances Kennedy. The story of wine in California. Berkeley: University of California Press, 1962. 125p. Illus. G20160

> This is Mrs. Fisher's major contribution to wine literature. It is an historical account of California wines from 1769 to the end of Prohibition. The text is beautifully illustrated with color and black and white photographs by Max Yavno. The Foreword is by Maynard Amerine.

FISHER, S.I. Observations on the character and culture of the European vine ... Also manual of the Swiss vigneron by Mons. Brun Chappuis and art of wine making by Mons. Bulos. Philadelphia: Key and Biddle, 1834. 244p. G20170

Appears to be the first viticultural work by an American traveler on the vineyards of Europe. Fisher was impressed with the skill of Swiss vignerons in producing satisfactory wines under the most difficult climatic conditions. He was convinced "that by adopting the system of Swiss cultivation, we shall in time succeed in the difficult task of acclimating to our country, the foreign vine." Although he hoped that American grapes might, with time, be used for winemaking, he advised the cultivation of specific European vines for certain regions of New Jersey and Pennsylvania and along the southern Atlantic coast. Fisher's text, as the title indicates, consists of general observations gathered over a five-year period in Europe. For practical viticultural information he included English translations of a Swiss vinedresser's manual by M. Chappuis and a French wine making guide by M. Bulos.

FISKE, John. Tobacco and alcohol I. It does pay to smoke; II. The coming man will drink wine. New York: Leypoldt and Holt, 1869. 163p. G20180

FISTER, Charles. Home winemaking. London: Ward, Lock, 1974. 128p. Illus. G20190

FITCHETT, L.S. Beverages and sauces of colonial Virginia. Richmond: William Boyd Press, 1938. 110p. G20200

FITTING, Greer. In praise of simple things. New York: McKay, c1975. 258p. G20210

Includes wine and wine making.

FITZGERALD, Edward J., Trans. The Rubaiyat of Omar Khayyam. G20220

This is the most famous of the poems that espouse wine as a hedonistic or epicurean device. It consists of a somewhat cynical collection of epigrams that hold that religion, patriotism and accomplishment do not really matter, for death comes all too soon. Thus it suggests that we should be content to live for the day, helped by liberal quantities of wine. Famous verses in the poem pertaining to wine include: "A jug of Wine, a Loaf of Bread, and thou . . .;" "I wonder often what the Vintners buy one half so precious as the stuff they sell."

Fitzgerald's translation of Khayyam is not literal. Rather, he developed rhymed paraphrases of the original verses which he then strung together to form a connected poem.

Fitzgerald's first version of his translation was published anonymously in 1859 and contained seventy-five quatrains. It was not a success. Other anonymous editions were published in 1868, 1872 and 1879. In 1889, six years after his death, a revised copy of the 1879 edition was found and published. It contains 101 quatrains and varies little from the third and fourth editions. Since 1889 it has been in print constantly and has gone through hundreds of editions by various publishers. It is often elaborately illustrated.

There is not a great deal of factual data about the life of Omar Khayyam. It is known that he was one of the outstanding mathematicians and astronomers of his time, and that in the late 1100's he undertook the reform of the Persian calendar. From the name he used for his poetry, Khayyam, it is popularly supposed that he was a tentmaker, but that name is either a reference to his father's occupation or a poetic one to his own occupation, for he once described himself as one "who stitched the tents of science."

FLAGG, William J. Handbook of the sulphur-cure, as applicable to the vine disease in America, and diseases of apple and other fruit trees. New York: Harper, 1870. 99p. G20240

_____. Three seasons in European vineyards: treating of vine-culture; vine disease and its cure; wine-making and wines, red and white; wine-drinking, as affecting health and morals. New York: Harper, 1869. 332p. Illus. G20250

> Flagg (1818-1898) discusses methods that he observed and how they might be applicable in the United States. Pages 211-283 contain the text of the third edition of *Manual for the Sulphuring of Diseased Vines* . . . by Henri P.L. Mares.

FLANDERS, Charles R. Gourmet au Vatel. An authoritative guide to the proper selection, handling, mixing and serving of wines and liqueurs. Boston: M.F. Foley, 1934. 119p. G20260

FLEISCHMAN, Joseph. The art of blending and compounding liquors and wines and valuable information concerning whiskies in bond. New York: Dick and Fitzgerald, 1885. 68p. G20270

FLETCHER, Wyndham. Port: an introduction to its history and delights. London: Philip Wilson Publishers, 1978. 128p. Illus. G20280

> Wyndham Fletcher retired in 1975 from his position as the managing director of Cockburn's, but he remains one of the port trade's personalities. This work varies from the usual book on the subject in that the author blends in his reminiscences of forty-five years in the port trade.
>
> Also published in 1981 by The Wine Appreciation Guild.

FLEURY, R. de. 1800 and all that. Drinks ancient and modern. London: The St. Catherine Press, 1937. 236p. G20290

FLOWER, Raymond. Chianti: the land, the people and the wine. London: Croom Helm, 1978. 305p. Illus. G20300

> Raymond Flower, an historical writer, chronicles Tuscany from ancient times to present. The book is well researched and is recommended reading for those interested in this area or its wines.

FLUCHERE, Henri Andre. Wines. New York: Golden Press, 1973. 160p. Illus. G20310

FOEX, G. Manual of modern viticulture: reconstitution with American vines. Translated from the 6th French ed. by R. Dubois and W.P. Wilkinson. Melbourne: Gov't. Print., 1902. 269p. G20320

FOGELSONGER, M.I. The secrets of the liquor merchant revealed; or, the art of manufacturing the various kinds and qualities of brandies, whiskies, gins, rums, bitters, wines, cordials, syrups . . . by the use of the different essential oils, essences . . . Alpena, MI: McPhail and Ferguson, 1898. 122p. G20330

_____. The secrets of the liquor merchant revealed . . . Washington: Mark Green and Bros., 1933. 122p. G20340

A reprint of the 1898 edition.

FOLWELL, Raymond J. and BARITELLE, John L. The U.S. wine market. Washington: Dept. of Agriculture; Economics, Statistics and Cooperative Service, 1978. 152p. G20350

FONSECA, A.M. da. Port wine. Notes on its history, production and technology. Oporto: Instituto do Vinho do Porto, 1981. Illus. G20360

Nicely illustrated with black and white and color photographs. The text provides a great deal of statistical data but avoids the controversial, i.e., the 19th century practice of adding elderberry juice to port. (See Forrester, Joseph James.)

FOOTE, E.J. Will you take wine? A guide to the purchase, serving and appreciation of wines, cocktails, spirits and liqueurs. London: Putnam, 1935. 72p. G20370

FORBES, Ellert. Wines for everyman. London: Herbert Joseph, 1937. 191p. G20380

FORBES, John Girtin. The morning after or to the rescue of those poor souls who have had one too many the night before. San Francisco: McLellan Publishing, 1947. 20p. G20390

FORBES, Patrick. Champagne. London: Victor Gollancz, 1967. 492p. Illus. G20400

Although somewhat dated, still the definitive modern work on Champagne. Fifth edition published in 1982.

_____. The story of the Maison Moet et Chandon. London: Moet and Chandon, 1972. 29p. Illus. G20410

A reprint (with a few small amendments) of the chapter on Moet et Chandon in _Champagne_.

FORBES, R.J. Short History of the art of distillation from the beginning up to the death of Cellier Blumenthal . . . Leidon: E.J. Brill, 1948. 405p. Illus. G20420

FORD or FOORD, Edward. Wine and women: a briefe description of the courtesie of a courtezan. Written solely for the benefit of immodest and intemperate youth. London: Printed by John Hammond, 1647. G20430

A poem with prose interspersions and warnings of the perils of debauchery. The author dedicated his work to one Robert Walloppe, an M.P. Walloppe, he says in his preface, is free of all such lusts, but "would your unworthy servant were as free, for I must confesse . . . that the excess of wine, inordinate affections, chambering and wantonness, hath bin habituall with me. . . ." First and only edition. Rare.

FORD, Gene. The ABC's of wine, brew and spirits. Seattle: Murray Publishers, 1980. 128p. G20440

_____. Gene Ford's illustrated guide to wines, beers and spirits. Dubuque, IO: William C. Brown Publishers, 1983. 392p. G20450

FOREST, Louis. See under *Wine Album*.

FOREVER young. Liverpool: Edward Young and Co, c1947. 95p. Illus. G20470

> A booklet published by Edward Young and Company, wine and spirit merchants, to commemorate its 150th anniversary. It gives the complete history of the firm and its trade in the wines of Burgundy, Bordeaux, Cognac, Cyprus, Oporto, Jerez, Sete. Includes notes on ancient wines.

The FORGE wine menu. Miami: Forge Restaurant, 1983. 280p. Illus. G20480

> The menu contains descriptions of the various wine districts and wines from all principal wine producing countries. The most expensive single bottle is priced at $35,000 for an 1822 Chateau Lafite. Contains fifty-one page supplement list.

FORNACHON, John Charles MacLeod. Bacterial spoilage of fortified wines. Adelaide: Australian Wine Board, 1943. 126p. Illus. G20490

> Second edition published in 1969.

_____. Studies of the sherry flor. Adelaide: Australian Wine Board, 1953. 146p. Illus. G20500

> A textbook for the Australian sherry maker. Second edition published in 1972.

JOSEPH JAMES FORRESTER (1809-1861)

In 1831, when James Forrester was twenty-two years old, he arrived in Oporto to work in the port trade with his uncle. At that time the adulteration of port by the blending of wines from throughout Portugal with elderberry juice and sugar was common practice. These wines were sold in large quantities in England and, in some circles, created a bad name for the port trade. Forrester became concerned for the future of the port trade, and in a series of articles, championed the fight against these practices. His actions were opposed and resented by most of his colleagues.

Forrester's position was that port should always be a natural wine and should not be adulterated in any fashion. Forrester's fight against these abuses contributed to the changes that were instituted prohibiting the blending of elderberry juice with wine. Perhaps it is fortunate that he lost on the issue of brandy being added to halt the fermentation of port, or we would have a wine dissimilar to what we enjoy today as port.

Besides being a brillant viticulturist, Baron de Forrester was a talented painter, writer and the first cartographer of the Douro River and its surrounding wine districts. He was drowned when his boat was swamped in the rapids of the Douro River.

FORRESTER, Joseph James (Baron de Forrester). The capabilities of Portugal, the advantages to be obtained by a reciprocal reduction of import duties, the effect of railroads in the Kingdom of Portugal, and the bearing of these inquiries upon the principle of free trade. London: S. Weale, 1853. 290p. Illus. G20530

      The essay for which the Oliveira Prize was awarded.

_____. Curious reflections on the use made of the elderberry, which is now grown in the wine district of the Alto Douro. London: 1845. G20550

_____. An illustrated paper of the vine disease in the districts of the Alto Douro. London: 1854. G20560

      This was a study of the fungus disease *Oidium Tuckerii*. It consists of nineteen sectional color illustrations portraying the various stages of the disease, with explanatory notes.

_____. Map of the wine districts of the Alto Douro. London: Published by Royston, Brown. G20570

_____. Mr. Forrester's vindication from the aspersions of the Commerical Association of Oporto; and his answer to the judge, a late member of the courts being the second part of "Observations on the attempts lately made to reform the abuses practiced in Portugal in the making of port wine". Edinburgh: J. Menzies, 1845. 49p. G20580

_____. Observations on port wine: together with documents proving the existence of these abuses, and letters on the same subject . . . published in his own defense. Edinburgh: J. Menzies, 1845. 80p. G20590

_____. Observations on the attempts lately made to reform the abuses practiced in Portugal, in the making and treatment of port wine. London: Richardson, 1845. G20600

_____. The Oliveira prize-essay on Portugal: with the evidence regarding that country taken before a Committee of the House of Commons in May, 1852; and the author's surveys of the wine-districts of the Alto-Douro . . . London: J. Weale, 1853. 290p. Illus. G20610

      Second edition, London, 1854.

_____. Original surveys of the Portuguese Douro and adjacent countries, and so much of the river as can be made navigable in Spain. London: 1848. Illus. G20620

_____. Original surveys of the wine-districts of the Alto Douro. London: 1845. G20630

_____. Papers relating to the improvement of the navigation of the River Douro . . . and a map of that river and of the wine district of Alto Douro. Oporto: Commercial Printing Office, 1844. [17]p. G20640

_____. Port and the wines of Portugal. 1845. G20650

_____. Portugal and its capabilities . . . together with a companion to the essay containing a word or two on port-wine trade from 1678 to 1860. 4th ed. London: Weale, 1860. Illus. G20655

_____. Representation made by Offley, Webber and Forrester of Oporto, to their correspondents, respecting the recent discussions on the subject of port wine. Oporto: Commercial Printing Office, 1845. 8p. G20660

_____. Second representation made by Offley, Webber and Forrester of Oporto, to their correspondents, respecting the recent discussions on the subject of port wine. Oporto: Commercial Printing Office, 1846. 27p. G20670

_____. A short treatise on the unequal and disproportionate imposts levied on port-wine shipped from Oporto to Great Britain. London: P. Richardson, 1850. 26p. G20680

_____. Short treatise on the chemical changes which often take place in Port-wines stored in England. London: 1858. G20690

_____. Statistics of the rise and progress of the port-wine trade from 1678 to 1851, with the author's evidence before a select committee of the House of Commons, on the wine duty question, as appears in the Blue Book of the Honourable House. London: 1852. G20700

_____. Third representation by Offley, Webber and Forrester of Oporto, to their correspondents, respecting the recent discussions on the subject of port wine. 2nd ed. Oporto: Commercial Printing Office, 1847. 28p. G20710

_____. Vindication of the author against the aspersions of the Commercial Associations of Oporto, the Royal Wine Company, and of the British Factory or Association; all of whom deny the truths conveyed in *word or two on Port-wine*. Oporto and London: 1845. G20720

In Portuguese and English.

_____. The wine question considered, or, observations on the pamphlets of Mr. James Warre and Mr. Fleetwood Williams, respecting the general company for the agriculture of the vineyards, on the Upper Douro, known in England under the name of the Royal Oporto Company. London: Printed for Wilson, Royal Exchange; Richardson, ditto, 1824. 65p. G20730

The fifteen-page appendix is a translation of a letter titled "New Instruction," sent by the English factors at Oporto to all their brokers purchasing port wines.

_____. Wine trade of Portugal: proceedings at the meeting . . . held . . . at Pezo-da-Regoa, 8th October 1844, at the invitation of Joseph James Forrester. Translated in London. London: Royston, 1844. 31p. G20740

Translated from the account of Forrester's meeting that appeared in the *Periodico dos Pobres* in Oporto. Second edition published by Pelham Richardson in London in 1845.

_____. A word or two on Port Wine! Addressed to the British public generally, but particularly to private gentlemen; shewing how, and why, it is adultered, and affording some means of detecting its adulterations . . . Edinburgh: J. Menzies, 1844. 19p. G20750

Also a London edition, 1844.

_____. A word on two on Port Wine . . . together with "Strictures" on the pamphlet entitled: "A Word of Truth on Port-Wine" . . . by T. Whittaker the younger. London: 1848. G20760

FORSHAY, Bill, ed. I'll drink to that; a compilation of toasts. B-F Publishers, 1977. G20770

> Unable to verify.

FORSYTH, J.S. The natural and medical dieteticon: or, practical rules for eating, drinking and preserving health, on principles of easy digestion . . . containing . . . remarks on different alimentary drinks . . . London: Sherwood, 1824. 360p. G20780

FOSTER, Alfred Edye Manning. Dining and wining. London: Geoffrey Bles, 1924. 118p. G20790

_____. London restaurants. London: Geoffrey Bles, 1924. 118p. G20800

_____. Through the wine list. London: Geoffrey Bles, 1924. 112p. G20810

FOSTER, Charles. Home winemaking. London: Ward, Lock, 1969. 64p. Illus. G20820

> Later editions of 64p. published by Drake of New York in 1972, and 128p. by Ward Lock of London in 1974.

_____. Home winemaking, brewing and other drinks. London: Ward, Lock, 1982. G20830

FOSTER, Peter and PETERS, John. Vitis Vera. The mystic symbol of the Church of Christ as used in passages from the Vulgate edition of the Holy Bible and from the translation of 1611. Huntingdon: Vine Press, 1957. G20840

FOSTER, William. Short history of the Coopers' Company. London: Published by the Worshipful Company of Coopers, 1944. 146p. G20850

FOUGNER, G. Selmer. Along the wine trail. 5 vols. New York: Sun Printing and Publishing Ass'n., 1934-1937. G20860

> Vol. 1, wines of the world, 108p.; vol. 2, distilled liquors, 113p.; vol. 3, cocktails, 127p.; vol. 4, a tour through European wine lands, 128p.; and vol. 5.

_____. Along the wine trail. Boston: Stratford, 1935. 306p. G20870

> After the repeal of Prohibition, Fougner wrote a daily column in *The New York Sun* on matters pertaining to wines, spirits and beers. These columns formed the basis for this book. The foreword says: "The purpose of this book is to tell in a simple manner the story of all alcoholic beverages which were banned by the Prohibition laws. . . ."

FOWLES, Gerald Wilfred Albert. Straight-forward winemaking. Reading, England: By the Author, 1975. 97p. G20880

FOWLES, Gerry. Wine for all seasons. Berkshire, England: By the Author, 1977-78. G20890

Seven booklets of approximately twenty-eight pages each.

FRANCIS, Alan David. The wine trade. London: A. and C. Black, 1972. 353p. G20900

> Deals with the English wine trade, especially that in Portugal. An American edition was published by Barnes and Noble in 1973.

FRANCIS, Grant R. Old English drinking glasses; their chronology and sequence. London: Herbert Jenkins, 1926. 222p. Illus. G20910

FRANCIS, L.R. 100 years of wine making: Great Western, 1865-1965. B. Seppelt and Sons, 1966. 26p. Illus. G20920

FRANKLYN, H. Mortimer. A glance at Australia in 1880 or food from the south. Melbourne: The Victoria Review Publishing Co., 1881. 414p. G20940

FRANZ, Arnulf. The new wine book; information and directions for making wine from grapes, raisins, oranges, berries . . . Los Angeles: Western Beverage Corp., c1934. 57p. Illus. G20950

FREDERICKSEN, Paul. The authentic Haraszthy story. An historical research project by the Wine Institute for the Wine Advisory Board. San Francisco: 1947. 12p. Illus. G20960

FREELS, S.C. The X-ray; or, compiled facts and figures of unequaled interest to the retail liquor dealer; or the art of buying, rectifying, reducing, blending, compounding, preserving and selling all wines and liquors common to the traffic. San Francisco: Press of H.S. Crocker, 1900. 96p. Illus. G20970

FRENCH wine correspondence course. New York: Le Comite National des Vins de France, 1959. 47p. Illus. G20980

FRENCH, John. The art of distillation, or a treatise of the choisest spagyricall preparations performed by way of distillation, being partly taken out of the most select chymicall authors of several languages, and partly out of the author's manual experience; together with the description of the choisest furnaces and vessels used by ancient and modern chymists . . . London: Printed by Richard Cotes and are to be sold by T. Williams, 1651. 199p. Illus. G20990

> French (1616?-1657), an army physician, was well versed in the literature of the period and in 1651 or 1652 he published a translation of Glauber's *Furni, Novi Philosophici,* considered by many to be the most important chemical treatise of the 17th century. "Spagirie" is derived from two contradictory Greek verbs meaning "to extract" and "to combine" and denoted early chemistry or alchemy. A spagisiste was a doctor who diagnosed diseases purely on chemical theories. The application of chemistry to medicine was popular with medical schools in the Netherlands in the 17th century.

> Many of the woodcuts in this work are also used in Glauber's and are copied from the original edition of that work (1646-49). Subsequent editions were published in 1653, 1664 and 1667 with slightly modified titles. Rare.

_____. The London-distiller, exactly and truly shewing the way (in words at length and not in mystesterius [sic] characters and figures) to draw all sorts of spirits and strong-waters; to which is added their vertues, with additions of many excellent waters. London: T. Williams, 1652. 64p. Illus. G20995

> Second edition published in 1667 of 44p. and appended to his *The Art of Distillation*.

FRENCH, Richard Valpy. The history of toasting; or, drinking of healths in England. London: National Temperance Publishing Depot, c1881. 104p. G21000

_____. Nineteen centuries of drink in England: a history . . . London: Longmans, 1884. 398p. G21010

> A subsequent revised edition was published by the National Temperance Depot, without date, circa 1900.

FREWIN, Leslie, ed. The Cafe Royal story. London: Hutchinson Benham, 1963. 151p. Illus. G21020

> No restaurant in Great Britain has a finer wine tradition associated with its history. Text includes the Cafe Royal wine list and the photographs cover the restaurant's history. Foreword by Graham Greene.

FRIED, Eunice. What every woman should know about wine. Garden City, NY: Doubleday, 1974. 144p. G21030

FRIENDS of Wine. Short guide to wine. London: The Friends of Wine, n.d. 19p. G21040

FRITZSCHE Brothers. Fritzsch's manual . . . formulas and suggestions for . . . preparation of liquors, cordials, flavorings . . . A practical manual prepared by a well-known flavoring house. New York: Fritzsche Brothers, c1897. 117p. G21050

The FRUIT industry in New York State. New York: 1916. Illus. G21060

> Published in two parts, with 120 pages on grapes. Includes Liberty Hyde Bailey's article on the history and varieties of grapes.

FRUMKIN, Lionel. The science and technique of wine. London: H.C. Lea, 1965. 208p. Illus. G21070

> Subsequent editions published in 1967 and 1974.

FRYE, Melinda Young. Thomas Jefferson and wine in early America: art and artifacts reflecting the cultural history of wine in the Colonies and the early Republic . . . San Francisco: The Wine Museum, c1976. 24p. Illus. G21080

FULLER, Andrew S. The grape culturist: a treatise on the cultivation of the native grape. New York: Davies and Kent, 1864. 262p. Illus. G21090

> Gives full directions for planting, training, grafting, etc. Native grapes are emphasized, foreign vines are confined to indoor cultivation and hybridization and pest conrol are significant topics. Illustrated with 150 engravings. This was one of the most popular

American texts and numerous revised and enlarged editions were published by Orange Judd including editions of 1865, 1866, 1867, 1894, 1899 and 1907.

FUNK, Wilfred John. If you drink. New York: By the Author, 1940. 170p. Illus. G21100

FURNESS, Rex. The fermentation industry. London: Ernest Benn, 1924. 19p. G21110

GABLER, James and GABLER, JoAnn. Wines of the founding fathers. Columbus, OH: Warren-Teed Pharmaceuticals, 1976. Illus. G21130

> Three pamphlets: No. 1, George Washington, 10p.; No. 2, Thomas Jefferson, 13p.; No. 3, Benjamin Franklin, 10p. These pamphlets, based entirely on original research, outline the wine drinking habits of these three great Americans.

GABLER, James M. Wine into words: a history and bibliography of wine books in the English language. Baltimore: Bacchus Press Ltd., 1985. 403 p. Illus. G21131

GAGE, Joseph H. The beckoning hills. Philadelphia: John C. Winston, 1951. 233p. G21140

> A novel with a California wine industry setting.

GAIGE, Crosby. Dining with my friends. New York: Crown Publishers, 1949. 292p. G21150

GALE, Hyman, ed. The how and when: An authoritative guide to origin, use and classification of the world's choicest vintages and spirits. Chicago: Marco Importing, 1937. 203p. Illus. G21160

> Subsequent editions published in 1940 and 1945.

GALE, R. The marketing of wine and vines in Australia. Adelaide: 1970. 68p. G21170

GALET, Pierre. A practical ampelography: grapevine identification. Ithaca, NY and London: Cornell University Press, 1978. 248p. Illus. G21180

> This is the English version of Professor Galet's *Precis d'ampelographie pratique* as translated and adapted by Lucie T. Morton. Ampelography is the science concerned with the description of vine species and cultivated varieties. Unlike most of his predecessors, who concentrated on the fruit clusters, Professor Galet goes about grapevine identification by concentrating on the leaf structure. The book covers all major *vinifera,* includes French and American hybrids, and native American species. The work offers over 100 descriptions and is well illustrated. This is the definitive work in English on this subject.

GALLO, Ernest and GALLO, Julio. Gallo vineyards. Modesto, CA: 1967. 18p. Illus. G21190

> Gallo is not only the largest winery in the world, but the training ground for many prominent California winemakers.

[GALLOBELGICUS]. Wine, beere, ale and tobacco: contending for superiority. A dialogue. 2nd ed. London: Printed by T.C., for John Grove, 1630. [26p] G21200

>   Another edition printed by J.B. for John Grove, 1658.

————. Wine, beere, ale and tobacco: a seventeenth century interlude. Chapel Hill, NC: The University, 1915. 54p. G21210

>   A facsimile reprint.

GARDNER, John, ed. The brewer, distiller and wine manufacturer; giving full directions for the manufacture of beers, spirits, wines, liquors . . . Philadelphia: P. Blakiston Son, 1883. 278p. Illus. G21220

>   Also a 1902 London edition.

GAREY, Thomas A. Orange culture in California with an appendix on grape culture by L.J. Rose. San Francisco: By the Author, 1881. 227p. G21230

GARNSEY, William. Garnsey's new wine tables . . . London: 1797. 5p. G21240

————. Table of the customs, excise and convoy duties upon importation of wines into the Port of London and other ports of Great Britain . . . London: Printed by T. Plummer, 1801. 40p. G21250

>   "Signed by the author to prevent any spurious edition."

————. Table of duties of customs upon wine imported into London, with the drawbacks thereof allowed upon exportation. London: Printed by T. Plummer, 1797. G21260

>   Unable to verify.

GARRETT, Blanche Pownall. Canadian country preserves and wines. Toronto: Lewis and Samuel Publishers, 1974. 133p. Illus. G21270

GARRETT, Paul. The art of serving wine. Norfolk, VA: By the Author, 1905. 48p. Illus. G21280

GARVIN, Fernande. French wines. New York: Le Comité National des Vins de France, 1968. 64p. Illus. G21290

>   Subsequent editions.

GASKIN, Catherine. Summer of the Spanish woman. Garden City, NY: Doubleday, 1977. 503p. G21300

>   A novel with a Spanish wine (sherry) setting.

GATHERINGS from the wine-lands. London: Foster and Ingle, 1855. 192p. Illus. G21320

>   Interesting wine scene etchings.

GAY, John. Wine, a poem . . . to which is added old England's new triumph: or, the battle of Audenard, a song. London: Printed by H. Hills, 1708. 16p. G21330

_____. Wine, a poem. A facsimile reprint of Gay's first work with an introductory note by Iolo A. Williams. London: Dulaund, 1926. 14p. G21340

> This is a fascimile reprint of John Gay's poem, *Wine*, published in May, 1708 when Gay was not quite twenty-three years old. Limited to 500 copies. Scarce.

GAYON, Ulysse. Studies on wine-sterilizing machines. Translated by Raymond Dubois and W. Percy Wilkinson. Melbourne: R.S. Bain, 1901. 103p. Illus. G21350

GAYRE, G.R. Wassail! In mazers of mead. An account of mead, metheglin, sack, and other ancient liquors, and of the mazer cups out of which they were drunk, with some comment upon the drinking customs of our forebears. London: Phillimore, 1948. 176p. Illus. G21360

> This work is mainly about fermented beverages made from honey, with references to classical literature. Contains a discussion of the origin of "sack."

GEISS, Lisbet. The gay language of wine. West Germany: 1981. 166p. Illus. G21370

> A compendium of wine terminology, illustrated with drawings by Wilhem Busch. Translated from the German.

GEORGE, J. and ANDERSON, B. Easy wine making in 21 days. London: Hamlyn, 1976. 64p. Illus. G21410

GEORGE, Rosemary. The wines of Chablis and the Yonne. London: Philip Wilson, 1984. 184p. Illus. G21420

> Also published by The Wine Appreciation Guild.

GERMAN wine atlas and vineyard register. London: Davis-Poynter, 1977. 88p. G21430

The GERMAN wine market until 1990. Kuno Pieroth, 111p. G21440

GERMAN wines - a correspondence course. New York: The German Wine Information Bureau, c1983. 56p. Illus. G21450

GESNER, Conrad. Newe jewell of health. 1576. G21455

> A translation by George Baker of a famous German treatise on distillation. He discouraged the distilling of "strong waters" from wine regarding it as wasteful.

GIBBONS, Henry. The wine culture in California. San Francisco: H.H. Bancroft, 1867. 48p. G21460

> An early anti-prohibition treatise.

GIBBS, William H, III. Wine tour: central coast. St. Helena, CA: Vintage Image, 1980. 88p. Illus. G21470

> Chapters on food, lodging and wine shops and a winery index.

GILBEY, W. and A. The vintage of 1912; 38th annual report on the produce of the vineyards of France, Germany . . . London: W. and A. Gilbey, c1912. 42p. G21480

_____. Wines and spirits of the principal producing countries. London: W. and W. Gilbey, 1869. G21490

GILDING, Bob. The journeyman coopers of East London. Workers control in an old London trade with historical documents and personal reminiscences by one who has worked at block and an account of unofficial practices down the wine vaults of the London dock. Oxford: Truex Press, 1971. 86p. Illus. G21500

GILKES, Thomas. Strictures on the sixth chapter of "Anti-Bacchus," on the character of scripture wines, shewing the delusion under which tee-totalers labour, in adopting it as part of their creed. London: Simpkin, 1842. 40p. G21510

> *Anti-Bacchus* was an essay by Benjamin Parsons that was originally published in the *Princeton Review.*

GILLESPIE, Duncan. Lighthearted winemaking. Andover, England: Amateur Winemaker, 1971. 109p. G21520

_____. The winemaker's garden. Andover, England: Amateur Winemaker, 40p. G21530

_____. Winemaking and brewing. 2nd ed. Andover, England: Amateur Winemaker, 1980. 265p. G21540

GILLESPIE, Duncan, comp. Full to the bung! A bedside book for winemakers, beermakers and kofyars! Andover, England: Standard Press, 1974. 151p. G21550

GILLETTE, Paul. Enjoying wine. New York: New American Library, 1976. G21560

GILLETTE, Peter A. and GILLETTE, Paul. Playboy's book of wine. Chicago: Playboy Press, 1974. 252p. Illus. G21570

GIORDANO, Frank. Texas wines and wineries. Houston: Texas Monthly Press, 1984. 192p. Illus. G21575

> Until the mid-1970's, only one small winery existed in Texas. This book covers fifteen wineries and their owners who are trying to prove the botanist and viticulturist, T.V. Munson, correct when he exclaimed of Texas in 1876: "I have found my grape paradise!"

GLASS drinking vessels from the Franz Sichel collection. San Francisco: Franz W. Sichel Foundation, 1969. 62p. Illus. G21580

> The history and description of the Franz W. Sichel collection is provided in conjunction with the history from the beginnings of glassmaking to use in the Roman world and in Eastern and Western Europe through the 18th century.

GLASS in Germany from Roman times to present. Catalog by Dr. Ernst Thiele of an exhibition sponsored by the German Arts Council. Opladen, West Germany: 1965. G21590

GLAUBER, Johann Rudolph. A description of new philosophical furnaces, or a new art of distilling, divided into five parts. Whereunto is added a decription of the tincture of gold, or the true aurum potabile; also the

first part of the mineral work. Set forth and published for the sakes of
them that are studious of the truth. Set forth in English by J.F.D.M.
[John French]. London: Printed by Richard Coats for Tho. Williams,
1651. 452p. G21600

> Each part of the "Description of new philosophical furnaces," and
> each of the other two treatises has a separate title page, all dated
> 1652. Translated by John French. [See French, J.]

GLEANINGS amongst the vineyards, by an F.R.G.S. London: Beeton, 1865.
170p. Illus. G21610

A GLIMPSE of a famous wine cellar in which are described the vineyards of
Marne and the methods employed in making champagne. Translated
from the French. New York: Frances Draz, 1906. 28p. G21620

GLOOR, Robert L. A guide to American and French hybrid grape varieties.
Fredonia, NY: Foster Nursery, [197-]. 27p. G21630

GLOVER, J. Drink your own garden. London: Batsford, 1979. 112p. Illus.
G21640

> 140 recipes for wines, mead, beers and other drinks. Measurements
> are given in imperial, U.S. and metric units.

GODFREY, Boyle, M.D. Miscellanea vere utilia: or miscellaneous observations
and experiments on various subjects. In three parts. Part I. Upon ali-
ments, in order to promote health and longer life; wherein divers kinds
of foods are daily in use that are repugnant to health are mentioned;
and teas and wines particularly considered . . . London: Printed for J.
Robinson, c1735. 138p. G21650

> Second edition, with additions, of 152p. published in London in
> 1737.

GOFF, Michael. Food and wine; an annotated list. London: National Book
League, 1972. 40p. G21660

GOFFINET, Sybil. Cream, butter and wine. London: Andre Deutsch, 1955.
120p. G21670

GOHDES, Clarence Louis Frank. Scuppernong, North Carolina's grape and its
wines. Durham, NC: Duke University, 1982. 115p. Illus. G21680

GOLD, Alex, ed. Wines and spirits of the world. London: Virtue, 1968. 707p.
Illus. G21700

> The various chapters were written by acknowledged experts in
> their fields such as M. Gonzales (sherry), S.F. Hallgarten (German
> wines), F.F. Hennessy (cognac), G.F. Robertson (port), Edmund Pen-
> ning-Rowsell (armagnac), David Peppercorn (bordeaux), etc. A fully
> revised edition of 753 pages was published in 1972.

GOLD SEAL wine and champagne guide. Hammondsport, NY: Gold Seal
Vineyards, 1963. 32p. Illus. G21690

GOLDING, Louis and SIMON, André L. We shall eat and drink again. London:
Hutchinson, 1941. 275p. Illus. G21710

> An anthology of articles on food and wine.

GOLDWYN, Craig. Goldwyn's grape vine; a . . . scrapbook . . . of the best wine-induced ruminations of the Chicago Tribune's wine critic. Ithaca, NY: Wine Stains, 1980. G21720

GONZALES-GORDON, M.M., *Marques de Bonanza*. Sherry, the noble wine. London: Cassell, 1972. 236p. G21730

GOOD sherry. London: 1889. 25p. G21760

The GOOD wine guide, 1981. London: Hodder, 1981. G21770

GOOD wine guide, 84. London: Sunday Telegraph. G21780

> Gives prices, tasting notes and availability in 11,500 wine shops and supermarkets.

GOOD wine. A fifteenth century song. Cernel Press, 1963. G21790

> An edition of thirty-six copies.

GOOD wine. A song from a 15th century manuscript in the Bodleian Library. Shaftesbury: Privately printed by James E. Masters and Beatrice M. Masters for their friends, 1929. 5p. G21800

> Limited to ninety copies.

GORDON, A.J. Of vines and missions. Flagstaff, AZ: Northland Press, 1971. 89p. Illus. G21810

> A book of poems celebrating wine and grapes.

GORDON, Ethel Edison. The French husband. New York: Thomas Crowell, 1977. 257p. G21820

> A novel with a Burgundy setting.

GORDON, William Reed. Keuka Lake memories, 1835-1935. Hammondsport, NY: By the Author, 1967. 239p. Illus. G21830

> Although this book is essentially about the transportation systems of this area, there is also an interesting history of the Hammondsport wineries and the development of the grape growing industry. The author compares the Keuka hillsides to those of the Rhine River Valley in Germany. Many historic photographs of the wineries and vineyards are reproduced. The author spent fourteen years researching his material.

GORE-BROWNE, Margaret. Let's plant a vineyard; 6000 vines or 600 or 60 or 6. London: Mills and Boon, 1967. 59p. Illus. G21840

GORMAN, Robert. Gorman on California premium wines. San Francisco: Ten-Speed Press, 1975. 289p. G21850

GOSSIP about wines. Extracted from the "Edinburgh Review," and edited with notes by T. Hardy. Adelaide: 1869. 20p. G21860

GOSWELL, R.W. Fortified wines. Part I: the production of port. Bristol: John Harvey and Sons, 1966. 25p. G21870

GOTTFRIED, John and GOTTFIRED, Patricia. A wine tasting course; the practical way to know and enjoy wine. New York: McKay, 1978. 214p. G21880

GOULD, Francis L. Bottles and bins; recipes. St. Helena, CA: C. Mondavi and Sons, Charles Krug Winery, 1965. 129p. Illus. G21890

> Art by Mallette Dean.

_____. Charles Krug Winery 1861-1961. St. Helena, CA: C. Mondavi and Sons, 1961. 16p. Illus. G21900

_____. My life with wine. St. Helena, CA: By the Author, 1972. 71p. Illus. G21910

> The author tells of his long life with wine, from his introduction to wine (cut with water) at the age of six in 1890, to his experiences as an amateur, then as a professional, and for over twenty-five years as a writer. The book covers many famous vintages and several memorable meals, and ends with a selection from the author's *Bottles and Bins* newsletter of the Charles Krug Winery and a small anthology of poems in praise of wine.

GOURLIE, John. Home wine and cider making simplified. Noroton: Country Book Store, c1949. 24p. Illus. G21920

GRACE, Virginia R. Amphoras and the ancient wine trade of Athens. Princeton, NJ: American School of Classical Studies, 1969. 32p. G21930

GRAHAM, J.C. Know your New Zealand wines. Auckland: Collins, 1980. 96p. Illus. G21940

GRAHAM, M.E., comp. Wine and Food Society of Southern California; a history with a bibliography of A.L. Simon. Los Angeles: The Society, 1957. 60p. G21950

GRAHAM, William. The art of making wines from fruits, flowers, and herbs, all the native growth of England: particularly grapes, goose-berries . . . London: Printed for J. Williams, 1780. 64p. G21960

> There are prior and subsequent editions.

GRAMP, G. and Sons. 100 years of wine making . . . 1847-1947. Adelaide: Gillingham, 1948. 45p. Illus. G21970

_____. Orlando vineyards. Adelaide: Mail Newspapers, 1932. 8p. G21980

GRANT, C.W. Descriptive catalogue of vines plus a price list of autumn 1860. Iona, NY: 1859-60. 48p. G21990

> Grant's was one of the foremost nurseries for grapevines at the time. Numerous prior and subsequent editions published.

_____. Manual of the vine, including illustratead catalogue of vines (8th ed.); and, grape vines: description of stock of vines for sale at Iona Island (3rd ed.). Iona, NY: By the Author, 1864. 101p. Illus. G22000

GRANT, J. McB. Report of the fact-finding inquiry into matters relating to the Australian wine industry. 1972. G22010

> Unable to verify.

GRANT'S of St. James's. A gateway to wine. London: Grant's of St. James's, 1964. 76p. Illus. G22020

This book was produced by the London wine merchant firm of Grant's of St. James's to "help those who would like to learn more about wine." It discusses most of the wines of the world and provides recipes and a useful glossary. Nicely illustrated with black and white and color photographs and maps.

The GRAPE and wine industries of British Columbia. Richmond: B.C. Legislative Assembly, Select Standing Committee on Agriculture, 1978. 147p. G22030

GRAPE and wine production in the Four Corners region. Tucson, AZ: University of Arizona, 1980. 116p. Illus. G22040

GRAPE growing and wine making. London: Grey Owl Research Laboratories, 1951. G22050

GRAPES and grape vines of California; published under the auspices of the California State Viticultural Association, oleographed by Wm. Harring. San Francisco: Edward Bosqui, 1877. Unpaged. Illus. G22060

The California State Viticultural Association commissioned Miss Hannah Millard to do a series of watercolors illustrating varieties of grapes grown in California. Millard produced ten paintings; one each of the Mission Grape, the Johannisberg riesling, the rose chasselas, the white muscat of Alexandria, the black hamburgh, the flame tokay, the zinfandel, the sultana, the catawba, and the emperor. Edward Bosqui, a famous San Francisco printer, was given the task of reproducing the paintings. Bosqui engaged William Harring to do the lithography from the original water color paintings by Miss Millard. The results were so astonishing that a group of judges at the Paris Exposition of 1878 could not believe that *Grapes and Grape Vines of California* had been produced in far-off San Francisco. Each illustration is accompanied by text describing the history of that grape. There are only eight known copies of the original publication.

GRAPES and grape vines of California. Facsimile reprint. New York: Harcourt Brace Jovanovich, Inc., 1981. Unpaged. Illus. G22070

This facsimile reprint is beautifully reproduced and includes an introduction by Kevin Starr, covering the history of Edward Bosqui, his printing company and the production of *Grapes and Grape Vines of California*. It also includes a historical note about the various grapes by Leon D. Adams. Folio.

GRAPEWIN, Charley (pseud). The flowing-bowl. Privately published, 1933. 17p. Illus. G22090

GRATRIX, Dawson. In pursuit of the vine. London: Herbert Jenkins, 1953. 228p. Illus. G22100

Foreword by André L. Simon.

GRAY, Arthur, ed. Toasts and tributes. New York: Rohde and Haskins, 1904. 301p. G22110

GRAY, James. After Repeal; what the host should know about serving wines and spirits, proper glassware and cocktail recipes. St. Paul: Brown Blodgett, 1933. 32p. Illus. G22120

GRAZZI-SONCINI, G. Wine: classification, wine tasting, qualities and defects. Sacramento: State Print. Off., 1892. 57p. G22130

    Translated by F.T. Bioletti.

The GREAT wines of Bordeaux. Bordeaux: Feret et Fils, c1933. Illus. G22140

GREENBERG, E. and M., eds. The great cooks' guide to wine drinks. New York: Beard Glaser, 1977. G22150

GREG, Thomas Tylston. Through the glass lightly. Essays on wine. London: J.M. Dent, 1897. 143p. G22160

GREGER, Max. Notes upon pure and natural wines of Hungary. London: Printed by Haddon, 1869. 52p. G22170

    Mr. Greger was a London wine merchant who imported Hungarian wines. He was a member of the Jury of the International Exhibition at Vienna in 1873. Subsequent editions.

GREGORY, C. Caterer's guide to drinks. A guide for the professional English caterer covering the marketing and production of wines and spirits, licensing law, and the sale of alcoholic drinks. London: Northwood, 1979. 240p. G22180

GREGORY, Thomas Jefferson. History of Solano and Napa Counties, with biographical sketches of the leading men and women of the counties who have been identified with its [sic] growth and development from the early days to the present time. Los Angeles: Historic Record Company, 1911. 1112p. Illus. G22190

    Has a short chapter on the "Viticulture of Napa County," as well as a section on the pioneer grape growers of the Napa Valley. Several prominent pioneer wine producers are discussed.

GREIG, Peter, ed. Catalogue of the wines and spirits from the estate of Mrs. Henry Walters. New York: William Bradford Press, 1943. 60p. Illus. G22200

    The sale was at the Ritz Carlton Hotel, New York City, November 29-30, 1943. The catalog contains much historical information on madeira. Mr. Greig, a director of the wine and spirit firm of Greig, Lawrence and Houyt, purchased and sold on November 29-30, 1943, some 400 cases of wines, cognacs and whiskies that were part of the cellar accumulated by Henry Walters of Baltimore and New York. Mr. Walters' art collection was the foundation of the Walters Art Gallery in Baltimore, Maryland. Mr. Greig reported that "what I saw in the cellar of her [Mrs. Henry Walters'] sixty-first street house here in New York made me gasp. To a wine man it was like stumbling on a vault full of gold nuggets." To list and describe the cellar, Mr. Greig prepared this catalog. Since the cellar contained a treasure chest of old madeiras, Mr. Greig visited Baltimore and Savannah to gather first-hand information about the pedigree and history of the madeiras, some of which were dated 1820, 1827, 1828, etc. Mr. Greig found that none of the madeira experts of the Old South had written down their knowledge for future generations. An example in point is Douglas H. Thomas, a Baltimore banker, who held numerous madeira parties in the early 1900's. At the time of his death, he was reported to have been engaged in writing a history of madeira, with special emphasis on madeira in Baltimore, but it was never completed. Mr. Greig's account of these old madeiras is, therefore, particularly significant.

Before the Civil War, especially in Savannah, Charleston and Baltimore ". . . almost every important family collected madeiras just as many active ladies today collect antiques. But the old madeiras were authentic! Wines were passed down from father to son, and such was the pride of the owner in the quality of his wines he often named them after his own clan.

"They were shipped from abroad in cask and left in the wood for ten years or so, and then were transferred, not to bottles, but to five-gallon demijohns. In those early days no smaller container would serve, for 'Madeira likes it own company.' "

"When a dinner party was given or one of the famous wine tastings was arranged, the wines were syphoned, not poured, into beautiful decanters. Sometimes these preparations commenced three weeks before the date of the party."

The importance of madeira in the social life of the upper-class in certain eastern American cities continued until about the time of Prohibition. But the demise of madeira as a popular wine probably had more to do with its decline in quality than with changing lifestyles or Prohibition. Douglas H. Thomas of Baltimore (who was recognized by his peers as an expert on madeiras) wrote to a friend in 1909: "There is very little really good madeira in existence. I meet 'Old Madeiras' sometimes at dinners, but almost invariably it turns out to be strong, 'roachy' stuff which politeness compels me to drink and smack my lips over."

Also, see comments under Mitchell, S. Weir. *The Madeira Party.*

GRIFFIN, John Joseph. The chemical testing of wines and spirits. London: John J. Griffin and Sons, 1866. 150p. Illus. G22210

Deals with wine primarily from a medical point of view, but also contains other interesting wine information. Second edition published in 1872.

GRINSTEAD, Raymond M. Modern wine and liquor control, wine cellar control, public service bar controls. Stamford, CT: Jodahl, 1934. 42p. Illus. G22220

GRISWOLD, Frank Gray. French wines and Havana cigars. New York: Dutton, 1929. 101p. Illus. G22230

A study of bordeaux and burgundy wines with consideration given to champagnes, brandy, chartreuse and the wine trade; with a chapter on Havana cigars.

————. The Gourmet. New York: Dutton, 1933. 121p. G22240

Limited edition of 200 copies. Scarce.

————. Old Madeiras. New York: Dutton, 1929. 65p. G22250

This is essentially a republication of Dr. S. Weir Mitchell's story *A Madeira Party* preceded by twelve pages of notes by the author about madeira. Limited edition of 200 copies. Scarce.

GROHUSKO, Jacob Abraham. Jack's manual on the vintage and production, care and handling of wines, liquors . . . New York: Knopf, 1933. 234p. G22260

Subsequent editions.

GROSSMAN, Harold J. Beverage dictionary with the pronunciation, use . . . of over 200 alcoholic beverages. Stamford, CT: The Dahls, 1938. 62p. G22270

————. Grossman's guide to wines, spirits and beers. New York: Sherman and Spoerer, 1940. 404p. Illus. G22280

Provides general information on all countries but notable for its coverage of all aspects of retail liquor store management and bar, restaurant and hotel service. Many subsequent editions including completely revised editions by Harriet Lembeck. (See Lembeck, Harriet.)

————. Imported wines and spirits. New York: 1961. 64p. Illus. G22290

GROSVENOR, Judith. Home wine and beer. London: Langham Press, 1983. 96p. Illus. G22300

GROVER, Linda. Napa Valley. Burbank, CA: Blackjack Productions, 1980. G22320

A novel with a California wine industry setting.

GUEST, Catherine. Winemaking. London: E.P. Publishing, 1979. G22330

GUIDE to Australian wineries. Melbourne: Southdown Press, 1978. 95p. Illus. G22340

A pamphlet for tourists of 356 vineyards with general chapters on wine.

GUIDE to California wines. Los Angeles: California Museum of Science and Industry, c1978. 48p. Illus. G22350

GUIDE to California's wine country. Menlo Park, CA: 1982. 160p. Illus. G22360

GUIDE to good wine. London: Chambers, 1952. 208p. Illus. G22370

Allan Sichel, Leslie Seyd, H.B. Lanson, Lance K. Cock, Ian MacKenzie, Alfred Langenbach are contributors. Revised editions published in 1959 and 1973.

GUIDE to good wine. Huguenot, S.A.: Monis Wineries Ltd., 16p. G22380

GUIDE to importers and purchasers of wines, containing an account of all the known vineyards in the world, a description of the kind and quality of their produce, and a classification. London: 1828. G22390

GUIDE to selected wines. San Francisco: The Wine Spectator, 1983. G22400

> This is a compilation of wines either recommended or highly recommended in 1982 by *The Wine Spectator,* a newspaper about wine published every two weeks. 596 wines are reviewed. Published annually.

GUNN, John and GOLLAN, R. McK. Report on the wine industry of Australia. Canberra: Gov't. Print., 1931. 63p. G22410

> Parliamentary paper of folio size of which only 840 copies were printed.

GUNN, Peter. Burgundy: landscape with figures. London: Victor Gollancz, 1976. G22420

GUNTRUM Family. History of the Guntrum Family: 150 years of Weingut Louis Guntrum. Nierstein am Rhein, 1974. G22430

GUNYON, R.E.H. The wines of central and south-eastern Europe. London: Duckworth, 1971. 132p. Illus. G22440

GUTHRIE, William. Remarks on claret, burgundy, champagne. Their dietetic and restorative uses, treatment, and service. London: Simpkin, Marshall, 1889. 38p. Illus. G22450

GUTTADAURO, Guy J., comp. A list of references for the history of grapes, wines and raisins in America. Davis, CA: University of California at Davis, 1976. 70p. G22460

GUYOT, Jules. Culture of the vine and wine making. Translated from the French by L. Marie. Melbourne: Walker, May, 1865. 108p. Illus. G22470

_____. Growth of the vine and principles of winemaking. Melbourne: Leader Office, 1896. 28p. G22480

GWYNN, Stephen Lucius. Burgundy: with chapters on the Jura and Savoy. London: George G. Harrap, 1930. 283p. Illus. G22490

> A later edition was published by Constable, London, in 1934. The Constable edition is edited by André L. Simon and an 1935 edition published by Farrar and Rinehart of New York.

_____. In praise of France. London: Nisbet, 1927. 300p. Illus. G22500

> The author writes: "Travelling in France . . . is like falling in love - the greatest of all voyages of discovery." A very large part of the author's love affair was initiated by his taste for the wines of France, which he discusses in detail.

_____. Memories of enjoyment. Tralee, Ireland: The Kerryman Limited, 1946. 148p. G22510

> An anthology of articles about life's pleasures of which the delights of the grape prevail with "In Praise of Wine," "What did Shakespeare Drink," "What the Augustans Drank" and other wine stories.

GYORGY, Paul. The fine wines of Germany and all the world's wine lore. Berlin: Paul Funk, 1965. 172p. G22520

HAARLEM, J.R. Variety tests for grapes for wine. Toronto: 1954. 151p. G22530

HACKETT, F. Michael. English cottage wines. The art of making wine in the home. Morpeth: English Cottage Wine Co., 1960. 53p. G22540

HACKWOOD, Frederick W. Good cheer: the romance of food and feasting. London: T. Fisher Unwin, 1911. 424p. Illus. G22550

_____. Inns, ales and drinking customs of Old England. London: T. Fisher Unwin and New York: Sturges and Walton, 1909. 392p. Illus. G22560

> Although essentially about inns and taverns, there is much about wine, e.g., old English vineyards, the establishment of vintners in London, types of wines imported, etc.

HADFIELD, John. The Saintsbury oration. London: The Curwen Press, 1950. 13p. G22570

HAGGARD, H.W. and JELLINEK, E.M. Alcohol explained. Garden City, NY: Doubleday, Doran, 1942. 297p. Illus. G22580

HAHN, Dr. Report on some questions connected with viticulture at the Cape. Cape Town: 1882. G22590

> Unable to verify.

HAIMO, Oscar. Cocktail and wine digest. 13th ed. New York: By the Author, 1955. 142p. Illus. G22600

> Many subsequent editions.

HALASZ, Zoltan. The book of Hungarian wines. Budapest: Corvina Press, 1981. 210p. Illus. G22610

_____. Hungarian wine through the ages. Budapest: Corvina Press, 1962. 186p. Illus. G22620

HALES, Dr, of Teddington. Compleat treatise on practical husbandry. London: 1727. G22630

> Covers grapes and wine.

HALES, Stephen. A friendly admonition to the drinkers of brandy . . . 2nd ed. London: Printed for J. Downing, 1734. 24p. G22640

> Subsequent editions 1735, 1751, 1754, 1800 and 1818.

HALL, Charles Victor. California, the ideal Italy of the world . . . Philadelphia: Cooperative Printing, 1875. 32p. G22650

HALL, George, ed. Invitations to dine in London and Greater London. London: Gray's Inn, 1956. 372p. Illus. G22660

> Contains wine recommendations.

HALL, Harrison. Hall's distiller . . . adapted to the use of farmers and distillers. Philadelphia: By the Author, 1813. 244p. Illus. G22670

Describes the different kinds of stills in use in this country during the early nineteenth century. The second edition published in 1818 contains ninety additional pages.

HALL, Holworthy and KAHLER, Hugh. The six best cellars. New York: Dodd, Mead, 1919. 106p. G22680

Set in an affluent suburb of New York City, this is a satirical period piece on the problems of social survival under the burdens of an empty wine cellar and Prohibition.

HALL, James J. and BUNTON, John. Wines. London: W. and G. Foyle, 1961. 93p. Illus. G22690

HALLGARTEN, Peter. Chateauneuf-du-Pape. London: S.F. and O. Hallgarten, 1961. 15p. Illus. G22700

_____. Cotes-du-Rhone. The vineyards and villages of the Rhone Valley. London: Wineographs, 1965. 30p. G22710

_____. Guide to the wines of the Rhone. London: Pittman, 1979. 137p. Illus. G22720

_____. Liqueurs. London: Wine and Spirit Publications, 1967. 135p. Illus. G22730

_____. The problem of acidity in white wines. 1966. 6p. G22740

_____. Spirits and liqueurs. Faber and Faber, 1979. 176p. G22750

HALLGARTEN, S.F. (Fritz). Alsace and its wine gardens. London: André Deutsch, 1957. 187p. Illus. G22760

Second edition published in 1969.

_____. A guide to vineyards, estates and wines of Germany. Dallas: Publivin, 1974. 262p. Illus. G22770

Hundreds of wine labels reproduced in color.

_____. German wines. London: Faber and Faber, 1976. 397p. Illus. G22780

Fritz Hallgarten was a German wine merchant who left Nazi Germany to found a successful London wine business—one which still bears his name. His more than forty years as a wine merchant specializing in German wines make him particularly qualified to write a book about German wine history, techniques and laws. It explains the complex changes in the 1971 wine laws and is a standard reference on the subject.

Later edition of 399p. by Publivin of Dallas, published in 1981. Also published by The Wine Appreciation Guild in 1981.

_____. Rhineland wineland. London: Elek Books, 1951. 199p. Illus. G22790

Subsequent and greatly expanded editions.

_____. The great wines of Germany and its famed vineyards. See André L. Simon and S.F. Hallgarten.

_____. The wines and wine gardens of Austria. Watford, Great Britain: Argus Books, 1979. 339p. Illus. G22810

HALLIDAY, James. Coonawarra, the history, the vignerons and the wines. N.S.W., Australia: Yenisey Ltd., 1983. 188p. Illus. G22820

_____. Vintage Halliday. Magazine Promotions, Ltd., 1982. 232p. Illus. G22823

_____. Wine and wineries of Victoria. St. Lucia, Queensland: University of Queensland Press, 1982. 152p. Illus. G22845

_____. Wines and wineries of Western Australia. St. Lucia, Queensland: University of Queensland Press, 1982. 144p. Illus. G22847

_____. Wines and wineries of New South Wales. St. Lucia, Queensland: University of Queensland Press, 1980. 128p. Illus. G22830

_____. Wines and wineries of South Australia. St. Lucia, Queensland: University of Queensland Press, 1981. 144p. Illus. G22840

HALLIDAY, James and JARRATT, Ray. The wines and history of the Hunter Valley. Sydney: McGraw-Hill, 1979. 144p. Illus. G22850

HAMMOND, H. Notes on wine and vine culture in France. Beech Island, SC: By the Author, 1856. 21p. G22860

HANCKEL, Norman. Australian and New Zealand complete book of wine. 1973. 466p. G22870

HANCOCK, George Charles. Report on the composition of commoner British wines and cordials (alcoholic and non-alcoholic). London: 1924. 58p. G22880

A HANDBOOK on wines: to all who drink them. An essay more than passing useful. London: Tyas, 1840. 67p. G22900

HANDS, Phyllis. The complete book of South African wine.
> (See Kench, John.)

HANKERSON, Fred Putnam. The cooperage handbook. Brooklyn: Chemical Publishing, 1947. 182p. Illus. G22920

> Exclusively about barrels, and covers their history, method of manufacture, uses, types, specifications, dimensions, etc. A limited portion of the book is applicable to the wine industry.

HANN, George E. Some notes on the technical study and handling of wines. London: Merritt and Hatcher, 1948. 82p. G22930

HANNA, Phil Townsend. Good wine needs no bush. Los Angeles: Ward Ritchie Press, 1944. 13p. G22940

> "An address delivered before the Society of the Medical Friends of Wine at the Bohemian Club, March 22, 1944, and reprinted for those interested in the aesthetics and therapeutics of wine, by the Wine Institute." See Brathwaite, Richard for an historical account of the expression, "good wine needs no bush."

HANNUM, Hurst and BLUMBERG, Robert S. Brandies and liqueurs of the world. Garden City, NY: Doubleday, 1976. 278p. G22950

HANSEN, Emil. Practical studies in fermentation. Being contributions to the life history of micro-organisms . . . London: Spon, E. and F.N., 1896. 277p. G22970

HANSEN, Jens P. Wine in the Bible. Evanston, IL: Signal Press, 1955. 22p. G22980

HANSON, Anthony. Burgundy. London: Faber and Faber, 1982. 378p. Illus. G22990

> For those of us who have felt cheated after opening a bottle of burgundy, Mr. Hanson tells us why. The "why" is because many wine producers in Burgundy cheat. They sell wines labeled Burgundy that have been blended, or as Hanson calls it, "bone set", with more southerly wines that never saw the pinot noir grape. They also engage in excessive production, over-sugaring and heating or pasteurization of wines. Although all of this is illegal, Hanson says it is widely practiced. "One regrets having to say it, but most red burgundies today are mediocre wines without quality and poor value for money. Briefly, a rip-off. The Burgundians are coasting along on their reputation." He even calls into question the quality of that holy-of-holies, Domaine de la Romanée-Conti. This book is excellent reading for anyone who has purchased or intends to purchase burgundy wines.

HANSSEN, Maurice and DINEEN, J. Wines, beers and spirits. A straightforward approach to making wines and beers at home, including descriptions of the small-scale production of spirits. Wellingborough, England: Thorsons, 1977. 96p. G23000

AGOSTON HARASZTHY (1812-1869)

Agoston Haraszthy, a vade-mecum for success: brilliant, energetic, imaginative, personable and with a nose for money.

Emerging on the losing side of Hungarian politics, Haraszthy emigrated to Salk City, Wisconsin, in 1842 with his wife, three sons and his father. Almost immediately he became the center of activity in his community; operating a sawmill, brickyard, dabbling in politics, winemaking and land speculation.

Seven years later he left for California and for the next nineteen years proved himself one of the most remarkable of the '49ers. He first went to San Diego, where he became sheriff and town marshall. In 1852, he was elected to the State Assembly and moved to San Francisco. He became director of the San Francisco Mint and experimented with a variety of agricultural activities on a farm in San Mateo County, south of San Francisco.

His interest in making wine commercially didn't take root until he purchased the Buena Vista Ranch in Sonoma Valley in 1856. Although Haraszthy was not the first to establish a vineyard in Sonoma Valley, his letters to San Francisco newspapers and articles for agricultural journals on everything from planting vines and growing grapes to making and bottling wine probably did more to focus attention on

BUENA VISTA RANCHE, SONOMA COUNTY, CALIFORNIA : RESIDENCE OF A. HARASZTHY.

Sonoma Valley as a prime grape-growing area than those of any other person.

By 1858, Haraszthy had planted nearly 140 acres, mainly in the mission grape. Because Haraszthy knew great wine could not be made from that grape, he convinced Governor Downey to send him to Europe to collect grapevines. Before leaving he stopped in New York and arranged with Harper and Brothers for publication of a book about his trip.

During his travels Haraszthy collected and imported over 1,400 vinifera vine varieties. When the California legislature rejected his request for reimbursement for his expenses and the costs of the vines, Haraszthy planted the vines at Buena Vista and published a catalog for their sale. Many of the vines were purchased and planted throughout California. However, there remains to this day serious dispute as to how much influence Haraszthy's collection of foreign vines has had on the development of today's California vines.

Haraszthy went on to incorporate his vineyards into the Buena Vista Viticultural Society and be became "its superintendent." Three years later, after a series of financial setbacks, the Society's directors removed him.

Ever restless, he went to Nicaragua in 1868 and bought a sugar plantation with the intention of distilling rum. He disappeared one day in 1869, and it is believed that while attempting to cross an alligator-infested stream he fell in and drowned.

HARASZTHY, Agoston. Grape culture, wines, and wine-making. With notes upon agriculture and horticulture. New York: Harper and Brothers, 1862. 420p. Illus. G23020

> Haraszthy's account is of his travels through ". . . parts of France, the Netherlands, Holland, Rhenish, Prussia, Bavaria, Nassau, Baden, Switzerland, Spain, Italy and England." The object of his trip, sanctioned by Governor J.G. Downey, was to examine the different varieties of grapes and the methods of making wines in the wine growing countries of Europe.

> Aside from its historical value as a reference on 19th century European methods of viticulture and wine making, Haraszthy's descriptions of the wines he drank, the towns he visited, the countrysides through which he traveled and anecdotes of the people he met make for entertaining reading.

> After inspecting the cellars at Steinberg, in the Rheingau, he was treated to a tasting of that celebrated vineyard's wines from the years 1822 to 1859. "To describe the wines," he said, "would be a work sufficient for Byron, Shakespeare, or Schiller, and even those geniuses would not do full justice to them until they had imbibed a couple of glasses full." Later that day, Haraszthy visited Schloss Johannisberg and was equally impressed by its wines. Recalling his journey on the train from Frankfurt to Switzerland, Haraszthy tells an amusing story of a Russian lady and her baggage problem, of her astonishment, and that of the rest of the train car, when he revealed he was a Californian. "Everybody in the car looked at me, and I became the lion of the time. My fair neighbor asked me many questions about gold; how long I had lived in California. . . . I told her eleven years. 'Why,' she said, 'and you have not been killed! How have you escaped so many years without having been

murdered?' " Haraszthy's explanation of why Europe had such a distorted view of America and crime might well apply today to other equally distorted views of America, ". . . other nations wash their dirty linen in secret, and we do it openly. . . ."

In spite of incredibly wretched travel and lodging facilities in Spain, Haraszthy never seems to have lost his patience or his sense of humor. Upon arriving in a small town in Spain he tells of being surrounded by thirty beggars. "They really besieged us. Resistance was out of the question. In the first place it would not look well to attack a lot of old men and women, all blind, lame, or diseased; then they were in greater number than we. I was struck by an idea: putting my hand in my pockets, I pulled out a handful of copper coins and threw it among the crowd. The move was most successful; there was a general scramble, in which the lame walked and the blind saw."

The text also includes a chapter on "Grapes and Wines in California," which consists of extracts from an essay written by Haraszthy in 1858 for the State Agricultural Society but modified to the extent that Haraszthy's opinions had been changed. There is also a ten-part appendix of extracts from European texts on grape growing, wine making, the manufacture of potato starch and grape sugar, the culture of the silkworm, etc.

_____. Grape culture, wines and wine-making. Hopewell, NJ: Booknoll Reprints, 1971. 420p. Illus. G23030

HARASZTHY, Arpad. California grapes and wines . . . and the vineland of the west; or champagne and its manufacture. San Francisco: Bosqui Engraving and Printing, 1883. 30p. G23040

_____. "The Haraszthy family.". Berkeley: Bancroft Library, University of California, 1866. G23050

_____. Wine-making in California. San Francisco: The Book Club of California, 1978. 69p. G23060

> Limited edition of 600 copies. Contains four articles by Arpad Haraszthy that appeared in *The Overland Monthly* in 1871 and 1872.

HARDMAN, William. The wine-growers' and wine-coopers' manual. New York: Howard Lockwood, 1877. 181p. G23070

> The author was associated for twenty-four years with a prominent wine firm in Sicily. Much of this information was compiled from the works of Jullien, McCulloch, Busby, Shaw, Redding, Mulder and others. The information regarding sherry is based on the author's personal visit to that area in 1869. An English edition of 166p. was published in 1878 by W. Tegg of London.

HARDWICK, Homer. Winemaking at home. New York: Wilfred Funk, 1954. 253p. Illus. G23080

> Lists 220 wines that can be made from 84 different raw materials ranging from apples to wheat. Second edition published in 1970.

The HARDY tradition; tracing the growth and development of a great wine-making family through its first hundred years. Adelaide: Thomas Hardy and Sons, 1953. 50p. Illus. G23090

HARDY, Thomas. Notes on the vineyards of America and Europe. Adelaide: L. Henn, 1885. 134p. G23100

—————. A vigneron abroad; trip to South Africa. Adelaide: W.K. Thomas, 1899. 34p. G23110

HARINGTON, Sir John. The school of Salernum; regimen sanitatis salerni, the English version . . . by Sir John Harington. 1953. 92p. Illus. G23120

HARPER, Charles G. Queer things about London. Strange nooks and corners of the greatest city in the world. London: Cecil Palmer, 1923. 256p. Illus. G23130

> A fascinating book for anyone interested in the history of London, and doubly so for the wine lover. It traces the sentry walk of the old Roman wall to the wine vaults of Barber's bonded warehouse at Coopers Row. There is another wine vignette which describes an ancient processional ritual still carried out from the Hall of the Vintners' Company.

HARPER'S manual; standard work of reference for the wine and spirit trade. London: The Wine and Spirit Gazette, 1941. 495p. Illus. G23140

> Many subsequent editions.

HARRIMAN, Karen, ed. The art of drinkmanship. London: Marshall, Cavendish, 1972. 64p. Illus. G23150

HARRIS, Mollie. Drop o' wine. London: Chatto and Windus, 1983. G23160

HARRIS, Robert. The drunkard's cup. (A sermon). London: Printed by Felix Kyngston for Thomas Man, 1619. 29p. G23170

> Subsequent editions in 1622, 1626 and 1630.

HARRISON, Brian. Drink and Victorians. London: Faber and Faber, 1971. 510p. Illus. G23180

> The temperance question in England, 1815-1872.

HARRISON, Godfrey. Bristol Cream. London: Batsford, 1955. 162p. Illus. G23190

HARRISON, Leonard. After repeal: a study of liquor control administration. New York: Harper, 1936. G23200

HARROLD, Marshall C. The Ohio winemakers. Dayton, OH: 58p. Illus. G23210

> Contains a history of the early days and a tour guide for today.

HART, M.A., comp. Eating and drinking; a miscellany. London: Sampson Low, 1947. 232p. Illus. G23220

HARTLEY, Joseph. The wholesale and retail wine and spirit merchant's companion and complete instructor to the trade . . . London: By the Author, 1835. 208p. G23230

Subsequent editions published in 1839, 1843 and 1850.

HARTLEY, Walter N. Fermentation and distillation. London: 1884. 26p. G23240

HARTMAN, Dennis. Wines and liqueurs, what, when, how to serve. Washington, DC: Congressional Press, 1933. 23p. G23250

HARTMAN, George. The family physician, or a collection of choice . . . remedies for the cure of almost all diseases . . . together with the . . . method of making English wines . . . London: Printed for Richard Wellington, 1696. 528p. G23260

_____. Hartman's curiosities of art and nature of the true preserver and restorer of health . . . being a choice collection of . . . as also for preserving and making of . . . cherry-wine. London: Printed by T.B. for the Author, 1682. 352p. G23270

HARTSHORNE, Albert. Antique drinking glasses. New York: Brussel and Brussel, 1968. 490p. Illus. G23280

A reprint of *Old English Glasses,* below.

_____. Old English glasses. An account of glass drinking vessels in England, from early times to the end of the eighteenth century. With introductory notices, original documents . . . London and New York: E. Arnold, 1897. 490p. Illus. G23290

HARVEY, John and Sons. Harvey's pocket guide to wine. London: Octopus, 1981. 160p. G23300

Provides information concerning grapes and grape hybrids, methods of making wine and major shippers. Also includes maps locating major wine-producing areas and vintage charts.

_____. Harvey's wine guide. Bristol: John Harvey and Sons, 1948. 48p. Illus. G23310

This is the first edition. There have been almost yearly subsequent editions.

_____. Wine list. Bristol: John Harvey and Sons, 1962. 88p. Illus. G23320

Contains advice on serving and laying down wines. Second edition of 92p. published in 1963.

HASELGROVE, C.P. About vines and wines. Sydney: Wine and Food Society of N.S.W., 1956. 14p. G23340

HASKELL, George. Account of various experiments for the production of new and desirable grapes . . . Ipswich, MA: 1877. 18p. G23350

_____. A narrative of the life, experience, and work of an American citizen. Ipswich, MA: 1896. 156p. G23360

Autobiography. Contains an account of the author's work with American grapes.

————————. Wines, liqueurs and brandies. London: By the Author, 1922. 98p. G23370

> The author furnishes 250 recipes for the manufacture of imitation wines, liqueurs and brandies. The author contends that by using his recipes the British wine merchant "can produce wines and liqueurs quite as good as those produced in any other country. . . ." The imitation of wines through chemical and other means was in vogue during the last half of the 19th century, even in France and Germany.

HASKIN, Steve and FINGERHUT, Bruce. Read that label: how to tell what's inside a wine bottle from what's on the outside. South Bend, IN: Icarus Press, 1983. 124p. Illus. G23380

HASLER, G.F. Wine service in the restaurant. Professional guide for the sommelier. London: Wine and Spirit Publications, 1967. 84p. Illus. G23390

> A handbook for the professional wine waiter written by a founding member of the Guild of Sommeliers.

HASLER, Hall R.J. Wine-art recipe booklet. Vancouver: Wine-Art, 1977. 62p. G23400

HASZONICS, Joseph J. and BARRATT, Stuart. Wine merchandising . New York: Ahrens, 1963. 214p. Illus. G23410

HATCH, Evelyn M. Burgundy past and present. London: Methuen, 1927. 239p. Illus. G23420

HATCH, Ted. The American wine cookbook. New York: Putnam's, 1941. 315p. G23430

> Also contains wine as a beverage, mixed drinks and wine service.

HAWKER, Charlotte. Chats about wine. London: Daly, 1907. 158p. G23440

> Another edition, 1910.

————————. Wine and wine merchants. London: 1909. G23450

HAYNES, Irene W. Ghost wineries of the Napa Valley; a photographic tour of the 19th century. San Francisco: Sally Taylor and Friends, 1980. 78p. Illus. G23460

HAZAN, Victor. Italian wine. New York: Knopf, 1982. 337p. Illus. G23470

HAZELTON, Nika Standen. American wines. New York: Grossett and Dunlap, c1976. 96p. Illus. G23480

MAURICE HEALY (1887-1943)

Maurice Healy, a lawyer, was admitted to the Irish Bar in 1910 and the English Bar in 1914. He was a teetotaler until the First World War. After the war he practiced law in London, where he became the friend of André Simon, who referred to Healy as "my dearly beloved disciple." It was Healy's proposal that they honor George Saintsbury (see Saintsbury) by forming a dining club that would meet to dine twice a year: on October 23, the Professor's birthday, and April 23, his nameday - St. George's Day.

HEALY, Maurice. A bibliography of memorabilia, trivia, jocose jocoseria and other odd notes upon wine and its lore. A supplement to his paper on "Irish Wine.". London: Private circulation only, 1927. 10p. G23500

_____. Claret and the white wines of Bordeaux. London: Constable, 1934. 165p. G23510

> Healy, a lover of claret, wrote this book at André Simon's request for Constable's Wine Library, a series of popular books on wine. Simon considered it the best of the series, if for no reason other than it sold the most copies.

_____. Opusculum: Irish wine. London: Privately printed, c1926. G23520

> Healy was a member of Ye Sette of Odd Volumes, a literary dining club of mostly lawyers and writers. New members were expected to make a literary communication to the Sette and this was Healy's. "Irish" wine was claret.

_____. Stay me with flagons. London: Michael Joseph, 1940. 290p. G23530

> An account of the wines of the world delivered in a conversational and personal style. Subsequent editions.

HEATH, Ambrose. Good drinks. London: Faber and Faber, 1939. 239p. Illus. G23540

_____. Home-made wines and liqueurs: how to make them. London: Jenkins, 1961. 96p. G23550

HEATON, Nell St. John. Wines, mixed drinks and savouries. London: Arco Publications, 1962. 160p. G23560

HEATON, Nell and SIMON, André. A calendar of food and wine. London: Faber and Faber, 1949. 268p. Illus. G23570

> Subsequent edition of 270p. published by Crest Books of London.

HEATON, Vernon. Choose a wine and cheese party. London: Elliott Right Way Books, 1969. 127p. Illus. G23580

HEBERT, Malcolm R. California brandy drinks, the one bottle bar. San Francisco: The Wine Appreciation Guild, 1981. 154p. G23590

> Includes over 1,000 brandy drinks.

_____. The wine lovers' cookbook. San Francisco: The Wine Appreciation Guild, 1984. 176p. Illus. G23595

> Contains an informative essay of California wines by Brian St. Pierre of the Wine Institute along with suggestions for matching food and wine.

HECKMANN, Manfred. Corkscrews. An introduction to their appreciation. San Francisco: The Wine Appreciation Guild, 1981. 124p. Illus. G23600

HEDDLE, Enid Moodie. Story of a vineyard: Chateau Tahbilk 1860-1960. Melbourne: F.W. Cheshire, 1960. 56p. Illus. G23610

> Limited edition of 500 copies. 1968 edition by Hawthorne Press.

HEDRICK, Ulysses Prentice. Grapes and wines from home vineyards. New York: Oxford University Press, 1945. 326p. Illus. G23620

> This work is, in the author's words, "a by-product of a life-long experience in viticulture." The book is in two parts: the home vineyard; and wines made from native grapes grown in the home vineyard. There are also chapters on recipes for wine drinks and food seasoned and flavored by wine. Chapter ten contains information on why the native American grapes have been replaced with European varieties.

_____. The grapes of New York. Albany: J.B. Lyon, 1908. 564p. Illus. G23630

> This is a significant and comprehensive ampelography covering American grapes and an important reference. The contents cover Old World grapes, grape-growing and the grape regions in New York state, and detailed discussions of the leading and minor American grape varieties, including a brief history of each variety, the place, date and circumstances of origin and a technical description of the vine and its fruit. Footnotes contain biographical sketches of important early American wine growers. There are 101 color plates of grapes, which add greatly to the text. To prepare these plates, four negatives were taken of a grape varietal and the colors of red, yellow, blue and black were assigned to each negative, respectively. This was the second in a series of fruit publications by the Board of Control of the New York Agricultural Experimental Station.

_____. A history of horticulture in America to 1860. New York: Oxford University Press, 1950. 551p. Illus. G23640

> Contains the early history of grape culture in the United States.

_____. Manual of American grape growing. New York: Macmillan, 1919. 458p. Illus. G23650

> This manual was written for both commercial and amateur grape growers. The author admits that it relies heavily on his monumental work, *The Grapes of New York*. The chapter on grape pruning in California is a republication of parts of F.T. Bioletti's Bulletin 246, published in 1919. The text is illustrated with thirty-two black and white photographs of grape varietals and fifty-four text drawings.

HEIDE, Ralph Auf Der. The illustrated wine making book. Garden City, NY: Doubleday, 1973. 206p. Illus. G11620

HEINTZ, William F. Freemark Abbey Winery of Tychson Hill, St. Helena, California; highlights from its early history. Research of Glen Ellen. 1975. G23660

> Unable to verify.

HELLMAN, R. Food and wine in Europe. London: Charles Letts, 1970. 128p. G23670

HELMONT, Jean Baptiste van. Ternary of paradoxes. The magnetick cure of wounds. Nativity of tartar in wine. Image of God in man. Written originally by Jon. Bapt. van Helmont, and tr., illustrated and ampl[ified] by Walter Charleton. London: Printed by J. Flesher for W. Lee, 1650. 147p. Illus. G23680

HENDERSON, Alexander. The history of ancient and modern wines. London: Baldwin, Cradock and Joy, 1824. 408p. Illus. G23690

> Alexander Henderson (1780-1863) graduated as a doctor of medicine from Edinburgh University in 1803. Although he established a medical practice in London, he applied himself chiefly to literature, contributing to the *Encyclopedia Britannica* and other publications. Most writers credit Henderson with writing the first book in English that describes in detail what are today called modern wines [see, however, Shannon, R.]. Before writing this book, Henderson had visited the principal wine-growing districts of France, Germany and Italy.

> For wine tasters caught up in the practice of attempting to identify wines "blind," Henderson has a fascinating account of the vagaries of wine tastes and smells. In discussing the tastes of wines, he comments: ". . . but what terms will convey an adequate notion of that peculiar ethereal flavour which distinguishes each of these liquors when duly mellowed by age, and which, in fact, is only developed by long keeping? To tell us that it is penetrant, volatile, transient, and so forth, is nothing to the purpose: and the only satisfactory and intelligible way in which the description can be given, as has been already observed, is by a comparison with some other known sensation of taste, respecting which all men are agreed. In like manner, those properties of wine which we recognize by the origin of smell, - 'Foolish delights, and fond abusions, Which do this sense besiege with light illusions,' are equally various and difficult of investigation and definition."

> Henderson devotes fourteen chapters and 228 pages to modern wines and many of his observations are as valid now as then. It is a large, well-printed text, tastefully illustrated with thirty-two vignettes and initial engravings portraying various mythological Bacchian experiences.

> An attempt through the British Library to determine the number of copies printed was unsuccessful. Baldwin, Cradock and Joy, a bookselling firm best known for its periodical publication, *London Magazine,* left very little archival information, none of which sheds light on edition sizes. Scarce.

HENDERSON, James Forbes. Startling profits from wine making, in combination with the wine, spirit, and aerated water trades. 2nd ed. Dundee, Scotland: W. and D.C. Thomson, 1897. 110p. G23700

> First edition, 1896.

HENDERSON, Robert, Attorney-at-Law. An inquiry into the nature and object of the several laws restraining and regulating the retail sale of alcohol,

THE

HISTORY

OF

ANCIENT AND MODERN WINES.

INTRODUCTION.

OF THE PRINCIPLES OF FERMENTATION, AND THE CONSTITUENTS OF WINE IN GENERAL.

 HE invention of Wine, like the origin of many other important arts, is enveloped in the obscurity of the earliest ages of the world; but, in the history of ancient nations, it has generally been ascribed to those heroes who contributed most to civilize their respective countries, and to whom divine honours were often rendered, in return for the benefits which they had conferred upon mankind. Without dwelling on the fabulous traditions

B

beer, wine and spirits . . . with . . . an appendix of cases illustrative of individual calamity . . . suffered under the existing mode of granting and withholding licenses to inns, taverns, ale-houses . . . without the power of appeal; in a letter to the Hon. Henry Grey Bennett, M.P. London: 1817. 144p. G23710

HENRIQUES, E. Frank. The Signet encyclopedia of whiskey, brandy and all other spirits. New York: New American Library, 1979. 243p. Illus. G23720

_____. The Signet encyclopedia of wine. New York: New American Library, 1975. 350p. G23730

Numerous subsequent editions.

HENSCHKE, C.A. Observations of winemaking in Europe in relation to the wine industry in Australia. Canberra: Winston Churchill Memorial Trust, 1970. 36p. G23740

HENSHAW, Dennis. Brush your teeth with wine. London: Hammond, Hammond, 1960. 284p. Illus. G23750

HERBEMONT, N. A treatise on the culture of the vine and on wine making in the United States. Baltimore: Irving Hitchcock, 1833. G23760

Unable to verify.

HERE'S how . . . [a book about wine and other alcoholic beverages]. London: Victoria Wine Co., 1965. 80p. Illus. G23770

HERN, A. What are you drinking? World's Work, 1982. 32p. Illus. G23780

HEROD, William P. An introduction to wines; with a chapter on cordials and aperitives. New York: Fortuny's, 1936. 63p. G23790

HERSTEIN, Karl M. and GREGORY, Thomas C. Chemistry and technology of wines and liquors. New York: D. Van Nostrand, 1935. 360p. Illus. G23800

A technical work more suited to the chemist but with many descriptions of wines, spirits and liquors. One reviewer called the second edition of this work ". . . the poorest treatise on wine production that can be written for current conditions." He went on to add: "Under no circumstances should the book be permitted to fall into the hands of a newcomer. . . . It is ghastly to contemplate what might happen if all winemakers were suddenly to disappear from the earth, and all wine henceforth to be made in accordance with the principles laid down here." The second edition of 436p. was published in 1948.

HERTER, George Leonard. How to make the finest wines at home in old glass or plastic bottles and jugs for as little as ten cents a gallon! Rev. 2nd ed. Waseca, MN: By the Author, 1967. 144p. Illus. G23810

First edition of 70p. published in 1965.

HERTZ, Emanuel. The use of wine by Jews for religious purposes. New York: By the Author, 1922. 8p. G23820

HEUBLEIN, Inc. Third premiere national auction of rare wines. Heublein, 1971. 104p. Illus. G23830

> In 1969 Heublein, Inc. initiated the first auction of rare wines. The auction has been held annually since in various cities throughout the United States. The catalogs describe in detail the various wines being offered and their sources. Preview tastings are held in selected cities prior to the auction and admission to the tastings and the auction is by catalog only. Issued annually.

HEUCKMANN, Wilhelm. The grafted vine; European scions; American stocks; the end of phylloxera. London: Trata Maria Drescha, 1964. 16p. Illus. G23840

> Translated by Margaret Gore-Browne, produced and hand-painted by Trata Maria Drescha.

HEWETT, Edward and AXTON, W.F. Convivial Dickens: The drinks of Dickens and his friends. Athens, OH: Ohio University Press, 1983. 191p. Illus. G23845

> There are literally hundreds of references to drinking in the words of Charles Dickens. Using these as a key, the authors have opened the drinking habits of all classes of Victorian society for study. They have also "reconstructed" the drinks themselves from early recipe books and Dickens' own hand. Over 130 authentic recipes follow the chapters pertaining to them.

> This is a very handsome and entertaining book. The illustrations are, for the most part, old prints, many by George Cruikshank, taken from the original editions of Dickens novels.

> Dickens' two tours of the United States are also closely followed and there is a chapter on U.S. drinking habits of the time. Much of the drinks and the drinking involved wine.

> The Dickensian scholar, B.W. Matz, authored two books on the inns and taverns of Dickens. *Convivial Dickens* is the perfect complement to those volumes, but stands on its own as a valuable study of drinking habits and social customs.

> An appendix lists the contents of Dickens' cellar as auctioned August 13, 1870. Dickens apparently did not comtemplate such an early death, for the cellar included about 185 dozen bottles of various wines; heavy on sherry, clarets, champagne and port and less than two dozen of red burgundy. The authors' note that the fifty-three dozen of "hard liquors are what we might expect to find in a cellar of that time." (Also see Dickens, Cedric.)

HEWITT, John Theodore. Chemistry of winemaking: a report on oenological research. London: His Majesty's Stationery Office, 1928. 56p. G23850

HEYNE, Ernest B. Complete catalogue of European vines, with their synonyms and brief descriptions. San Francisco: Pacific Press Office, 1881. 63p. G23860

HICHENS, Phoebe. Wineman's bluff. London: Macmillan, 1973. 188p. Illus. G23870

How to make wines at home from grape concentrates.

HIGHTOWER, Penny. Cocktails with wine. 1977. G23880

Unable to verify.

HILGARD, Eugene W. The phylloxera or grapevine louse, and the remedies for its ravages. Sacramento: University of California College of Agriculture, Bulletin 23, 1875. G23890

_____. Report on experiments on fermenting red wines and related subjects during the years of 1886-7. Sacramento: State Office Publication, 1888. 48p. G23900

HILL, Kenneth. Wine and beermaking at home. London: Luscombe, 1974. 116p. Illus. G23910

_____. Wines that win prizes. London: Mills and Boon, 1972. 96p. Illus. G23920

HILLMAN, Howard. The diner's guide to wines. New York: Hawthorne, 1978. 203p. G23930

General introduction to wine selection. Lists over 500 international dishes with appropriate wines for each. Also includes a list of "least wanted" food and beverages that do not go with wine.

HILLS, William M. Small fruits. Their propagation and cultivation including the grape . . . Boston: Cupples, Upham, 1886. 138p. Illus. G23940

HINES, Philip R. The wines and wineries of Ohio. Franklin, OH: By the Author, 1973. 152p. Illus. G23950

HINKLE, Richard Paul. Central coast wine book. St. Helena, CA: Vintage Image, 1980. 210p. Illus. G23960

_____. Napa Valley wine book. St. Helena, CA: Vintage Image, 1979. 178p. Illus. G23970

HINTON, L. Redman wine; the story of a winemaker. Adelaide: Gillingham, 1971. 40p. G23980

HIRSCH, Irving. Manufacture of whiskey, brandy, and cordials. 2nd ed. Newark: Sherman Engineering, 1937. 183p. G23990

HIRSCHFELD, Albert M. The standard handbook on wines and liquors. New York: Wm. C. Popper, 1907. 103p. G24000

HISTORY of the organization and progress of the Italian-Swiss Colony. Asti, CA: 1903. 27p. Illus. G24010

HITZ, Vajen E., comp. The grape industry: a selected list of references on the economic aspects of the industry in the United States, 1920-1931. Washington: Department of Agriculture, 1932. 141p. G24020

HOARE, Clement. Descriptive account of an improved method of planting and managing roots of grape vines. London: Longman, Brown, Green and Longmans, 1844. 82p. G24030

_____. A practical treatise on the cultivation of the grape vine on open walls. 3rd ed. London: Longman, Brown, Green and Longmans, 1841. 210p. Illus. G24040

> The first and second editions of this popular treatise were published in 1835 and 1837. Vines were cultivated in England at the time of these publications only against walls, upon roofs of buildings and under glass. Hoare's treatise on the cultivation of the grape vine in this manner became the standard reference work. Subsequent editions were published in 1840, 1844, 1845, 1847 and 1848. The first American edition in 1837 contains a dedication by George Brimmer to the Horticultural Society of Massashusetts. Brimmer proposed that the application of Hoare's principles would "restore the confidence of the horticulturists of Boston and its vicinity in the capacity of their climate to mature in open air some of the best varieties of foreign grapes." Subsequent editions were published in Boston in 1840 and 1845 and in New York in 1847.

HOBART, Alice Tisdale. The cup and the sword. New York: Bobbs-Merrill, 1942. 400p. G24050

> A novel about power and intrigue in a family's attempt to control the wine industry (Napa/Sonoma) between the World Wars.

HOCKER, E. Curtis. Hocker's alcoholic beverage encyclopedia. San Francisco: By the Author, 1941. 159p. G24060

HOCKING, Anthony. Wine: pride of South Africa. Purnell, South Africa: 1973. 24p. Illus. G24070

HOFER, A.F. Grape growing, a simple treatise on the single pole system, or how grapes are cultivated in the Upper Rhine Valley. New York: E.H. Libby, 1878. 32p. Illus. G24090

HOFFMAN, Melvin Butler. Grape production in New York. Rev. ed. Ithaca, NY: New York State College of Agriculture at Cornell University, 1944. 375p. Illus. G24100

HOGG, Anthony. Cocktails and mixed drinks. Everything the home bartender wants to know about: setting up shop, spirit and wine aperitifs, coolers, warmers and planning for a party. London: Hamlyn, 1979. 128p. Illus. G24110

_____. Guide to visiting vineyards. London: Michael Joseph, 1976. 196p. Illus. G24120

> Nearly 200 vineyards are listed by country and district. Each district has a preamble about the grapes grown and the wines made. The author then provides a selection of vineyards where visitors are welcomed, giving their names, addresses and telephone numbers. He gives directions on how to find them, and brief descriptions of what the visitor will see. A handy reference for those planning a vineyard tour. A second edition of 229p. was published in 1981.

HOGG, Anthony, ed. Off the shelf. 2nd ed. Harlow: Gilbey Vintners, distributed by Peter Dominic Publications, 1972. 184p. Illus. G24130

_____. WineMine: a first anthology. London: Souvenir Press, 1970. 223p. Illus. G24140

> An anthology of wine information originally published in the magazine *WineMine* produced by the wine firm of Peter Dominic. Subsequent publications.

_____. WineMine, autumn, 1962. Horsham, Sussex: Peter Dominic, 1962. 144p. Illus. G24150

_____. WineMine, winter 1972, no. 24. London: Peter Dominic, 1972. 144p. Illus. G24160

_____. The winetasters' guide to Europe. New York: Dutton, 1980. 256p. Illus. G24170

> Information, including directions and hours, for over 300 vineyards and cellars.

HOGGSON, Thomas. The squire's home-made wines as described and set-forth in the journal of Thomas Hoggson, gent., 1765. Newly augmented and enlarged and done into a booke by Charles Edmund Merrill, Jr. New York: Pynson Printers, 1924. 37p. G24180

HOLDEN, E.A. The history of viticulture and wine making in Australia. Sydney: Pratten Bros., 1935. 12p. G24200

HOLDEN, Ronald and ROTE, Glenda. Touring the wine country of Oregon. Portland: Holden Travel Research, 1982. 208p. G24210

_____. Touring the wine country of Washington. Seattle: Holden Pacific, 1983. 234p. G24220

HOLDSWORTH, J.H. Memoranda on Tours and Touraine . . . also on the wines and mineral waters of France . . . Tours: A. Aigre, 1842. 235p. G24230

HOLIDAY book of food and drink. New York: Hermitage House, 1952. 346p. G24240

> Collection of essays by noted wine experts.

HOLIDAY drink book. Mt. Vernon, NY: Peter Pauper Press, 1952. 67p. Illus. G24250

HOLLAND, Tim. Behind the label. London: By the Author, 1974. 141p. Illus. G24260

> Written as a training guide for persons starting in the English wine trade.

HOLLAND, Tim and BONE, Arthur. French wines. London: Macdonald, 1978. 96p. G24270

HOLLAND, Vyvyan. Drink and be merry. London: Victor Gallanz, 1967. 173p. G24280

HOLLINGWORTH, Jane. Collecting decanters. New York: 1980. 128p. Illus. G24290

> Discusses the history of the decanter from ancient times to the present. Detailed descriptions of the decanters are complemented by ninety-two illustrations, twenty-seven in color.

HOLT, Raymond M. The fruits of viticulture in Orange County. Los Angeles: The Quarterly Historical Society of Southern California, 1946. 27p. G24300

> Much about wine and the deadly disease known as the Anaheim or Pierce disease that destroyed almost every vineyard in Southern California by 1889.

HOLTGRIEVE, Don. The California wine atlas. Hayward, CA: Ecumene Assoc., 1978. G24310

HOME wine-making: a WI home skills guide to basic techniques and recipes. London: Macdonald Educational for WI Books, 1979. 64p. G24330

HOME-MADE wines, beers, liqueurs, cordials, cups and cocktails. London: Ward, Lock, 1937. 63p. G24340

HONNEYMAN, William. Calculating alcohol yields from specific gravities. Lecture of considerable interest to winemakers who rely on the hydrometer alone for estimating alcohol yields. Belfast: By the Author, 1966. G24350

HOOPS, John Herman Henry. How to make grape culture profitable in California, with explanation of California vine or Anaheim disease. San Jose, CA: Press of the Pacific Tree and Vine, 1904. 40p. Illus. G24370

HOPE, W.H. St. John. On the English medieval drinking bowls and on other vessels such as standing cups, chalices, etc. Westminster: Society of Antiquaries, 1887. 65p. Illus. G24380

HORNE, Eric. What the butler winked at. London: T. Werner Laurie, 1924. 281p. G24390

HORNICKEL, Ernst. The great wines of Europe. First American ed. New York: Putnam's, 1965. 229p. Illus. G24400

HOW to make your own wine. Sydney: Hamyln, 1973. 112p. Illus. G24410

HOWARD, Frances. Landscaping with vines. New York: Macmillan, 1959. 230p. G24420

HOWARD, Kathleen. Making wine, beer and merry. Norman, OK: Popular Topics Press, 1973. 183p. Illus. G24430

HOWE, E., comp. Viniana; a collection of ephemera associated with the wine trade. n.p., n.d. Unpaged. G24440

HOWELL, Charles Coes. The case of whiskey. Altadena, CA: By the Author, 1928. 238p. G24445

The author was an executive of a major distilling and a wine importer and his business was, of course, destroyed by Prohibition, "without compensation."

Various Protestant groups had led the fight for Prohibition and had painted the distillers, brewers and winemakers as very bad people indeed.

Mr. Howell, retaliating, paints some of them in the same colors but, quoting his sources, says his is an historically accurate portrayal.

He also has a great deal of comment on "what we use to drink." The section on wine is interesting as to its history in the United States during Prohibition. For example, the wine industry was ruined but the grape growers thrived, for prior to 1920 an average of 13,500 railroad cars of wine grapes were shipped from California but that figure jumped to 64,394 carloads in 1926.

In the author's presence, the Commissioner of Internal Revenue told a luncheon group that his agents had found numerous shipments of unfermented juice with a large red sticker on the head of each barrel printed, "Warning: the contents of this barrel is unfermented grape juice. Do not add yeast, and do not keep barrel in a warm place or the contents will ferment and become wine."

Although farmers were allowed, under permit, to make 300 hundred gallons of wine or cider in their homes for family use, the practice spread to the cities, where salesmen delivered ten and twenty gallon kegs with printed warnings as to what would happen if the bung was removed.

An excellent insider's account of the hypocrisy and fundamental weaknesses of the Volstead Act and similar state laws.

HOWKINS, Ben. Rich, rare and red: The International Wine and Food Society's guide to port. London: The International Wine and Food Society and Heinemann, 1982. 169p. Illus. G24450

HUBBARD, T.S. Descriptive catalogue of grape vines and small fruits. A nursery based on grapes in particular. Fredonia, NY: 1884. G24460

Prior and subsequent editions. Issued Annually.

HUDSON, Horace Bushnell. California vineyards. A favored section of the Golden State as it appears to an eastern writer. Scenes in Fresno County, the vineyard center. Minneapolis: By the Author, 1902. 84p. Illus. G24470

HUDSON, William. Wines of Italy. London: 1888. 33p. G24480

HUGEL, Jean. And give it my blessing. Riquewihr, France: By the Author, 1967. 32p. Illus. G24490

HUGGETT, Henry E.V. Rhenish, a paper on Rhine wines. London: Privately printed, 1929. 41p. G24500

Privately printed by the Ye Sette of Odd Volumes dining club in London, of which André Simon and Maurice Healy were members.

After election, each member was expected to present a literary or artistic address to the Club, of which copies would be printed and distributed to the members and friends. Limited edition of 199 copies. Scarce.

HUGHES, A. Cyprus wines. An island industry. London: Cyprus Wine Board, 12p. Illus. G24510

HUGHES, Bernard G. English, Scottish and Irish table glass from the sixteenth century to 1820. New York: Bramhall House, 1956. 408p. Illus. G24520

HUGHES, David. The complete book of South African wine.

(See Kench, John.)

HUGHES, John. An itinerary of Provence and the Rhone. London: Cawthorn, 1822. 267p. G24540

HUGHES, William. The complete vineyard: or, an excellent way for the planting of vines according to the German and French manner and long practiced in England. Wherein is set forth the ways, and all the circumstances necessary for the planting of a vineyard with the selection of the soil; the situation thereof the best way for the planting of young plants; the best time and manner of pruning; the turning and translation of the ground; with other necessary observations. London: Printed by J.C. for Royal Crook, 1670. 92p. G24550

There is a 1665 edition of 27p.

HUNT, Peter, comp. Eating and drinking; an anthology for epicures. London: Ebury Press, 1961. 320p. Illus. G24570

Introduction by André L. Simon. Much about wine.

HUSENBETH, Frederick Charles. A guide for the wine cellar; or a practical treatise on the cultivation of the vine, and the management of the different wines consumed in this country. London: Effingham Wilson, 1834. 133p. G24590

Husenbeth was a British wine merchant.

GEORGE HUSMANN (1827-1902)

The German heritage was as strong in California as it was in the East. A handbook for German immigrants to California, published in San Francisco in 1885, states: "Of particular importance is wine-growing, originally introduced by the missionaries and now mainly cultivated by Germans."

By the 1870's California was the leading wine growing state in the Union surpassing Missouri and Ohio. Symbolic of this shift was the move of George Husmann from Missouri to California. Husmann, professor of horticulture at the University of Missouri, became instrumental in the rejuvenation of the phylloxera-ravaged vineyards of Europe when he supplied pest-resistant American vines as root stock for grafting the Old World grapes. In 1881, with the vineyards of Missouri in decline, he moved to Napa Valley; convinced "that this was the true home of the grape, and that California . . . was destined to be the vine land of the world."

Husmann wrote three books on viticulture whose titles mirrored his changing perspective: *The Cultivation of the Native Grape* (1866); *American Grape Growing and Wine Making* (1880); and *Grape Culture and Wine-Making in California* (1888). The second book is an informative text on grape culture throughout the country; it describes vinifera as reserved for California and only native grapes as suitable for all other regions. An enlarged edition (c1883) of this manual marks his move to Napa, with its appendix of sixty-six pages devoted to the details of grape culture and wine making in California.

HUSMANN, George. American grape growing and wine making. With contributions from well-known grape growers, giving a wide range of experience. New York: Orange Judd, 1880. 242p. Illus. G24680

> Numerous subsequent editions, including 1881; 310p. in 1883; 1885; 269p. in 1888; 1892; 1896; 1906. Also published in 1912, 1915 and 1919.

_____. The cultivation of the native grape and manufacture of American wines. New York: Woodward, 1866. 192p. Illus. G24690

> The spine reads: *Grapes and Wine* and the book is often quoted under that title. Subsequent editions published including 1868 and 1870. The fourth edition, published in 1896, contains several added chapters on the grape industries of California.

_____. An essay on the culture of the grape in the great west . . . Hermann, MO: Printed by C.W. Kielmann, 1863. 43p. Illus. G24695

_____. Grape culture and wine making in California. A practical manual for the grape-grower and wine-maker. San Francisco: Payot, Upham, 1888. 380p. Illus. G24700

_____. Illustrated descriptive catalogue of western and southern . . . grape vines . . . Columbia, MO: c1879. 72p. Illus. G24704

_____. The present and future of the California wine interest. c1886. 6p. G24708

HUSMANN, George Charles Frederick (1861-1939). Currant-grape growing: a promising new industry. Washington: Gov't. Print. Off., 1920. 16p. G24600

_____. Grape districts and varieties in the United States. Washington: Gov't. Print. Off., 1932. 33p. Illus. G24610

_____. Grape investigations in the vinifera regions of the United States with reference to resistant stocks, direct producers, and viniferas. Washington: Gov't. Print. Off., 1910. 86p. G24620

_____. Grape propagation, pruning and training. Washington: Gov't. Print. Off., 1911. 29p. Illus. G24630

> Subsequent editions in 1917, 1922 and 1932.

_____. Grape, raisin, and wine production in the U.S. USDA Yearbook, 1902. G24640

> Eleven photographic illustrations add interesting graphics to the information. Husmann is listed here as expert in viticultural investigations, Bureau of Plant Industry.

_____. Muscadine grapes. Washington: Gov't. Print. Off., 1916. 28p. Illus. G24643

_____. The present condition of grape culture in California. USDA Yearbook, 1898. G24650

Includes a retrospective look at California's grape industry.

_____. Testing grape varieties in the vinifera regions of the United States. Washington: Gov't. Print. Off., 1915. 157p. G24658

_____. Testing vinifera grape varieties grafted on phylloxera resistant rootstocks in California. Washington: United States Dept. of Agriculture, 1939. 64p. Illus. G24665

_____. Testing phylloxera-resistant grape stocks in the vinifera regions of the United States. Washington, DC: Gov't. Print. Off., 1930. 54p. G24660

HUSMANN, George Charles Frederick and DEARING, Charles. The muscadine grapes. Washington: Gov't. Print. Off., 1913. 64p. G24710

HUSMANN, George Charles and SNYDER, Elmer. Testing vinifera grape varieties grafted on phylloxera-resistant rootstocks in California. Washington: Gov't. Print. Off., 1939. 64p. G24720

HUTCHINSON, Claude B. California agriculture. Berkeley: University of California Press, 1946. 444p. G24730

Contains sections on the development of the grape industry.

HUTCHINSON, Peggy. Peggy Hutchinson's do's and dont's of wine making. London: W. Foulsham, 1959. 120p. G24740

_____. Peggy Hutchinson's home-made sparkling wine secrets. London: W. Foulsham, 1957. 128p. G24750

_____. Peggy Hutchinson's home-made wine secrets. London and Philadelphia: W. Foulsham, c1943. 124p. G24760

Several subsequent editions.

_____. More Peggy Hutchinson's home-made wine secrets. London and New York: W. Foulsham, c1959. 127p. G24770

_____. Tonic wine-making secrets. London: W. Foulsham, 1960. 94p. G24780

HUTCHINSON, Peggy and WOODMAN, Mary. Homemade wines: how to make them. Liverpool: W. Foulsham, 1970. 96p. Illus. G24790

HUTCHINSON, Ralph B. The California wine industry. 2 vols. Los Angeles: University of California, 1969. G24800

_____. A method for evaluating the economic impact of the grape planting of 1969-1973 on the California wine industry. 1974. G24810

HUTCHINSON, Ralph B. and BLUMMER, Sydney. The Williamson Act and wine growing in the Napa Valley. Pomona, CA: California State Polytechnic College, 1970. 23p. G24820

HUTCHINSON, William G., ed. Songs of the vine with a medley for malt-
worms. London: A.H. Bullen, 1904. 344p. G24830

> This first-rate collection of poetry about wine and ale and drink-
> ing-in-general includes poems by William Blake, A.E. Housman,
> John Masefield, Robert Herrick, John Keats, William Shakespeare,
> and many other famous English writers. The collection ranges
> from the 12th to the late 19th centuries and is testimony to the
> allure that drink, especially wine, has had for English literature.
> Many are impassioned paeans to the vine; some are cleverly hu-
> morous. A few, such as Herrick's "Ode to Ben Johnson" and Keats'
> "Lines on the Mermaid Tavern," are well-known from poetry an-
> thologies, but others are gems we would know little of had they not
> been given another life by Mr. Hutchinson.

HUTTON, Isaac G. The vigneron; an essay on the culture of the grape and the
making of wine. Washington: By the Author, 1827. 60p. G24840

> Hutton was a member of the New York State Society for the Pro-
> motion of Agriculture and the Arts. In the appendix Hutton ac-
> knowledges John Adlum's contributions to "planting and managing
> a vineyard," and includes seven pages of extracts from *The To-
> pography of all the Known Vineyards.*

HYAMS, Edward. Dionysus: a social history of the wine vine. New York: Macmillan, 1965. 381p. Illus. G24850

> This is the history of the grapevine, Vitis vinifera, from its pre-
> historic origins in western Asia to its conquest of the world with
> the planting of vines in the Southern hemisphere in the last cen-
> tury. The book includes a survey of American wines from colonial
> times through the 1860's and contains 128 illustrations with eight
> in color. Edward Hyams began growing vines in England in 1945.

_____. Grapes under cloches. London: Faber and Faber, 1951. 133p.
Illus. G24860

> Hyams describes the method of cultivating grapes under cloches in
> a manner useful to the amateur or commercial grower. The book
> includes a chapter on making wine.

_____. The grape vine in England. The history and practice of the
cultivation of vines in England, an account of their origin and introduction. London: The Bodley Head, 1949. 208p. G24870

> Thirty-five years after the publication of this book, the spirit of the
> book, i.e., that vines can be grown and good wines made in Eng-
> land, has become a reality. An important reference source for those
> interested in growing grapes in cold climates. Illustrated with
> photographs and drawings.

_____. Vin; the wine country of France. London: Newnes, 1959. 208p.
Illus. G24880

_____. The wine country of France. New York: Lippincott, 1960. 208p.
Illus. G24890

HYAMS, Edward, ed. Vineyards in England; a practical handbook for the restoration of vine cultivation and wine making to Southern Britain. London: Faber and Faber, 1953. 229p. Illus. G24900

HYATT, Thomas Hart. Hyatt's handbook of grape culture; or, why, where, when, and how to plant and cultivate a vineyard, manufacture wine . . . especially adapted to California . . . also the United States, generally. San Francisco: H.H. Bancroft, 1867. 279p. Illus. G24910

> This is the first book on wine that bears a California imprint. Similar to the books then published in the East, it is a general viticultural manual which includes a discussion of wine making and a description of recommended grape varieties. Hyatt emphasizes California viticulture and the European grapes, but he indicates that native grapes, grown in California, have their "ascidity of taste very much toned down by our genial climate and friendly soil."

> The book also contains an interesting description of operations at the Buena Vista Vinicultural Society at Sonoma, founded by Haraszthy. Buena Vista, with over a million vines, was considered the largest vineyard in the world. Aided by Chinese labor, it claimed to produce wine at the cost of four cents per gallon. As Hyatt's words were being written, Buena Vista was on the verge of financial collapse. Haraszthy was being forced out for alleged mismanagement, and the vines were soon to be ravaged by phylloxera. Second edition published in 1876.

ILLUSTRATIONS of Napa County with historical sketch. Oakland, CA: Smith and Elliott, 1878. 28p. Illus. G24920

> Facsimile edition published by Valley Publishers, Fresno, in 1974. Folio.

The IMPOSTORS detected, or the vintners' triumph over B-e and H-r. A farce occasioned by a case lately offered to the members of the H-se of C-ns by the said B-ke and H-r London: 1712. G24930

> Unable to verify.

IN praise of claret. London: Wine Trade Club, 1926. G24940

> This booklet was issued by the Education Committee of the Wine Trade Club and was widely circulated throughout England and Scotland. It is made up of extracts from the publications of André L. Simon, W.J. Todd and H. Warner Allen.

IN Vino Veritas, or a conference betwixt Chip the cooper and Dash the drawer (being both boozy), discovering some secrets of the wine-brewing trade. London: Printed for J. Nutt, 1696. 35p. G24950

IN Vino Veritas, or secrets of the wine trade discovered. London: 1628. G24960

> Unable to verify.

The INNKEEPER, and public brewer; containing hints for managing spirits and wines . . . by a practical man. London: G. Biggs, n.d. 152p. G24970

INSTITUTO Do Vinho Do Porto. Toast your friends in port. Oporto: n.d. 29p. G24980

INTERNATIONAL Congress of Viticulture. Official report. San Francisco: Dettner Printing, 1915. 324p. G24990

INTERNATIONAL First Symposium on Wine and Health, Univ. of Chicago, 1968. Wine and health proceedings. Pacific Coast Pub. by Wine Advisory Board, 1969. G25000

The IRON gate of Jack and Charlie's "21". New York: Jack Kriendler Memorial Foundation, 1950. 220p. Illus. G25010

> "Thru which is presented a vivid portrayal of a unique institution — by a distinguished group of authors, artists and celebrities."

ITALIAN Swiss Colony, growers and producers of choice California wines. San Francisco: c1911. 32p. Illus. G25025

ITALIAN Swiss Agricultural Colony, producers of fine wines and brandies. Dry wine vineyards, Asti, Sonoma County, California. Sweet wine vineyards, Madera, Madera County, California. San Francisco: 1898. 30p. Illus. G25020

JACK and Charlie's "Twenty-One" wine list. New York: 21 Club, 1954. 72p. Illus. G25030

> Limited edition of 1,000 copies.

JACK, Florence B. Homebrewed wines and beers including cordials and syrups. Milwaukee: Casper, 1934. 56p. G25040

_____. One hundred drinks and cups. London: Country Life, 1927. 52p. G25050

_____. One hundred home-brewed wines including cordials, beers and syrups. London: Country Life, 1927. 56p. G25060

> Several subsequent editions.

JACKISCH, Philip. Modern Winemaking. Ithaca, NY: Cornell University Press, 1985. 288p. Illus. G25065

JACKSON, Agnes. Fruit and wine farming in South Africa. London: Oxford University Press, 1958. 32p. G25070

JACKSON, David and SCHUSTER, Danny. Grape growing and wine making: a handbook for cool climates. Martinsborough, New Zealand: Alister Taylor, 1981. 194p. Illus. G25080

> Covers geographical distribution of the grape, grape growing and winemaking. Descriptions of cultivation and winemaking techniques are augmented by eighteen pages of color photographs of grape varieties, various black and white photographs, diagrams, illustrations, and tables and appendices containing analytical methods used by wine makers from the time of harvest to bottling. Also published by Altarinda Books of Orinda, CA in 1981.

JACKSON, George H., M.D. The medical value of French brandy. Montreal: By the Author, 1928. 315p. Illus. G25090

Covers far more material than its title suggests. Dr. Jackson spent seventeen years in Charente. During that time he studied the making of cognac from the planting of the vineyards to blending, bottling and shipping. The first four chapters cover potable spirits, a history of the cognac area, the soil of the Charente vineyards, the species of vines, various vine diseases and the vintage. The next four chapters deal with the aging of cognac, its chemical composition and the different methods used to detect quality, age and frauds. The last three chapters should interest the physician because they deal with the physiologic and therapeutic value of cognac.

JACKSON, Henry. An essay on bread . . . to which is added an appendix; explaining the vile practices committed in adulterating wines, cider, porter, punch, vinegars and pickles. London: J. Wilkie, 1758. 55p. G25100

_____. An essay on British isinglass intersperced with hints for further improvement of malting, brewing, fermenting . . . London: J. Newbury, 1765. 94p. G25110

JACKSON, Joseph Henry and HART, James D. The vine in early California. San Francisco: Book Club of California, 1955. Illus. G25120

Consists of thirteen folders. The first has the table of contents for the series and the text of a letter written in 1866 by J. Ross Browne to Congressman James A. Garfield about California wines. The other twelve folders each contain a reproduction of an early vinous item and cover eleven vineyards and other subjects.

JACKSON, Michael. Michael Jackson's pocket wine book. London: Mitchell Beazley, 1979. G25130

JACOB, Harry Ernest. Grape growing in California. Revised by A.J. Winkler. Berkeley: Circular No. 116, University of California, 1950. 80p. Illus. G25140

JACQUELIN, Louis and POULAIN, Rene. The wines and vineyards of France. London: Hamlyn, 1962. 416p. Illus. G25150

Revised edition published in 1965.

JAGENDORF, M.A. Folk wines, cordials, and brandies. Ways to make them, together with some lore, reminiscences, and wise advice for enjoying them. New York: Vanguard Press, 1963. 414p. Illus. G25160

Folk wines are wines made from fruits, flowers, vegetables, cereals, herbs, berries and other combinations. Brandies, liqueurs and cordials are made from many of the same flowers, fruits, etc. Before giving the reader the various recipes, the author tells us about the aesthetics of winemaking, what is needed to make wine and even the bottling procedures. The author covers seventy-three wines and thirty-two brandies, cordials and liqueurs plus a number of exotic drinks.

The book is illustrated with prints taken from a variety of sources. Subjects include the Spanish way of drinking wine from leather bottles, by Gustave Doré, and George Washington's wine cooler.

JAMES, Margery Kirkbride. Studies in the medieval English wine trade. Oxford: Clarendon Press, 1971. 232p. Illus. G25170

JAMES, Marquis and JAMES, Bessie R. Biography of a bank: the story of the Bank of America. New York: Harper and Brothers, 1954. 521p. G25180

> Includes a history of the bank's involvement with the California wine industry.

JAMES, W. Bosville. Wine duties considered financially and socially: being a reply to Sir James Emerson Tennent on *Wine, its taxation and uses* . . . London: Longman, 1855. 195p. G25190

WALTER JAMES

Walter James abandoned journalism to become a winemaker. When his winery burned down, he turned his attention to writing about wine and life. His books are filled with personal anecdotes and philosophy.

JAMES, Walter. Antipasto. Melbourne: Georgian House, 1957. 100p. Illus. G25210

> A potpourri of the author's thoughts on wine, food and literature.

_____. Ants in the honey. Melbourne: Hawthorn Press, 1972. 76p. G25220

> More thoughts on wine and life.

_____. The bedside book of Australian wine. An Australian winemaker's diary. Adelaide: Rigby, 1974. 199p. Illus. G25230

_____. Barrel and book: a winemaker's diary. Melbourne: Georgian House, 1949. 109p. Illus. G25240

> The author's first book about his experiences as a winemaker.

_____. The fear of wine. Sydney: The Wine and Food Society of N.S.W., 1954. 22p. Illus. G25250

> The 1953 J.K.Walker Lecture to the Wine and Food Society of New South Wales. Limited edition of 500 copies.

_____. The gadding vine. Melbourne: Georgian House, 1955. 118p. Illus. G25260

> Reflections on life, wine and literature.

_____. The 1971 Wynn Winegrowers diary and cellar notebook. Australia: Wynn Winegrowers, 1971. G25270

_____. Nuts on wine. 2nd ed. Melbourne: Georgian House, 1952. 85p. Illus. G25280

_____. What's what about wine: an Australian wine primer. Melbourne: Georgian House, 1953. 45p. Illus. G25290

_____. Wine; a brief encyclopedia. New York: Knopf, 1960. 208p. Illus. G25300

_____. Wine in Australia; a handbook. Melbourne: Georgian House, 1952. 168p. Illus. G25310

A general survey of the Australian wine scene, in dictionary form. Several subsequent editions.

_____. A word book of wine. London: Phoenix House, 1959. 208p. Illus. G25320

_____. Winegrowers diary. Melbourne: Lothian Publishing, 1969. Illus. G25330

JAMIESON, Ian. The Simon and Schuster pocket guide to German wines. New York: Simon and Schuster, 1984. 144p. G25335

JANSEN, Chris. Winelands of the Cape. Cape Town, South Africa: Don Nelson, 1980. 113p. Illus. G25340

  111 beautiful color photographs of the vineyards and the people.

THOMAS JEFFERSON (1743-1826)

Historians have thoroughly studied the life of Thomas Jefferson and yet have largely failed to acknowledge one of his principal loves - wine. Dumas Malone spent decades detailing in six volumes the life of Thomas Jefferson but mentions his involvement with wine only four times. Fortunately, this neglect by historians did not prevent history from recording Thomas Jefferson as one of the greatest wine connoisseurs of the 18th century.

Jefferson's interest in wine developed early. When he built Monticello, he designed a wine cellar and a double dumbwaiter to transport wine from the cellar to each side of the dining room fireplace. In these early years he also met Phillip Mazzei, who had been banished from Italy for his revolutionary activities and hoped to begin a new life growing grapes and making wine in Virginia. Jefferson quickly deeded 474 acres adjacent to Monticello to Mazzei, and to raise funds, Mazzei sold shares to Virginia's landed gentry. The original subscribers included such promiment colonials as George Washington, George Mason, Governor Earl Dunmore, Peyton Randolph, Thomas Adams, John Park Custis (Washington's stepson) and Jefferson. Unfortunately, the vineyard they hoped would turn the Virginia land into another Médoc was never to be. War intervened, and Mazzei was sent to France on a secret mission by the Virginia Assembly. Before leaving, he rented his estate, Colle, to the interned German General, Reidesel, whose horses, according to Jefferson, "in one week destroyed the whole labor of three or four years."

When the war ended a new life began. Jefferson was appointed by Congress to serve as Minister to France. He left from Boston on July 5, 1784, with his oldest daughter, Martha, and four dozen bottles of hock (a white Rhine wine).

Within two weeks of his arrival in Paris, Jefferson purchased 276 bottles of wine, largely Bordeaux. When Jefferson met with his fellow ministers, Benjamin Franklin and John Adams, at Franklin's Villa in Passy, a Paris suburb, he discovered that Franklin had acquired a wine cellar of over 1,200 bottles. Most of Franklin's bordeaux wines had been selected by John Bondfield, the American Consul in Bordeaux, and Bondfield served Jefferson in the same capacity. Within less than a year of Jefferson's arrival, Adams had become minister to the Court of Great Britain and Franklin had gone home at his own request, leaving Jefferson the sole minister.

Jefferson (bored with ministerial duties that seemed to consist of "the receipt of whale oils, salted fish and salted meats on favorite terms; the admission of our rice on equal terms with that of Piedmont,

Egypt and the Levant; a mitigation of the monopolies of our tobacco")
decided to learn firsthand about the wines he loved.

His tasting notes from this trip are of value to contemporary wine
drinkers for they constitute the first detailed modern account of wine
in English and cover many of the wines still drunk today.

He left Paris on February 28, 1787, for Burgundy (not Champagne
as Jefferson recorded) where he remained for a few days - the beginning of an education about the region's wines that would continue for
the rest of his life. He thought Chambertin the best of the reds, followed by Clos de Vougeot and Vosne because they were the "strongest
and will bear transporation and keeping." He considered Volnay's flavor the equal of Chambertin, but gave it fourth rating because it was
lighter in body and lacked the longevity of its more celebrated northern neighbors. The best white wine of Meursault, he thought, came
from the vineyards of Goutte d'Or (drop of gold), at one-eighth the cost
of Montrachet. It, and Volnay, remained two of his favorite table wines
during his two and half remaining years in France.

The land grew richer as the road turned southward to Beaujolais -
"the richest country I ever beheld." As he traveled, he ordered wines
for his home in Paris, to be stored in his cellar for dinners with the
aristocrats and intellectuals of Parisian society.

The wines of Cote Rotie, he thought, had "a quality which keeps
well, bears transportation and cannot be drunk under four years. . . ."
He felt that Chateau Grillet, now the smallest vineyard in France with
its own Appellation Controlee, was in a class of its own.

In his "Hints on European Travel," he recommends Hermitage and
the panoramic view from the hill where it's produced: "On the hill
impending over this village [Tain] is made the wine called hermitage
so justly celebrated. Go up to the top of the hill, for the sake of the
sublime prospect from thence. . . ." Jefferson became so fond of white
Hermitage that he considered it and champagne the best white wines
of France.

Leaving Tain, Jefferson's journey next took him through Orange.
Surprisingly, he doesn't comment on the red wines of the Southern
Rhone, famous today for Chateauneuf-du-Pape. The wine was well
known in England and America at least ten years before his visit. As
he traveled from Nimes to Aix-en-Provence, he saw a countryside covered with vines. In the sea at the mouth of the Rhone, he bathed a
hard-to-heal wrist, injured in Paris. "The man who shoots himself in
the climate of Aix must be a bloody-minded fellow indeed. I am now in
the land of corn, wine, oil and sunshine. What more can man ask of
heaven? If I should happen to die at Paris, I will beg of you to send me
here, and have me exposed to the sun. I am sure it will bring me to
life again. . . ."

Rice, not wine, drew him to Italy, for as he traveled he searched for
products suitable for transplanting to American soil. He crossed the
Maritime Alps on muleback through picturesque mountain villages.
Crossing the Po by boat, he arrived in Turin and began sampling the
predecessor of today's nebbiolo grape, which is used to make Italy's
great Barolos, Barbarescos, Gattinaras and Ghemmes. He found the
wines as "sweet as silky madeira, as astringent on the palate as bordeaux and as brisk as champagne."

Before leaving for France, he arranged with Poggio, a muleteer, to
smuggle a sack of rough rice to him in Genoa "it being death to export
it in that form." He spent several days clambering across the Apenaine
mountain precipices on his return trip. In Avignon, he discovered a
white wine he rated the equal of montrachet and sauternes - vin blanc
de Rochegude. He ordered a quantity for his Paris home, and two
years later shared his find with President Washington, describing it as
one of France's best wines. Unfortunately, the red wines produced
there today bear no resemblance to the white that he liked so well.

Other popular white wines in his day were frontignan and vin Muscat de Lunel, which was consumed so rapidly, Jefferson noted, that it was impossible to buy aged bottles.

Entering Bordeaux country, he passed through Sauternes, "where the best white wines of Bordeaux are made." His selection of Bordeaux's best wine-producing localities included Médoc, famed for its reds; Graves and Sauternes, both for their whites. Although his trip through Bordeaux took place sixty-eight years before the 1855 classification of the vineyards, he correctly categorized four vineyards of "first quality: Margaux, Latour, Lafite and Haut-Brion." Three-quarters of a century before the French classification, Jefferson had chosen Chateau d'Yquem the best Sauternes.

Jefferson left Bordeaux without mentioning the respected wines of St. Émilion or Pomerol, and continued to Touraine.

On his return to Paris, Jefferson began ordering wine from the vineyard owners and merchants. One, M. Parent, whom he had met in Beaune, supplied him with over a thousand bottles of burgundy during the next two years.

A year later, with a comprehensive background on France's viticulture locked in his encyclopedic mind, Jefferson traveled down the Rhine to learn more about German wines. Although he didn't visit the Moselle, he was advised the best moselle was made near Koblenz on the mountain of Brownberg. He rated Wehlen second; Graach and Piesport third; Zelting fourth and Bernkastel fifth.

He felt that it was "only from Rudesheim to Hochheim that wines of the very first quality are made, and even in this canton, it is only hochheim, johannesberg and rudesheim that are considered as of the very first quality." The German reds Jefferson dismissed as "absolutely worthless."

Hurrying home to Paris, he stopped in the sun-drenched city of Épernay, in Champagne. He classified Épernay's white wines as mousseux (sparkling) and non-mousseux (still). Today, virtually all champagne is sparkling, but in the 18th century, many connoisseurs, including Jefferson, preferred the non-sparkling variety. Jefferson also disagrees with the contemporary taste for blanc de blanc champagne, preferring champagne made of pinot noir. He also preferred it aged rather than young, as the current trend dictates.

After five years in France and with two years of his appointment remaining, he asked for a six-month leave of absence to return to America for personal reasons - leaving everything behind except his daughter, thirty-eight trunks and hampers including thirty-eight bottles of meursault, sixty bottles of sauternes, thirty-six bottles of montrachet, thirty-six bottles of champagne, sixty bottles of rochegude and fifty-eight bottles of frontignan.

Jefferson's return to France was aborted when Washington notified him of his appointment as Secretary of State. In this office, Jefferson soon began guiding the Chief Executive through the perilous waters of foreign affairs and, in addition, the ordering of French wines. Through him, Washington was drinking the wines of Chateau d'Yquem, Chateau Calon-Segur and the best frontignan and champagne before his first term was over.

The roads leading to the raw, new capital [Washington], were dirt when Thomas Jefferson became President in 1801. The federal city, a noble concept on paper, was in reality a forest encircling about fifteen boarding houses grouped around the still unfinished Capitol building. The boarding houses had as their residents a transient society, for virtually none of the members of Congress had bought homes in Washington. They spent only the winter months there when Congress was in session.

No sidewalks or lamps interrupted the darkness along the few roads in Washington. Houses were so isolated that numbers weren't necessary; instead, they were identified as "near the President's house, west of the war office, opposite the treasury" or whatever. There were no hotels, restaurants or coffee houses. For public entertainment, the residents had their choice of a race track or theatre that was "astonishingly dirty and void of decoration."

The camping-out quality of the makeshift city was reinforced by the executive mansion. Although over $300,000 had been spent, the structure was unfinished, not only in frame but in furnishings. Irish architect James Hoban, who designed the mansion, complained that workmen had left out the upper story and "built no cellars which President Jefferson, after experiencing great losses in wines, had been obliged to add at a depth of sixteen feet underground. . . ."

Monticello's overseer, Edmund Bacon, on a visit to the White House, recalls the social demands made on President Jefferson: "He was perfectly tired out with company. He had a very long dining room, and his table was chock-full every one of the sixteen days I was there. There were Congressmen, foreigners and all sorts of people to dine with him. He dines at four o'clock and they generally sat and talked until night. . . ."

John Quincy Adams, who dined with President Jefferson on more than one occasion, once remarked "as usual the talk turned to wine." The wines served were the best. Among clarets, Jefferson's favorites included Chateau d'Yquem; Chambertin among burgundies; white Hermitage, Champagne and Frontignan.

Two Presidential terms later, Jefferson returned to Monticello as a private citizen. Instead of the hectic pace of "turning the White House into a general tavern," his daily discipline began with correspondence in the morning, riding among his farms and visiting plantation shops and gardening until dusk. "From dinner to dark," he wrote to a friend, "I give to society and recreation with my neighbors and friends; and from candlelight to early bedtime I read, my health is perfect and my strength considerably reinforced by the activity of the course I pursue. . . ."

His wine tastes were changing to lesser-known wines, particularly from southern France. His choices included casked wines from Rousillan and Muscat de Rivesaltes; from Italy, Chianti, Poncina, Artiminio and Montepulciano. His obvious favorites were all reds: Claret de Bergasses from Languedoc or Provence, Limoux and Ledenon. He remained remarkably active during the seventeen years of his retirement - including beginning a home brewery and corresponding with John Adlum, the father of American viticulture, about Adlum's efforts to cultivate native grapes. Jefferson felt that old age was depriving him of the sensual enjoyment of life and its pleasures. He wrote to Abigail Adams in 1817, one year before he founded the University of Virginia: "To see what we have seen, to taste the tasted, and at each return, less tasteful; o'er our palates to decant, another vintage." On July 4, 1826, the fiftieth anniversary of the United States, Thomas Jefferson died.

JEFFERSON, Thomas. As sweet as Madeira . . . as astringent as Bordeaux . . . as brisk as champagne: Thomas Jefferson on wines, facsimile of a document. A collection of Herbert R. Strauss with an introduction by Lawrence W. Towner. Chicago: Privately printed, 1965. 6p. G25360

> During his wine tour of France, Jefferson stayed three days at the Hotel de York in Nice. Through a Parisian friend, Abbé Arnaud, Jefferson was introduced to a local wine merchant, Monsieur de Sasserno. At Sasserno's house he sampled the wines of Bellet, which is a few miles northeast of Nice. Jefferson found them "remarkably good."

He felt differently when, after retirement, he tasted one of the 300 bottles of the same wine ordered from Sasserno's son. Its sour taste provoked a definition of Jefferson's wine standards.

"My taste for the wine of Nice, and for the particular quality of it which I drank at your father's house in Nice [1787], and which M. Spreafico sent me in 1816, will, I fear, become a troublesome circumstance to you; and chiefly perhaps because the expressions characterizing subjects of taste and flavor in one language have not always terms synonymous in another. To remove this difficulty, I will explain to you the particular terms we use to designate particularly different flavors or characters of wine. These are 1. *sweet* wines, such as Frontignan and Lunel of France, Pacharetti doux of Spain, Calcavallo of Portugal, vin du Cap, etc. 2. *acid* wines, such as the vins de Grave, du Rhin, de Hochheim, etc. 3. *dry* wines, which have not the least either of sweetness or acidity as Madere sec, Pacharetti sec, vin d'Oporto, etc. 4. *silky* wines, which are in truth a compound in their taste of the dry dashed with a little sweetishness, barely sensible to the palate. The silky Madeira we sometimes get in this country is made so by putting a small quantity of Malmsey into the dry Madeira. There is another quality which is often found in the *dry* and the *silky* wines, which quality we call *rough* or *astringent,* and the French also, I believe, call it astringent. There is something of this in all the wines of Nice which I have seen, and so much of it in those of Oporto as to approach to bitterness while it is also dry. Our vocabulary of wines being thus explained, I will observe that the wine of Bellet sent to me by Mr. Spreafico in 1816 was *silky* and a little *astringent,* and was the most delicious wine I ever tasted, and the most esteemed here generally. That of 1817 was *dry,* a little *astringent,* and an excellent wine. That of 1818, last received, has its usual astringency indeed, but is a little acid; so much acid so as to destroy its usual good flavor. Had it come in the summer, I should have suspected its having acquired its acidity by fretting in the hold of the ship, or in our hot warehouses, on a summer passage. But it was shipped at Marseille in October, the true time for shipping delicate wines for this country. With these explanations of the meaning of our terms, I will now pray you, Sir, to send me through Mr. Cathalan, 150 bottles of the wine of Bellet of the *silky* quality sent me in 1816 by Mr. Spreafico, if to be had; and if that was of an accidental recolte [vintage] not always to be had, then send it of the *dry* quality, such as was sent me in 1817."

JEFFS, Julian. The dictionary of world wines, liqueurs and other drinks. Toronto: Pagurian Press, 1973. 144p. Illus. G25370

—————. Little dictionary of drink. London: Pelham, 1973. 144p. G25380

—————. Sherry. London: Faber and Faber, 1961. 268p. Illus. G25390
Subsequent editions published in 1970 and 1978.

—————. Wine and food of Portugal and Madeira. London: Wine and Food Society, 1965. 30p. Illus. G25400

_____. The wines of Europe. London: Faber and Faber, 1971. 524p. G25410

JENKINS, D.H. Vines for every garden. Garden City, NY: Doubleday, 1937. 95p. G25420

JESSOP, George H. Judge Lynch: a romance of the California vineyards. Chicago: Belford, Clarke, 1889. 232p. G25440

A novel with a California wine industry setting.

JEWETT, Edward H. The two-wine theory. "Communion wine". New York: E. Steiger, 1888. 176p. G25450

JOBE, Joseph, ed. The great book of wine. Cleveland: World Publishing, 1970. 437p. Illus. G25460

Originally published in Switzerland in 1969 by Edita Lausanne. Translated by Michael and Angela Kelly and Peter Dewhirst. Subsequent American editions were published by Galahad Books, New York and Chartwell Books. This is one of the best illustrated of all major wine books with many color reproductions and original full cover maps by Robert Flack. It contains a full index of 7,500 different wines from thirty-four nations. The text contributions are mainly by European experts and suffer from the translation.

Later Galahad editions, not dated, are much poorer in quality than the earlier ones and omit some of the text and illustrations.

JOHNSON, Frank. Professional wine reference. New York: Beverage Media, 1977. 354p. Illus. G25470

A beginner's encyclopedia written as a reference source for those in the wine trade. Over 830 alphabetically arranged entries with phonetic pronunciations. An appendix is devoted to wine service and care. Subsequent editions.

JOHNSON, George William and ERRINGTON, Robert. The grape vine; its culture, uses and history. London: R. Baldwin, 1847. Illus. G25480

Subsequent edition published in 1853 by Bohn of London.

JOHNSON, Grove. Practical studies for the wine-maker, brewer and distiller. Perth: Imperial Printing, 1939. 91p. G25490

JOHNSON, Harry J. Eat, drink, be merry and live longer. 4th ed. Garden City, NY: Doubleday, 1968. 243p. G25500

HUGH JOHNSON (1939)

Hugh Johnson is acknowledged to be one of the very best writers on the non-technical aspects of wine. He achieved this literary pinnacle at an early age. Shortly after graduating from King's College, Cambridge University, he became the second secretary (replacing André Simon) of the Wine and Food Society and the editor of the *Wine and Food Society Journal*. In 1966, at the age of twenty-seven, he wrote his first book, *Wine*, an instant best seller. This was followed five years later by his remarkable treatise, *The World Atlas of Wine*. A full-time writer, Johnson writes in a style that reveals in subtle imagery his love for wine.

"For me, wine is all pleasure, which is doubled by my having opportunities to write about it. One really looks for words to describe it, because it is a true experience."

Mr. Johnson was awarded, in 1982, *Wines and Vines* "Perpetual Trophy for Excellence in Wine Writing."

JOHNSON, Hugh. The best of vineyards is the cellar. London: Hedges and Butler, 1965. 36p. Illus. G25520

> This book was written for Hedges and Butler, wine merchants. The first part of six pages details the history of Hedges and Butler. The second part of twelve pages is titled "Lunching and Dining in London" and gives Mr. Johnson's opinions on a variety of London's better-known restaurants. The book is interestingly illustrated with eighteen full-page drawings by England's well-known wine artist, Charles Mozley.

_____. Hugh Johnson's modern encyclopedia of wine. New York: Simon and Schuster, 1983. G25530

See *Hugh Johnson's Wine Companion.*

_____. Hugh Johnson's wine companion. The new encyclopedia of wine, vineyards and winemakers. London: Mitchell Beazley, 1983. 544p. Illus. G25540

> Documents some 40,000 of the world's wines and lists 7,000 winemakers in thirty countries. The U.S. section covers California, the Pacific-Northwest, New York State, New England, the Mid-West, Mid-Atlantic and Southwest. A valuable reference. Published by Simon and Schuster under the title *Hugh Johnson's Modern Encyclopedia of Wine.*

_____. Pocket encyclopedia of wine. London: Mitchell Beazley and: Simon and Schuster, 1977. 144p. Illus. G25550

> Sized for a vest pocket but packed full of wine information. Rates the wines by vineyard and vintage, etc. Published annually. The 1985 edition was the eighth edition, revised and enlarged. The British edition is published by Mitchell Beazley. It is the world's best selling wine book with more than 1,700,000 copies in print.

_____. Wine. London: Thomas Nelson and New York: Simon and Schuster, 1966. 264p. Illus. G25560

> This was Mr. Johnson's first wine book. In addition to covering most of the world's wine areas, the book contains a history of winemaking, an explanation of wine labels, notes on the nomenclature of wines, advice on which wines to serve with various foods and descriptions of numerous personal wine experiences. Many subsequent editions.

_____. The world atlas of wine. A complete guide to the wines and spirits of the world. London: Mitchell Beazley and New York: Simon and Schuster, 1971. 272p. Illus. G25570

> This is the book that every wine writer wishes he had written and is the second best-selling wine book ever published, with over one

million copies sold. The entire book was designed by the author: the proportions of space, the graphics, the more than 300 illustrations, the idea of having labels (over 900 in color), the 154 superbly accurate maps by Harold Fullard, cartographer, and, of course, 80,000 words of text that cover the history of wine, its geography, how and where it is made, etc. An essential reference. Numerous subsequent editions.

JOHNSON, Hugh, ed. The Pan book of wine (articles selected from House and Garden). Rev. ed. London: Pan Books, 1964. 176p. G25580

JOHNSON, Samuel. Indulgence in wine. St. Catharines, ONT: Modern Publications, 1966. 21p. G25590

Reprint of original London edition of 1825.

JOHNSON, Stephen William. Rural economy: containing a treatise . . . as recommended by the Board of Agriculture in Great Britain . . . on the culture of the vine; and on turnpike roads. New Brunswick, NJ: Printed by W. Elliot for I. Riley, 1806. 246p. Illus. G25600

JONAS, Peter. The distiller's guide, comprehending the whole art of distillation and rectification . . . 2nd ed. London: Printed for Sherwood, Neely, and Jones, 1816. 292p. G25610

Third edition, 1818.

_____. Distiller's, wine and brandy merchant's vade mecum. Hull: By the Author, 1808. G25620 Subsequent editions.

_____. A key to the distillery . . . Also the art of making British wines from fruits, flowers and herbs . . . London: By the Author, 1813. 292p. G25635

_____. The theory and practice of gauging. New ed. by W. Tate. London: Sherwood, Neely and Jones, 1823. 392p. G25640

JONES, Idwal. Chef's holiday. New York: Longmans, Green, 1952. 210p. Illus. G25650

An interesting account of a Parisian restaurant owner on a holiday with a companion who owns a circus. Contains more about food than wine, but wine plays a part.

_____. Don Luis de Aliso. Westways, 1948. Illus. G25660

Recounts the settling of Jean Louis Vignes, from Bordeaux, as a cooper in Los Angeles in 1829 or 1831, and his establishment of the vineyard at El Aliso.

_____. High bonnett. New York: Prentice-Hall, 1945. 184p. G25670

A novel.

_____. Vermilion. New York: Prentice-Hall, 1947. 495p. G25680

_____. Vines in the sun. A journey through the California vineyards. New York: William Morrow, 1949. 253p. Illus. G25690

An account of pioneer wine days in California with anecdotes, character sketches and descriptions of scenes and places.

_____. The vineyard. New York: Duell, Sloan and Pearce, 1942. 279p. G25700

>A novel.

JONES, R. Page. Wines of the generals. New York: Harcourt Brace, 1978. 284p. G25720

>A novel that contains much about wine.

JONES, Robert. The imbibers guide to wine pronunciation. Forest Grove, OR: Hydra Book Co., 78p. G25730

JORDAN, Joseph V. Simple facts about wines, spirits, liqueurs . . . Los Angeles: Los Angeles School of Bartending, 1937. 90p. G25750

JORDAN, Rudolf, Jr. Quality in dry wines through adequate fermentations . . . A manual for progressive winemakers in California. San Francisco: Pernau Publishing, 1911. 146p. Illus. G25760

>This manual was privately published in San Francisco for "progressive winemakers in California." Jordan's father had been a pioneer Napa winegrower whose vineyard is now the site of the Christian Brother's Novitiate of Mont La Salle. Jordan's book, *Quality in Dry Wines through Adequate Fermentations,* in contrast to Rixford's, is thoroughly Californian. Its inspiration was the scientific studies on wine making by Professor Frederic T. Bioletti and others at the University of California, to which the author added the results of his own work conducted at Castle Rock Vineyard in Napa. Jordan advocated a "new style" of California wine, one which was light, dry and fruity, produced by controlled, low-temperature fermentation and by the use of carefully selected, pure yeast strains. This style anticipates the trend in white wine currently being produced in California.

JORGENSEN, Alfred Peter Carlslund. Micro-organisms and fermentation. 7th English ed. Revised by Albert Hansen. London: Griffin, 1948. 550p. Illus. G25770

_____. Practical management of pure yeast. The application and examination of brewery, distillery and wine yeast. 3rd ed. Revised by Albert Hansen. London: Griffin, 1936. 111p. G25780

JOSKE, Prue and HOFFMAN, Louise. Wineries of Western Australia. Sydney: Second Back Row Press, 1979. 138p. Illus. G25790

JOSLYN, Maynard A. A technologist views the California wine industry. 1974. 151p. G25795

>See California Wine Oral History Series.

JOSLYN, Maynard Alexander and AMERINE, Maynard A. Commercial production of brandies. Berkeley: University of California, 1941. 80p. Illus. G25800

_____. Commercial production of dessert wines. Berkeley: University of California, 1941. 186p. G25810

_____. Dessert, appetizer and related flavored wines; the technology of their production. Berkeley: University of California Press, 1964. 483p. Illus. G25820

JOSLYN, Maynard Alexander and CRUESS, William Vere. Elements of wine making. Berkeley: University of California, College of Agriculture, 1934. 64p. G25840

_____. Laboratory examination of wines and other fermented fruit products. New York: Avi Publishing, 1934. G25850

JUDGING home-made wine and beer. A handbook for the guidance of judges. 4th ed. Andover, England: Amateur Winemakers National Guild, 1971. 37p. G25860

JULLIEN, André. The topography of all the known vineyards; containing a description of the kind and quality of their products and a classification. Translated from the French and abridged so as to form a manual and guide to all importers and purchasers in the choice of wines. London: Printed for G. and W.B. Whittaker, 1824. 264p. G25870

> Jullien (1766-1832) was a wholesale wine-merchant in Paris who regularly visited the principal wine-producing districts of France. According to André Simon, "he obtained a vast amount of practical knowledge about the vineyards he visited, the different species of vines he saw and the different wines he tasted, and he made it a practice to write down everything that interested him; later on in life he undertook to visit most of the vine-growing districts of Europe, and even passed into Asia. In 1816, he published in Paris a book entitled *Topographie de tous les Vignobles Connus,* which is of the highest interest because most of the information it contains is absolutely original." This English translation is not complete, but is the only one published.

_____. Wine merchant's companion and butler's manual containing the best information on the selection and management of French wine. From the French. London: W. Anderson, 1825. 107p. G25880

JUNIPER, William (pseud). The law of drinking. San Francisco: Herbert and Peter Fahey, 1935. 27p. G25890

_____. The true drunkard's delight. London: Unicorn Press, 1933. 375p. G25900

> The title is misleading. The contents are a Bacchic medley of songs, poems and philosophies from Shakespeare, Leigh Hunt, the 18th century dramatists and poets and other literary sources. The book contains interesting and obscure material involving obvious research and a wide knowledge of literature.

K.,G.A. Clarets and sauternes; classed growths of the Médoc and other famous red and white wines of the Gironde. London: The Wine and Spirit Trade Record, 1920. 398p. Illus. G25910

K.,T.D. Know the drink: wine. Leeds: Educ. Prod., 1968. G25920

KAFKA, Barbara. American food and California wine. New York: Chalmers, 1981. 84p. Illus. G25930

KAISER Stuhl story. Adelaide: Barossa Co-operative Winery, 1974. Unpaged. G25940

KAPPELER, George J. Modern American drinks. Akron: Sealfield, 1907. G25950

KARN, C. Armagnac, Beaune, Bordeaux . . . London: Golden Cockerel Press, 1938. Unpaged. G25960

WILLIAM I. KAUFMAN

Mr. Kaufman has written over 100 books. His 1971 series of books of children's poems, songs, prayers, legends and stories, done for UNICEF, won the Christopher award. He has also had many one-man exhibitions of his photographs.

KAUFMAN, William I. California wine drink book, cocktails, coolers, punches and hot drinks made with wine. San Francisco: The Wine Appreciation Guild, 1982. 128p. G25980

_____. Champagne. New York: Viking Press, 1973. 212p. Illus. G25990

One would not read this book to learn how the vine is cultivated and champagne made because these subjects are treated relatively briefly. This book is about the "spirit" of champagne. It is above all an art book, and its folio size enhances the magnificent photographs, many the author's own, which capture the beauty and antiquity of champagne. In addition, many old posters, drawings and paintings pertaining to champagne have been reproduced. The book is a beautiful example of the art book "in-action;" for if one wants to get the essence of champagne and its province, he could do no better than peruse this book, preferably with a glass of champagne.

_____. Encyclopedia of American Wine including Mexico and Canada. New York: Jeremy P. Tarcher, 1984. 640p. Illus. G25995

Provides the names of 844 wineries, 1,016 vineyards, 8,834 award winning wines and hundreds of definitions, historical facts and biographies.

_____. Pocket encyclopedia of American wineries east of the Rockies. Watkins Glen, NY: Association of American Vintners, 1984. 128p. G25995

_____. The traveler's guide to the vineyards of North America. New York: Penguin, 1980. 203p. G26000

Includes names of persons to contact, phone numbers, visiting hours, schedules of tours and tastings along with recommendations for local restaurants, hotels and points of interest.

_____. The whole-world wine catalog. New York: Penguin, 1978. 224p. Illus. G26010

_____. William I. Kaufman's pocket encyclopedia of California wine, 1981. San Francisco: Wine Appreciation Guild, 1980. 131p. Illus. G26020

_____. Wine and cheese tasting party. California: Buzza Book, 1971. 26p. Illus. G26030

KAY, Billy and McLEAN, Cailean. Knee deep in claret. London: Mainstream Publishing, 1983. Illus. G26040

> Covers the history of the development of the wine trade in Britain, particularly in Scotland, from the earliest times to present. The book's title is taken from a Robert Burns poem.

KEANE, Eve. The Penfold story. Sydney: Oswald L. Ziegler, c1951. 78p. Illus. G26050

KEECH, J. The grape grower's guide, a plain and practical work upon the management of the grape vine. Waterloo, NY: By the Author, 1869. 15p. Illus. G26060

KEENE, James B. A handbook of practical gauging with instructions in the use of Sykes's hydrometer. 5th ed. London: Pitman, 1883. 106p. G26070

KEIR, Ursula. The vintage. London: Collins and New York: Sloane, 1953. 255p. G26080

> A novel set in Beaujolais.

KELLER, Gayle. Vintagewise. St. Helena, CA: Vintage Image, 1980. 205p. Illus. G26090

ALEXANDER CHARLES KELLY (1811-1877)

Alexander Charles Kelly was born in Leith, Scotland, and received his doctorate in medicine from the University of Edinburgh. For reasons of health, Kelly emigrated to South Australia in March, 1840, and began medical practice at Port Adelaide. Three years later he purchased eighty acres south of Adelaide and planted a vineyard. Although not a rich man, his medical practice became secondary to that of vigneron.

In 1861 Kelly published *The Vine in Australia,* and its popularity quickly ran to a second printing of 1,000 copies in 1862. In November, 1862, Kelly and five prominent Adelaide businessmen formed the Tintara Vineyard Company. Kelly became the manager of the project at a salary of 200 pounds and he devoted full time to the business. In June, 1866, he reported sixty acres under vines. In 1867 he published *Wine-Growing in Australia* and along with *The Vine in Australia* they were considered the best works then available. The eventual failure of the Tintara Vineyard Company in 1873 was not because of the production of wines but the difficulty of selling them. In 1876 Tintara Vineyards was bought by Thomas Hardy and Sons. Dr. Kelly retired in 1876 and died one year later.

KELLY, Alexander Charles. The vine in Australia. Melbourne: Sands, Kenny, 1861. 215p. Illus. G26110

> A handbook on how to plant vineyards and make wines. Climate, soil and choice of grape varieties are discussed and instructions are provided for pruning and other aspects of vineyard management.

The chapters on fermentation give an insight into oenological thinking before information became available on the role of yeasts in fermentation and bacteria in spoilage. Rare.

_____. Wine-growing in Australia, and the teaching of modern writers on vine-culture and wine-making. Adelaide: E.S. Wigg, 1867. 234p.

G26120 Primarily a critical discussion of grapes and practices in France, especially Bordeaux. Rare.

_____. Winegrowing in Australia/The vine in Australia. 2 Vols. Sydney: The David Ell Press, 262/265p. Illus. G26130

Facsimile editions - numbered and limited to 1,000 copies.

KELLY, C.B. The grape in Ontario. Toronto: Ontario Department of Agriculture, 1944. 38p. Illus. G26140

KELLY'S directory of the wine, spirit, brewing and tobacco trades, 1926. 13th ed. London: Kelly's Directories, 1926. G26150

This directory, like its predecessors, deals with the alcoholic beverage and tobacco trades of England, Scotland, Wales, Ireland, the Channel Islands and the Isle of Man. It names 5,000 wine and spirits merchants and 13,000 grocers and chemists who deal in wine and spirits.

KENCH, John, HAND, Phyllis and HUGHES, David. The complete book of South African wine. Cape Town: Struik Publishers, 1983. 352p. Illus. G26160

This book is illustrated with over 700 color photographs, maps, wine labels and diagrams. The detail of the text allows this book to live up to its title, making it a significant reference for South African wines. Includes hundreds of tasting notes by David Hughes, the director of the Nederburg Wine Auction.

KENDERMANN, Hermann. Kendermann export price list. Germany: Hermann Kendermann, 1981. 90p. Illus. G26170

Color photographs of wine labels, cellars, estates, grapes, scenery, etc. with information on all the major German growers and shippers.

KENTISH, Thomas. The gauger's guide and measurer's manual. London: Dring and Page, 1861. 346p. G26180

KERCHT, J.S. Improved practical culture of the vine especially in regular vineyards. Translated from the 5th ed. Sydney: W. Baker, 1843. 44p. G26190

KERR, Norman Shanks. Unfermented wine a fact: A review of the latest attempts to show that the existence of unfermented wine among the ancients was impossible . . . Liverpool: Argus Printing and Stationary, 1878. 21p. G26200

_____. Wines, scriptural and ecclesiastical. London: National Temperance Publication, 1881. 173p. G26210

Second edition published in 1887.

KEW, Kenneth W. A search for rarities: my trip through Europe's vineyards. San Francisco: c1963. 19p. Illus. G26220

KHAYYAM, Omar. The rubaiyat of Omar Khayyam. Translated by Edward Fitzgerald. See Fitzgerald, Edward.

KILBY, Kenneth. The cooper and his trade. London: John Baker, 1971. 192p. Illus. G26240

> Once integral to the storage and transportation of wine and other products, the craft of coopering is a dying trade. Fortunately, this book will help preserve the skills and heritage of the cooper. The book is divided into two parts. The first part, "The life of the craftsman," is autobiographical but also describes the tools and techniques of the trade. The second part deals with the social history of coopering from earliest times to present. The text is well illustrated with fifty-six pages of black and white photographs and eighty-six drawings. Second edition of 192p. published in 1977.

_____. The village cooper. Shire Publications, 1977. G26250

KING, James. Historical summary of the proceedings and reports of the Hunter River Vineyard Association from its organization to its first annual meeting in the year 1853. Sydney: 1854. G26270

KING, James. Australia may be an extensive wine growing country. Edinburgh: 1857. 16p. G26260

KIRK, Alexander. Grape culture up-to-date. London: Simpkin, Marshall, Hamilton, Kent, 1909. 75p. Illus. G26280

KIRK, H.B and Co. Wines and wine drinkers of today. Wynkoop: Hallenback, 1885. G26290

> Unable to verify.

KIRTON, John William. A glass of foreign wine. London: By the Author, c1880. G26300

> Interesting discussion on claret, port and sherry.

_____. Intoxicating drinks, their history and mystery. London: Ward, Lock, 1879. 144p. G26310

KIRWAN, Andrew Valentine. Host and guest. A book about dinners, dinner-giving, wines, and desserts. London: Bell and Daldy, 1864. 410p. G26320

KITCHINER, Dr. Wm. The art of invigorating and prolonging life, by food, clothes, air, exercise, wine, sleep . . . London: 1824. 341p. Illus. G26330

KLERK, W.A. de. The white wines of South Africa. Cape Town: Balkema, 1967. 110p. Illus. G26340

KNIGHT, Richard Payne. An analytical inquiry into the principles of taste. 2nd ed. London: T. Payne and J. White, 1805. 470p. G26350

KNITTEL, John. Cyprus wine from my cellar. London: John Long, 1933. 288p. G26360

KNOWLTON, J.M. Our hardy grapes. New York: Coutant and Baker, 1863. 96p. G26370

KNOX, Graham. Estate wines of South Africa. Cape Town: David Philip, 1979. Illus. G26380

> Second edition of 240p. published by Creda Press in 1982.

KNOX, J. Wine and beer making made easy. London: Coles, 1974. 88p. G26390

KNOX, Oliver. Croft, a journey of confidence. London: Collins, 1978. 40p. Illus. G26400

> A history of Croft's first 300 years in the port trade. Eight color plates.

KO-OPERATIEVE WINJNBOUWERS VERENIGING (KWV)

> KWV is a South African co-operative winegrowers association representing the interests of some 5,700 wine growers. It is directed by a board of twelve directors elected from eight constituencies, with two directors from the constituencies of Paarl, Stellenbosch, Worcester and Robertson, and one director from Malmesbury, Montagu, Olifants River and Orange River. The co-operative was founded in 1918 by Dr. C.W.H. Kohler and today has over 1,000 employees.

KO-OPERATIEVE WINJNBOUWERS VERENIGING. Brandy. Paarl: KWV, 26p. G26420

_____. Brandy and Liqueurs. Paarl: KWV, c1982. 23p. Illus. G26430

_____. Cultivars. Paarl: KWV, c1982. 23p. Illus. G26440

_____. Co-operative winegrowers' association. Paarl: KWV, c1982. 24p. Illus. G26450

_____. Entertaining with wines of the Cape: choosing, cellaring, serving, cooking, recipes. 3rd ed. Rev. and enlarged. Suider-Paarl: KWV, 1968. Illus. G26460

_____. Fortified wines. Paarl: KWV, c1982. 23p. Illus. G26470

_____. A handbook on wine for retail licensees. Paarl: KWV, c1956. 78p. Illus. G26480

_____. The history of S.A. wine. Paarl: KWV, c1982. 24p. Illus. G26490

_____. Planning a wine and cheese party. Cape Town: ABC Press, 1967. 16p. G26500

_____. Red wines. Paarl: KWV, c1982. 23p. Illus. G26510

_____. South African sherry. Suider-Paarl: KWV, 10p. G26520

_____. The South African wine industry. Its growth and development. Suider-Paarl: KWV, n.d. 34p. G26530

_____. South African wines of origin. Cape Town: KWV, c1974. 30p. G26540

_____. A survey of wine growing in South Africa. Suider-Paarl: KWV G26550

> Published annually since 1956.

_____. A survey of wine growing in South Africa; 1967-68. Paarl: K.W.V., c1968. 52p. Illus. G26560

_____. White wines. Paarl: KWV, c1982. 23p. Illus. G26570

_____. Wine tasters notebook. Suider-Paarl: KWV, 32p. G26580

_____. The wine grower in South Africa. Suider-Paarl: KWV, 1961. 40p. G26590

_____. Wine guide. Paarl: KWV, c1982. 28p. Illus. G26600

_____. Wine and good health. Paarl: KWV, c1982. 23p. Illus. G26610

_____. Wine in the home. Paarl: KWV, c1982. 27p. Illus. G26620

_____. The history of South African wine. Paarl: KWV, 24p. G26630

KOEBEL, W.H. Madeira: old and new. London: Francis Griffiths, 1909. 216p. Illus. G26640

> Contains a chapter on the wines of Madeira which covers the history of the grape; the vicissitudes of the industry; local customs; the estuffas and transport of the wines.

KOENEN, Anton J. From vineyard to table. A practical wine-growers account of the making of hocks and moselles. London: By the Author, 1930. 33p. Illus. G26660

KOHLER, Charles William Henry. The memoirs of Kohler of the K.W.V. London and New York: Hurst and Blackett, 1946. 128p. G26670

> Charles Kohler was the founder of Ko-operatieve Winjnbouwers Vereniging (KWV). His success as a gold prospector in the Johannesburg gold rush was brought to an abrupt end when his health broke. On the advice of several physicians, he left the Rand and bought a 140-acre farm on the Berg River. "At this time (1890) a devastating depression had settled like a black cloud on the Western Province. . . . The wine farmers, in particular, were facing disaster, for the price of wine had droppped to a desperately low level and that pernicious insect Phylloxera had destroyed tens of thousands of vines. . . ." The book details Kohler's success as a winemaker and leader in the South African wine industry.

KOHNLECHNER, Manfred. Healing wines. Autumn Press, 1981. 153p. Illus. G26680

KOKEN, John Marshall, ed. Here's to it; toasts for all occasions from all over the world. New York: Barnes, 1960. 146p. G26690

KONNERTH, W. Michael. Beginners book of wine making. Presque Isle Wine Cellars, 1977. G26700

KORNFELD, Anita Clay. Vintage. New York: Simon and Schuster, 1980. 599p. G26710

A novel with a California wine industry setting.

KORSHIN, Nathaniel. Better wines for less money. New York: 1974. 263p. G26720

Guide to the wines of Europe, U.S., Israel, and Australia.

KRAFFT, Michael. The American distiller, or, the theory and practice of distilling, according to the latest discoveries and improvements, including the most improved methods of constructing stills, and of rectification. Philadelphia: For Thomas Dobson, 1804. 219p. Illus. G26730

KRAUSE, Steven. Wine from the wilds. Harrisburg, PA: Stackpole Books, 1982. 191p. Illus. G26740

KRESSMAN, Edouard. Wonder of wine. New York: Hastings House, 1968. 227p. Illus. G26750

KRICKAUFF, Freidrich E.H.W. The future of our wine industry and the results of manuring vineyards in Europe and Australia. Adelaide: Basedow, Eimer, 1899. 36p. Illus. G26760

KURTH, Heinz. Winemaking at home. London: Batsford, 1983. 80p. Illus. G26770

KYNGDON, F.B. Wine-culture in New South Wales. Sydney: Agriculture Department, New South Wales, 1899. 14p. G26780

L., A.G. Correspondence regarding "fortification" of Bordeaux and Burgundy wines before and after importation into the United Kingdom. London: 1914. 18p. G26790

Consists of an interesting exchange of letters between a London wine merchant designated "A.G.L." and goverment agencies between May 5, 1913 and March 21, 1914. A.G.L. is attempting to alert the authorities of the illegal fortification of burgundy and bordeaux wines. In one letter A.G.L. asserts: "I . . . invite your attention to the fact that it is universally acknowledged that practically the whole of the Burgundy and Bordeaux wine, sold in this country (including Chateau wines) are adulterated with alcohol or other spirit added either before or after importation." All of the various agencies blame some other agency with responsibility and, in the end, A.G.L.'s efforts to have the situation corrected are effectively avoided through bureaucratic maneuvers.

LA-VOGUE, Bruno [pseud]. The art and secrets in the manufacture of wines and liqueurs according to ancient and modern international methods - requiring no machinery. New York: La-Vogue Publishing, c1934. 63p. G26800

The LABEL: wine's identity card. Paris: Comité National des Vins de France, c1967. 28p. Illus. G26810

LACOUR, Pierre. The manufacture of liquors, wines and cordials without the aid of distillation . . . New York: Dick and Fitzgerald, 1853. 3l2p. G26820

The author provides recipes for the manufacture of imitation sherry, port, madeira, claret, red wine, white wine, champagne, malaga, and even cheaper versions of these wines. Another book that provides information on how to make "wine without grapes." Several later editions.

LADY's companion; or, an infallible guide to the fair sex . . . Also rules and receipts for making all the choicest cordials for the closet: brewing beers, ales, and making all sorts of English wines . . . 2nd ed. London: Printed for T. Read, 1740. 684p. Illus. G26830

LAFFER, Henry E. The wine industry of Australia. Adelaide: Australian Wine Board, 1949. 136p. Illus. G26840

Summary of the industry before modern expansion took place.

LAFKAS, Nicholas. The story of wine. San Francisco: California Academy of Sciences, 1961. 25p. G26850

LAKE Roland Garden Club. Wine and dine with the Lake Roland Garden Club. Ruxton, MD: 1935. 236p. Illus. G26860

LAKE, E.R. The grape in Oregon. Corvallis: Oregon Agricultural Printing Office, 1901. 84p. G26870

LAKE, Max Emory. Cabernet - notes of an Australian wineman. Adelaide: Rigby, 1977. 64p. Illus. G26880

Max Lake is a Sydney surgeon who loves wine. He operates a winery in the Hunter Valley which he named Lake's Folly. The cabernet sauvignon, he tells us, "is a difficult child but a splendiferous adult." Preface by Maynard A. Amerine.

_____. Classic wines of Australia. Melbourne: Jacaranda Press, 1966. 134p. Illus. G26890

_____. Hunter wine. Brisbane: Jacaranda Press, 1965. 94p. Illus. G26900

A second edition was published in 1974.

_____. Hunter winemakers: their canvas and art. Melbourne: Jacaranda Press, 1970. 188p. Illus. G26910

_____. The flavour of wine: a qualitative approach for the serious wine taster. Brisbane: Jacaranda Press, 1969. 60p. Illus. G26920

_____. Vine and scalpel. Brisbane: Jacaranda Press, 1967. 72p. Illus. G26930

The role of medical men in the early wine industry.

LAKE, Max and DUNSTAN, David. The winery walkabout seminar. 1981. 6p. G26940

LAMB, Douglas L. Guide to Bordeaux wines and cognac. Sydney: J. Sands, 1948. 34p. Illus. G26950

_____. Notes on Hocks and Moselles. Sydney: J. Sands, 1950. G26960

LAMB, Richard and MITTELBERGER, Ernest G. In celebration of wine and life. New York: Drake Publishers, 1974. 255p. Illus. G26970

The book's aim is to acquaint the reader with the origin, customs and traditions of wine as recorded throughout history. Contains interesting prints from the Wine Museum of San Francisco. A second edition was published in 1980.

LaMONTAGNE'S, Sons, E. The wines of Bordeaux. New York: E. LaMontagne's Sons, 1911. 53p. Illus. G26980

LAMSHED, Maxwell Robert. The house of Seppelt, 1851-1951. Being an historical record of the life and times of the Seppelt family through four generations. Adelaide: Advertiser Printing, 1951. 51p. Illus. G26990

LANDFIELD, Jerome. California: America's vineyard. San Francisco: Verdier Cellars, 1945. 36p. Illus. G27000

_____. Cellar chats in the Verdier Cellars. San Francisco: Verdier Cellars, 1950. 44p. G27010

LANGENBACH, Alfred. German wines and vines. London: Vista Books, 1962. 190p. G27020

_____. The wines of Germany. London: Harper, 1951. 180p. Illus. G27030

When first published, this was the most authoritative work on German wines in English, and it probably remains so on the subject of German wines that pre-date the reclassification of 1971.

LANGFORD, T. Plain and full instructions to raise all sorts of fruit trees that prosper in England. With the best directions for making liquors of several sorts of fruits. London: Printed by J.M. for R. Chiswel, 1681. 148p. G27050

Second edition, 1696 and third edition, 1699, both of 220p.

LANSDELL, J. Grapes and how to grow them: a handbook. London: Collingridge, 1907. 122p. Illus. G27060

Subsequent editions, including one of 114p. in 1919 and a revised and modernized edition of 144p., with an altered title, in 1946.

LANSDOWN, Charles William Henry. The South African liquor law. A treatise upon the laws controlling and regulating intoxicating liquor in the Union of South Africa, including, as amended to 1948, the Liquor Act 30 of 1928; the liquor proclamations of the Transkeian Territories; the wine, spirits and vinegar acts; the wine and spirits control acts; and the excise liquor control laws. 3rd ed. Cape Town: Juta, 1948. 656p. G27070

LANZA, Horace O. and BACCIGALUPPI, Harry. California grape products and other wine enterprises. 1971. 150p. Illus. G27075

See California Wine Oral History Series.

LASZKIEWICZ, Olga T.M. Wine and viticulture; a classified list of books in the Public Library of South Australia. Adelaide: Public Library of South Australia, 1967. 69p. G27080

_____. Wine and viticulture; a classified list of material held in the reference services branch of the State Library of South Australia. Adelaide: State Public Library of South Australia, 1977. 176p. G27090

An important scientific reference source, especially for those interested in academic papers covering technical wine subjects, e.g., "Influence of yeast strain, pH, and temperature on degradation of fumeric acid in grape juice fermentations," etc. Contains over 1,500 entries.

LATIMER, Patricia. California wineries: Sonoma and Mendocino Counties. Vol. 2. St. Helena, CA: Vintage Image, 1976. 191p. Illus. G27100

Limited edition of 2,000 copies signed by Sebastian Titus, artist. For Vol 1 see Topolos, Michael.

LATIMER, Patricia and KENLY, Deborah and TOPOLOS, Michael. Sonoma and Mendocino wine tour. St. Helena, CA: Vintage Image, 1977. Illus. G27110

LAUGHRIDGE, Jamie. Rising star: Domaine Chandon; a decade of sparkle. New York: Hopkinson and Blake, 1983. Illus. G27120

LAUMER, William F., Jr. About wines. Some curiosities, odds and ends, facts and fancies. St. Petersburg, FL: National Rating Bureau, 1962. 154p. G27130

LAUNAY, Andre. Caviare and after. London: MacDonald, 1964. 160p. Illus. G27140

_____. Eat, drink and be sorry. M. and J. Hobbs, 1970. G27150

Unable to verify.

_____. The merrydown book of country wines. London: New English Library, 1968. 118p. G27160

LAVER, James. Victorian vista. London: Hulton Press, 1955. 256p. G27170

LAW, Ernest. King Henry VIII's newe wyne seller at Hampton Court. Historically described. London: G. Bell, 1927. 29p. Illus. G27180

LAWRENCE, R. de Treville, Sr., ed. Jefferson and wine. The Plains, VA: Vinifera Wine Growers Association, 1976. 192p. Illus. G27190

A collection of papers, by numerous contributors, on Jefferson's interest in viticulture and wine.

LAXER, Bernard H. Bern's Steak House wine book. 36th ed. Tampa: Bern's Steak House Restaurant, 1976. 2,435p. Illus. G27200

Three volumes in one. Volume 1 has 990 pages on French wines. Volume II consists of 510 pages and covers "Wines from Around the World." Volume III, "Domestic Wines," contains 935 pages. Each volume contains descriptions of the wines and wine areas, phonetic pronunciations and photographs of the vineyards, chateaux, winemakers and wine labels. The *Wine Book* was first issued in 1960. Bern's claims to have the world's largest wine cellar with 5,400 different wines available.

THOMAS LAYTON (1910)

Thomas Layton has spent his life with wine. He was editor of *Wine Magazine* from 1958 through 1960, president of the *Circle of Wine Tasters* and a successful London wine merchant and restaurant owner. Michael Broadbent, a director and head of Christie's Wine Department, got his first job under the tutelage of Mr. Layton and has acknowledged that he "learned more about wine and the wine trade in those stimulating twelve months than during any other comparable period since." Mr. Layton still lists wine and traveling in Spain as his principal recreations.

LAYTON, Thomas. Choose your wine. London: Duckworth, 1940. 168p. G27220

> Information on the selection of wines from the merchant's point of view.

_____. Cognac and other brandies. London: Harper Trade Journals, 1968. 153p. Illus. G27230

_____. Dining 'round London. London: Transatlantic Arts, 1945. 57p. G27240

_____. Five to a feast. London: Duckworth, 1948. 219p. G27250

> Mainly autobiographical notes, but containing a list of classical wines and comments on wine and food in England during the war.

_____. Modern wines. London: Heinemann, 1964. 190p. G27260

_____. Restaurant roundabout. London: Duckworth, 1944. 252p. G27270

_____. Table for two. London: Duckworth, 1943. 232p. G27280

On his career as a wine merchant and restaurant proprietor.

_____. Wine's my line. London: Duckworth, 1955. 256p. Illus. G27290

_____. Winecraft. The encyclopedia of wines and spirits. London: Harper, 1961. 285p. G27300

> A second edition of 312p. was published in 1974.

_____. Wines and castles of Spain. London: Michael Joseph and New York: Taplinger Publishing, 1959. 246p. G27310

> An entertaining account of Mr. Layton's 6,000-mile trip through Spain, covering its wines, wine districts, winemakers, chateaux, monuments, museums, roads and history. A revised edition was published in 1971 by White Library.

_____. Wines and chateaux of the Loire. London: Cassell, 1967. 225p. Illus. G27320

_____. Wines and places of Alsace. London: Cassell, 1970. 209p. G27330

_____. Wines of Italy. London: Harper Trade Journals, 1961. 221p. Illus. G27340

_____. A year at the Peacock. London: Cassell, 1964. 216p. Illus. G2735

> An account of the author's experiences as the owner of a country pub.

LE BROCQ, Phil. A description with notes of certain methods of planting, training, and managing all kinds of fruit trees, vines . . . London: 1786. 43p. G27360

LE POSTE, Pierre. Vin rude, an alcoholic alphabet. London: Macmillan, 1980. Illus. G27370

LEBEGUE, J.L.P. and Co. The French wine trade, an appreciation of the present situation in Bordeaux and Burgundy. London: January, 1957, 12p.; January, 1958, 8p.; January, 1959, 8p.; January, 1960, 20p. G27380

LEE, Susan. Inexpensive wine; a guide to best buys. New York: Quadrangle, 1974. 182p. Illus. G27390

Subsequent editions.

LEE, William and FENTON, Samuel. The use of brandy and salt as a remedy for various internal as well as external diseases. 4th rev. ed. New York: 1844. 40p. G27400

LEEDOM, William S. The vintage wine book. New York: Vintage Books, 1963. 264p. Illus. G27410

LEENAERS, R. The Mitchell Beazley atlas of German wines. London: Mitchell Beazley, 1980. 306p. Illus. G27420

The LEGEND of liqueurs, wines and spirits. What to serve, when to serve, how to serve it. 4th ed. Lincoln: Ginrum Alpha Co. and Chicago: Reilley and Lee, c1938. 229p. G27430

LEGGETT, Herbert B. Early history of wine production in California. San Francisco: Wine Institute, 1941. 126p. G27440

LEGRAND, N.E. Champagne. 2nd ed. Reims: 1899. G27450

Unable to verify.

LEIPOLDT, C. Louis. 300 years of Cape wine. Cape Town: Stewart, 1952. 230p. G27470

_____. 300 years of Cape wine. Tafelberg, South Africa: 1974. 218p. Illus. G27480

Facsimile edition of the original text with additional photographs and a biography of the author.

LEMBECK, Harriet, ed. Grossman's complete guide to wines and spirits. 7th ed. rev. New York: Scribners, 1983. 638p. Illus. G27490

When Mr. Grossman died in 1967, Mrs. Lembeck undertook the job of keeping *Grossman's Guide* current. The latest edition gives comprehensive and detailed information on all types of alcoholic beverages. She was also responsible for the sixth edition published in 1977. The *Guide* has sold over 250,000 copies.

Mrs. Lembeck is a director of the Society of Wine Educators, a director of the New York City Wine and Food Society, vice-chairman of the New York Wine Writer's Circle, a wine lecturer, writer, judge and consultant. She was awarded the 1983 *Wines and Vines* "Perpetual Trophy for Excellence in Wine Writing." The only other recipients of this award are Leon D. Adams, Frank Prial, Hugh Johnson and Gerald Asher.

LEMERY, L. Treatise of all sorts of foods, both animal and vegetable: also of drinkables, giving an account how to choose the best sort of all kinds, and of the good and bad effects they produce. Translated by D. Hay, M.D. London: T. Osborne, 1745. 372p. G27500

> Includes a discussion of wine, its qualities and effects, the changes it undergoes in fermentation and how to make it. It advises that "wine moderately drank, fortifies the stomach, helps digestion, increases the spirits, heats the imagination, helps the memory, gives vigor to the blood, and works by urine."

LESKO, Leonard. King Tut's wine cellar. Berkeley: By the Author, 1977. 46p. Illus. G27510

LESLIE, Francis C. From port to port. Reminiscences, 1896-1946. Glasgow: National Guardian Publishing, 1946. 24p. Illus. G27520

> Recounts the author's fifty years in the port trade.

LESTER, Mary. Hand me that corkscrew Bacchus. Minnesota: Piper, 1973. 157p. G27530

A LETTER from a member of Parliament to his friends in the country, concerning the duties on wine and tobacco . . . London: T. Cooper, 1733. 36p. G27540

> Sometimes attributed to Robert Walpole.

LETTERS on wine. [Translated from the French by Ingersoll Lockwood]. London: 1865. 47p. G27550

LEVERETT, B. Winemaking month by month. London: Prism Press, 1979. 112p. G27560

LEVETT, Jack. Making wines at home. London: W. and G. Foyle, 1957. 87p. G27570

> Reprinted in 1958, 1962 and 1963.

LEVI, Leone. Consumption of spirits, beer and wine, in its relation to licences, drunkenness and crime: a report to M.T. Bass. London: Ridgway, 1872. 14p. G27580

LEVINSON, Harry A., comp. A resume of the great Herr Schraemli collection of books and manuscripts relating to cookery, gastronomy, wine, drink and related subjects. Beverly Hills, CA: n.d. [49]p. Illus. G27590

LEVY, Hermann. Drink. An economic and social study. London: Routledge and Kegan Paul, 1951. 256p. G27600

LEWIS, Robert A. The wines of Madeira. Herts, England: Shire Publications, 1968. 40p. Illus. G27610

ALEXIS LICHINE (1913)

Born in Moscow, Lichine spent his youth in Paris and came to the United States in his late teens. He eventually entered the wine business with the late Frank Schoonmaker. During the Second World War, he became the protocol aide-de-camp for General Eisenhower and is alleged to have liberated many a great bottle of wine on behalf of General Eisenhower and his staff. In the 1950's, he formed a group of investors and purchased Chateau Cantenac Prieure (later renamed Chateau Prieure-Lichine), and Chateau Lascombes. In 1955 he founded Alexis Lichine and Co., a wine shipping and exporting company. Known for his indefatigable energy and talented palate, Mr. Lichine over the past thirty years has done more to promote wine drinking in the United States than any other individual. He remains an outspoken critic of the 1855 classification of Bordeaux wines.

LICHINE, Alexis. Alexis Lichine's encyclopedia of wines and spirits. New York: Knopf, 1967. 713p. G27630

> An essential reference. It has sold over 250,000 copies and has been issued in many editions, the latest of which was published in 1981.

_____. Guide to the wines and vineyards of France. New York: Knopf and London: Weidenfeld and Nicholson, 1979. 449p. G27640

> This is a totally revised version of Lichine's popular *Wines of France*. It covers all the wine regions in France and lists hotels and restaurants for each region. A book for reference and to take along when traveling through the French wine country.

_____. Wines of France. In collaboration with William E. Massee. New York: Knopf, 1951. 364p. Illus. G27650

> Many subsequent editions.

LIEBLING, Abbott Joseph. Between meals. New York: Simon and Schuster, 1962. 191p. G27660

LIGHTBODY, James. Every man his own gauger: wherein not only the artist is shown a more ready and exact method of gauging than any hitherto extant. But the most ignorant, who can but read English, and tell seventy in figures, is taught to find the contents of any sort of cask or vessel, either full, or in part full; and to know if they be right sized . . . London: c1687. 72p. G27670

_____. Every man his own gauger . . . [with] the true art of brewing beer . . . [and] the vintner's art of fining . . . [and] the compleat cofeeman. 1695. 115p. G27680

LIMA, Jose Joaquim da Costa. A few words about port. Institute Do Vinho Do Porto, 1956. 31p. Illus. G27690

_____. Port wine. Portugal: n.p., 1938. G17600

LINDEMANN, E.H. The practical guide and receipt book for distillers, winegrowers, druggists, manufacturers of wines, liquors, cordials . . . San Francisco: M. Weiss, 1875. 41p. Illus. G27710

LINDEMANN, Richard Henry Ferdinand. Viticulture and wine economic and social life in the thirteenth-century. Valais: By the Author, 1975. G27720

> Unable to verify.

LINDEN, Keith. Making wine at home. Sydney: Angus and Robertson, 1973. 94p. Illus. G27730

LINDSEY, William. Red wine of Roussilion. Boston: Houghton Mifflin, 1915. 174p. G27740

LIQUOR Publications, Inc. 1946 red book. Encyclopedic directory of the alcoholic beverages industries. New York: Liquor Publications, 1946. 588p. Illus. G27750

> Lists wineries, brands, etc. and includes regulations, statistics, distributors, production methods, dictionary. Published annually.

LITTLEWOOD, Joan. Milady vine: the autobiography of Philippe de Rothschild. London: Jonathon Cape, 1984 and New York: Crown, 1984. 272p. Illus. G27760

LITTLEWOOD, Joan and PENNING-ROWSELL, Edmund. Mouton - Baronne Philippe. London: Christie's Wine Publications, 1981. 60p. Illus. G27770

LIVINGSTONE-LEARMONTH, John and MASTER, Melvyn C.H. The wines of the Rhone. London: Faber and Faber, 1978. 235p. Illus. G27790

> Describes the main wine areas and details of grape varieties, the important producers, vintage comparisons and basic maps. A worthwhile addition to an area of wine literature that has been largely neglected. Revised edition of 392p. in 1983.

LLOYD, Frederick Charles. The art and technique of wine. London: Constable, 1936. 270p. G27800

LLOYD, Paul. Concordance among wine judges. Pomona, CA: n.p., 1955 and 1956. 31p. G27810

LOCKE, John. Observations upon the growth and culture of vines and olives; the production of silk; the preservation of fruit . . . now first printed from the original manuscript in the possession of the present Earl of Shaftesbury. London: Printed for W. Sandby, 1766. 73p. G27820

LOEB, O.W. and PRITTIE, Terence. Moselle. London: Faber and Faber, 1972. 221p. Illus. G27830

LOEB, Robert H., Jr. How to wine friends and affluent people. Chicago: Follett Publishing, 1965. 131p. Illus. G27840

LOFTUS, Lansdell J. Grapes, peaches and nectarines and melons. London: Collingridge, n.d. 144p. Illus. G27850

LOFTUS, Simon. Adnams Sole Bay Brewery 1982 wine list. Suffolk, England: Adnams and Company, 1983. 64p. Illus. G27860

> An informative and well-written account of wine districts throughout the world and current vintages, their availability and prices. Issued annually.

LOFTUS, William Robert. Loftus' legal handbook for . . . wine sellers in England: containing an abstract of all the laws . . . relating to the licenses, liabilities and privileges of those trades . . . London: 1862. G27870

_____. Loftus' wine calculator; adapted to the present rate of duty on wine . . . shewing the relative cost in bond and duty paid per pipe, butt, hogshead, quarter cask, gallon and dozen bottles . . . London: 1860. 48p. G27880

Subsequent editions of 1865 and 1877. A revised edition was published in 1885.

_____. The brewer: a familiar treatise on the art of brewing, with directions for the selection of malt and hops . . . instructions for making cider and British wines. Also, a description of the new and improved brewing saccharometer and slide rule . . . London: 1856. 192p. G27890

_____. The wine merchant: a familiar treatise on the art of making wine, with introductory remarks on ancient and modern wines . . . London: By the Author, 1865. 160p. G27900

_____. The wine and spirit merchant. A familiar treatise for practical men, on the management of wines and spirits in all their varieties, with an appendix . . . London: By the Author, c1870. 300p. Illus. G27910

> Contains illustrations of corking machines, packing and sampling tools, corkscrews, bottling tapes, funnels, bottling machines, bottle seals, paper bottle labels, etc.

LOGAN, Anne M. Wine and wine cooking. Richmond, VA: Westover Publishing, 1972. 328p. Illus. G27920

> Primarily about wine and not cooking, although it contains some interesting recipes.

LOGOZ, Michel. Wine label design. New York: Rizzoli, 1984. 160p. Illus. G27925

> This book should prove as interesting to graphic artists as to wine lovers. Of the 500 illustrations, 480 are in color, reproducing a collection of labels that range from Cold Duck to Mouton-Rothschild. The publisher, Rizzoli, is noted for the fidelity and beauty of its color reproductions.

> An essential book to the increasing group of wine label collectors. Some of the most interesting labels are on relatively unknown Swiss wines.

> As the publisher says, "A book of great seductiveness, one that will delight the eye and stimulate the palate."

LOLLI, Giorgio, M.D. Alcohol in Italian culture. Food and wine in relation to sobriety among Italians and Italian - Americans. New Haven: Yale Center of Alcohol Studies, 1958. 140p. G27930

The LONDON distiller. Compiled and set forth by the special license . . . for the sole use of the company of distillers of London . . . London: R. Bishop, 1639. 67p. G27940

> Also 1668 and 1698 editions.

LONG, Alistair. The winemakers of the Clare Valley. Melbourne: Decalon, 1978. 80p. Illus. G27950

LONG, James. Century companion to brandy and cognac. London: Century, 1983. 98p. Illus. G27960

LONG, Joseph. Description and use of the sliding rule for gauging, ullaging, valuing and reducing spirits: also directions for cask and malt gauging. London: Printed by Perry, 1836. 43p. G27970

LONGONE, Janice B. and LONGONE, Daniel T. American cookbooks and wine books, 1797-1950; being an exhibition from the collections of, and with historical notes by, Janice Bluestein Longone and Daniel T. Longone. Ann Arbor, MI: By the Authors, 1984. 68p. Illus. G27980

> Daniel Longone's chronological account of early American wine books and their authors is the most complete extant. Jan Longone is the proprietress of The Wine and Food Library and specializes in wine and cook books. Her husband, Daniel, is a professor of chemistry at the University of Michigan and collects early wine books.

LONGWORTH, Nicholas. On the cultivation of the grape and manufacture of wine. Cincinnati: Hommedieu and Co., 1846. 19p. Illus. G27990

> Printed at the order of the Cincinnati Horticultural Society as addendum to their first volume of transactions, which included their charter, constitution and by-laws, and listed among its members some of the outstanding vine growers of that era, including Robert Buchanan, Nicholas Longworth and Robert Warder. This is followed by Longworth's important work on the strawberry - *Character and Habits of the Strawberry Plant.*
>
> Nicholas Longworth (1783-1863), born in Newark, New Jersey, went west as a young man and settled in Cincinnati. Although he acquired substantial wealth as a lawyer, banker and businessman, he maintained a lifelong interest in horticulture, specializing in grapes, strawberries and blackberries. He encouraged German immigrants to settle in Ohio and grow vineyards. Longworth's own vineyards were extensive and he was the first American vineyardist to make wine on a large scale and to refine methods of making wine from the native grapes.
>
> He was one of the men to whom John Adlum sent the catawba grape variety, and he became its leading disseminator and promoter, making this grape the first widely popular American grape and Cincinnati the foremost grape-growing region of the continent. His "Sparkling Catawba" wine found a following all over the United States and was celebrated in a poem by Longfellow, who found its taste, "more dulcet, delicious and dreamy than that of Champagne."
>
> Although Longworth successfully grew native grapes, he experimented in vain for thirty years with European grapes. In *Transactions of the New York Agricultural Society, 1846,* he told of his experience: "I have tried the foreign grapes extensively for wine at great expense for many years, and have abandoned them as unfit for our climate. In the acclimation of plants I do not believe. . . . I have obtained 5,000 plants from Madeira, 10,000 from France; and one-half of them, consisting of twenty varieties of the most celebrated wine grapes from the mountains of Jura, in the extreme

northern part of France, where the vine region ends; I also obtained them from the vicinity of Paris, Bordeaux and from Germany. I went to the expense of trenching one hundred feet square on a side hill, placing a layer of stone and gravel at the bottom, with a drain to carry off the water, and to put in a compost of rich soil and sand three feet deep, and planted on it a great variety of foreign wine grapes. All failed; and not a single plant is left in my vineyards. I would advise the cultivation of native grapes alone, and the raising of new varieties from their seed."

Robert Buchanan in his book, *The Culture of the Grape and Winemaking,* paid the following tribute to Longworth: "But to Mr. Longworth, more than to any other man in the west, we are most indebted for our knowledge in grape culture. Mr. Longworth has, within the last twenty-seven years, with unwearied zeal and a liberal expenditure of money, in numerous experiments with foreign and native grapes, succeeded in enabling himself and others to present to the public, a Sparkling Catawba rivaling the best French Champagne, and a dry wine from the same grape that compares favorably with the celebrated Hock wine of the Rhine."

LOOS, Mary and DURANTY, Walter. Return to the vineyard. Garden City, NY: Doubleday, Doran, 1945. 243p. G28000

A novel.

LORD, Tony. The world guide to spirits, liqueurs, aperitifs and cocktails. London: Macdonald, 1979. 256p. Illus. G28010

The co-founder and editor of *Decanter* has produced a handsome volume on the subject of the world's spirits, including fortified wines like sherry and port. The text material is well-researched. Illustrated with color photographs of local scenes, posters, labels, old engravings, etc. A significant reference.

LOUBAT, Alphonse. The American vine dresser's guide. New York: G. and C. Carvill, 1827. 137p. G28020

The text in this and the two subsequent editions is printed in both English and French on facing pages. Loubat states he has planted two vineyards in New Jersey and Long Island of 11,000 grape vine roots from his father's extensive vineyards and nurseries in the district of Bordelais, Damazan, Clerac and Buzat (Depts. of Gironde and Lot).

_____. The American vine dresser's guide. 2nd ed. New York: G. and C. Carvill, 1829. 142p. G28030

Changes in the translation (the type was completely reset) show this as a different edition. Loubat states that his Long Island vineyard now contains thirty-five acres with 72,000 grape roots. Pages alternate in English and French.

_____. The American vine dresser's guide. New and rev. ed. New York: D. Appleton, 1872. 123p. G28040

Contains further variations in the translation, plus a frontispiece portrait. Pages alternately in English and French.

LOUBERE, Leo A. The red and white; a history of wine in France and Italy in the 19th century. Albany: State University of New York Press, 1978. 401p. Illus. G28050

Contains a wealth of information about every aspect of the wine industry of 19th century France, but is far less informative about the Italian wine industry.

LOUGHEAD, Flora Haines Apponyi. The abandoned claim. Boston: Houghton Mifflin, 1891. 330p. G28060

A novel with a California wine industry setting.

LOUW, Alison, ed. Do-it-yourself wine and beer making. London: Marshall Cavendish, 1975. 96p. Illus. G28070

Subsequent editions.

LOYD, Rev. J.F. Wine as a beverage. New York: Hitchcock and Stevens, 1874. 52p. G28080

LUCAS, Cyril. Making sparkling wine. London: Mills and Boon, 1971. 95p. Illus. G28090

SALVATORE PABLO LUCIA (1901-1984)

Dr. Lucia was for years the head of the Department of Preventive Medicine at the University of California Medical School in San Francisco. In addition to his many books he authored over 125 scientific papers.

LUCIA, Salvatore Pablo, M.D. Alcohol and civilization. New York: McGraw-Hill, 1963. 416p. G28110

_____. Dessert wine: the elixir of the grape. San Francisco: Wine Institute, 1946. 10p. G28120

_____. A history of wine as therapy. Philadelphia: Lippincott, 1963. 234p. Illus. G28130

Extensive references to literature on the medical uses of wine. A subsequent edition was published in 1967.

_____. Some notes on the wines served at the "Bonanza Inn" dinner of the Wine and Food Society. San Francisco: Wine and Food Society, 1945. 11p. G28140

_____. Wine and health; proceedings . . . held at the University of Chicago, Center for Continuing Education. Menlo Park, CA: Pacific Coast Publishers, 1969. 86p. Illus. G28150

_____. Wine and the digestive system; the effects of wine and its constituents on the organs and functions of the gastrointestinal tract, a selected annotated bibliography. San Francisco: Fortune House, 1970. 157p. G28160

_____. Wine and your well-being. New York: Popular Library, 1971. 160p. Illus. G28170

_____. Wine as food and medicine. New York: Blakiston, 1954. 149p. Illus. G28180

_____. The wine diet cookbook. New York: Abelard-Schuman, 1974. 132p. Illus. G28190

LUCIA, Salvatore Pablo, ed. Final report of the national study on the medical importance of wine. San Francisco: Wine Advisory Board, 1973. G28200

LUDOVICI, Anthony M. Man's descent from the gods or the complete case against Prohibition. London: Heinemann, 1921. 255p. G28210

LUKAS, Jan. The book of wine. Praha, Czechoslovakia: Artia, 1964. 73p. G28220

LUNDY, Desmond. Leisure winemaking. Calgary, Canada: Detselig Enterprises, 1978. 223p. Illus. G28230

LURIA, A.N. A.N. Luria wine merchants since 1892. New York: H. Wolff, c1937. 40p. G28240

LUTZ, Henry Frederick. Viticulture and brewing in the ancient Orient. New York: G.E. Stechert and Leipzig: J.C. Hinrich'ssche Buchhandlung, 1922. 166p. Illus. G28260

LYALL, Alfred. Rambles in Madeira and in Portugal in the early part of 1826. London: Rivington, 1827. 380p. Illus. G28270

LYON, Alexander Victor. Problems of the viticultural industry. Melbourne: H.J. Green, 1924. 84p. Illus. G28280

LYON, Peter. Tulips, stilts and balloons. Hertfordshire: Kit-Cat Press, 1963. Unpaged. G28290

On wine glasses.

LYONS, Nan and Ivan. Champagne blues. New York: Simon and Schuster, 1979. 304p. G28300

A novel.

MAANEN-HELMER, Elizabeth and MAANEN-HELMER, J. Van. What to do about wines. New York: Harrison Smith and Robert Haas, 1939. 184p. G28310

MABON, Mary. ABC of America's wines. New York: Knopf, 1942. 233p. Illus. G28320

Describes 350 American wines.

MacARTHUR, William. Letters on the culture of the vine, fermentation and the management of the wine cellar. Sydney: Statham and Foster, 1844. 153p. G28330

As a child, William MacArthur (1800-1882) played in his father's Camden Park vineyards in Australia. At twenty he established his own vineyard on the Nepean River and brought German vignerons to the colony to tend the vines. His achievements as a winemaker were known as far as London, where in 1841 he was given an award for his brandy. In the early 1840's, he wrote, under the pseudonym "Maro," a series of articles that appeared in Australian newspapers on viticulture and wine-making. These articles form the content for MacArthur's only book.

MacAULAY, Rose. They went to Portugal. London: Jonathan Cape, 1946. 443p. Illus. G28340

Pages 229 through 252 are on the port wine trade.

MacCOLLOM, William. Vines and how to grow them. London: The Garden Library, 1911. 315p. G28350

MacCULLOCH, John. Remarks on the art of making wine, with suggestions for the application of its principles to the improvement of domestic wines. 2nd ed. London: Longman, Hurst, Rees, Orme and Brown, 1817. 261p. G28360

The first edition was published in 1816 and later editions were published in 1821 and 1829. MacCulloch first published his *Remarks* in the *Transactions of the Caledonian Horticulture Society* in 1815.

MacDONALD, Barbara. Wine in cooking and dining. Chicago: The Institute, c1976. Illus. G28380

MacDONALD, Kenneth and THROCKMORTON, Tom. Drink thy wine with a merry heart. Ames: Iowa State University Press, 1983. 109p. Illus. G28390

MacDONALD, Lyn. Bordeaux and Aquitaine. London: Batsford, 1977. G28400

MacDOUGALL, Katrina. Winery buildings in South Australia, 1836-1936: Part I, the Barossa Region. Adelaide: Dept. of Architecture, 1980. 140p. Illus. G28410

_____. Winery buildings in South Australia, 1836-1936: Part II, the Southern Region. Adelaide: Dept. of Architecture. G28420

MacGREGOR, James. Wine making for all. London: Faber and Faber, 1966. 144p. G28430

MacHOVAC, Frank J. Making wine at home. Mount Vernon, NY: Peter Pauper Press, 1974. 64p. G28450

MacKAY, Margaret. The wine princes. New York: John Day, 1958. 374p. G28460

A novel.

MacKAY, Muriel. Country winemaking and wine cookery. London: David and Charles, 1982. G28465

MacKENZIE, Alexander. California's top 10 wines. Los Angeles: Armstrong Publishing, 1978. Illus. G28470

MacQUITTY, Jane, ed. Which? Wine guide, 1983. London: Hodder, 1982. G28480

Gives advice on what to buy and where to buy it. Covers the best wine bars, wine-conscious restaurants, and is consumer oriented. Ms. MacQuitty's recommendations have created a "stir" in the conservative, male-dominated wine trade. 1984 edition of 667p.

MADDEN, John. Shall we drink wine? A physician's study of the alcohol question.. Milwaukee: Press of Owen and Weirbrecht, 1899. 220p. G28490

MADELEINE, B., comp. Savoury Rumanian dishes and choise [sic] wines. Bucharest: Luceafarul Co., 1939. 153p. Illus. G28500

MAGARY, Alan. Across the Golden Gate. California's North Coast, wine country and redwoods. New York: Harper and Row, 1980. 331p. Illus. G28510

MAGGS Bros., Ltd. Food and drink through the ages, 2500 B.C. to 1937 A.D. A catalogue of antiquities, manuscripts, books and engravings, treating of cookery, eating and drinking. London: Maggs Bros., 1937. 191p. Illus. G28520

M'AHARRY, Samuel. The practical distiller or an introduction to making whiskey, gin, brandy, spirits . . . Harrisburg, PA: John Wyeth, 1809. 184p. G28530

MAHONEY, John W. Wines and spirits; labelling requirements. 2nd ed. London: Wine and Spirit Publications, 1972. 54p. G28540

Third edition of 125p. published in 1979. Includes latest EEC regulations.

MAIGNEN, P.A. Cognac in 1876. London: By the Author, 1876. 16p. Illus. G28550

MALET, William E. The Australian wine-growers' manual; containing full and practical instructions concerning the cultivation of the vine; and the art of making wine after the latest and most approved methods. Sydney: Belder and Foster, 1876. 255p. G28570

MALLET, P. A narrative of circumstances relating to the excise bill on wine. London: F.G. and J. Robinson, 1795. 44p. G28580

MANN, Gladys. Home wine and beer making. London: Octopus Books, 1975. 144p. Illus. G28590

Later edition of 144p. published in 1977 by Cathay Books.

MANNING, Sydney A. A handbook of the wine and spirit trade. London: I. Pitman, 1947. 170p. Illus. G28600

Second edition issued in 1950.

_____. The social wine guide. Cape Town: Central New Agency, 1952. 51p. G28610

MANNING, Carol and ROBERTS, Larry. Vineyards on the mission trail book. 1981. 31p. Illus. G28620

Profiles of the wineries of Santa Barbara and San Luis Obispo counties.

MANT, J.B. The pocket book of mensuration and gauging. London: Crosby, Lockwood and Son, 1891. 249p. G28630

MARAIS, J.F. The reconstitution of phylloxerised vineyards: with special reference to the American vine both as graft-bearer and direct producer. Cape Town: Dept. of Agriculture, 1893. 66p. G28640

IRVING H. MARCUS

For almost thirty years, Mr. Marcus was editor, publisher and owner of the wine industry magazine, *Wines and Vines*. He also wrote for many years the annual report on the American wine scene for the *Encyclopedia Britannica Yearbooks*. In 1965 he received the Merit Award of the American Society of Enologists, and in 1969 the Wine Institute honored him with a plaque "in appreciation for his extensive contribution to the progress of the industry."

MARCUS, Irving H. Dictionary of wine terms. 17th ed. Berkeley: Wine Publications, 1964. 64p. Illus. G28660

> This pocket-size booklet defines some 600 wine terms and outlines the wine-making process. It ran into nineteen editions and sold over 435,000 copies.

_____. How to test and improve your wine judging ability. Berkeley: Wine Publications, c1973. 96p. G28670

_____. Lines about wines, from the typewriter of Irving H. Marcus. Berkeley: Wine Publications, 1971. 214p. Illus. G28680

> The contents of this book first appeared as editorials in *Wines and Vines*.

MARGAN, Frank. The grape and I. N.S.W., Australia: Hamlyn, 1969. 141p. Illus. G28690

_____. A guide to the Hunter Valley. Sydney: Jason Publications, 1971. 51p. G28700

_____. The Hunter Valley: its wines, people and history. North Sydney: N.S.W. Hunter Vintage Festival Committee, 1973. 14p. Illus. G28710

MARIE, Ludovic. Notes and comments on the two prize essays [of M. Belperroud and M. Pettarrel] on the vine. Melbourne: W. Fairfax and Co., 1860. 30p. G28720

MARIO'S vineyard. New York: Souvenir Press G28730

> A novel with a Napa Valley, California, setting. Unable to verify.

The MARKET and economics of the U.S. wine market. Wantagh, NY: Specialists in Business Information, 1978. 124p. G28740

MARKET for wine in ten western European countries. Geneva: International Trade Centre, 1969. 402p. G28750

MARKETING California grapes; a report prepared for the California Vineyardists Association by the policy holders service bureau. Metropolitan Life Insurance Company, 1928. 128p. G28760

MARKS, Robert, ed. Wines; how, when and what to serve. New York: Schenley Import Corporation, 1934. 63p. Illus. G28770

MARRISON, L.W. Wines and spirits. Baltimore: Penguin Books, 1957. 320p. G28780

> An account of the making of all kinds of alcoholic drinks - wine, brandy, rum, whiskey, gin and cocktails. Numerous subsequent editions.

_____. Wines for everyone. New York: St. Martin's Press, 1971. 212p. Illus. G28790

MARTELL. The story of the brandy with the golden gleam: Martell cognac, from 1715 onwards. Martell: 1972. 32p. Illus. G28800

MARTIN, William, Sr. A rough sketch of the renewal system of pruning grape vines. Pittsburgh: 1854. 16p. Illus. G28810

MARTINI, Louis M. and MARTINI, Louis P. Winemakers of the Napa Valley. 1973. 94p. Illus. G28815

> See California Wine Oral History Series

MARTYN, Charles. The wine steward's manual. New York: Caterer Publishing, 1903. 120p. Illus. G28820

> Covers a variety of procedures on how to taste and judge wine. We are told "you cannot be a good taster if you smoke, or even if you drink too much; if you eat foods that are too hot, too spicy, or too rich as they vitiate your pallet; if you have bad teeth, or if your breath smells; if you have a cold or are otherwise unwell." The book also contains a wine list with prices of the Cafe des Beaux-Arts in New York from December 3, 1903 and a vintage chart of champagne, burgundy, rhine, moselle and sherry for the years 1878 through 1902.

MARVEL, Tom, ed. A pocket dictionary of wines. New York: Multi-Merchants Service, 1960. 47p. Illus. G28840

MASON, Dexter, comp. Art of drinking . . . New York: Farrar and Rinehart, 1930. 76p. G28850

[MASSARD, Secondin]. The art and secrets in the manufacture of wines and liquors according to ancient and modern international methods - requiring no machinery . . . supplemented with a chapter on the food value and medicinal properties of wines - with formulas for making them, compiled and written by Bruno La Vogue [pseud.], enologist, with special contribution by European mfrs. and other authorities. New York: La Vogue Publishing, c1934. 63p. G28860

MASSEE, William Edman. An insider's guide to low-priced wines. Garden City, NY: Dolphin Books, 1974. 230p. G28870

_____. Joyous anarchy. The search for great American wines. New York: Putnam's, 1978. 311p. G28880

_____. Just tell me what I want to know about wine (questions by D. Ivens). New York: Grosset and Dunlap, c1981. G28890

_____. Massee's 5-day-melt-way wine diet. Garden City, NY: Doubleday, Dolphin Books, 1977. 112p. Illus. G28900

_____. Massee's guide to eating and drinking in Europe. New York: McGraw-Hill, 1963. 219p. G28910

_____. Massee's guide to wines of America. New York: Dutton, 1974. 264p. G28920

_____. Massee's wine almanac. Englewood Cliffs, NJ: Prentice-Hall, 1980. 218p. Illus. G28930

_____. Massee's wine-food index. New York: Bramball House, 1962. 203p. Illus. G28940

_____. Massee's wine handbook. Garden City, NY: Doubleday, 1961. 217p. Illus. G28950

> Subsequent editions.

_____. McCall's guide to wines of America. New York: McCall Publishing, 1970. 120p. G28960

_____. The red, white and rose of wines. New York: Dell, 1972. 160p. Illus. G28970

_____. Wines and spirits: a complete buying guide. New York: McGraw-Hill, 1961. 427p. Illus. G28980

MASSEL, Anton. Applied wine chemistry and technology. London: Heidelberg Publishers, 1969. 288p. Illus. G28990

_____. Basic viticulture. London: Heidelberg Publishers, 1971. 45p. Illus. G29000

> There have been three subsequent printings.

_____. Dicta technica. Modern techniques in the beverage industry. 2nd ed. London: Oenological Research Labs, 1967. 95p. G29010

_____. No. 2 basic oenology. London: Heidelberg Publishers, 1971. 48p. Illus. G29020

MASSEL, Anton and BARTY-KING, Hugh. Classic wine making. London: Heidelberg Publishers, 1983. 202p. Illus. G29030

MASSON, G. Wine from Ontario grapes; a guide to winemaking with the new hybrids. Niagara-on-the-Lake, Ontario: By the Author, 1979. 196p. G29040

MASSON (Paul) Vineyards. The story of a winery. Saratoga, CA: 1961. 15p. Illus. G29050

> Gives the history of this winery, with photographs by Ansel Adams and Perkle Jones. Numerous subsequent editions.

_____. Ways with wine; a drink book and cook book. 7th ed. Saratoga, CA: Paul Masson Vineyards, 1966. 31p. Illus. G29060

> The recipes are originally by Morrison Wood. Many subsequent editions.

MATTHEWS, Charles George. Manual of alcoholic fermentation and the allied industries. London: Edward Arnold, 1902. 295p. Illus. G29080

> Chapter eight deals with wine, including descriptions of its production in Germany, Burgundy and Champagne. It also discusses the principal diseases of vines and their causes.

MATTHEWS, Patrick, ed. Christie's wine companion. London: Christie's Wine Publications, 1981. 191p. Illus. G29090

> An anthology of twenty-two articles by such well-known writers as Michael Broadbent, Hugh Johnson, Harry Waugh, and H.W. Yoxall. Nicely illustrated. This is the first issue of what is to be a bi-annual publication.

_____. Christie's wine companion 2. London: Christie's Wine Publications, 1983. 208p. Illus. G29100

> Articles about many different aspects of wine by Burton Anderson, Michael Broadbent, Patrick Grubb, Hugo Dunn-Meynell, Anthony Hanson, Ian Jamieson, Hugh Johnson, Make Lake, Edmund Penning-Rowsell, David Peppercorn, Jancis Robinson, Serena Sutcliffe, Bob Thompson, Bernard Watney and Harry Waugh.

MAURY, Emmerick A. Wine is the best medicine. London: Souvenir Press, 1976. 127p. G29110

> The author, a physician, gives a list of physical disorders and prescribes a wine to cure each but no clinical data is given. This is the first English edition. Translated from the French by Marie-Luce Monferran-Parker.

MAXWELL, George A. Winery accounting and cost control. New York: Prentice-Hall, 1946. 137p. G29120

MAXWELL, Herbert E. Half-a-century of successful trade; being a sketch of the rise and development of the business of W. and A. Gilbey, 1857-1907. London: Printed for private circulation by W. and A. Gilbey, Ltd., at the Pantheon Press, 1907. 80p. Illus. G29130

_____. Three-quarters of a century of successful trade; being a sketch of the rise and development of the business of W. and A. Gilbey from 1857. London: Printed for W. and A. Gilbey Ltd., by McCorquodale, 1929. 112p. Illus. G29140

MAXWELL, Kenneth. Fairest vineyards, being a description of the products of the vineyards of the Cape of Good Hope. Johannesburg: Hugh Keartland, 1966. 84p. Illus. G29150

MAY, William J. Vine culture for amateurs; being plain directions for the successful growing of grapes . . . London: "The Bazaar" Office, c1880. 34p. Illus. G29160

MAYER, C.. The making of wine and its bye products, brandy and vinegar. Cape Town: Dept. of Agriculture, 1901. 64p. G29170

MAYERNE, Sir Theodore. The distiller of London, compiled and set forth by the special license and command of the King's most excellent majesty;

for the sole use of the company of distillers of London [Examined and corrected by T. de Mayerne and T. Cademan]. London: R. Bishop, 1639. 67p. G29180

Mayerne was one of the most skillful physicians of his time.

MAYNARD, Theodore, ed. A tankard of ale; an anthology of drinking songs. London: Erskine MacDonald, 1920. 187p. G29190

MAZADE, M. First steps in ampelography: a guide to facilitate the recognition of vines. Translated by R. Dubois and W.P. Wilkinson. Melbourne: Gov't. Print., 1900. 95p. G29200

M'BRIDE, Duncan. General instructions for the choice of wines and spirituous liquors, dedicated to His Royal Highness the Prince of Wales. London: J. Richardson, c1793. 102p. G29210

M'Bride was an enterprising London wine merchant who obtained the support of some doctors concerning the curative powers of his own brand of Spanish wine, known as Toc-kay de Espagna. The book is divided into four parts: "Part I, describes those wines which are best to be used at the tables of the opulent. Part II, points out those wines which alone ought to be administered to the sick. Part III, contains instructions concerning spirituous liquors, with methods for detecting abuses in them, and Part IV, gives an account of many disorders cured by the wine called Toc-kay de Espagna, with copies of letters to some great personages on the subject of that wine; also copies of letters from persons of distinction, relative to its extraordinary effects. The whole essentially useful in all families."

McCALL, Peter. The winemaker's dictionary. Andover, England: Amateur Winemaker, 1974. 191p. G29220

Second edition, 1975.

McCULLY, Helen. Nobody ever tells you these things. London: Angus and Robertson, 1968. 308p. G29230

About food and wine.

McEWIN, George. The South Australian vigneron and gardener's manual, containing plain practical directions for the cultivation of the vine . . . Adelaide: James Allen, 1843. 124p. G29240

_____. The South Australian vigneron and gardener's manual . . . 2nd ed. Adelaide: Thomas and Clark, 1871. 134p. G29250

_____. The South Australian vigneron and gardener's manual . . . Facsimile copy of 1st ed. Adelaide: Public Library of South Australia, 1962. 124p. G29260

McGINTY, Brian. Vintage time in the Valley of the Moon. Santa Maria, CA: Santa Maria Printers and Stationers, 1960. 20p. Illus. G29280

Much about Agoston Haraszthy.

McGREGOR, James. Winemaking for all. England: 1966. 144p. G29290

McGREGOR, Marvin, D. Grapes, wine, and brandy (review and outlook for 1964-65). San Francisco: Bank of America, 1964. 24p. G29300

McGREW, J.R. Basic guide to pruning. Rev. ed. American Wine Society, 1978. 14p. G29310

McILNAY, Annabelle. Making wine at home. Secaucus, NJ: Citadel Press, 1974. 191p. Illus. G29320

McINDOE, David, ed. Chapman's New Zealand grape vine manual or plain directions for planting and cultivating vineyards and for making wine. Auckland: G.T. Chapman, 1862. 111p. G29330

> The text includes a reprint of James Busby's *A Manual of Plain Directions for Planting and Cultivating Vineyards and for Making Wine*. Also republished in 1875.

McIVER, L.L. Linda Vista Vineyards. Mission San Jose, Alameda Co., California. San Francisco: H.S. Crocker, 1894. 60p. Illus. G29340

McKEARIN, George S. and McKEARIN, Helen. American glass. New York: Crown, 1941. 634p. Illus. G29350

> The definitive work on the entire craft of early American glass-making, including wine glasses and wine bottles. There are over 3,000 illustrations, consisting of 2,000 original photographs and more than 1,000 line drawings by James L. McCreery.

McKEE, Irving. Historic Napa County wine-growers. n.p., n.d. 17p. G29360

> Research report prepared at the request of Wine Institute for Wine Advisory Board.

McKEOWN, Anthony G. Winemaking and brewing without tears. Wirral, England: Foremost Press, 1973. 176p. G29370

McLAREN Vale Winemakers Committee. Introducing the southern vineyards of South Australia: Happy Valley, Clarendon, Reynella, McLaren Vale, McLaren Flat, Langhorne Creek. Adelaide: Hunkin, Ellis and King, 1972. 40p. G29380

McLAREN, Moray. Pure wine, or *In Vino Sanitas*. A centenary celebration of, quotation from and comment on Dr. Robert Druitt's remarkable book, *A Report on Cheap Wines 1865*. Edinburgh: Alastair Campbell, 1965. 60p. Illus. G29390

McLEAN, James M. Book of wine. Philadelphia: Dorrance, 1934. 53p. G29400

McLEOD, Jeanette. Barossa Valley sketchbook. Sydney: Rigby, 1968. 64p. Illus. G29410

McMULLEN, Thomas. Handbook of wines, practical, theoretical, and historical; with a description of foreign spirits and liqueurs. New York: D. Appleton, 1852. 327p. G29420

> André Simon thought this book lacked originality. He commented: "McMullen's's book is merely a repetition of what had been better written before him by Henderson, Morewood, Jullien, M'Culloch, and Redding. Some chapters are even entirely transcribed from

Henderson and Redding, and acknowledged to be so." Nevertheless it is probably the first consumer-oriented book on wine published. It describes the character and quality of major wines of the world, from Portugal to Persia (but not the United States). It has chapters on the purchase, cellaring and appreciation of wines, as well as a tabular listing (sixty-three pages) of all known wines, spirits and liqueurs.

McMURTRIE, William. A report upon the statistics of grape culture and wine production in the United States for 1880. Washington: USDA, Special Report No. 36, 1881. 104p. G29430

McNEIL, Arthur, L., Rev. Mass wine. Its manufacture and church legislation. Los Gatos, CA: Novitiate of Los Gatos, 1938. 31p. Illus. G29440

A review of Catholic regulations concerning wines for sacramental purposes, with the author's comments.

McNEILL, Florence Marian. The Scots cellar, its traditions and lore. Edinburgh: R. Paterson, 1958. 290p. Illus. G29450

McNULTY, Henry. Drinking in vogue. 8th ed. New York: The Vendome Press, 1978. 159p. Illus. G29460

Five chapters on wine.

_____. The vogue wine book. New York: Harmony Books, 1983. Illus. G29465

McPHERSON, John H. How to choose and use wine at table. Sydney: Gregory's, 1968. 126p. Illus. G29470

McWILLIAM, D.M. Wine merchant's recipes. Glasgow: William Gilmour, 1930. 106p. G29480

Second revised edition of 126p. published by the Food Trade Press in 1947.

MEAD, Peter B. An elementary treatise on American grape culture and wine making. New York: Harper Brothers, 1867. 483p. Illus. G29490

Although not as popular as other viticultural books of its time, this is a handsome volume with an ornate, gilt-decorated spine, nearly two hundred illustrations by Henry Holton, and paper and typography of a quality uncommon in trade publications of the time.

While offering precise descriptions of native grapes, he recommends only a few as useful for wine making (the iona, delaware, diana, Allen's hybrid and catawba) and rejects the rest, especially the then ubiquitous concord. "A recently produced bottle of the pure Concord is before us as we write. We shall not undertake the impossible task of describing it, further than saying, that this, at least, resembles anything but wine. We can not drink it; neither can our friends. . . . If the leopard never changes his spots, neither does the 'fox' his odor." Mead condemns the practice of adding sugar to the must derived from unripe grapes and considers any adulteration in wine making as both unnecessary and even immoral. "But it is said that some of our native grapes will not make wine without sugar. That is very true; and it may be added that they will not make true wine with it. They are clearly not wine grapes . . . we have an innate dislike for deception in all its forms." Other interesting features of this book are a chapter on "taste," with respect to discernment of quality, and a discussion of Pasteur's then recent studies on fermentation and the stabilization of bottled wine by heat treatment (pasteurization).

MEADOWCROFT, Ernest. The essential facts of home winemaking. Essex: Emma, 1962. 12p. G29500

MEARNS, John. Treatise of the pot culture of the grape. London: W.S. Orr and Co., 1843. 96p. Illus. G29510

MEINHARD, Heinrich. German wines. Newcastle upon Tyne: 1971. 85p. Illus. G29520

_____. The wines of Germany. New York: Stein and Day, 1976. 276p. Illus. G29530

MEISEL, Anthony and ROSENWEIG, Shelia. On wine. New York: Excalibur Books, 1983. 192p. Illus. G29540

MELE, Pietro Francesco. Moet et Chandon: impressions of France. Rome: Moet et Chandon, n.d. Illus. G29550

MELVILLE, John Robert. Guide to California wines. Garden City, NY: Doubleday, 1955. 270p. G29560

Revised editions in 1960, 1968, 1972 and 1976.

MENDALL, Seaton C. Planting and care of young vineyards in the Finger Lakes area of New York State. Hammondsport, NY: Taylor Wine Company, 1960. 36p. Illus. G29570

_____. Vineyard practices for Finger Lakes growers. Hammondsport, NY: Taylor Wine Company, 1957. 21p. G29580

MENDELSOHN, Oscar A. The dictionary of drink and drinking. London: Macmillan, 1966. 382p. G29590

_____. Drinking with Pepys. London: Macmillan, 1963. 125p. Illus. G29600

Samuel Pepys, born 1632, kept a detailed diary of his activities from 1659 to 1669. The diary, written in a form of short-hand, was only partially deciphered in 1825. It was not until 1893 that a more complete (ten volumes) version appeared, but even this one was selectively edited. Pepys noted everything; bribes, his liaisons with women and his frequent "merriness." Since he held a rather high position in the Admiralty, he had access to all that was available to drink in England.

The diary is an extraordinarily valuable record of Restoration life in England under Charles II, "warts and all." Pepys loved wine, to excess, and the diaries record his frequent foreswearance and dereliction.

From the vast number of observations, Mr. Mendelsohn has selected only entries which, with his comments, provide some light on the subject of drinks and drinking, especially wines.

Part of the entry of April 10, 1663 reads, ". . . to the Royal Oak Tavern . . . and here drank a sort of French wine called Ho Bryan, that hath a good and most particular taste that I never met with."

Although that entry lay interred in the largely undeciphered diary for over 150 years, it is of interest in that it is the first reference in English literature to a named claret. It is also of interest that the wine was served in a tavern.

In 1600's clarets were not laid-down, so it must have been a young Haut-Brion, served from the cask. This gives some insight into the promise of the great Bordeaux wines that have held the affection of the British and Scottish upper-class to this day.

But the availability of French wines in taverns was coming to an end. After William III came to the throne in 1688 the great cycle of French-English wars began, and French wines were unobtainable to all but the wealthiest. Port and sherry were available, though, and became the wines of choice for the great majority of Englishmen.

Pepys was removed from office in 1688 but lived until 1703 as a man of wealth and importance.

_____. The earnest drinker. A short and simple account of alcoholic beverages. London: George Allen and Unwin, 1950. 241p. G29610

_____. The earnest drinker's digest; a short and simple account of alcoholic beverages for curious drinkers. Sydney: Consolidated Press, 1946. 229p. Illus. G29620

_____. From cellar and kitchen. Melbourne: Macmillan, 1968. 239p. Illus. G29630

_____. Nicely, thank you, (drunk 2,000 times). A frolic with some synonyms. Melbourne: National, 1971. 102p. G29640

MENEFEE, Campbell Augustus. Historical and descriptive sketch book of Napa, Sonoma, Lake and Mendocino . . . Napa City, CA: Reporter Publishing House, 1873. 356p. Illus. G29650

> Contains several biographical sketches of prominent wine men of that era.

The MERCHANT and seaman's expeditious measurer . . . also rules for determining the contents of all sorts of casks, in wine and beer measure. New York: D.A. Nash, n.d. 195p. G29660

MEREDITH, Joseph. Treatise on the grape vine. London: George Philip, 1876. 96p. G29670

MEREDITH, Ted. Northwest wine: the vinifera wines of Oregon, Washington and Idaho. Kirkland, WA: Nexus Press, 1980. 186p. Illus. G29680

MERWE SCHOLTZ, Hendrik van der. Wine country; journeys along the Cape wine routes. Cape Town: Buren Publishers, 1970. 239p. Illus. G29690

MESSENGER, Elizabeth Esson. The wine and food bank. Wellington, New Zealand: 1961. 39p. G29700

MEW, James and ASTON, John. Drinks of the world. London: Scribner and Welford, 1892. 362p. Illus. G29710

MEYER, Otto E. California premium wines and brandies. 1973. 71p. Illus. G29715

> See California Wine Oral History Series.

MEYLAN, Henry. The bright and fragrant wines of Switzerland. Lausanne, Switzerland: The Swiss Wine Growers Association, n.d. 27p. Illus. G29720

MEYNELL, Francis. Quicquid agunt homines. London: The Curwen Press, 1943. 10p. G29730

> An address in praise of George Saintsbury.

MICHAELS, Marjorie. Stay healthy with wine. Natural cures and beauty secrets from the vineyards. New York: Dial Press, 1981. 246p. Illus. G29740

> Specific wines are recommended for mixing with anything from onions to apples for use in the treatment of arthritis, diabetes, colds, flu and other complaints and illnesses. No clinical data is provided.

MIDDLETON, Scudder. Dining, wining and dancing in New York. New York: Dodge Publishing, 1938. 165p. Illus. G29750

MILBOURN, Thomas, ed. The Vintners' Company, their muniments, plate, and eminent members; with some account of the ward of Vintry. London: Vintners' Company, 1888. 136p. Illus. G29760

> A compilation of papers covering the history of the Vintners' Company. The papers address its charters and muniments, including the first charter of incorporation in 1437, and biographies of prominent members.

MILES, Cecil H. A glimpse of Madeira. London: Garnett, 1949. 147p. Illus. G29770

MILES, J.G., ed. Innkeeping: a manual for licensed victuallers. 5th ed. London: Barrie and Rockliff for the National Trade Development Association, 1969. 248p. G29780

MILLER, Mark. Wine, a gentleman's game: the story of Benmarl vineyards. New York: Harper and Row, 1984. 214p. G29790

> The story of the author's transition from painter and illustrator to wine grower and vintner in the Hudson River Valley.

MILLER, Philip. The Gardeners dictionary; containing the methods of cultivating . . . fruit and flower garden . . . and vineyard . . . together with accounts of the nature and use of barometers . . . and the orgin of meteors . . . London: By the Author, 1731. 843p. G29800

> The author (1691-1771) was gardener for the Chelsea Physic Gardens and the most respected gardener of his era.

Second edition, 1733; third edition of three volumes published in 1735 through a ninth edition published in 1835 with the inscription "Ebenus Cretica" - no more published.

MILLIGAN, David. All color book of wine. Octopus Books, 1974. 72p. Illus. G29810

A pictorial book - short on text.

MILLNER, Cork. Vintage valley. Santa Barbara, CA: McNally and Loftin, 1983. G29840

MILLION, Marc and MILLION, Kim. The wine and food of Europe. London: Webb and Bower, 1982. Illus. G29820

_____. The wine roads of Europe. London: Robert Nicholson Publications, 1983. 285p. Illus. G29830

Arrow/Hutchinson published it first, according to U.S. edition.

MILLS, Frederick C. The wine guide; being practical hints on the purchase and management of foreign wines; their history, and a complete catalogue of all those in present use, together with remarks upon the treatment of spirits . . . London: Groombridge, 1861. 64p. G29850

MILLS, Samuel A, comp. The wine story of Australia. Penfold and Co. Sydney: Attkins, McGuitty, 1908. 32p. Illus. G29860

MISAURUS, Philander (pseud). The honour of the gout, or a rational discourse demonstrating that the gout is one of the greatest blessings which can befall mortal man . . . by way of letter to an eminent citizen, wrote in the heat of a violent paroxysm. London: Astley, c1732. 53p. G29870

A satire against doctors. The author was also known as Philander Misiatrus.

MISCELLANIES over Claret: or the friends to the tavern . . . being a collection of poems . . . from the Rose Tavern without Temple-Bar. London: 1697. 20p. G29880

MISCH, Robert Jay. Quick guide to the wines of all the Americas. Garden City, NY: Doubleday, 1977. 164p. Illus. G29890

_____. Quick guide to wine. Garden City, NY: Doubleday, 1966. 98p. Illus. G29900

MISHKIN, David Joel. The American colonial wine industry: an economic interpretation. 2 Vols. Ann Arbor: University Microfilms International, 1966. 322/630p. G29910

Describes the role the industry played in the Spanish, French, Dutch, and British colonial policies, and establishes the primacy of economic motives in the viticultural schemes during the colonization of America. Based on the author's Ph.D dissertation, The *American Colonial Vineyard: An Economic Interpretation*, University of Illinois, 1966.

MITCHELL, John Richard. Improving your finished wine. Andover, England: Amateur Winemaker, 1978. 109p. G29920

_____. Scientific winemaking made easy. Andover, England: Amateur Winemaker, 1969. 253p. Illus. G29930

MITCHELL, Silas Weir, M.D. A little more burgundy. G29940

The story is one told by an American student named Michel who is living in Paris in 1853 (Mitchell Weir was studying medicine in Paris at about that time). Much of the tale is set in an ancient Parisian cellar that harbors fine old bottles of burgundy. This book is included in the 1895, 1897, 1900, 1902 and 1910 editions of the following entry, *A Madeira Party*.

_____. A Madeira party. New York: The Century Co., 1895. 165p. Illus. G29950

Madeira, which is often neglected in modern wine books, once had an extraordinary hold on the tastes and affections of the American upper-classes.

In 1895, S. Weir Mitchell, a prominent Philadelphia physician, wrote this small book, a fictional recreation of a madeira tasting for four in an upper-class home in Philadelphia "sometime early in the second quarter of the century."

The occasion is the return of a friend who has lived in Europe the past thirty years and remarks, "I have tasted no madeira for twenty years." At one point the host remarks, "There is but one wine. . . . No other, not even the finest claret, but is underbred compared to this aristocrat."

An interesting theory is brought out as to why madeira became the wine of preference. "Great Britain allowed no trade with France or Spain, but . . . we were permitted to trade with the Canary and Madeiras. . . . It so happened that the decisive changes of weather our winter and summer afforded did more to ripen this wine than its native climate."

They are a proper group of snobs. One remarks, "I have noticed that the acquisition of a taste for Madeira in middle life is quite fatal to common people." Also, "And then one must be careful not to have wine shaken; that bruises it." And, "it sours a wine to send it to the right. That is a fact, sir, a well known fact." Further, it spoils a wine to "fine it at the change of the moon. . . . Always fine a wine [with egg white or milk] during the decline of the moon."

Though pretentious, it is an excellent account that describes the madeira ritual: the tasting was preceded by a very light meal, in this case, "A trifle of terrapin, without wine in the dressing" and the breast of a canvasback duck. Then the cloth was removed from the table, and a crust of bread on a plate was set by each guest. (In 5th century B.C. Greece, a light meal preceded a drinking party which began when the meal was finished and the tables were cleared. See William Younger, *Gods, Men and Wine*.) No smoking was allowed and the talk was limited to madeira and pertinent reminiscences. Six quart decanters were placed on rolling coasters, for the finest madeiras were never bottled. A servant distributed the glasses. In the center of the table was set a notched silver bowl of water and in each notch in the bowl, the stem of an inverted glass was placed. Also, each guest received a glass bowl which held two glasses. Thus a glass for each wine and a means of rinsing a glass. The least esteemed wine was served first. The decanter was then passed by the host to his guest on the left saying, "With the sun, gentlemen." The wines were expertly discussed. An occasional toast was given preceded by the question, "Are you all charged," apparently meaning, "Are your glasses full; are you ready for the toast."

These gentlemen bore an extreme prejudice against bottled madeira (it was kept in five gallon demi-johns in moderate darkness under the roof), but there was one exception. One reminisces about long-gone wines and mentions "Constitution." Another says, "It was the class wine of 1802. . . . At Harvard each class used to import a tun of wine, which, after it was bottled, was distributed among the graduates. I still have two of the bottles with '1802' surrounded by 'Constitution' molded in the glass." Rare.

For other historical data on madeira in the United States see Greig, Peter.

_____. A Madeira party. Reprint edition. [Privately printed for E.J. Rousuck.] 1958. Unpaged. Illus. G29960

Edition limited to 100 copies. A facsimile reprint of the 1895 edition.

_____. A Madeira party. Reprint edition. Sacramento: Corti Brothers, 1975. 80p. Illus. G29970

A reprint of the 1895 edition, bound in boards with a leather spine. Introduction by William J. Dickerson and appendices on madeira wine by Roy Brady. Edition limited to 1,000 copies. Andrew Hoyem of San Francisco was the printer.

MITCHELL, Sir Thomas L. Notes on the culture of the vine and the olive and methods of making wine and oil in southern parts of Spain. Sydney: D.L. Welch, 1849. 28p. G29980

MITZKY and Co. Our native grape. Grapes and their culture; also a descriptive list of old and new varieties. Rochester, NY: W.W. Morrison, 1893. 218p. Illus. G29990

A compilation of hundreds of native and hybrid grapes, from the Adelaide to the Zinnia. In addition to black and white illustrations, it has three fine, color lithograph plates for the Green Mountain, Brillant and Early Ohio grapes.

M'MAHON, Bernard. The American gardener's calendar . . . Philadelphia: Printed by B. Graves, 1806. 618p. G30000

Much detailed information is available in the calendar on classes of wine, propagation, vineyards, and the making of red and white wines. It contains a fold-out table of growing times of the Munier Miller's Burgundy Penn grape between 1787 and 1800, and mentions the contemporary work of Peter Legaux of Spring Hill Vineyard. M'Mahon advocates the planting of European grapes and mentions only two American varieties, i.e. the Bland's grape and the Alexander grape. This important garden book was published from 1806 to 1857 in eleven editions with minor textual changes.

MODERATION: the treasure of the wise. 2nd ed. London: James L. Denman, 1926. G30010

> Written by a physician, its message is summed up in the foreword: "There is no one thing that holds so much good as a bottle of wine. It cheers the weary, soothes the troubled, nourishes the feeble, and promotes the amity of man."

MODI, Sir Jivanji Jamshedji. Wine among the ancient Persians; a lecture delivered before the Self-Improvement Association . . . Bombay: Bombay Gazette Steam Press, 1888. 16p. G30020

MOHR, Frederick. The grape vine. A practical scientific treatise on its management . . . New York: Orange Judd, 1867. 129p. Illus. G30030

> Dr. Frederick Mohr's work, *On the Treatment of the Grape Vine and on Wine Making (Der Weinstock Und Der Wein)* was considered in Germany to be the best book on the culture of the grapevine. Dr. Mohr, a doctor of physiology and medicine, was also one of the great chemists of his time.

> Translated from the German and accompanied with hints on propagation and general treatment of American varieties by Horticola (the pseudonym of Charles Siedhof). Siedhof notes that his translation of Mohr's *Der Weinstock Und Der Wein* begins with this first section because he felt that in the United States there was more demand for works on viticulture than on viniculture.

MOISY, Robert. Beaujolais. Neuchatel: 1956. 95p. G30040

MOLYNEAUX, Edwin. Grape growing for amateurs . . . with lists of varieties most suitable for the amateur. London: L.U. Gill, 1891. 124p. Illus. G30050

MONCRIEFF, R.W. The chemical senses. New York: John Wiley and London: Leonard Hill, 1944. 424p. G30060

MONSON-FITZJOHN, G.J. Drinking vessels of bygone days from the neolithic age to the Georgian period. London: Herbert Jenkins, 1927. 144p. Illus. G30070

MONTAGNE, Prosper. Larousse Gastronomique; the encyclopedia of food, wine and cookery. New York: Crown, 1961. 1101p. Illus. G30080

> Also published in London by Hamlyn.

MONTAGU, Basil. Some enquiries into the effects of fermented liquors. 2nd ed. London: Printed for R. Hunter, 1818. 397p. G30090

MONZERT, Leonard. The independent liquorist; or the art of manufacturing and preparing all kinds of cordials, syrups, bitters, wines, champagne, beer, punches, tincture, extracts, essences, flavorings, colorings . . . New York: John F. Trow, 1866. 193p. G30100

_____. Monzert's practical distiller; an exhaustive treatise on the art of distilling and rectifying spirituous liquors and alcohol . . . Danbury, CT: Behrens Publishing, 1889. 156p. Illus. G30110

> Also another 1889 edition published by Dick and Fitzgerald, New York.

MOONEN, L. Australian wines; a paper read at a special meeting of the Chamber on Monday, 23rd April, 1883. Melbourne: Victoria Chamber of Manufacturers, 1883. 20p. G30130

MOORE, Bernard. Wines of North America. Secaucas, NJ: 1983. 192p. Illus. G30140

> Describes over 180 wineries in all. There are 100 excellent color illustrations, many of them extending over two full pages. There are six detailed maps of wine-producing areas, and many obscure wine labels are reproduced including "Moody Blue" and "Pussycat" from Canada and Boordy Vineyards from Maryland and "Brahydel" in Michigan.

MOORE, Jonas. England's interests: or, the gentlemen and amour's friend. Shewing how land may be improved . . . the best and quickest way of raising a nursery . . . how to make cider . . . and . . . wines . . . London: A. Bettesworth, 1721. 188p. G30150

MOORE, Lew, comp. Dictionary of foreign dining terms. A concise guide to the food and wines of fifteen nations. London: W.H. Allen, 1958. 133p. G30160

_____. Diners' dictionary of foreign terms. New York: Sterling Publishing, 1958. 127p. G30170

MORE favorite recipes for home made wines and beers. Bristol: South Gloucestershire Wine Circle, 1977. 32p. G30180

MORE, D. Discovering country winemaking. London: Shire Publications, 1980. 95p. G30190

MOREL, Julian. Handbook of wines and beverages. London: Pitman, 1975. 138p. G30200

MOREWOOD, Samuel. An essay on the inventions and customs of both ancients and moderns in the use of inebriating liquors . . . London: Longman, Hurst, Rees, Orme, Brown and Green, 1824. 375p. Illus. G30210

> The author earned a living as an Irish collector of excise taxes, but during his spare time he collected an incredible amount of information about inebriating beverages in all times and all countries, including much about wine. The first edition, published in 1824, was the first publication on this subject in English. The second edition, published in 1838, is more complete. Morewood's efforts were obviously a labor of love since he describes them as having "beguiled many a tedious hour, and sweetened many a solitary evening." An interesting and worthwhile account.

_____. A philosophical and statistical history of the inventions and customs of ancient and modern nations in the manufacture and use of inebriating liquors, with the present practice of distillation in all its varieties. Dublin: William Curry, Jr., 1838. 745p. Illus. G30220

MORGAN, E. The tavern-keeper or publicans directory and family assistant, containing receipts for the managing, colouring and flavouring of foreign wines and spirits, and for making and managing British wines and compounds . . . London: Crabb and Burnham, c1820. 180p. G30230

MORGAN, Jefferson. Adventures in the wine country. San Francisco: Chronicle Books, 1971. 128p. Illus. G30240

  Revised edition published in 1976.

MORGAN, Louise. Home made wines. London: Hutchinson, 1958. 167p. Illus. G30250

MORGAN, Percy T. Purity and adulteration in native wines. Address by Percy T. Morgan . . . at the International Pure Food Congress, St. Louis. 1904. 16p. G30260

MORGAN, Roy. Sealed bottles: their history and evolution, 1630-1930. Staff, England: Midlands Antique Bottle Publishing, 1972. 120p. Illus. G30270

MORNY, Claude, ed. A wine and food bedside book. London: the International Wine and Food Society, 1972. 334p. Illus. G30280

MORO VISCONTI, Giancarlo. Something about Italian wines. A tentative market guide. Translated by Antonio Amato. Rome: Servizio Informazioni, 1958. 91p. G30290

MORRELL, J. An international guide to wines of the world. London: Bartholomew, 1980. 160p. Illus. G30300

MORRELL, J. and STEVENSON, T. Sunday Telegraph good wine guide, 82/83. London: Sunday Telegraph, 1982. 160p. Illus. G30310

  Issued annually.

MORRIS, Denis. ABC of wine. London: Daily Telegraph, 1977. 116p. G30320

_____. Daily Telegraph guide to the pleasures of wine. Glasgow: William Collins, 1972. 116p. Illus. G30330

_____. The French vineyard. London: Eyre and Spottiswoode, 1958. 223p. Illus. G30340

MORRIS, Roger. The genie in the bottle; unraveling myths about wine. New York: A and W Publishers, 1981. 218p. G30350

MORRIS, William. Praise of wine. Los Angeles: Ward Ritchie Press, 1958. 11p. G30360

MORTLOCK, Geoffrey and WILLIAMS, Stephen, eds. The flowing bowl, a book of blithe spirits and blue devils. London: Hutchinson, 1947. 259p. G30380

A selection from the "best things written through the ages on drinks, drinking, etc."

MORTON, Alexander. Just what you want to know about wine. New York: McMullen, 1890. 16p. G30390

MORWYNG, Peter. The treasure of Evonymous. London: 1559. G30395

The first treatise on distillation in English.

MOSER, Lenz. High culture system. Kiems, Donau, Austria: By the Author. G30400

Unable to verify.

MOUBRAY, Bonington (pseud). A practical treatise on breeding, rearing and fattening all kinds of domestic poultry, pheasants, pigeons and rabbits . . . with instructions for the private brewery on cider, perry and British wine making. London: Sherwood, Gilbert and Piper, 1834. 467p. Illus. G30410

MOURAILLE, L.P. Practical guide to treatment of wine in English cellars. London: Simpkin, Marshall, 1889. 124p. G30420

MOURNETAS, Andre and PELISSER, Henry. The vade-mecum of the wine lover. Paris: La Conception, 1953. 64p. Illus. G30430

Translated from the French by William Buckley and Claude Landry.

MOWAT, Jean, ed. Anthology of wine. Essex, England: W.H. Houldershaw, c1946. 78p. Illus. G30440

MUENCH, Friedrich. School for American grape culture: brief but thorough and practical guide to the laying out of vineyards, the treatment of vines, and the production of wines in North America. Translated from the German by Elizabeth H. Cutter. St. Louis: C. Witter and Philadelphia: J.A. Lippincott, 1865. 139p. G30520

In the mid-19th century Missouri was the second largest wine growing state in the Union. Vineyards cultivated to native varieties were concentrated along the Missouri River in and around the town of Hermann, west of St. Louis. The vinegrowers were mainly of German extraction, and much of the literature of the area was published in that language. Friedrich Muench was a Lutheran minister and noted hybridizer who produced esteemed wines at Mount Pleasant Vineyard at Augusta. His *Amerikanische Weinbauschule* describes his viticultural methods and evaluates the many grape varieties grown from New England to Texas.

MUESCH, John. A treatise on the use of wine from religious and organic standpoints. Malvern, AK: By the Author, 1902. 22p. G30460

MUIR, Augustus. Literature and wine: recollections of a Saintsbury student spoken at the 25th Meeting of the Saintsbury Club, 23 October 1944. London: Privately printed at Curwen Press for The Saintsbury Club, 1945. 12p. G30470

_____. The vintner of Nazareth. London: Macmillan, 1972. 156p. G30480

This is a "translation" of a series of fictional letters written by a vintner and rabbi who lived in Nazara in the first century.

The vintner, Barnabas, made a wine so popular that he opened ". . . a booth in the village where my wine can be bought from goatskins by anyone, Jew or Gentile, who will bring a pitcher." Barnabas writes of his contacts with Jesus, Ausonius, John the Baptist. The theme of wine dominates the letters.

MUIR, Augustus, ed. How to choose and enjoy wine. London: Odhams Press, 1953. 160p. Illus. G30490

Eleven authorities have each contributed a chapter. Subsequent editions.

MULDER, Gerardus, J. The chemistry of wine. London: John Churchill, 1857. 390p. G30500

The author was a professor of chemistry at the University of Utrecht, Holland. His treatise was originally translated into German and from German it was edited and translated into English by Dr. Henry Bench Jones, a physician. At the time of its publication, it was a distinctly original contribution, but according to André Simon "many of Mulder's definitions have now been proved to be quite erroneous." Although the text is technical, there are chapters on the grape, the cellaring of wine and the adulteration of wine.

MULLIGAN, Mary Ewing. Lets throw an Italian wine tasting. New York: The Italian Trade Commission, 1978. 24p. Illus. G30510

MUNSON, Thomas Volney. Address on native grapes of the United States. Read before the American Horitcultural Society, at New Orleans, January 20, 1885, and published in full in the Transactions of the Society for 1885. Indianapolis: Carlon and Hollenbeck, 1885. 13p. G30530

_____. Advantages of conjoint selection and hybridization and limits of usefulness in hybridization among grapes. New York: 1904. G30540

An important work included in the proceedings of the International Conference of Plant Breeding and Hybridization held in New York in 1902, and then printed as the Horticultural Society of New York Memoirs, Vol. I.

_____. Classification and generic synopsis of the wild grapes of North America. Washington: Gov't. Print., 1890. 14p. G30550

_____. Foundations of American grape culture. New York: Orange Judd, 1909. 252p. Illus. G30560

A significant contribution to the study of hybridization of American grapes.

_____. Investigation and improvement of American grapes at the Munson Experiment Station from 1876 to 1900. Austin, TX: Von Boeckmann, Schutze, 1900. 286p. Illus. G30570

MURPHY, Brian. Vino. San Franciso: Determined Productions, 1969. 67p. Illus. G30580

MURPHY, Dan F. The Australian wine guide. Melbourne: Sun Books, 1966. 215p. Illus. G30590

> Subsequent editions.

_____. Dan Murphy's classification of Australian wines. Melbourne: Sun Books, 1974. 216p. Illus. G30600

> Contains a table of every Australian vineyard of importance and a classification of great wines, very good wines, special binnings, blended wines, etc. The author compares Australian wines with European wines, and differentiates between them.

_____. A guide to wine. Melbourne: Macmillan, 1977. 101p. Illus. G30610

_____. What wine is that? A guide to Australian wines. Sydney: Ure Smith, 1973. 41p. Illus. G30620

> 268 labels reproduced in color. Revised edition of 57p. published by Ure Smith in 1975.

MURRAY, John Alan. Beverages. London: Constable, 1912. 84p. G30630

MURRAY, Samuel W. Wines of the U.S.A., how to know and choose them. Concord, MA: The Wine Press, 1957. 31p. Illus. G30640

MURTRIC, W.M. Report upon statistics of grape culture and wine production in the U.S. for the year 1880. Washington: Gov't. Print., 1881. G30660

MUSCATINE, Doris and AMERINE, Maynard A. and THOMPSON, Bob, eds. The book of California wine. Berkeley: University of California Press and London: Sotheby, 1984. 640p. Illus. G30665

> The editors have brought together forty-four knowledgeable wine-makers and wine authorities to explore all aspects of California wine.

MUSCHAMP, Michael. Wine and winemakers of Australia. Melbourne: Hill of Content Publishing, 1977. 155p. Illus. G30670

MYHILL, Henry. The Loire Valley. London: Faber and Faber, 1978. 148p. G30680

> Not about wine per se, but wine is discussed.

The MYSTERIE of vintners. London: Printed by William Whitwood, 1669. 91p. G30690

> The word "mysterie" meaning "trade" rather than mysterious.

NANOVIC, John. The complete book of wines, vineyards and labels. 252p. G30710

> Unable to verify.

NAPA Valley Wine Library Association. Book collection of the Napa Valley Wine Library. St. Helena, CA: Napa Valley Wine Library Association, 1979. 17p. G30720

About 1,500 entries. The Napa Valley Wine Library has a complete set of the Oral Histories Transcripts, featuring interviews with prominent California viticulturists and enologists. Noted under "Oral Histories Transcripts."

_____. History of Napa Valley; interviews and reminiscences of long-time residents collected by the Napa Valley Wine Library 1976, Volume II. St. Helena: 1977. 380p. Illus. G30730

NAPA Valley Wine Tour. St. Helena: Vintage Image, 1981. 88p. Illus. G30735

NELSON, James Carmer. Everybody's guide to great wines under $5. New York: McGraw-Hill, 1983. 290p. G30740

_____. The poor person's guide to great cheap wines. New York: McGraw-Hill, 1977. 247p. G30750

NETTLETON, Joseph Alfred. A study of the history and meaning of the expression "Original Gravity" as applied to beer, worts and distillers' wash: together with a detailed description of the various processes for finding the original gravity of any fermented liquors . . . London: 1881. G30770

NEUCHATEL: its lake, its mountains and its vineyards, by a member of the Alpine Club. London: McCracken, 1877. 32p. G30780

NEUWIRTH, Art. The German wines. By the Author, 1977. 63p. Illus. G30790

A NEW and easy way to make wine of English grapes and other fruit. London: 1672. G30800

Unable to verify.

NEW methods of grafting and budding, as applied to reconstitution with American wines. Melbourne: Victoria Dept. of Agriculture, 1901. 72p. G30810

NEW South Wales, Department of Tourism. Wineries of NSW and Northern Victoria. Sydney: 1976. 64p. Illus. G30820

NEWHALL, Charles S. The vines of northeastern America. New York: Putnam's, 1897. 207p. Illus. G30830

NEWMAN, Peter C. King of the castle. The making of a dynasty: Seagram's and the Bronfman empire. New York: Atheneum, 1979. 304p. G30840

NEWMARK, A. Tannin and its uses in wine. San Francisco: The Triton Co., 1935. 30p. G30850

Also published by Newmark Chemical Laboratories, Melbourne, 1935.

The NIAGARA grape. Fall season 1887, spring session 1888. Niagara White Grape Co., c1888. G30870

NICHOL, Alexander. Wine and vines of British Columbia. Vancouver, BC: Bottesini Press, 1983. 168p. G30880

NIEKERK, Tinus Van. Wine appreciation. Pretoria: Erroll Marx Publishers, 1981. 174p. Illus. G30890

NIESSEN, Carl Anton. Report on the vine culture and the wine trade of Germany for the years 1898-1900. London: Harrison and Sons, 1901. 16p. G30900

NOLING, A.W., comp. Beverage literature: a bibliography. Metuchen, NJ: Scarecrow Press, 1971. 865p. G30910

> In 1946, A.W. Noling was chief executive officer of Hurty-Peck Company, a major manufacturer of soft-drink flavor bases. In that year he began to collect beverage books, mostly relating to beverage bases. This collecting led to the present Hurty-Peck Library of Beverage Literature, the largest single collection in the world of beverage books written in English.

> This bibliography lists the titles of 1,200 books on wines and approximately 600 on beer and brewing. It also includes entries on cocoa and chocolate, coffee, inns and taverns, drinks and drinking and other beverge-related subjects. Most of these are in the Hurty-Peck Library in Orange, California.

> A convenience of the book is that it includes, in addition to the comprehensive listing by author, an alphabetical listing for each of the twenty-three subject categories. There is also a comprehensive section of books listed alphabetically by title.

> As massive an undertaking as it was, Noling did not claim that his bibliography was complete. Booksellers often catalog pre-1971 books as "Not in Noling," implying perhaps that such a book must be scarce, but that is not necessarily the case. Regardless of completeness, Noling accomplished the job of organizing the most comprehensive list of "beverage" titles then or now in existence.

_____. A bibliography of books and booklets on beverages, their history and manufacture. Indianapolis: Hurty-Peck and Company, 1961. 55p. Illus. G30920

> This booklet lists some 600 titles that were then in the Hurty-Peck Library. It has sometimes been confused with his bibliography listed above.

NOOLAS, Rab, ed. (pseud). Merry-go-down. A gallery of gorgeous drunkards through the ages. London: Mandrake Press, 1929. 231p. Illus. G30930

> Rab Noolas is a pseudonym of Philip Heseltine and read backward is Saloon Bar, but the scholarship of the book reveals the author to be a person of considerable knowledge. The illustrations by Hal Collins are quite good. This is a curious book and will appeal to collectors of the unusual. Limited edition of 600 copies.

NORMAN, W. More fun with wine. New York: Pocket Books, 1973. 248p. G30940

NORRIS, Sheila. Your life is more pleasant with wine. The Australian Wine Board, n.d. [16]p. Illus. G30950

NORTH, Derek and BROMPTON, Sally. How to choose French red wines. London: Elvendon, 1983. 95p. G30960

_____. How to choose French white wines. London: Elvendon, 1983. 95p. G30970

NORTH, Sterling, ed. So red the nose; or, breath in the afternoon. New York: Farrar and Rinehart, 1935. 72p. Illus. G30980

NORTHEY, Jo. Good housekeeping book of wine. London: Ebury Press, 1974. 206p. Illus. G30990

NORTHOVER, Robin and VAN ECK, Norma. The feminine touch: Wine and food. Melbourne: Decalon, 1978. 96p. Illus. G31000

NORTON, Charles. Modern blending and rectification, containing recipes and directions for producing gins, cordials, all types of bitters, drinking specials, and all kinds of punches . . . Chicago: 1911. 106p. Illus. G31010

_____. Modern manual for rectifiers, compounders, and all dealers in whiskies, wines and liquors. Chicago: Foote and Salomon, 1900. 86p. G31020

NOTES for an epicure. A handbook on the traditions and service of wine and other beverages. Toledo: Libby Glass Manufacturing Co., 1933. 44p. Illus. G31030

NOVITSKY, Joseph W.D. A vineyard year, 1984. San Francisco: Chronicle Books, 1984. 120p. Illus. G31040

> One hundred color and forty black and white photographs by Nick Pavloff, a former Time-Life photographer.

NOWAK, Carol E and CHRISTIAN, Vance A., eds. Society of Wine Educators guide to wine courses taught by instructor members. Salt Lake City: The Society of Wine Educators, 1980. G31050

> A second edition was published in 1981 and edited by Vance A. Christian.

NURY, F.S. and FUGELSANG, K.C. The winemaker's guide. Fresno, CA: Valley Publishers, 1978. 106p. G31060

NUTT, Frederic. The complete confectioner; or, the whole art of confectionery made easy; with receipts for liqueure, homemade wines, cordials . . . London: Printed by J. Sweeton for Mattews Leigh, 1809. 261p. G31070

> Subsequent editions in 1815 and 1819.

NYKANEN, Lalli and SUOMALAINEN, H. Aroma of beer, wine and distilled alcoholic beverages. Hingham, MA: D. Reidel Pub., 1983. G31080

OENOLOGICAL instruments of precision. English abridgement of the French. 4th ed. Paris: Dujardin-Salleron, 1907. 112p. G31090

OINOPHILIS, Boniface (pseud). Ebrietatis encomium: or, the praise of drunkenness . . . London: E. Curl, 1722. 151p. Illus. G31100

> Second edition of 204p. was published in 1743.

_____. Ebrietatis encomium: or, the praise of drunkenness . . . New York: 1922. 177p. Illus. G31110

> Reprint of the 1722 edition.

OKON, Leonard. Before the corkscrew, an index to French wines. Omaha, NB: Perch Publications. G31120

OLD English wines and cordials. Rules and recipes for making all sorts of English wines and all the choicest cordials for the closet. Reprint. Bristol: High House Press, 1938. 32p. G31130

> Published in a limited edition of 215 copies, of which numbers one to twenty-five are signed by the artist and printer. The book was printed on an Albion handpress by James E. Master and the illustrations, designed and engraved by Reynolds Stone, are printed directly from the original wood blocks. Originally published in 1737.

OLD sherry; the story of the first hundred years of Gonzalez Byass and Co., 1835-1935. London: Sir Joseph Causton and Sons, 1935. 155p. Illus. G31125

OLDHAM, Charles F. California wines. A paper read before the Society of Arts, John Street, Adelphi, London, on January 31st, 1894. London: 1894. 15p. Illus. G31140

OLDMEADOW, Ernest James. Not claret. London: Richards, c1936. 96p. G31150

_____. The Saintsbury succession. Words spoken at the 24th meeting of The Saintsbury Club, 20th April 1944. Exeter: Sydney Lee, 1944. 12p. G31160

OLIVE and the vine, adapted for South Australia. Gawler, 1871. 12p. G31170

OLIVER, Katherine Elspeth. The claw. Los Angeles: Out West Magazine, 1914. 384p. G31180

> A novel with a California wine industry setting.

OLIVER, Raymond. Gastronomy of France. Cleveland: The Wine and Food Society in Association with World Publishing Company, 1967. 335p. Illus. G31190

> Contains forty-three pages on wine. Translated from the French by Claude Durrell. Mr. Oliver was owner and chief chef of the LeGrand Vefour, a Michelin three-star restaurant. He also accumulated one of the world's greatest libraries of culinary texts.

OLIVIER, Stuart. Wine journeys. New York: Duell, Sloan and Pearce, 1949. 312p. G31200

> This is a series of anecdotes of the author's adventures in wine collecting throughout Europe. Most of the wines are long since gone, but the author's enthusiasm for his subject and unusual style of writing make for entertaining reading.

OLKEN, Charles E., SINGER, Earl G. and ROBY, Norman. The connoisseurs' handbook of California wines. New York: Knopf, 1980. 182p. Illus. G31210

> A second edition of 230p. was published in 1983 and a third edition of 256p. in 1984. Over 200,000 copies in print.

OLMO, Harold P. Plant genetics and new grape varieties. 1976. 183p. G31215
See California Wine Oral History Series.

OLMO, Harold Paul. California ampelography (Binder's title: Chardonnay). San Francisco: Wine Advisory Board, c1971. G31220

_____. Plant genetics and new grape varieties. University of California, 1974. G31230

_____. Report to the government of Malta on grape and wine production in the Maltese Islands. Rome: Food and Agriculture Organization of the United Nations, 1963. 45p. Illus. G31240

_____. Ruby Cabernet and Emerald Riesling: two new table-wine grape varieties. Berkeley: University of California, Agricultural Experiment Station, Bulletin 704, 1948. 12p. Illus. G31250

_____. A survey of the grape industry of Western Australia. Perth, Western Australia: Vine Fruits Research Trust, 1956. 80p. Illus. G31260

_____. Training and trellising grapevines for mechanical harvest: the duplex system. Berkeley: University of California, Agricultural Extension Service, 1968. 16p. Illus. G31270

OLMO, Harold Paul and KOYAMA, A. Rubired and Royalty, new grape varieties for color, concentrate and port wine. Berkeley: University of California, Agricultural Experiment Station, Bulletin 789, 1962. 13p. Illus. G31280

OLMO, Harold Paul, ed. Proceedings of the Third International Symposium of Grape Breeding, June, 1980. Davis, CA: University of California, 1980. 331p. Illus. G31290

OLNEY, Bruce. Liqueurs, aperitifs and fortified wines. London: Hills and Boon, 1972. 92p. Illus. G31300

ONE hundred recipes for making beer and wine . . . Columbus, OH: Big Features Publicity, 1919. 63p. G31310

ONE hundred sixteen uncommon books on food and drink; from the distinguished collection on gastronomy of Marcus Crahan. Friends of Bancroft Library, 1975. G31320

ONE hundred years in the good earth 1849-1949. Angeston, S.A.: S. Smith and Sons, 1949. G31330

ONE hundred years of wine making 1847-1947. Rowland Flat, S.A.: G. Gamp and Sons, 1947. G31340

OPPENHEIMER, Karl. Ferments and their actions. Translated from the German by C. Ainsworth Mitchell. London: C. Griffin, 1901. 343p. G31350

OPPERMAN, Diederik J. Spirit of the vine: Republic of South Africa. Cape Town: Human and Rousseau, 1968. 360p. Illus. G31360
Published on the occasion of the 50th anniversary of the K.M.V. An interesting review of wine in South Africa, including its influence on art and literature.

ORCHARDS and vineyards of Ontario, the premier province of Canada. Liverpool: Ontario Government Agency, c1897. 9p. Illus. G31370

ORDISH, George. The constant pest: a short history of pests and their control. New York: Scribner, c1976. 240p. Illus. G31380

> Includes vine diseases.

_____. The great wine blight. London: J.M. Dent, 1972. 237p. Illus. G31390

> This is the story of *Phylloxera vastatrix*, the devastating disease that swept throughout the world's vineyards in the latter part of the 19th century and almost destroyed them completely. It tells how the disease started, spread and was finally conquered, and why today all of the world's great vines are grown on American rootstock. The definitive work on *Phylloxera*. Also published by Scribner in 1972.

_____. Vineyards in England and Wales. London: Faber and Faber, 1977. 186p. Illus. G31400

_____. Wine growing in England. London: Rupert Hart-Davis, 1953. 128p. Illus. G31410

ORFFER, C.J., ed. The southern point of Africa: from spirit of the vine. Cape Town: Human and Rousseau G31420

_____. Wine grape cultivars in South Africa. Cape Town: Human and Rousseau, 1979. 111p. Illus. G31430

ORIGINAL documents respecting the injurious effects and the impolicy of a further continuance of the Portuguese Royal Wine Company of Oporto. Translated from the original Portuguese in the *Portuguese Investigator*. London: Richardson, 1813. 101p. G31440

> The documents are letters to the *Investigador Portuguez em Inglaterra*, and the earliest is dated 1777. They have been selected, translated and given an introduction by an anonymous editor.

ORSI, Richard J. A list of references for the history of agriculture in California. Davis: University of California, 1974. 141p. G31460

> Includes sections on grapes and wines.

ORTOLANI, Vinicio. Wines of Italy and Italian wines imported into Canada. Ottawa: Runge Press, 127p. Illus. G31470

OSBORN, John. Vineyards in America: with remarks on temperance . . . culture of grape vine in the United States. New York: By the Author, 1855. 24p. G31480

OSTERMAN, Edmund. Wine and the bottom line. Washington, DC: National Restaurant Association, 1980. 79p. Illus. G31490

> A restaurant training manual.

OTT, Edward. From barrell to bottle. London: Dennis Dobson, 1953. 61p. G31500

_____. A tread of grapes: the autovinography of a wine lover. Bidford-on-Avon, England: By the Author, 1982. 94p. G31510

> A diary of wine stories covering the author's thirty-year love affair with wine. There are a number of amusing ancedotes in this entertaining book and perhaps Mr. Ott has partly unraveled the mystery of why modern burgundies aren't what they used to be. On a visit to Clos de Vougeot, founded in 1150 by the Cistercian monks, he found an old blackboard behind the presses with notations chalked on it: "1P, 2P, 3P." Investigation disclosed that the letters stood for the French word *Pigeage* meaning a routine carried out by the monks in the olden days, when on three occasions during fermentation, the monks jumped naked into the vats to stir up the grape skins. According to Mr. Ott "it was the only occasion in the year when the monks had a bath and for many years after this unhygienic stirring was abandoned it was said that a real burgundy expert could declare by the taste whether a wine was pre- or post-*Pigeage*."

_____. The wines of France. Pershore, Great Britain: Pershore Print., 1980. 20p. G31520

OUGH, Cornelius Steven. Chemical, physical and microbiological stability of wines and brandies. Rehovot, Israel: Israel Wine Institute, 1964. 26p. G31530

_____. Report to the government of Israel on wine production and the development of the research winery. Rome: Food and Agricultural Organization of the United Nations, 1965. G31540

_____. Selection of judges and sensory evaluations of wines. Rehovot: Israel Wine Institute, 1964. 19p. G31550

OUGH, Cornelius Steven and AMERINE, Maynard. Effects of temperature on wine making. Berkeley: University of California, Division of Agricultural Sciences, 1966. 36p. Illus. G31560

OUSBACK, Anders, ed. The Australian wine browser. Sydney: David Ell, 1979. 123p. Illus. G31580

_____. Words on wine: a collection of quotations selected by Anders Ousback. Melbourne: Hill of Content, 1977. 44p. Illus. G31590

The OXFORD Cherwell wine book. Oxford: The Cherwell Office, 1934. G31600

> An anthology of articles by prominent wine writers which originally appeared weekly in *The Cherwell,* the leading undergraduate journal. H. Warner Allen writes on sherry, Maurice Healy on burgundy, André Simon on Graves and Sauternes, etc.
>
> Simon begins his article with the playful comment: "When Heywood's *Fair Maid of the West* — who is, of course, a barmaid — offers some Graves to some swaggering sailors, one of them will have none of it, and exclaims, 'None but sextons drink Graves wine.' This is perfectly good evidence that Graves was shipped to England in Shakespearean days.

OXFORD night caps: a collection of recipes for making various beverages used in the university. Oxford: Peppercorn Press, 1827. 54p. G31610

> Was reissued many times including 1847, 1860, 1871 and 1893 with additional recipes. In this edition, there are recipes for a variety of cider and perry cups, possets, wine cups, punches, mead and metheglin.

OZIAS, Blake. All about wine. New York: Crowell, 1967. 144p. Illus. G31620

> Subsequent editions, including one published in 1973.

————. A commentary on wines. New York: Anthony Oechs, 1934. 59p. Illus. G31630

————. How the modern hostess serves wine. New York: The Epicurean Press, 1934. 27p. Illus. G31640

PACKER, Joy. Valley of the vines. Philadelphia: Lippincott, 1955. 278p. G31650

> A novel about South Africa and wine.

PACKMAN, W. Vance. Gentlemen's own guide to wines and spirits. London: By the Author, 1902. 91p. G31660

————. Wine and spirit manual and Packman's handy agency list. London: 1903. 264p. G31670

PACOTTET, Paul and GUITTONNEAU, L. Wines of Champagne and sparkling wines. 2nd ed. Paris: J.B. Bailliere, 1930. 401p. G31680

PAGE-ROBERTS, James. Vines in your garden. Andover, England: Amateur Winemaker, 1982. G31690

PAGUIERRE, M. Classification and description of the wines of Bordeaux . . . Edinburgh: William Blackwood, 1828. 164p. G31700

PAIGE, William Victor. Is this your wine? London: C. Johnson and New York: McBride, 1957. 76p. Illus. G31710

PAKENHAM, Michael. The first 100 columns. Philadelphia: By the Author, 1976. 113p. G31720

> The author wrote a syndicated weekly wine column for the *Philadelphia Inquirer* and published the first 100 of these, covering the period from September 16, 1973 through September 21, 1975.

PALLADIUS. Palladius on husbondrie. 2 Vols. Early English Text Society, 1872 and 1879. 387p. G31725

> The only known translation (from a manuscript of about 1420) into early English with a somewhat paraphrased modern English translation. Contains sections on vine growing and a little on wine.

PALMER, Bruce. Wine-making at home. New York: Workman Publishing, 1975. 119p. Illus. G31730

PALMER, E.F. and VAN HAARLEM, J.R. The grape in Ontario. Toronto: Ontario Department of Agriculture, 1938. 39p. Illus. G31740

PALMER, Edward. The spirit, wine dealer's and publican's director . . . London: G. and W.B. Whittaker, 1824. 276p. Illus. G31750

PALMER, J.S. Palmer's popular receipts; proper guide for making wines. London: 1850. 36p. G31760

PAMA, Cor. Cape wine homesteads. Johannesburg: A.D. Donker, 1980. 120p. Illus. G31770

_____. The wine estates of South Africa. Cape Town: Purnell, 1979. 103p. Illus. G31780

PANARELLA, Giancarlo. Italian wine and brandy buyer's guide. Rome: 1975. G31790

PARK, Robert, M.D. The case for alcohol: or, the actions of alcohol on body and soul. London: Rebman, 1909. 85p. G31800

PARKER, Robert Eugene. Place a drop of wine near my lips when I die. New York: Vantage Press, 1977. 73p. G31820

PARKER, Robert H. In praise of wine. New York: Dial Press, 1933. G31830

PARKER, Robert M. Jr. Bordeaux: a definitive guide 1961-1983. New York: Simon and Schuster, 1985. Illus.

PARKES, B. The domestic brewer and family wine maker. 1824 London: Wetton and Jarvis, 1821. 127p. Illus. G31860

PARKINSON, James. Observations on the nature and cure of gout: on nodes of the joints, and on the influence of certain articles of diet. London: Symonds, 1805. 174p. G31870

   Wine is believed to be one of the culprits.

PARONETTI, Lamberto. Chianti: A history of Florence and its wines. London: Wine and Spirit Publications, 1970. 224p. Illus. G31880

PARRACK, Anne. Commonsense wine-making. Andover, England: Amateur Winemaker, 1978. 206p. G31890

   A second edition was published in 1981.

PARRISH, M.F. The story of wine in California. Berkeley: University of California Press, 1962. 125p. Illus. G31900

PARSONS, Herbert. Grapes under glass. London: Collinridge and New York: Transatlantic Arts, 1955. 64p. Illus. G31910

PART, Alexander Francis. The art and practice of innkeeping. London: Heinemann, 1922. 308p. Illus. G31920

PARTRIDGE, Bruno. A history of orgies. London: 1958. G31930

PASCALL, Frank. Old-time recipes, AD 1720 to 1780. Wines, bitters, preserves, confections of two hundred years ago. London: By the Author, c1913. 38p. G31940

PASTEUR, Louis. Studies on fermentation. London: Macmillan, 1879. G31950

PATERSON, John. Choosing your wine. London: Hamlyn, 1980. 128p. Illus. G31960

_____. The Hamlyn book of wines. London: Hamlyn, 1975. 176p. Illus. G31970

_____. The Hamlyn pocket dictionary of wine. London: Hamlyn, 1980. 256p. G31980

_____. The international book of wines. London: Hamlyn, 1975. 176p. Illus. G31990

PATERSON, Wilma. A country cup. Old and new recipes for drinks of all kinds made from wild plants and herbs. London: Pelham, 1980. 96p. Illus. G32000

PATRICK, Ted. Great restaurants of America . Philadelphia and New York: Lippincott, c1960. Illus. G32010

> Contains a section on wine appreciation.

PATTEN, Marguerite. 500 recipes for home-made wines and drinks. London: Hamlyn, 1963. 96p. G32020

> A revised edition in 1971.

PATTON, William. Bible wines. New York: National Temperance Society, 1874. 139p. G32030

_____. The laws of fermentation and the wines of the ancients. New York: National Temperance Society, 1871. 129p. G32040

PAYNE, Brigham. Story of Bacchus and centennial souvenir. Hartford, CT: Brooks, 1876. 111p. Illus. G32050

PEABODY, Richard R. The common sense book of drinking. Boston: Little, Brown, 1931. 207p. G32070

PEARKES, Gillian. Complete home wine-making. London: Herbert Jenkins, 1962. 143p. Illus. G32080

> Subsequent editions in 1976, 1978 and 1983.

_____. Growing grapes in Britain. A handbook for winemakers. Andover, England: Amateur Winemaker, 1969. 156p. Illus. G32090

> Four subsequent editions were published through 1978.

_____. Vinegrowing in Britain. London: Dent, 1982. 324p. Illus. G32100

PEARL, Raymond. Alcohol and longevity. New York: Knopf, 1926. 273p. G32110

PEARSON, John R. Vine culture under glass. 3rd ed. London: Journal of Horticulture and Cottage Gardener, 1873. 40p. G32120

> Subsequent revised editions, including one of 52p. in 1885 and one of 56p. in 1901.

PEARSON, Ken. Heritage of the soil and sun. Livermore, CA: Cresta Blanca Wine Co., 1950. [21]p. Illus. G32130

PEEKE, Hewson Lindsley. Americana ebrietatis; the favorite tipple of our forefathers and the laws and customs relating thereto. New York: Privately printed, 1917. 154p. G32140

The subtitle on the half-title page of this book is "Byegone Ways of Byegone Days," and it is apparently the purpose of this scarce book ("one hundred copies of this edition have been printed for sale and the type distributed") to describe the drinking habits of Americans, including the clergy. By 1917, these habits had led to the sentiment that would result in the Volstead Act of 1919.

When Congress met in 1774 in Philadelphia, John Adams, after dining with a young Quaker couple, notes in his diary: "A mighty feast again; nothing less then the very best of claret, madeira and burgundy. I drank madeira at a great rate and found no inconvenience." William Byrd, a prominent 17th century Virginian, ordered for the Council of Lower Norfolk twenty dozen of claret, and six dozen of canary, sherry and rhenish, respectively. A quarter cask of brandy was also added.

Thaddeus Stevens noted, about 1820, that for his examination for the Maryland Bar there was one indispensable requirement: "There must be two bottles of madeira on the table and the applicant must order it in." After passing the exam, he was told that the ceremony closed as it opened. He willingly supplied two more bottles.

The Supreme Court imported madeira every year. Justice John Story recalled that this was "labelled 'The Supreme Court', as their Honors . . . used to make 'a direct importation every year and sip it as they consulted over the cases before them every day after dinner, when the cloth had been removed.' "

Among other things, the book documents the hold that madeira had on the upper-classes. It was by far the most-consumed wine in pre- and post-Revolutionary days. As Justice Story wrote of Chief Justice John Marshall, "The Chief was brought up on Federalism and Madeira, and he is not the man to outgrow his early prejudices."

_____. Americana ebrietatis; the favorite tipple of our forefathers and the laws and customs relating thereto. Reprint. New York: Hacker Books, 1970. G32150

PEIXOTTO, Ernest. A bacchic pilgrimage. French wine. New York: Scribner's, 1932. 201p. Illus. G32160

The author's skill as a writer and artist enliven this account of his trip through France's vineyards. The text is complemented by thirty-one pen and ink drawings by the author and Staats Cotsworth.

PELLEGRINI, Angelo. The unprejudiced palate. New York: Macmillan, 1948. 235p. G32170

Essays on food and wine by a university professor. Includes recipes, methods of making wine at home and advice regarding alcoholic beverages.

_____. Wine and the good life. New York: Knopf, 1965. 307p. G32180

PELLICOT, Andre. The wine and winemaking in southern France. Melbourne: A. Walker May, 1868. 76p. G32190

PELLUCCI, Emanuele. Antinori: Vintners in Florence. Florence: Vallecchi, 1981. 116p. Illus. G32200

_____. Brunello di Montalcino. Florence: By the Author, 1981. 131p. Illus. G32210

> The history, production, techniques, and wineries of Italy's most expensive wine.

PENINOU, Ernest P. A history of Orleans Hill Vineyard and Winery of Arpad Haraszthy and Company. Winters, CA: Yolo Hills Viticultural Society, 1983. 33p. Illus. G32220

> Also an account of the wine growing activities in Capay Valley, Yolo County, California (northeasts of Napa) in the 1880's and 1890's.

_____. Peter Lassen's Bosquejo Rancho 1844-1851. Red Bluff, CA: By the Author, c1965. [40]p. G32230

> About the history of viticulture and winemaking at Vina, Tehama County, California.

_____. Winemaking in California. 2 vols. San Francisco: Peregrine Press, 1954. Illus. G32240

> Designed, handset and hand printed by Henry Evans. The illustrations and cover blocks were designed and cut by Patricia Evans. Vol. 1 of 37p. covers: "How wine is made" and "From the missions to 1894." Vol. 2 of 36p. covers: "The California Wine Association" and index. Limited edition of 150 copies.

PENINOU, Ernest and GREENLEAF, Sidney. A directory of California wine-growers and winemakers in 1860 with biographical and historical notes and index. Berkeley: Tamalpais Press, 1967. 84p. Illus. G32250

> 263 persons are listed as engaged in growing grapes or making wine in California. When known, biographical and historical sketches are given. Of the many sites where wine was being made in 1860, the authors conclude "that there seem to be only six occupied by wineries today. However, there are many sites of 1860 vineyards still planted to grapes." There are historical sketches of the Kohler and Frohling vineyard in Los Angeles, Jacob Gundlach's vineyard in Sonoma and Agoston Haraszthy's vineyard in Sonoma. Limited edition of 450 copies.

PENNING-ROWSELL, Edmund. The International Wine and Food Society's guide to the wines of Bordeaux. London: Michael Joseph, 1969. 320p. Illus. G32260

> Also published in 1970 by Stein and Day of New York. Subsequent editions.

_____. Red, white and rose. A guide to wines and spirits. London: Pan Books, 1967. 129p. Illus. G32270

> A second edition was published in 1973.

PENZER, Norman Mosley. The book of the wine label. London: Home and Van Thal, 1947. 143p. Illus. G32280

> This is the definitive work on the historical development of silver, enamel and Sheffield plate decanter labels in England. Although collectors' items today, they were used in past centuries to identify the wine brought to the table in decanters. A second edition of 143p. was published by White Lion Publishers of London in 1974.

PEPPERCORN, David. Bordeaux. London: Faber and Faber, 1982. 428p. Illus. G32290

PEPPERCORN, David and COOPER, Brian and BLACKER, Elwyn. Drinking wine: a complete guide for the buyer and consumer. London: Mac-Donald, 1979. 256p. Illus. G32300

> The most original feature of this book is Peppercorn's ratings, by which 1000 wines are given from one to five stars to indicate not only the quality of each wine but its value in relation to its price.

PERDIX, Elizabeth. Wine for the vintage. New York: Raley, 1939. 256p. G32310

PERELLI-MINETTI, Antonio. A life of wine making. 1975. 174p. Illus. G32315

> See California Wine Oral History Series.

PERKINS, Arthur, J. Vine-pruning: its theory and practice. Adelaide: Printed by Vardon and Pritchard, 1895. 74p. Illus. G32320

PEROLD, Abraham Izaak. A treatise on viticulture. London: Macmillan and Stellenbosch: Stellenbosch University, 1927. 696p. Illus. G32330

> For many years this was the standard text on viticulture.

PERRY, Evan. Corkscrews and bottle openers. Princes Risborough, Bucks: Shire Publications, 1980. 32p. Illus. G32340

PERRY, Martin H. And to drink Sir! London: St. Giles Publishing, 1947. 72p. G32350

> Includes wine.

PERSOZ, Juan F. New process of the culture of the vine. New York: C.M. Saxton, 1857. 58p. Illus. G32360

> Translated by J. O'C. Barclay.

PETEL, Pierre. The little wine steward. 155p. G32370

> Unable to verify.

PETERSON, Harold Leslie. Cups of valor. Harrisburg, PA: Stackpole, 1968. 106p. Illus. G32380

PETERSON-NEDRY, Judy. Showcase Oregon wineries. Portland: H. Dieter Rickford, 1981. 68p. Illus. G32390

PETRI, Louis A. The Petri family in the wine industry. 1971. 67p. G32394

> See California Wine Oral History Series.

PEYNAUD, Emile. Knowing and making wine. New York: John Wiley, 1984. 400p. Illus. G32395

Emile Peynaud (1913) has had more influence on the style of today's Bordeaux wines than any other single person. His influence
has been so strong that it is often referred to as the "Peynaudiza-
tion of Bordeaux."

PEYSER, Jefferson E. The law and the California wine industry. 1974. 71p.
Illus. G32398

See California Wine Oral History Series

PHELPS, Richard Harvey. The vine: its culture in the United States. Wine
making from grapes and other fruit, useful recipes . . . Hartford: Press
of Case, Tiffany, 1855. 83p. Illus. G32400

Directed toward the home grower and wine maker.

PHILLIPS, Dr. Gilbert. The appreciation of wine. Sydney: 1950. 14p. G32410

Sixth J.K. Walker lecture to the Wine and Food Society of N.S.W.
dealing with the physiology of wine tasting. 500 copies were issued.

PHILLIPS, Keith. Barossa Valley. Sydney: Rigby, c1972. 32p. Illus. G32420

PHILLIPS, Marion, ed. The vineyard almanac and wine gazetteer. Los Altos,
CA: The Vineyard Almanac and Gazetteer, 1980. 96p. Illus. G32430

A yearbook compendium of wine information.

PHIN, John. Open air grape culture: a practical treatise on the garden and
vineyard culture of the vine, and the manufacture of domestic wine.
Designed for the use of amateurs and others in the northern and middle states; to which is added a selection of examples of American vineyard practice, and a carefully prepared description of the celebrated
Thomery system of grape culture. New York: C.M. Saxton, 1862. 375p.
Illus. G32440

A revised edition was published in 1876 with the advice to women
that they could earn more money by cultivating the grapevine than
by making shirts.

PHIPPS, William. The vintner's guide, containing useful information as well
for the vintner as for the brewer, distiller, and merchant. Dublin: John
Bromell, Boyle, 1825. 248p. G32450

PHYLLOXERA Vastatrix. Report of the Secretary for Agriculture Australia:
1879. 6p. G32460

Contains a map of the Geelong vineyards in 1879 showing up-
rooted and still existing vineyards. Limited printing of 775 copies.

PIAZ, Antonio dal. Brandy distillation. Appendix A to the biennial report of
the board of State Viticultural Commissioners. For 1891-1892. Sacramento: A.J. Johnston, Supt. State Print., 1892. 125p. Illus. G32465

Brandy production in California had become so important that it
was one of the leading branches of the viticultural industry. The
book consists of two parts. The first part covers historical and sta-
tiscial data, grapes suitable for fine brandy, stills in use in California, how to establish and operate a distillery and foreign markets

for brandies. The second part is a translation of a German work by Antonio Dal Piaz concerning the distillation and manufacture of cognac. There are two color plates of the folle blanche leaf and grape together with numerous illustrations of stills and related equipment.

PICKERING, Clarence R. The early days of Prohibition. New York: Vantage, 1964. 145p. G32480

A PICTORIAL history of Australian wine. London: Emu Wine Co., c1960. 20p. Illus. G32490

PIERCE, Newton Barris. The California vine disease. A preliminary report of investigations. Washington: Gov't. Print. Off., 1892. 222p. G32500

Includes information on the origins of the California wine industry.

PIEROTH, Kuno F. The great German wine book. New York: Sterling, 1982. 220p. Illus. G32510

An interesting book in three parts. Part I relates the history of wines from ancient times to present day Germany. This section is illustrated with color reproductions of paintings, mosaics and statuary. Part II is a word-and-picture tour through the eleven German winemaking districts. The color photography is imaginative and beautifully reproduced. Part III is far less laborious than the title "The Long Road from Vine to Glass" might imply. The text and photographs cover drinking utensils and bottles from Roman times to present, wine labels, great vintages, wine tasting and wine and health.

PINNEGAR, Francis. How to make home wines and beers. London and New York: Hamlyn, 1978. 80p. Illus. G32520

PINONI, Pietro and BURGER, Robert F. Pietro on wine. San Francisco: Delphio Press, 90p. Illus. G32530

PITTMAN, David J. and SNYDER, Charles R., eds. Society, culture and drinking patterns. New York: John Wiley, 1962. 616p. G32540

PLATTER, John. John Platter's book of South African wines. Derek Butcher, 1980. 119p. Illus. G32550

A subsequent edition was published in 1982.

PLAYBOY'S wine guide; the ABC's of selecting, storing and serving wine. Chicago: Playboy, 1975. G32560

PLIMMER, R.H.A. The chemical changes and products resulting from fermentation. London: Longmans, 1903. 184p. G32570

POGASH, Jeffrey. How to read a wine label. New York: Hawthorne, 1978. 216p. Illus. G32580

A dictionary of French and California wine terms, including prices, serving suggestions and methods for evaluating your wine merchant.

POHREN, D.E. Adventures in taste: the wines and folk foods of Spain. Madrid: Society of Spanish Studies, 1972. 302p. Illus. G32590

An account of the author's trips through Spain. It includes descriptions of the wines, foods and places and provides recipes for Spanish food and details about how the wines are made.

POISTER, John J. Wine lover's drink book. London: Collier Books, 1983. 204p. G32600

POLLACK, Pam. Dining and drinking. New York: Hart, 1977. G32610

PONGRACZ, D.P. Practical viticulture. Cape Town: David Philip, 1978. 240p. Illus. G32620

PONSOT, Maurice. Complete yearbook of French quality wines. 1945. G32630

Unable to verify.

POPRMILOVIC, Boris, ed. Wines and wine-growing districts of Yugoslavia. Zagreb: Zadruzna Stampa, 1969. 98p. Illus. G32640

PORTER, John D. The chef suggests. London: Robertson and Mullens, 1950. 203p. Illus. G32660

Contains information on Australian wines.

POSTGATE, Raymond. An alphabet of choosing and serving wine. London: Herbert Jenkins, 1955. 94p. G32670

_____. The home wine cellar; with chapters on home bottling and other advice on the care of wine. London: Herbert Jenkins, 1960. 94p. Illus. G32680

_____. The plain man's guide to wine. 14th ed. London: Michael Joseph, 1967. 164p. Illus. G32690

_____. Portuguese wine. London: Dent, 1969. 102p. Illus. G32700

POTTER, Mike. The wines and wineries of South Australia. Adelaide: Rigby, 1978. 226p. Illus. G32710

POTTER, S. A Christmas miscellany containing good cheermanship, with notes on winemanship. London: Blumenthals, c1950. 20p. G32720

POTTICARY, John F. Potential for the development of a wine and supporting wine grape industry in Oregon. Portland: State Department of Commerce, Economic Development Division, 1968. 12p. G32730

POULTER, Nick. Growing wines. Andover, England: Amateur Winemaker, 1972. 109p. Illus. G32740

Subsequent editions.

_____. Wines from your vines. Andover, England: Amateur Winemaker, 1974. 106p. G32750

POUPON, Pierre and FORGEOT, Pierre. A book of Burgundy. London: Lund Humphries, 1958. 78p. Illus. G32760

Introduction by André L. Simon; translated by Siriol Hugh-Jones. The text was written to accompany the beautiful handmade color illustrations by Denis Mathews and was never published in French.

_____. The wines of Burgundy. 6th ed., rev. Paris: Presses Universitaires de France, 1979. 231p. G32770

POWERS, Lucius. The Fresno area and the California wine industry. 1974. 54p. Illus. G32775

  See California Wine Oral History Series.

The PRACTICAL distiller: or, a brief treatise of practical distillation in which the doctrine of fermentation is methodically explained in a new method. With the description of a new engine-still . . . to which is added . . . a treatise of making artificial wines from several fruits of the British production . . . London: B. Lintot, 1718. 54p. G32780

A PRACTICAL man. The butler, the wine-dealer and private brewer. London: G. Biggs, c1840. 134p. G32790

A PRACTICAL man. The innkeeper and public brewer. London: G. Biggs, c1840. 152p. G32800

PRATT, Edwin A. The licensed trade: an independent survey . . . London: John Murray, 1907. 329p. G32810

PRATT, James Norwood. The wine bibber's bible. San Francisco: 101 Productions, 1971. 191p. Illus. G32820

  Also 1975 and 1981 editions.

[PRENTISS, Albert Nelson] My vineyard at Lakeview, by a western grape grower. New York: Orange Judd, 1866. 143p. G32830

  This is the personal account of a New Englander who left the printing trade and moved to Ohio resolved to change his life style. The author chronicles his selection of land, choice of native vines and year-by-year failures, followed by successes that led eventually to a profitable commercial vineyard. Prentiss reveals the daily life of a hard-working pioneer viticulturist who wrote to share his experiences but who was too modest to put his name to the book.

PRESCOTT, Albert B. Chemical examination of alcoholic liquors. New York: Van Nostrand, 1875. 108p. G32840

  Much about wine. Also 1880 edition.

PRESTON, William A. Cork and wine. St. Helena, CA: Illuminations Press, 64p. Illus. G32850

  Written by an executive of one of the principal suppliers of corks and stoppers to the wine industry, this little monologue will answer most questions one might have about this subject.

PRETTYMAN, Mrs. Hannah. Recipes for homemade wines. London: Wren Books, 1946. 30p. G32860

_____. Thirty-three recipes for homemade wines. London: Wren Books, 1947. 81p. G32870

PRIAL, Frank J. Wine talk. New York: Times Books, 1978. 264p. Illus. G32880

  Frank Prial has been the wine editor for *The New York Times* except for a three year period when he served as a foreign correspondent. In 1981 he was awarded the *Wines and Vines* "Perpetual Trophy for Excellence in Wine Writing." This is a compilation of eighty-four short, well-written articles or profiles on subjects such as Friedrich Engel's preference for 1848 Chateau Margaux, Thomas Jefferson's fondness for 1784 Haut-Brion, corkscrews, the history of Mouton-Rothschild's famous artist labels, and the judging of hundreds of red wines at the 1977 Los Angeles County Fair. An informative travel companion.

PRICE, Pamela Vandyke. Companion to the wines of Bordeaux. London: Century, 1983. 121p. Illus. G32890

_____. A directory of wines and spirits. London: Northwood Publications, 1974. 118p. Illus. G32900

A greatly expanded and revised edition of 394p. was published in 1980.

_____. Eating and drinking in France today. London: Stacy and New York: Scribner's, 1972. 324p. Illus. G32910

Subsequent editions.

_____. Enjoying wine: a taster's companion. London: Heinemann, 1982. 202p. Illus. G32920

_____. Entertaining with wine. London: Northwood Publications, 1976. 196p. Illus. G32930

_____. France: a food and wine guide. London: Batsford and New York: Hastings House, 1966. 328p. Illus. G32940

_____. Guide to the wines of Bordeaux. Pitman, 1977. 121p. G32950

_____. Guide to the wines of Champagne. Pitman, 1979. 140p. Illus. G33020

_____. The Penguin book of spirits and liqueurs. Penguin, 1980. 334p. G32960

_____. The taste of Kinloch. London: Kinloch and Co., 1961. 42p. Illus. G32970

A handbook of wines and spirits based on the experience of Charles Kinloch and Co., wine and spirit merchants. The book was published to celebrate 100 years in the wine trade.

_____. The taste of wine. London: Macdonald and Jane's, 1975. 192p. Illus. G32980

Of more value as a reference to the history of wine, soil, grapes, methods of vinification, what to drink, maps, wine areas, etc. than on tastes of different kinds of wines. Nicely illustrated with color photographs.

_____. Understanding wines and spirits. London: Corgi, 1982. 233p. G32990

_____. Winelovers handbook. New York: Simon and Schuster and

London: Conde Nast Publications, 1969. 80p. and 97p. Illus. G33000

_____. Wines and spirits. London: Corgi, 1972. G33010

PRICE, Pamela Vandyke and FIELDEN, Christopher. Alsace wines and spirits. London: Sotheby Publications, 1984. 216p. Illus. G33025

PRINCE, William Robert. A treatise on the vine; embracing its history from the earliest ages to the present day . . . with a complete dissertation on the establishment, culture, and management of vineyards. New York: T. and J. Swords, 1830. 355p. Illus. G33030

> William Robert Prince (1795-1869) was the fourth proprietor of the famous Prince Nursery and Linnaean Botanic Garden at Flushing, Long Island. During his lifetime the Prince Nursery was the most important nursery in the United States. Prince was a capable horticulturist, and his book presents what was known of both the European and American grape. It includes a history of the vine from Roman times and a summary of regional European viticultural practices. A major portion of the text is the detailed description and classification of hundreds of European and American grape varieties, most of which were being cultivated at the Prince Nursery. Among them is listed the "Black Zinfardel [sic] of Hungary." Thus, the Zinfandel was cultivated in the eastern United States at least twenty-six years before Agoston Haraszthy (who has often been credited with the introduction of that grape into the United States) began his viticultural efforts at his Buena Vista Ranch in Sonoma Valley. Prince specified which grapes were best for the table and which for wine. He advocated the hybridizing of European and American vines, and at the request of European vinegrowers he had American varieties sent to France, Germany and Madeira. Although the Prince Nursery had cultivated European vines for decades and his text contains much information on them, Prince's own preference for native varieties is unmistakable. He concluded that "to establish vineyards of the most profitable description, with a certainty of regular crops in localities north of the highlands in this state, native varieties alone should be selected. . . ."

PRINTS and drawings of the grape and wine in the historical collection of The Christian Brothers of California. San Francisco: n.p., 1968. 22p. Illus. G33040

PRISNEA, Constantin. Bacchus in Rumania. Bucharest: Meridiana, 1964. 244p. Illus. G33050

PROCEEDINGS of 1st International Symposium on Sparkling Wines. Italy: Chiriotti Editori, 1981. 194p. Illus. G33060

> Reports of the symposium were published in the language in which they were read, with summaries in the official languages: English, French, German and Italian.

PRONSINI, Bill. Twospot. New York: Putnam, 1978. G33070

> A novel with a California wine industry setting.

PROSKAUER, Julien J., ed. What'll you have? New York and Chicago: Burt, c1933. 128p. Illus. G33080

PROSSER, Richard Bissell. Birmingham inventors and inventions - being a contribution to the industrial history of Birmingham. Birmingham: The "Journal" Printing Works, 1881. 251p. G33090

> Describes Thomason's "Ne plus ultra" corkscrew patented in 1802. This corkscrew combined the novelty ". . . that one continuous motion of the handle causes the worm to inter the cork and also withdraws it from the bottle. Another advantage is that the cork is discharged . . . by simply turning the handle in the reverse direction. . . ." Thomason made 130,000 of these corkscrews during a fourteen-year period.

PUISAIS, J. Initiation into the art of wine tasting. Madison, WI: Interpublish, 1974. G33100

> Translated from the French.

PURSER, J. Elizabeth. The winemakers. Vashon Island, WA: Harbor House Publishing, 1977. 224p. Illus. G33110

> The story of winemaking in the states of Washington and Oregon. The text has been beautifully illustrated with 241 color photographs by Lawrence Allen that capture the spirit and activity of the people involved in winemaking, and the natural beauty of the Northwest.

PYNE, William Henry. Wine and walnuts; after dinner chit-chat. London: Longman, Hurst, Rees, Orme and Brown, 1823. G33120

> Second edition, 1824.

QUACK-vintners; or a satyr against bad wine, with directions where to have good. Inscribed to B   ks and H   R. London: 1712. 24p. G33130

> Edward Ward, 1667-1731, is the attributed author of this poem.

QUARLES, Francis. Barnabas and boanerges: or, wine and oyle for afflicted soules. 2nd ed. London: James Lindesay, 1645. 222p. G33140

QUIMME, Peter. The Signet book of American wine. New York: New American Library, 1975. 276p. Illus. G33160

> Subsequent revised editions.

QUINN, George. Fruit tree and grape vine pruning; a handbook for fruit and vine growers, working under the climatic and economic conditions prevailing in temperate Australia. 4th ed. Adelaide: Gov't. Print., 1913. 278p. Illus. G33170

> Many subsequent editions.

_____. Influence of the season of planting on the rooting of grape vine cuttings. Adelaide: South Australia Agriculture Department, 1931. G33180

QUITTANSON, Charles and DES AULNOYES, Francois. The elite of the wines of France; spirits, eaux-de-vie and liqueurs. Paris: Centre National de Coordination, c1967. 199p. Illus. G33190

RABELAIS, Francois. The works of Rabelais. The Urquhart-Le Motteux translation, edited with an introduction and notes by Alfred J. Nock and

Catherine Rose Wilson. 2 Vols. New York: Harcourt, Brace, 1931. 952p. Illus. G33200

> It is not our purpose, even had we the ability, to review the works of Francois Rabelais (1495-1553) for there is a good sized library of scholarly - and often contradictory - books on the subject. However, the five books of *Gargantua* and *Pantagruel* merit some mention among wine books.
>
> Gargantua was born saying Drink! Drink! Drink! and his son, Pantagruel, went on a memorable quest in search of the wisdom of the "Divine Bottle."
>
> In fact, wine drinking is so pervasive throughout the five books, both as a literary and, as some allege, a symbolic device, that many scholars have theorized about it. To some it is a form of religious cryptography; to others it is an exhortation to drink deeply of all of life's mysteries, including philosophy, knowledge and God. Still others have taken the drinking and scatology literally and see in it that Rabelais was, though a genius, only a drunken and bawdy teller of heretical tales.
>
> The controversy has gone on for centuries and will probably never be resolved. One of the latest books on the subject is Florence Weinberg's *The Wine and the Will: Rabelais's Bacchic Christianity.* (See listing.)
>
> Perhaps it was fitting that in only the fourth meeting of the Wine and Food Society in 1934, André Simon presided over a luncheon of 300 in honor of Francois Rabelais.

RACK, John. The French wine and liquor manufacturer. A practical guide and receipt book for the liquor merchant . . . including complete instructions for manufacturing champagne wine . . . 2nd ed. New York: Dick and Fitzgerald, 1865. 268p. Illus. G33210

> First edition, 1863; subsequent editions, including 1868 and 1873.

RAELSON, Jeffrey E. Getting to know German wines. Miami: Banyan Books, 1979. 80p. Illus. G33220

RAFINESQUE, Constantine Samuel. American manual of the grape vine and the art of making wine: including an account of sixty-two species of vines, with nearly 300 varieties. An account of the principal wines, American and foreign. Properties and uses of wines and grapes. Cultivation of vines in America; and the art to make good wines. Philadelphia: By the Author, 1830. 64p. Illus. G33230

> Rafinesque (1783-1840) was born in Turkey. He came to Philadelphia when he was nineteen years old and studied botany as a hobby. In 1805, he went to Sicily where he spent the next ten years and commenced his scientific publications, which numbered more than 400 at the time of his death in 1840. In 1815, he returned to the United States and became a professor at Transylvania University in Lexington, Kentucky.
>
> Although his botanical studies of the grape are now discredited by botanists, Rafinesque gave an account of vineyard acreage in the

United States between 1825 and 1830. This is the earliest vineyard acreage estimates of this country. Rafinesque reported: "In 1825 I collected an account of our principal vineyards and nurseries of vines. They were then only sixty of one to twenty acres each, altogether 600 acres. While now, in 1830, they amount to 200 of three to forty acres, or nearly 5,000 acres of vineyards. Thus having increased tenfold within five years, at which rate they promise to become a permanent and increasing cultivation."

RAGAN, William Henry. The home vineyard, with special reference to northern conditions. Washington, DC: USDA, 1902. 22p. G33240

RAINBIRD, George M. Escape to sunshine. A story of a happy holiday. London: Collins, 1952. 256p. Illus. G33250

_____. An illustrated guide to wine. New York: Harmony Books, 1983. 224p. Illus. G33260

Over 300 color photographs.

_____. The pocket book of wine. London: Evans Brothers, 1963. 157p. G33270

_____. Sherry and the wines of Spain. London: McGraw-Hill, 1966. 228p. Illus. G33280

_____. The subtle alchemist. London: Michael Joseph, 1973. Illus. G33290

_____. The wine handbook. New York: Hawthorn Books, 1964. 157p. Illus. G33300

RAINFORD, Bentham. Sicily and its wines. London: n.d. G33310

Unable to verify.

RAMBLES in Madeira and in Portugal with details illustrative of the health, climate, produce and civil history of Madeira. London: C. and J. Rivington, 1827. 380p. G33320

RAMEY, Bern C. The great wine grapes and the wines they make. Burlingame, CA: The Great Wine Grapes, 1977. [252]p. Illus. G33330

Bern Ramey graduated from the University of California, Davis, with a degree in Enology and Viticulture in 1946. He describes thirty of the greatest grapes grown in California and the wines they make. In addition, a viticultural profile of each grape has been supplied by Dr. Lloyd A. Lider, Professor of Viticulture and Enology at the University of California, Davis. Each grape variety is illustrated with a full color photograph. The photographs were taken over a three-year period in the experimental vineyards at Davis by the author's son, Tim. The photographs are of superb quality and have not been altered or retouched in any way. For the photography buff, the manner in which the prints were taken is described in the biographical sketch of Tim Ramey. The book has been produced on eighty-pound vellum paper stock. The Foreword is by Maynard Amerine. A beautiful book for reading and viewing.

_____. Pocket dictionary of wines. Skokie, IL: Wineco Publishing, 1970. 64p. Illus. G33340

_____. The still white table wines of America. New York: Sommelier's Society, n.d. 9p. G33350

_____. The winesap is not necessarily an apple. American Society of Enologists, 1955. [8]p. G33360

RAMOS, Adam and RAMOS, Joseph. Ramos' guide - 680 mixed wine drinks. San Francisco: Apple Pie Press, 1974. 163p. Illus. G33370

RAMSDEN, Eric. Busby of Waitangi - resident of New Zealand. Wellington: A.H. and A.W. Reed, 1942. 396p. Illus. G33380

_____. James Busby, the prophet of Australian viticulture and British resident at New Zealand (1833-40). 2nd ed. Sydney: D.S. Ford, 1941. 28p. G33390

RANDOLPH, Thomas. The drinking academy. Cambridge: Harvard University Press, 1930. 64p. G33400

RANKINE, Bryce Crossley. Observations on wine making and wine research in France, Germany, Switzerland and California; a report to the Council of the Australian Wine Research Institute. Adelaide: Australian Wine Research Institute, 1967. 55p. G33410

_____. Wines and wineries of the Barossa Valley. Melbourne: Jacaranda, 1971. 114p. Illus. G33420

RANNIE, William F. Wines of Ontario. Lincoln, Ontario: By the Author, 1978. 171p. Illus. G33430

> An historical account of grape growing and wineries in Ontario from 1860 to the present.

The RATIONAL manufacture of American wines. St. Louis: Oesterreicher and Co., 1872. 144p. Illus. G33440

RAWNSLEY, Kenneth. Homemade wine, how to go about it. London: Thorson's, 1979. 79p. G33450

CYRIL RAY (1908)

After leaving Oxford, Mr. Ray eventually became journalist and professional writer. During the Second World War he was correspondent for the *Manchester Guardian* and the BBC and he had a distinguished war record. Following the war, he served as chief consultant to the *Good Food Guide* and was the founder and first president of the Circle of Wine Writers. One of Mr. Ray's most significant contributions to wine literature was his editorship of the *Compleat Imbiber* series, which was awarded in 1964 the Wine and Food Society's first André Simon Prize. In addition to his many books on wine, he has written extensively on this subject for numerous newspapers, magazines and periodicals.

RAY, Cyril. Bollinger; the story of a champagne. London: Peter Davies, 1971. 179p. Illus. G33470

Largely a discourse about a single champagne house, but includes a description of the Champagne riots of 1911 and other worthwhile information. A revised and enlarged edition of 217p. was published by Heinemann/Peter Davies in 1982, which includes a new chapter on Madame Bollinger, who ran the firm for thirty years until her death in 1977.

_____. Cognac. New York: Stein and Day, 1974. 171p. Illus. G33480

_____. The complete book of spirits and liqueurs. London: Cassell, 1978. 139p. Illus. G33490

_____. Cyril Ray's book of wine. New York: William Morrow, 1978. 125p. Illus. G33500

_____. Fide et fortitudine. The story of a vineyard: Langoa-Leoville Barton 1821-1971. Oxford: Pergamon Press, 1971. 29p. Illus. G33510

_____. The gourmet's companion. London: Eyre and Spottiswoode, 1963. 505p. Illus. G33520

_____. The house of Warre 1670-1970. London: Warre and Co., 1971. [22]p. Illus. G33530

_____. Introduction to wines. London: Observer, 1960. 35p. Illus. G33540

_____. Lafite. The story of Lafite-Rothschild. 2nd ed. New York: Stein and Day, 1971. 162p. Illus. G33550

A revised edition of this monograph first published in 1968. There are appendices of vintage notes from 1847 to 1977, comparative prices of recent vintages and those of other first growth clarets, tasting notes from 1918 to 1976, and Lafite auction prices from 1806 to 1971.

_____. Lickerish limericks. London: Dent, 1979. 48p. Illus. G33560

The limericks are spiced by Charles Mozley's drawings.

_____. Mouton-Rothschild. London: Christie Wine Publications, 1974. 64p. Illus. G33570

_____. The new book of Italian wines. London: Sidgwick and Jackson, 1982. 240p. Illus. G33580

_____. Ray on wine. London: Dent, 1979. 198p. Illus. G33590

A personal expression of the pleasure Ray has derived from wine during forty-plus years.

_____. Robert Mondavi of the Napa Valley. London: Peter Davies/ Heinemann, 1984. 171p. Illus. G33600

_____. Ruffino: the story of a Chianti. Italy: I.L. Ruffino, 1978. 158p. Illus. G33610

_____. The wines of France. London: Allen Lane, 1976. 205p. Illus. G33620

_____. The wines of Germany. London: Allen Lane, 1977. 224p. Illus. G33630

—————. The wines of Italy. London: McGraw-Hill, 1966. 136p. Illus. G33640

RAY, Cyril and RAY, Elizabeth. Wine with food. London: Sidgwick and Jackson, 1975. 159p. Illus. G33650

RAY, Cyril, ed. The compleat imbiber no. 1. London: Putnam, 1956. 256p. Illus. G33660

> *The Compleat Imbiber* consists of twelve volumes edited by Cyril Ray and published between 1957 and 1971.
>
> Each volume is an anthology of stories about food and drink by many of England's most prominent writers, and is nicely illustrated with pictures of paintings, engravings, drawings, and photographs covering a period of 4,000 years from ancient Egypt to Picasso.
>
> *The Compleat Imbiber* anthologies first appeared in 1953 as the magazine of W. and A. Gilbey, distillers and wine shippers. Mr. Ray edited a selection of those stories and it was published as Vol. 1 by Putnam in time for Gilbey's centenary held at the Cafe Royal from May 23 to June 7, 1957 and titled *The Compleat Imbiber, a Centenary Exhibition of Drinking Through the Centuries.*
>
> Volume 1 was so successful that Gilbey's continued its sponsorship through Volume 4. John Harvey and Sons of Bristol sponsored Volumes 5 through 9. Volumes 10 and 11 were sponsored by the London wine shippers, F.S. Matta. Volume 12 was jointly sponsored by F.S. Matta and the wine firm of Findlater, Mackie, Todd and Co. Charles Hasler designed each volume beginning with Volume 4.

—————. The compleat imbiber no. 2. London: Putnam, 1958. 208p. Illus. G33670

—————. The compleat imbiber no. 3. London: Putnam, 1960. 176p. Illus. G33680

> Scarce.

—————. The compleat imbiber no. 4. London: Vista Books, 1961. 208p. Illus. G33690

—————. The compleat imbiber no. 5. London: Vista Books, 1962. 206p. Illus. G33700

—————. The compleat imbiber no. 6. London: Vista Books, 1963. 224p. Illus. G33710

—————. The compleat imbiber no. 7. London: Vista Books, 1964. 224p. Illus. G33720

—————. The compleat imbiber no. 8. London: Collins, 1965. 224p. G33730

—————. The compleat imbiber no. 9. London: Collins, 1967. 224p. Illus. G33740

—————. The compleat imbiber no. 10. London: Hutchinson, 1969. 224p. Illus. G33750

Contains an interesting article on Cyrus Redding by Anthony Powell.

_____. The compleat imbiber no. 11. London: Hutchinson, 1970. 224p. Illus. G33760

_____. The compleat imbiber no. 12. London: Hutchinson, 1971. 224p. Illus. G33770

_____. Vintage Tales. London: Century Publishing, 1984. Illus. G33780

A collection of prose and verse including contributions from Graham Greene, Evelyn Waugh, John le Carre and others.

RAY, Georges. The French wines. Translated from the French and revised by Paul Capon. New York: Avenel Books, 1965. 153p. Illus. G33790

First published in France, 1946.

RAYMOND, Irving Woodworth. The teaching of the early Church on the use of wine and strong drink. New York: Columbia University Press, 1927. 170p. G33800

REACH, Angus Bethune. Claret and olives, from the Garonne to the Rhone; or, notes social, picturesque, and legendary, by the way. London: D. Boque, 1852. 264p. Illus. G33810

READ, Jan. Companion to the wines of Spain and Portugal. London: Century, 1983. 137p. Illus. G33820

_____. Guide to the wines of Spain and Portugal. London: Pitman, 1977. 125p. Illus. G33830

_____. The pocket guide to Spanish wines. London: Mitchell Beazley and New York: Simon and Schuster, 1983. 144p. Illus. G33840

_____. The wines of Portugal. London: Faber and Faber, 1982. 190p. Illus. G33850

_____. The wines of Rioja. London: Sotheby Publications, 1984. 184p. Illus. G33855

_____. The Wines of Spain. London: Faber and Faber, 1982. 267p. G33860

_____. The wines of Spain and Portugal. London: Faber and Faber, 1973. 380p. Illus. G33870

Discusses the lesser-known wines of both countries in addition to port, madeira and sherry. The book is enhanced by reproductions of old prints, quotes from two master travelers of the past, Richard Ford and Cyrus Redding, and six appendices largely of wine production statistics.

READ, Jan and MANJON, Maite. Paradores of Spain. London: Macmillan, 1977. 224p. Illus. G33880

REAY-SMITH, John. Discovering Spanish wines. London: Robert Hale, 1976. 159p. Illus. G33890

The RED wines of Australia. Lane Cove, N.S.W.: Project Publishing Company, 1981. G33900

CYRUS REDDING (1785 - 1870)

As a young man, Cyrus Redding moved from Cornwall, where his family had lived since the 15th century, to London to become a journalist. He became successful as an author of a variety of books and poems including *A Biography of William IV*, and *A History of Shipwrecks and Disasters at Sea*. Redding's involvement with wine, and French wine in particular, came about by accident. In 1814 he was sent to Paris as correspondent for *The Examiner* and remained in Paris as editor of *Galignani's Messenger* until 1819. Redding spent this time visiting the vineyards of France and Italy and recalled in the introduction to *A History and Description of Modern Wines*, "I cannot look back without pleasure to seasons spent in lands of the vine, not in the town, but in the heart of the country. . . ."

Redding writes in an unpretentious style that makes him more readable than Barry or Henderson, both of whom he criticizes in the introduction to *A History and Description of Modern Wines*.

REDDING, Cyrus. Every man his own butler. London: Whittaker, 1839. 200p. Illus. G33920

Scarce. There is also an 1853 edition.

_____. French wines and vineyards; and the way to find them. London: Houlston and Wright, 1860. 240p. G33930

Scarce.

_____. A history and description of modern wines. London: Whittaker, Treacher and Arnot, 1833. 407p. Illus. G33940

This is the first book in English that deals exclusively with modern wines. It was an immediate success and required a second edition in 1836, a third in 1851 and subsequent printings thereafter. According to André Simon, ". . . no other book written in English on the subject of wines has ever been more popular nor so copiously copied from by later writers than Redding's *History*." As a reference for information about wines of the late 18th and early 19th centuries that are still produced today, there is nothing better in the English language. Scarce.

_____. A history and description of modern wines. 2nd ed. London: Whittaker, 1836. 423p. G33950

_____. A history and description of modern wines. 3rd ed. London: M.G. Bohn, 1851. 440p. G33960

André Simon's listing in his *Bibliotheca Vinaria* of 1871 as the publication date for the third edition is erroneous, although the third edition was republished subsequent to 1851 and in 1871.

_____. A History and description of modern wine. Reprint. Ilkley, West Yorkshire: Andrew Low Fine Wines, Ltd., 1980. 407p. Illus. G33970

A facsimile of the 1833 edition limited to five hundred copies.

A

HISTORY AND DESCRIPTION

OF

MODERN WINES.

BY

CYRUS REDDING.

LONDON:

WHITTAKER, TREACHER, & ARNOT,

AVE MARIA LANE.

1833.

Quarter-bound in sheepskin and green cloth with marbled end papers. The binding and paper are of high quality.

REDDINGTON, D. Essay on grape culture and wine making as a lucrative
business. [Keokuk, IA: 1866]. 8p. G33980

REDI, Francesco. Bacchus in Tuscany: a dithyrambic poem from the Italian of
Francesco Redi, with notes. Translated by Leigh Hunt. London: Printed
for John and H.L. Hunt, 1825. 298p. G33990

> Physician to Ferdinando and Cosimo III, Redi (1626-1698) was a
> student of many subjects. Though a writer of many books, Redi is
> best known for this poem. As the years passed, this poem expanded
> in scope by virtue of improvisions. The poem had six substantial
> revisions, changing even its title as it was passed about in man-
> uscript form. Finally, in 1685, it took the long polymetric form in
> which it was printed.
>
> The preface by Leigh Hunt describes how he first encountered the
> poem and how he came about translating it. The preface also de-
> tails Redi's life. First edition in English. Scarce.

REDUCTION of the wine duties. Report of the meeting of the Wine Duties
Reduction Committee, and the Anglo-French Free-Trade Association,
at the Crystal Palace, July 9th, 1856. Debate in the House of Commons
on Mr. Oliveira's motion for the wine duties reduction . . . 15 July, 1856
. . . London: Ward, Lock, c1856. 64p. G34000

REED, Myrtle. Master of the vineyard. New York and London: Putnam, 1910.
372p. G34010

REED, Stan. The wine world at a glance. Seattle: Rustan Pub. House, 1969.
64p. G34020

REEMELIN, Charles. The vine-dresser's manual, an illustrated treatise on
vineyards and wine-making. New York: C.M. Saxton, 1855. 103p. Illus.
G34030

> This was a very popular manual which went through numerous
> subsequent editions including the years 1856, 1857, 1858, 1859,
> 1860, 1868 and 1898. A practical guide written "so that even the
> most inexperienced may, with this book in hand, start, plant, per-
> fect and cultivate a vineyard, and make good, wholesome wine." An
> immigrant from Germany, the author had a vineyard in Ohio and
> recommended planting only the native Catawba in the Ohio Valley
> and the Isabella in the East.

REEVE, Lloyd Eric and REEVE, Alice Means. Gift of the grape; based on Paul
Masson vineyards. San Francisco: Filmer Publishing, 1959. 314p. Illus.
G34050

REICHARDT, Alfred. The future of German viticulture in the E[uropean]
C[ommon] M[arket]. Mannheim: Veroffentlichungen der
Wirtschafthochschule, 1960. 123p. G34060

> Potential economic effects of the Common Market on the German
> grape and wine industry.

REID, Hilary F. A century in commerce; the story of John Reid and Co., Ltd., 1869-1969. Auckland: J. Reid, 1969. 86p. Illus. G34070

REID, J.G.S. The cool cellar. Auckland: Southern Cross Books, 1969. G34090

REID, J. John Reid's LCBO wines and spirits guide book: a comprehensive buyer's guide to the wines and spirits available in Ontario. Newly rev. Toronto: G. de Pencier, 1978. 383p. G34080

RENDLE, Wm. E. England a wine-producing country: being a treatise on the new patent fruit tree and plant protectors. London: Allan, 1868. 71p. Illus. G34100

RENNER, Hans Deutch. Pocket guide to wine. London: Citizen Press, c1945. 16p. G34110

RENWICK, Cyril. A study of the wine in the Hunter region of N.S.W. Newcastle, N.S.W: Hunter Valley Research Centre, 1977. 67p. Illus. G34120

REPETTO, Victor and BLOCK, Sydney J. Perspectives on California wines. 1976. 65p. Illus. G34125

> See California Wine Oral History Series.

REPORT of a jury of experts on brandy made by Gen. Henry M. Naglee, at San Jose, together with testimonials of physicians and gentlemen as to its purity and wholesomeness; to which is added a short essay upon it, and other spirits, both pure and adulterated, and their effects on the human system, in health, disease, and convalescence. San Francisco: Spaulding, Barto, 1879. 114p. G34130

REPORT of the Cape of Good Hope Department of Agriculture for the year 1889-90. In two parts. Cape Town: 1890-91. G34140

> Unable to verify.

REPORT of the Commissioner of Agriculture for the year 1862. Washington: Gov't. Print. Off., 1863. 632p. Illus. G34150

> Contains several articles on viticulture and wine.

The REPORT of the Commissioner of Patents for the year 1858. Washington: Agriculture Department of U.S. Gov't., 1859. 552p. Illus. G34160

> Contains articles on "The Grape and Wine-Culture of California" by Andrew W. M'Kee of San Francisco; "The Grapes and Wine of Los Angeles" by Matthew Keller.

REPORT on Cyprus viticulture. Limassol: c1939. 40p. G34170

REVIEW of the discussions relating to the Oporto wine company. London: Cadell and Davies, 1814. 81p. G34200

> The last twenty-five pages form an appendix of letters, petitions, etc.

REYNOLDS, Bruce. A cocktail continentale. 6th ed. George Sully, 1926. 200p. Illus. G34210

RHEBERGEN, G. Jan. 24 exlibris med vin-motiver. Exlib Risten, 1979. 60p. G34220

It was the idea of Norbert Lippoczy, a Hungarian who lives in Poland, to publish this book. Mr. Lippoczy is a specialist in the field of collecting "wine-exlibris," bookplates, and he has more than 3,000 plates, many of which he commissioned.

This small but elegant volume, with text in Danish, German and English, has twenty-four tipped in plates, many signed by the artist, from the collections of prominent collectors. They are of outstanding quality. At least twenty of them are woodcuts, linocuts or wood engravings. Many are by well-known graphic artists. Limited edition of 225 copies.

RHODES, Anthony. Princes of the grape: great wine makers through the ages. London: Weidenfeld and Nicolson, 1975. 160p. Illus. G34230

RICHARDSON, Collette, ed. House and Garden's drink guide; what drinks to serve when — and how to make them. Recipes compiled by Elizabeth Lambert de Ortiz. New York: Simon and Schuster, c1973. 285p. G34240

Includes wine.

RICKET, E. and THOMAS, C. The gentlemen's table guide. Recipes, wine cups, American drinks . . . London: By the Authors, 1871. 53p. G34250

RIEHL, Edwin Hugo. Growing grapes. Saint Joseph, MO: The Fruit-grower Company, 1906. 39p. Illus. G34260

RIKER, Douglas H. The wine book of knowledge. A comment upon and compilation of facts pertaining to the use and enjoyment of wine, and a little about its romance and history. Los Angeles: Ascot Press, 1934. 71p. Illus. G34270

RILEY, Norman and DUNN-MEYNELL, Hugo. Wine record book - a log of bottles cellared and tasted. London: Wine and Spirits Publications, 1968. 140p. G34280

Includes an introduction by Harry Waugh, a vintage rating guide and vintage chart, an analysis of the grape, vinification charts, a temperature chart, a section on wine labels, bottle openers and bottles, and a supply of record forms entitled "bibliography." Second edition 1970, third edition 1972, reprinted 1976 and 1978.

RITTICH, Virgil J. and RITTICH, Eugene. European grape growing in cooler districts where winter protection is necessary. Edited by Norley F. Tunbridge. Minneapolis: Burgess Publishing, 1941. 83p. Illus. G34290

RIXFORD, Emmet H. The wine press and the cellar. A manual for the winemaker and the cellar-man. San Francisco: Payot Upham and New York: D. Van Nostrand, 1883. 240p. Illus. G34300

The earliest California imprint devoted solely to wine making as distinct from vine growing. The author produced prized wines from the cabernet grape at his La Questa Vineyard in San Mateo County, south of San Francisco. His book is a detailed manual for California winemakers based largely on methods used in France, where, the author states, "the finest wines of the world are produced." Includes a bibliography of works consulted.

ROATE, Mettja Cappon. How to make wine in your own kitchen. New York: Macfadden, Bartell, 1963. 175p. G34310

>Subsequent editions.

ROBARDS, Terry. California wine label album. New York: Workman Pub., 1981. 176p. Illus. G34320

_____. The New York Times book of wine. New York: Quadrangle, 1976. 467p. Illus. G34330

>Mr. Robards, formerly the wine columnist of *The New York Times,* is now a wine columnist for The *New York Post* and the New York bureau chief for the *Wine Spectator*, a bi-weekly wine newspaper.

_____. Terry Robard's new book of wine: the ultimate guide to wines throughout the world. New York: Putnam, Illus. G34340

_____. A votre santé. A complete guide to French wines. New York: Bantam Books, 1982. 127p. Illus. G34350

_____. Wine cellar journal. New York: Quadrangle, 1974. G34360

ROBERGE, Earl. Napa wine country. 2nd ed. Oregon: Graphic Arts Center Publishing, 1975. 207p. Illus. G34370

>A fine pictorial account of the Napa Valley by a talented professional photographer.

ROBERTS, George Edwin. Cups and their customs. London: John van Voorst, 1863. 52p. Illus. G34380

>An interesting historical account of drinking vessels and wine drinking through the ages. Included is the following reference to the qualities that distinguished a good wine in the 12th century: "It should be clear like tears of a penitent, so that a man may see distinctly to the bottom of the glass; its colour should represent the greenness of a buffalo's horn; when drunk, it should descend impetuously like thunder; sweet-tasted as an almond; creeping like a squirrel; leaping like a roebuck; strong like the building of a cistercian monastry; glittering like a spark of fire; subtle like the logic of the schools of Paris; delicate as fine silk; and colder than crystal." Unfortunately, we are not told the name of this extraordinary wine. Second edition of 62p. published in 1869.

ROBERTS, Ivor. Great Australian wines. Sydney: Ure Smith, 1974. 224p. Illus. G34390

ROBERTS, Ivor and BAGLIN, Douglas. Australian wine pilgrimage. Sydney: Horwitz, 1969. 167p. G34400

>Second edition, 1970. Also issued under title *Exploring Australian Wines* in 1971 by Ure Smith of Sydney.

ROBERTS, Jeremy and NORTHEY, Jose, ed. The wines of the world. London: Orbis, 1974. 176p. Illus. G34410

ROBERTS, John. A comprehensive view of the culture of the vine under glass. London: Longman, 1842. 83p. G34420

ROBERTS, William Henry. The British wine-maker, and domestic brewer; a complete, practical and easy treatise on the art and management of British wines, and liqueurs, and domestic brewing. Edinburgh: Oliver and Boyd, 1835. 292p. G34430

—————. The British wine-maker and domestic brewer, a complete, practical, and easy treatise on the art of making and managing every description of British wines, ales, beers . . . containing also a supplement on the rhubarb plant, showing it to be a basic nearly as valuable as that of the grape, for producing champagne, hock, madeira and constantia. 5th ed. Edinburgh: Black and London: Whittaker, 1849. 384p. G34440

ROBERTSON, George. Port. London: Faber and Faber, 1978. 188p. G34450

ROBERTSON, Jean and Andrew. Food and wine of the French provinces: a traveller's guide. London and Glasgow: Collins, 1968. 218p. Illus. G34460

ROBINSON, James. The art and mystery of making British wines, cider and perry, cordials and liqueurs; with directions for the management of foreign wines and spirituous liquors; and recipes for the manufacture of agreeable and wholesome beverages, medicinal wines, and the distillation of simple waters . . . London: Chapman and Hall, 1865. 273p. Illus. G34470

—————. The whole art of making British wines, liqueurs, brewing fine and strong Welsh ales. London: Longman, Brown, Green and Longmans, 1848. 275p. G34480

Scarce.

JANCIS ROBINSON (1950)

Ms. Robinson was educated at St. Anne's College, Oxford, and from 1975-1980, was assistant editor and then editor of *Wine and Spirit* magazine. In 1977, she started Britain's first monthly wine newsletter and has been the wine correspondent for the *Sunday Times* since 1980. She was founder-editor of the annual publication *Which? Wine Guide*. In 1983, she was the presenter-writer of Britain's first television wine series "The Wine Programme" and has started production on a second series to be shown in 1985. In 1984, she passed the Masters of Wine examination and became the first non-trade Master of Wine and the ninth woman "MW".

ROBINSON, Jancis. The great wine book. London: Sidgwick and Jackson and New York: Morrow, 1982. 240p. Illus. G34490

The special quality of Ms. Robinson's book is in her emphasis on the personal qualities of the great wine makers. She writes, "it seems extraordinary how little has been written about wine *people*. This book largely ignores the historical aspects which have already been covered so well, and concentrates on the personalities behind the world's greatest wines. For the character of a wine and, especially, the will to produce really fine wine, is inextricably bound up with the personality, psychology and philosophy of its maker."

She also notes that "this is a very exciting time for wine" in that the range of good wines has greatly expanded, but that "the wine world has shrunk dramatically in the last twenty years so that communications between producers and their peers and customers have improved enormously."

This communication is enhanced greatly by the speed of travel and the fact that wine producers, as a group, are generous in sharing their production secrets. Even so, there remains great diversity about soil conditions and the best time to pick the grapes.

This book deals only with the heavyweights, but the author lists the properties that would have been included if the "book could have been twice or three times its present length. . . ."

A handsome book that includes over 300 color photographs, wine labels and maps.

_____. Masterglass. A practical course in wine tasting. London and Sydney: Pan Books, 1983. 176p. Illus. G34500

_____. The wine book: a straight-forward guide to better buying and drinking for less money. London: Fontana, 1979. 255p. Illus. G34510

Second edition, revised and updated in 1983.

ROBINSON, Jancis, ed. Which? Wine guide, 1981. London: Consumers Association and Hodder Stoughton, 1980. G34520

Subsequent edition of 426p. was published in 1981. Published annually thereafter (see MacQuitty, Jane).

ROBOTTI, Peter J. Much depends on dinner (or the tablecloth game). New York: Fountainhead, 1961. 306p. Illus. G34530

Contains several chapters on wines.

ROBOTTI, Peter J. and ROBOTTI, Frances. Key to gracious living; wine and spirits. Englewood Cliff, NJ: Prentice-Hall, 1972. 402p. Illus. G34540

ROBSON, Edgar Iliff. A guide to French fetes. London: Methuen, 1930. 238p. Illus. G34550

_____. A wayfarer in French vineyards. London: Methuen and Boston and New York: Houghton Mifflin, 1928. 212p. Illus. G34560

ROBY, Norman. America's brandyland. California Brandy Advisory Board, 1977. 20p. G34570

ROGER, J.R. The wines of Bordeaux. London: Andre Deutsch and New York: Dutton, 1960. 166p. Illus. G34580

ROGERS, C. Full and by; being a collection of verses by persons of quality in praise of drinking. London: Heinemann, 1925. 153p. G34590

ROLLAT, Edouard. Wine guide and cocktail book. New York: Vendome Liquor Co., 1934. 60p. G34600

[ROLLESTON, Samuel.] A dissertation concerning the original antiquity of barley wine. Oxford: Printed at the Theatre for J. Fletcher and sold by J. and J. Rivington. London: 1750. 38p. G34610

ROLLI, Otto Christian. Wine for home and medicinal use. Canton, OH: 1933. 30p. G34620

_____. Wines and cordials for home and medicinal use. Canton, OH: 1934. G34630

RONCARATI, Bruno. D.O.C. The new image for Italian wines. London: Harper Trade Journals, 1971. 89p. Illus. G34640

_____. Viva vino, D.O.C. wines of Italy. London: Wine and Spirit Publications, 1976. 206p. Illus. G34650

> A worthwhile reference book containing technical information on the D.O.C. system and the main wines of Italy according to region.

ROOK, Alan. The diary of an English vineyard. London: Wine and Spirit Publications, 1969. 123p. Illus. G34660

> A record of the establishment of the most northerly vineyard and its product, Lincoln Imperial Wine, 1967-1969. Republished in 1972.

ROOS, L. Wine making in hot climates, translated by R. Dubois and P. Wilkinson. Melbourne: Victoria Dept. of Agriculture, 1900. 273p. Illus. G34670

An important work which corrected previous publications that were not pertinent to the Australian climate.

ROOSE, Samuel. New and complete treatise on ullaging. London: 1832. 23p. G34680

_____. Wine and spirit dealer's guide. London: 1835. 124p. G34690

ROOT, Waverley Lewis. The food of Italy. New York: Atheneum, 1971. 750p. Illus. G34700

> Contains wine information.

ROPER, Elmo. A study of people's attitudes toward and usage of wine. Prepared for Wine Advisory Board of State of California by Elmo Roper and Associates, August, 1955. 2 vols. Illus. G34710

ROSE, John. The English vineyard vindicated. London: J.M. and John Crook, 1669. 48p. G34720

> Another edition published in 1675.

_____. The English vineyard vindicated. Reprint. Falls Village, CT: Herb Grower Press, 1966. G34730

> A reprint of the 1675 edition.

ROSE, L.J., Jr. L.J. Rose of Sunny Slope, 1827-1899: California pioneer, fruit grower, wine maker, horse breeder. San Marino, CA: The Huntington Library, 1959. 235p. Illus. G34740

> Biography of an early Los Angeles wine producer.

ROSE, Robert Selden. Wine making for the amateur. New Haven: Printed for members of the Bacchus Club, 1930. 100p. Illus. G34750

>   Limited edition of 515 copies.

ROSEN, Ruth C. Pop Monsieur: Champagne recipes for everyday food and drink. New York: Richard Rosen, 1956. 140p. Illus. G34760

ROSENBERG, Joe. Joe Rosenberg's grapenutz guide to California wines with imported wines supplement and dining with wines in Italy. Rev. Baltimore: Winemayven Productions, 1983. 100p. G34770

ROSS, George. Tips on tables, being a guide to dining and wining in New York . . . New York: Covici, Fried, 1934. 301p. G34780

>   Interesting for the 1934 wine prices.

ROSSATI, Guido. Descriptive account of the wine industry of Italy. Translated from the Italian by Guido Rossati. Rome: Societa generale dei viticoltori italiani, 1888. 103p. G34790

ROSSI, Edmund A. Italian Swiss Colony and the wine industry. 1971. 103p. Illus. G34795

>   See California Wine Oral History Series.

ROSSI, F. An investigation into the vine industry of Cyprus. Nicosia, Cyprus: Gov't. Print. Off., 1956. 24p. G34800

ROTHSCHILD, Philippine de and BEAUMARCHAIS, Jean-Pierre de. Mouton Rothschild paintings for the labels, 1945-1981. Boston: Little, Brown, 1983. 132p. Illus. G34810

>   In 1922, Philippe de Rothschild, then only twenty, took over the management of Mouton. Two years later he initiated the idea of bottling all of his wine at the chateau. This move caused great consternation within the English wine trade, but it revolutionized the distribution of the great clarets, because Chateaux Lafite, Latour, Margaux and Haut-Brion immediately followed Mouton's example. Until 1924, the *Premiers Crus* estates had traditionally chateau-bottled some of each vintage, but most of their wine was sold in barrels to wine merchants who bottled, labeled and sold it. Whether the buyer ultimately got the wine he paid for was known only to the wine merchant.
>
>   To draw attention to this innovation, Baron Philippe commissioned Jean Carlu, a twenty-four year old poster designer, to design the label. Carlu created a striking Cubist composition. In 1934 Baron Philippe carried the authentication of Mouton a step further; he added to the label the total number and sizes of bottles produced and signed the labels.
>
>   In 1945, in celebration of the Allied victory, he conceived the idea of decorating the Mouton label with a work of art. Since 1945 (except for 1953 and 1977) an artist has been commissioned (payment is in wine only) to illustrate the label. The Mouton label alumni read like a who's who of contemporary art: Jean Hugo, Jean Cocteau, Dignimont, George Brague, Salvadore Dali, Henry Moore,

Joan Miro, Marc Chagall, Pablo Picasso, Robert Motherwell, Andy Warhol, etc.

The book is divided into three parts. The first part gives the story of the labels. Two pages are devoted to each artist, a short description of each work of art submitted and used, with color reproductions. The second part tells the history of Mouton and the development of its wine museum, which houses many of the great wine related masterpieces of all periods. Part three covers notes on the wines behind the labels (1945-1981 and from Michael Broadbent's *Great Vintage Wine Book*), a listing of exceptional vintages and a glossary of terms. The book is profusely illustrated throughout with black and white and color photographs.

ROUECHE, Berton. Alcohol: the neutral spirit. New York: Berkeley Publishing, 1971. 127p. G34820

ROUX, Michel Pierre. A guide to the vineyards and chateaux of Bordeaux. Dallas: Publivin, 1972. 229p. Illus. G34830

ROUX, Michel Pierre, POUPON, Pierre and FORGEOT, Pierre. A guide to the vineyards and domains of Burgundy. Dallas: Publivin, 1973. 175p. Illus. G34840

ROWE, Percy. The wines of Canada. Toronto and New York: McGraw-Hill, 1970. 200p. Illus. G34850

ROWE, Vivian. French wines - ordinary and extraordinary. London: Harrap, 1972. 111p. Illus. G34860

ROWNTREE, Joseph and SHERWELL, Arthur. Public control of the liquor traffic: being a review of the Scandinavian experiments in the light of recent experience. London: Grant Richards, 1903. 296p. G34870

_____. The taxation of the liquor trade. Abridged ed. London: Macmillan, 1909. 212p. G34880

ROY, K.K., comp. A directory of wine and alcoholic beverages. Calcutta: Intertrade Publications, 1963. 94p. G34890

RUDD, Hugh R. Hocks and Moselles. London: Constable, 1935. 165p. Illus. G34900

Hugh R. Rudd was a partner of the famed English wine merchants, Berry Bros. and Rudd. This book is a compact guide to the wine districts of the Rhine and Moselle, the differences between the two valleys and their wines, the meaning of various terms such as spatlese, past vintages and of the youthful days the author spent among the vineyards of the Nahe Valley.

RULAND, Wilhelm. The finest legends of the Rhine. Bonn: Verlag Hoursch and Bechstedt., 125p. Illus. G34920

RUSSELL, Mark. The paragon of wines and spirits. Vol. 2. London: Heidelberg Press, 1973. 193p. Illus. G34930

See Baker, John V., ed. for reference to Vol. 1.

RUSTICUS (pseud). How to settle in Victoria. Melbourne: Slater, Williams and Hodgson, 1855. 118p. G34940

Contains information on wines of the area.

RYALL, R.B.C. Catalogue of the extensive collection of wine labels . . . formed by R.B.C. Ryall . . . which will be sold at auction by Christie, Manson and Woods . . . on . . . June 14, 1968 . . . London: White Bros., 1968. 36p. G34950

SABIN, A. Wine and spirit merchants' accounts. London: McGee, 1904. 176p. G34960

SABIN, Mrs. Belle Carpenter. Wines and fresh fruit beverages. Chicago: American Publishing, 1919. 75p. G34970

SABINE, H. Complete cellarman or innkeeper and publican's sure guide. London: By the Author, 1818. 48p. G34980

SADLER, E. and FLETCHER, C.R.L. Wine ghosts of Bremen. Oxford: W. Hauff, 1939. 64p. G34990

SADOUN, Roland and LOLLI, Georgi and SILVERMAN, Milton. Drinking in French culture. New Brunswick, NJ: Rutgers Center of Alcohol Studies, 1965. 133p. G35000

Much about wine.

SAILLAND, Maurice-Edmond. Traditional recipes of the provinces of France. Garden City, NY: Doubleday, 1961. 494p. Illus. G35010

Much information on local wines. Translated and edited by Edwin Lavin.

SAINT PIERRE, Louis de. Art of planting and cultivating the vine and also of making, fining and preserving wines according to the most approved methods in the most celebrated wine - counties in France. London: Printed by J. Wilkie, 1772. 344p. Illus. G35020

The author left France because of his religious beliefs and settled in Granville County, New-Bordeaux, South Carolina. He wrote this book to benefit his new countrymen and felt that grape growing and wine making were a panacea for ". . . families, groaning under the iron hand of oppression and poverty . . . and in the end give bread, wealth and affluence to millions, as well as contribute to aggrandize this nation . . ." and ". . . to promote this important object, shall be the grand aim and business of my life." Saint Pierre devoted full time to the cultivation of the vine and reported: "Neither pains, sollicitations, hazard, nor expence, have been spared to procure a supply of plants of the best growths of Champagne and Burgundy. These are now flourishing and by propagation will furnish vines in sufficient numbers, wherewith to stock the vineyards of my colonists, as well as those of the new-settlers, to the number of one hundred and fifty families." There is no evidence, however, to substantiate that Saint Pierre's noble plans survived his enthusiasm.

GEORGE SAINTSBURY (1845-1933)

After graduation from Oxford, George Saintsbury began a journalistic career that lasted twenty-years, followed by a twenty-year tenure as the Professor of Rhetoric and English Literature at the University of Edinburgh. It was during his professorship that most of his prodigious literary efforts took place. He wrote twenty-two literary histories, fifteen biographical and critical works and hundreds of introductions, prefaces, translations and other edited matters. This came after his journalistic efforts, modestly described by him as "The equivalent of at least a hundred volumes of the 'Every Gentlemen's Library' type — and probably more." It is ironic that the magnum opus for which he is best remembered is a small book about wine, *Notes on a Cellar-Book*, written in retirement when he was seventy-five years old.

Saintsbury acquired a taste for wine while an undergraduate at Oxford, and it remained his friend and constant companion throughout his life. Saintsbury's comment in *Notes on a Cellar-Book* that he was no longer able to drink claret or burgundy has been interpreted by some writers to mean that he was "wineless" during his last years. Fortunately, such was not his fate. According to Dorothy Margaret Stuart, a friend and frequent visitor, he stuck pretty much to a "chicken and champagne formula" but on at least one occasion substituted whiskey and soda for champagne.

His memory is perpetuated by the Saintsbury Club, founded by André Simon and three friends in 1931. They first decided to honor Saintsbury at a lunch or dinner but, when he turned them down, they decided to have a dinner in his honor without him. The first dinner of the Saintsbury Club was held at Vintners' Hall on October 23, 1931, George Saintsbury's eighty-sixth birthday. Saintsbury was elected president "in perpetuity." The Saintsbury Club still meets twice a year.

SAINTSBURY, George, E.B. The last scrap book. London: Macmillan, 1924. 344p. G35040

> One of the best "scraps" in this little volume is an 1803 wine list from a Paris guide with the Professor's comments. In one entry he states: "And though I cannot say I have ever drunk wine of Migraine, I shouldn't have expected it to be so frankly advertised as such."

> One of the few references to the wine of Migraine is found in Cyrus Redding's *A History and Description of Modern Wines*.

_____. Notes on a cellar-book. London: Macmillan, 1920. 228p. G35050

> Saintsbury had originally intended to write a history of wine but instead wrote this chronicle of his wine experiences over the years. His love of wine is revealed by his comment: "There is no money among that which I have spent since I began to earn a living, of the expenditure of which I am less ashamed or which gave me better value in return, than the price of the liquids chronicled in this book."

> First edition July 1920; reprinted August 1920; reprinted with notes November 1920; edition de luxe 1921; reprinted 1921; 1923; 1924; 1927; 1931; 1933; 1939; 1951; 1953; 1963 with preface by Andrew Graham; 1978 with preface by H.W. Yoxall.

_____. Notes on a cellar-book. Deluxe ed., reprint. London: Macmillan, 1978. 166p. Illus. G35060

Special edition by Christie's Wine Publications. Limited to 500 numbered copies. In slip cover, with marbled boards and a preface by H.W. Yoxall.

_____. A scrap book. London: Macmillan, 1922. 298p. G35070

A collection of what the author calls "scraps" - some eighty of them with much about good wines and good books.

_____. A second scrap book. London: Macmillan, 1923. 371p. G35080

The first part of *A Second Scrap Book* is made up of the professor's reminiscences of his undergraduate days at Oxford, sixty years before. We are treated to this account of Oxford drinking customs of about 120 years ago: "I was told some time ago, to my great horror, and I hope falsely, that undergraduate wines are things of the past. If so, it may be all the better to correct an impression derivable from some books and sure to be encouraged by the Pussyfoots [tee-totallers] that the 'wine' was necessarily an orgy. I know not what it may have been when Mr. John Thorpe's young friends drank five pints per man of his very particular port, or even in Mr. V. Green's time, when he conceived that touching affection for the 'joll lill birds.' But in mine, if not everywhere, certainly at Merton, whether in club-form or privately, 'wine' simply meant the dessert of an ordinary dinner, supplementing Hall, at which men dropped in or not as they liked, and went out to billiards or cards or reading as their fancy or habit took them. 'Supper' was quite a different thing, and had rather a tendency to become orgiastic. 'Leave' for it was required, and not indiscriminately given, but naturally was sometimes taken in the French manner. Whence another Merton story. A clandestine feast was being held when tidings came that the dean was on the warpath. The feasters fled; but the dignitary's progress was slow, and it so happened that an innocent strayed into the empty banquet-hall before his arrival, and was found there. 'Then he taxed him as he axed him, to quote a beautiful poem, Mr. W., have you been having supper?' Receiving a well-justified denial, the Dean walked round the table, inspecting every plate and dish and holding up glasses to the light. 'Then somebody else has,' he observed at last. And it was so." Wine runs as a theme throughout the essays and the professor addresses the evils of Prohibition and has a chapter on "The Order of Drinks."

SALLENGRE, Albert Henrik. Ebrietatis encomium: or, the praise of drunkenness. (See OINOPHILIS, Boniface.)

SALLEY, A.S. Narratives of early Carolina, 1655-1708. New York: Scribner's, 1911. 388p. Illus. G35100

SALMON, Alice Wooledge and DUNN-MEYNELL, Hugo. The Wine and Food Society menu book; recipes for celebration. London: International Wine and Food Society and Heinemann, 218p. Illus. G35105

Contains a compilation of recipes by Miss Salmon for lunch and luncheons, dinners, suppers and special occasions. Mr.Dunn-

Meynell (the Director General of the International Wine and Food Society) supplies comments for the wines to accompany the meals.

The SALTRAM vineyards 1859-1959, being a history of the Saltram vineyards and their one hundred years of wine making. Adelaide: Griffin Press, 1959. 28p. G35110

SALTUS, Francis S. Flasks and flagons. Buffalo: Charles Wells Moulton, 1892. 177p. G35120

SAMALENS, Jean and SAMALENS, Georges. Armagnac. London: Christie's Wine Publications, 1980. 60p. Illus. G35130

France is noted for two great brandies: Cognac and Armagnac. Armagnac differs most obviously from Cognac in the way it is distilled using the locally known Jet Contino distillation process which combines features of both the pot still (as used in Cognac) and the continous still (used for the distillation of most whiskies). It provides information on the making of this brandy and on the lives and customs of those who make it.

SAMPSON, Betty and SANDERS, Rosanne. The illustrated guide to home winemaking. London: Aurum Press, 1982. G35140

SAMSON, George Whitefield. The divine law as to wines. 2nd ed. Philadelphia: Lippincott, 1885. 613p. G35150

The first edition was published in New York, 1880, 326p.

SAMUELSON, James. The history of drink. A review, social, scientific and political. London: Trubner, 1878. 288p. G35160

A second edition was published in 1880.

SANCEAU, Elaine. The British factory Oporto. Barcelos: 1970. G35170

SANDEMAN, Fraser. History of cognac, brandy. Carlisle: Hudson, Scott, 1905. 41p. G35180

SANDEMAN, Geo. G., Sons and Co. The House of Sandeman. 3rd ed. London: 1972. 61p. Illus. G35190

A history of George Sandeman Sons and Company, including its wines and spirits and especially sherry and port. Subsequent editions.

_____. Jerez and its wine, sherry. London: Sandeman, 1953. 8p. G35200

_____. Port and sherry. The story of two fine wines. London: Sandeman, 1955. 63p. Illus. G35210

SANDERS, Bob and JENSEN, Seb. The vineyards of the Hunter Valley. Sydney: Jason Publications, 1971. 51p. Illus. G35220

SANDERS, F.W. Grapes: and how to grow them. A handbook dealing with the history, culture, management, propagation and insect and fungoid enemies of the grape vine and vineries, greenhouses, and in the open-air. London: 1907. G35230

Unable to verify.

SANDERS, John. A practical treatise on the cultivation of the vine, under glass as well as in the open air. London: Reeve and Benham, 1851. 31p. Illus. G35240

> Third edition published in 1862.

SANDERS, Leonard. Sonoma. New York: Delacorte Press, 1981. G35250

> A novel with a California wine industry setting.

SANDFORD, William. A few practical remarks on the medicinal effect of wine and spirits; with observations on the oeconomy of health: intended principally for the use of parents, guardians, and others intrusted with the care of youth. London: 1799. 151p. G35260

SARLES, John. ABC's of Italian wines. San Marcos, CA: 1981. 221p. Illus. G35270

SAROYAN, William. The laughing matter. Garden City, NY: Doubleday, Doran, 1953. 254p. G35280

> A novel with a California wine industry setting.

SARVIS, Shirley. American wines and wine cooking. Des Moines: Creative Home Library, 1973. 182p. Illus. G35290

SAUCIER, Ted. Bottoms up. New York: Greystone Press, Hawthorne Books, 1951. 288p. Illus. G35300

SAUER, Paul. A toast; spirit of the vine. Cape Town: Human and Rousseau. G35310

> Unable to verify.

SAUNDERS, Peter. A guide to New Zealand wine. Auckland: Wineglass Publishing, 1976. 56p. Illus. G35320

> Revised 1984 edition of 128p.

_____. Wine label language. Auckland: Wineglass Publishing, 1976. 138p. G35330

SAVILL, Stanley. The licensed victuallers' and liquor trades' law book: an easy guide to the police and excise code and the regulation of licensed premises. 2nd ed. London: Licensed Victuallers' Central Protection Society, 1903. 267p. G35340

SBARBORO, Andrea. The fight for true temperance. San Francisco: 1908. 67p. Illus. G35350

> Andrea Sbarboro, founder of the Italian Swiss Colony Winery and a spokesman for the then not formally organized California wine industry, wrote and published this booklet in 1908.
>
> At that time a wave of prohibition sentiment was sweeping the country and the "drys" had already been successful in getting a number of states to make it illegal to sell any alcoholic beverage.
>
> From internal evidence the pamphlet was probably meant for distribution to influential Americans, especially members of the U.S. Congress. It is an earnest attempt to obtain an exemption for wine from a general ban on alcoholic beverages. He advocates wine as a

necessity of life and as a true beverage of temperance. He cites eminent Americans who propose its use and points out the relatively minor alcohol-related problems of such countries as France and Italy, where much greater per capita amounts of wine were drunk. At the same time, the brewers, with vastly greater economic and political clout, were promoting beer as a temperance beverage. Of course, neither group prevailed.

Mr. Sbarboro's predictions as to what would occur in the event of Prohibition were ominously accurate. He erred only in underestimating the extent of the damage that actually occurred. Rare.

_____. Temperance versus Prohibition; important letters and data from our American consuls, the clergy and other eminent men. San Francisco: Designed and printed by H.S. Crocker, c1909. 56p. Illus. G35360

Second edition published in 1914.

_____. Wine as a remedy for intemperance: address delivered by Cav. Andrea Sbarboro, Hanford, Cal., December 4, 1906. Hanford, CA: 1906. 17p. G35370

An address delivered at the California Fruit Growers Convention.

SCHALCH, Edward A., comp. The glory of the grape: an anthology of wine verse. [London]: n.d. [94]p. Illus. G35380

Twenty articles comprising this anthology first appeared in *The Wine and Spirit Trade Record*. The anthology covers the period from ancient Greece and Rome to the middle of the 19th century with quotations from some eighty poets and thirty-two illustrations.

SCHENK, Henry A., ed. The new medical wine book. Written in conformity with the Volstead Act. San Francisco: By the Author, 1922. 24p. G35390

SCHENLEY Import Corporation. An introduction to wines. New York: Schenley, 1934. 56p. G35400

_____. Wine without frills; everyday enjoyment of imported wines and spirits. New York: Schenley, 1939. 61p. Illus. G35420

SCHMIDT, A. William. Fancy drinks and popular beverages, how to prepare and serve them. New York: Dick and Fitzgerald, 1896. 155p. G35430

_____. The flowing bowl: when and what to drink. By the only William. Full instructions on how to prepare, mix and serve beverages. New York: C.L. Webster, 1892. 294p. G35440

SCHMIDT, J.A. Diseases of the vine, how to prevent and cure them, according to doctrines of M. Pasteur. New York: 1868. 47p. G35450

SCHMITTHENNER, Dr. F. After turbidities of white bordeaux wines in bottle. Translated by G. Good, B.A. London: Communication from the Scientific Department of the Seitz-Works, Kreuznach (Rhineland), 7p. G35460

SCHNEIDER, Steven J. The international album of wine. New York: Holt, Rinehart and Winston, 1977. 288p. Illus. G35470

> Full-size reproduced labels are provided, over which actual labels may be pasted and space is available to make notes. Schneider, a member of the wine trade, is surprisingly critical of some famous wines.

SCHOENMAN, Theodore, ed. The father of California wine: Agoston Haraszthy. Santa Barbara, CA: Capra Press, 1979. 126p. Illus. G35480

> This book is essentially a reprint of Haraszthy's *Grape Culture, Wines and Wine Making* that was published in 1862 and is now scarce. For those bibliophiles who cannot obtain the original, this is a modestly priced alternative. It also includes a short history about Agoston Haraszthy, the accuracy of which has been questioned.

SCHOENSTEIN, Ralph, ed. The booze book, the joy of drink. Chicago: Playboy Press, 1974. 246p. Illus. G35490

SCHOLTZ, Merwe, ed. Wine country. Cape Town: Buren Publishers, 1970. 239p. Illus. G35500

> Describes journeys along the Cape wine routes. Photos by Cloete Breythenbach.

FRANK SCHOONMAKER (1905-1976)

Frank Schoonmaker began his career as a travel writer in Europe in the late 1920's and during this time developed an interest in wine. As the repeal of Prohibition approached, he wrote a series of wine articles for *The New Yorker* that was expanded into *The Complete Wine Book*. Shortly thereafter, he founded his own wine importing business. Mr. Schoonmaker was an early supporter of American wines, was critical of American vintners who labeled their wines after European wine-type names such as chablis, burgundy and chianti rather than by specific geographic and varietal appellations. His prophecy of forty-three years ago "That light, wholesome wine will one day occupy its rightful place in every American household . . ." has essentially been achieved.

SCHOONMAKER, Frank. The complete wine book. New York: Simon and Schuster, 1934. 315p. G35520

> Covers the principal wine regions of the world. A chapter on wine in the kitchen includes special recipes from continental innkeepers. Chapter twenty-two includes a history of American wine making.

> An anglicised edition of this book was published by George Routledge in 1935 with a foreword by P. Morton Shand.

_____. Distinguished American wines. New York: "21" Brands, c1946. 23p. Illus. G35530

_____. Frank Schoonmaker's encyclopedia of wine. New York: Hastings House, 1964. 410p. Illus. G35540

> An alphabetically arranged reference work covering the major wine areas of the world, the history of wine making, terms used in

describing wines and the vineyards, with phonetic pronunciations. Appendices cover vintage information, area classificiations, production and consumption statistics, etc. There were six editions of this very popular work from 1964 to 1975. Following Mr. Schoonmaker's death, a revised seventh edition was released with Julius Wile as the editor. [See Wile, Julius.]

_____. Vintage chart, 1945-1954. New York: Sherry Wine and Spirits Co., 1954. 19p. G35550

_____. Vintages of the nineteen-sixties: 1959-1967. New York: Hastings House, 1968. 27p. Illus. G35560

_____. Wines, cocktails and other drinks by F.A. Thomas (i.e. Frank Schoonmaker). New York: Harcourt, 1936. 228p. G35570

_____. The wines of Germany. New York: Hastings House, 1956. 152p. Illus. G35580

Later 1966 edition has 156 pages. A completely revised and edited version of this work by Peter Sichel was published in 1980. [See Sichel, Peter.]

SCHOONMAKER, Frank and MARVEL, Tom. American wines. New York: Duell, Sloan and Pearce, 1941. 312p. Illus. G35590b

An account of American vineyards and the factors which influence the quality of their products. Notes on wine nomenclature, legislative restrictions on wine, and the uses of wine in cooking. Chapters four and seven contain historical surveys of California and eastern American wines.

_____. Frank Schoonmaker's dictionary of wines; edited by Tom Marvel. New York: Hastings House, 1951. 120p. Illus. G35600

Subsequent editions.

SCHROEDER, Dr. H. Essay on a new system of grape culture. Bloomington, IL: 1866. G35610

SCHULTZ, Charles, Prof. Manual for the manufacture of cordials, liquors, fancy syrups. New York: 1862. G35620

Unable to verify.

SCHUTZENBERGER, P. On fermentation. London: Harry S. King, 1876. 331p. Illus. G35630

The author was the director of the chemical laboratory at the Sorbonne.

SCOTT, Dick. Winemakers of New Zealand. Auckland: Southern Cross Books, 1964. Part 1, 79p.; Part 2, unpaged. Illus. G35640

SCOTT, George E. Wine. Chicago: By the Author, 1936. 103p. G35650

SCOTT, J.M. The man who made wine. New York: E.P. Dutton, 1954. 125p. Illus. G35660

A novel.

SCOTT, James Maurice. The vineyards of France. London: Hodder and Stoughton, 1950. 163p. Illus. G35665

_____. Vineyards of France. London: Hodder and Stoughton, 1950. 163p. Illus. G35670

>A visually beautiful book with twelve tipped in water color plates and many black and white illustrations by Keith Baynes.

SCRIBNER, Frank Lamson. Report on the fungus disease of the grape vine. Washington: Gov't. Print. Off., 1886. 136p. G35680

>A government publication with plates to illustrate the research being done to help grape growers control disease problems.

SEABROOK, T.C. Some observations on wine. J.K. Walker lecture for 1948 to the Wine and Food Society of NSW. Sydney: 1949. 15p. G35690

>Limited to 500 copies that were privately printed on art paper and signed by Gilbert Phillips, president of the Society.

SEARLE, G. Grape-vine and its cultivation in Queensland. Brisbane: Gov't. Print. Off., 1888. 17p. G35700

>Popular series No. 18 of "Papers for the People by Practical Men on Agriculture, Horticulture and Pastoral Farming in Queensland, Australia."

SEARLE, Ronald. The illustrated winespeak, Ronald Searle's wicked world of wine tasting. London: Souvenir Press, 1983. 100p. Illus. G35710

>Mr. Searle, a cartoon artist, has fun caricaturing the wine buff.

SEARS, Fred Coleman. Productive small fruit culture; a discussion of the growing, harvesting, and marketing of strawberries . . . and grapes . . . 2nd ed. Rev. Philadelphia and London: J.B. Lippincott, 1925. 368p. Illus. G35720

SECOND report of the commercial relations between France and Great Britain. Silks and wines. Presented to both Houses of Parliament by command of his Majesty. London: Printed by W. Clowes for His Majesty's Stationery Office, 1835. 251p. G35730

>Binder's title: *Bowring's Reports.*

SEDGWICK, James. A new treatise on liquors: wherein the use of and abuse of wine, malt-drinks, water . . . are particularly considered, in many diseases, constitutions and ages. With the proper manner of using them, hot or cold, either as physick, diet, or both. Containing plain and easy rules for the preservation of health, and the attainment of long life. The whole being a full determination of all that hath lately been published on those subjects: tho' chiefly contrary to the opinions of Dr. Cheyne, Dr. Rouse, Dr. Short, Lommius, Van der Heyden, Dr. Hancocke, Mr. Smith and others. London: Printed for Charles Rivington, 1725. 407p. G35740

SEIBEL, George. The wine bills of Omar Khayyam. Pittsburgh: The Leasing Co., 1919. 34p. G35750

SEKERAK, John M., comp. Grapes, viticulture, wine and wine making: a subject bibliography of books and periodicals in the Peter J. Shields Library, University of California, Davis. Sacramento: Mark Larwood, 1975. 804p. G35760

> Only fifty copies published.

SELDES, Gilbert Vivian. The future of drinking. Boston: Little, Brown, 1930. 173p. Illus. G35770

SELDON, Philip. The *Vintage Magazine* consumer guide to wine. Garden City, NY: Doubleday, 1983. 402p. Illus. G35780

SELDON, Philip, ed. The great wine chateaux of Bordeaux. New York: Hastings House, 1975. 199p. Illus. G35790

> See also Duijker, Hubrecht.

SELIVANOVA, Nina. Dining and wining in old Russia. New York: Dutton, 1933. 154p. G35800

SELLERS, Charles. Oporto, old and new; being a historical record of the port wine trade, and a tribute to British commercial enterprise in the north of Portugal. London: Harper, 1899. 314p. Illus. G35810

> Rare.

SELTMAN, Charles. Wine in the ancient world. London: Routledge and Kegan Paul, 1957. 196p. Illus. G35820

SENATE Standing Committee on Trade and Commerce. Tax and the wine and grape industries: 1976-77, 2 vols. Canberra: 2024p. G35830

> Sworn evidence by winemakers and their accountants. A different description of the wine industry.

SENSORY identification of wine constituents. Royal Oak, MI: American Wine Society, 1979. 12p. G35840

SEPPELT, B. and Sons. Views of Seppeltsfield, South Australia. Adelaide: 1899. 76p. G35850

> Second edition of 64p. published in 1903.

SERJEANT, Richard. A man may drink. London: Putnam, 1964. 191p. G35870

> Deals with the physiological effects and medical aspects of wine.

SERLIS, Harry G. Wine in America. New York: Newcomen Society in North America, 1972. 18p. Illus. G35880

> Contains a history of wine making and of the California Wine Institute. Mr. Serlis is a former president of the Wine Institute.

SETRAKIAN, Arpaxat A. Setrakian, a leader of the San Joaquin Valley grape industry. 1977. 107p. Illus. G35885

> See California Wine Oral History Series.

SEWARD, Desmond. Monks and wine. London: Mitchell Beazley, 1979. 208p. Illus. G35890

In his foreword to this book, Hugh Johnson notes that, "When we think what we owe to them [monks] it is strange that no book that I know has ever before told the story."

Our debt is great, for "Monks largely saved viticulture when the Barbarian invasions destroyed the Roman Empire, and throughout the Dark Ages they alone had the security and resources to improve the quality of their wines slowly and patiently. For nearly 1,300 years almost all the biggest and best vineyards were owned and operated by religious houses."

The author proceeds to document that thesis and provides us with a well-researched millennium overview of the monks' contributions to wine, and of their contribution to the development of various liqueurs and whiskies. Included are histories of the various orders and descriptions of notable monasteries such as Clos de Vougeot, which was owned for centuries by the Cistercians.

The appendices provide a listing of wines with monastic associations and information about various wine tours.

SHACKLETON, Basil. The grape cure: a living testament. Thorsons, 1969. 128p. G35900

SHAND, Phillip Morton. Bacchus; or wine today and tomorrow. London: Kegan Paul, Trench, Trubner, 1927. 96p. G35910

"Teetotalism and castration are analogous abnegations, just as drunkenness and vicarious venery are analogous abuses. . . ." Shand develops the thesis that wine has many present dangers or enemies but teetotalism is not one of them. Eliminating Prohibition as a danger to rational nations, he proceeds to consider the dangers "to the survival of wine in that state of purity and excellence in which it is now obtainable, though by no means necessarily always obtained." These dangers are three in number - mass production; adulteration; and prostitution, so as to flatter vulgar palates in the form of so-called type wines, i.e. "*Monopoles*." Mr. Shand presents his arguments in a slashing style that at the time was not appreciated by some members of the English wine trade.

_____. A book of food. 2nd ed. London: Jonathan Cape, 1930. 319p. G35920

Some comments on wine with food.

_____. A book of French wines. 2nd ed. rev. and enlarged by Cyril Ray. London: Jonathan Cape, 1960. 415p. G35930

This edition is more valuable as a reference than the first. A scholarly, historical and factual account of the wines of France. Another edition by Penguin Books in 1964.

_____. A book of other wines than French. New York: Knopf, 1929. 183p. G35940

Written during Prohibition, there is only a two-page mention of California wines.

_____. A book of wine. New York: Brentano's, 1925. 320p. Illus. G35950

_____. A book of French wines. New York: Knopf and London: Cape, 1928. 247p. G35960

SHANKEN, Marvin, ed. The Wine Spectator guide to selected wines. 1985. 96p. G35965

> This pocket-sized book concentrates on the wines of California and covers the past year recommendations from the *Wine Spectator*, a wine periodical. Published annually.

SHANNON, R[obert], M.D. Practical treatise on brewing, distilling and rectification, with the genuine process of making brandy, rum, and hollands gin. The London practice of brewing porter, ale, and table beer, of brewing country ales, . . . of making wines, cider and vinegar. With an appendix on the culture and preparation of foreign wines, . . . London: Robert Scholey, 1805. 906p. G35970

> Although Simon lists this book in his *Bibliotheca Vinaria*, he does not list it under the chapter on "General Treatises on the Growing, the Making and the Management of Wines." Shannon's work qualifies in every respect. It consists of four sections: Book I - Brewing for malt liquors; Book II - Brewing for distilling; Book III - Made wines, vinegar, cider and perry; and Book IV, an Appendix on the ". . . growth, or culture, gathering, pressing, fermentation . . . of German, French, Spanish, Portugal, Italian and Grecian wines. . . ."
>
> Most writers attribute to Alexander Henderson the first detailed account in English of modern wines. Shannon's work, written nineteen years before Henderson's, deals not only with specific modern wines, but with such details as how the vines are planted, the grapes, the soils, how the wines are made and tasted and even how burgundy should be shipped to England: "It remains for me to relate how these wines may be brought to England. It has always been the custom to bring those wines from Burgundy in their casks; but as the carriage is long, and there is oftentimes a risque run, so the carriers, as well by land as by sea, are not always faithful; for notwithstanding all the precaution that can be taken to hinder them from drinking the wine, they will always find out stratagems to do it. . . . It ought to be brought in bottles from Beaune to London."
>
> Shannon's treatise covers all of the world's known wines including red and white Constantia, but he leaves no doubt as to his favorite region when he remarks, "If I had the office of providing the King's wine, I would go into Burgundy to choose it." Shannon goes on to tell us that the two best wines are Montrachet and Chambertin. "Chambertin produces, to my liking, the most valuable wine of all Burgundy," and Montrachet ". . . produces a white wine the most curious and most delicious in France. This wine has those qualities that neither the Latin nor the French tongue can express. I have drank it of six or seven years old and am not able to express its delicacy and excellence." An important reference for those interested in the history of "modern" wines. Rare.

SHARMAN, Fay. The taste of France. A dictionary of French food and wine. Boston: Houghton Mifflin, 1982. 320p. Illus. G35980

SHARP, Andrew. Wine taster's secrets, the consumer's guide to wine tasting, a step by step guide to the art of wine tasting. Ontario, Canada: Vintage House. 1981. 144p. Illus. G35990

SHARP, William J. Wine: how to develop your taste and get your money's worth. New York: Prentice-Hall, 1976. 176p. Illus. G36000

SHARPE, C.B. Hints on vines and peaches. Bath: Herald Office, 1900. 8p. G36010

SHAULIS, Nelson Jacob. Cultural practices for New York vineyards. Ithaca, NY: New York State College of Agriculture, 1950. 47p. Illus. G36040

SHAVER, Gordon O. Wines and liquors from the days of Noah. A safe guide to sane drinking. By the Author, 1939. 19p. G36050

SHAW, Henry. The vine and civilization. St. Louis: 1884. 71p. G36060

SHAW, Peter, M.D. An essay on the business of distillation and a practical essay on concentrating wine and other fermented liquors . . . London: 1731. G36070

>Peter Shaw, 1694-1763, served as physician "extraordinary" to King George II. Unable to verify this entry.

_____. The juice of the grape; or, wine preferable to water: a treatise, wherein wine is shewn to be the grand preserver of health, and restorer in most diseases. With many instances of cures performed by this noble remedy; and the method of using it, as well for prevention as cure. London: Printed for W. Lewis, 1724. 56p. G36080

_____. Three essays in artificial philosophy or unusual chemistry . . . An essay for the improvement of distillation . . . An essay for concentrating wines and other fermented liquors . . . London: Printed for J. Osborn and T. Longman, 1731. 192p. G36090

THOMAS GEORGE SHAW

Thomas George Shaw, a Scotsman, worked his way up from a position as a London wine dock clerk, to salesman for a port and sherry house, to his own business as a London wine merchant. Shaw has been credited with almost single-handedly bringing about the reduction of duties on wines imported into Great Britain and Ireland. Shaw's letter-writing campaign against excessive wine duties began in 1826 when Poulett Thompson was Chancellor of the Exchequer and was successfully completed on April 3, 1862, when William Gladstone, Chancellor of the Exchequer, to whom his book is dedicated, yielded and announced the reduction of duties, signed into law on April 4, 1862.

SHAW, Thomas George. Notes on the wine duty question and Mr. Shaw's pamphlet [entitled: "Wine Trade and its History"]. London: P. Richardson, 1851. 16p. G36110

_____. Wine in relation to temperance, trade and revenue. London: Gilbert Bros., 1854. 46p. G36120

"Letters published in the *Times* by Shaw and extracts from a pamphlet by Mr. Whitmore," edited by A.I. Robertson.

_____. Wine, the vine, and the cellar. London: Longman, Green, Longman, Roberts and Green, 1863. 505p. G36130

Seventy years ago, André Simon called this "one of the most interesting books we have on the subject," and it still is. Shaw's wit, sense of humor and love of wine pervades every page. Although there is much historical data, of real interest in the book are Shaw's reminiscences and ancedotes of his forty-two years in the wine trade.

The author tells us that he "was convinced forty years ago, and the conviction remains to this day, that in wine-tasting and wine-talk there is an enormous amount of humbug." And he admits that "I often form a very erroneous opinion, and like a wine one day and dislike it the next. . . ."

Reminded that "wine like love, has been a fertile and favorite subject for poets" we are brought back to reality by being told that Bordeaux wines were regularly mixed with wines from the south of France. In fact, Shaw did not believe that "a fiftieth part of the wine sent from Bordeaux to all parts of the world . . . as Claret, and to others, as vin de Bordeaux, is Médoc, or Bordeaux wine, at all." In Burgundy, "sugaring was so common that there was not the slightest desire to conceal it." A current wine writer (See Hanson) has accused some Burgundian vintners of heating or pasteurizing their wines but 120 years ago a few Burgundians had a different approach - they froze their wines!

Shaw's insatiable curiosity took him momentarily out of the vineyards and wine cellars and into the prison in Oporto. His description of the horrors it contained is a chilling account of man's inhumanity to man.

As for the wines of America, the author admits his ignorance and concedes that "the American wine best known by name in this country is the Catawba [Longworth's] just mentioned which reminds me of the sparkling Vouvray, made near Tours, but is not so good." He concludes his comments regarding American wines with the prophetic remark: "California seems better adapted for producing good wine." Scarce.

A considerably revised edition of 540p. was published in 1864.

_____. The wine trade, and its history . . . London: Charles Skipper and East, 1851. 15p. G36140

SHAY, Frank, comp. Drawn from the wood; consolations in words and music for pious friends and drunken companions. New York: Macaulay, 1929. 186p. Illus. G36150

_____. More pious friends and drunken companions. New York: Macaulay, 1928. 190p. Illus. G36160

_____. My pious friends and drunken companions; songs and ballads of conviviality. New York: Macaulay, 1927. 192p. Illus. G36170

_____. My pious friends and drunken companions and more pious friends and drunken companions. New York: Dover, 1961. 235p. Illus. G36180

SHEA, Patrick. The taxation of wine. Kent, England: The Center for European Agricultural Studies, Wye College, 1981. 40p. G36190

SHEAR, S.W. Economic status of the grape industry. Berkeley: University Print. Off., 1927. 127p. G36200

SHEARD, Frank. Tips of wine. Dewsbury: By the Author, c1950. G36210

SHEEN, James Richmond. Wines and other fermented liquors; from the earliest ages to the present time. London: R. Hardwicke, 1864. 292p. Illus. G36220

> A well-written account of the wines of the world, written in an instructive style free of technical terms. The text includes a chapter "On the Cellar and General Management of Wines," which offers useful hints on the construction of a wine cellar as well as the fining, bottling, and binning of wines. Second edition of 304p. published in 1865.

SHEPHERD, Cecil William. Wines, spirits, and liqueurs. London: Ward, Lock, 1958. 160p. Illus. G36230

> Subsequent editions.

_____. Wines you can make; a practical handbook on how to make these cheap and delicious wines in one's own home. London and Melbourne: Ward, Lock, 1954. 128p. Illus. G36240

> Subsequent editions.

SHERRARD-SMITH, Walter. Make mine wine. London: P.R. Macmillan, 1959. 173p. Illus. G36250

_____. Make your own wine. London: Phoenix House, 1964. 120p. Illus. G36260

_____. A new approach to wine making at home. Herne Bay, Kent: 1958. 61p. Illus. G36270

_____. Wine book for beginners. Herne Bay, Kent: 1962. 62p. Illus. G36280

_____. Wine facts and figures. Herne Bay, Kent: 1962. 31p. G36290

> Another edition of this pamphlet was published by Gibbs and Sons of Canterbury.

_____. Wine-making in earnest. Canterbury, England: 1962. 95p. G36300

SHERRY as seen by the British. Collection "Sherry in the world." Jerez de la Frontera, Spain: n.d. 57p. G36305

SHIDELER, James H. and LEE, Lawrence B. A preliminary list of references for the history of agriculture in California. Davis: University of California, Agricultural History Center, 1967. 62p. G36310

> Contains sections on grapes and wines.

SHOEMAKER, James Sheldon. Small-fruit culture; a text for instruction and reference work and a guide for field practice. Philadelphia: Blakiston, 1934. 434p. Illus. G36320

> More than 100 pages of the text concern grape cultivation, although mainly non - *Vitis vinifera* varieties. Subsequent editions.

A SHORT account of port and sherry: the vintaging and treatment of the wines together with a few hints as to their choice and invaluable properties. 2nd ed. London: Chiswick Press, 1889. 25p. Illus. G36330

> Consists of two pamphlets titled: "Good Sherry. How the wine is vintaged and reared with hints respecting the sherries to drink and the sherries to be avoided" and "Pure Port wine. The vintaging and after treatment of wine, and its invaluable properties."

SHORT, Thomas. Discourses on tea, sugar, milk, made-wines, spirits, punch, tobacco . . . with plain and useful rules for gouty people. London: T. Longman, 1750. 424p. G36340

SICHEL, Allan. A guide to good wine. London: Chambers, 1952. 200p. Illus. G36350

> Revised editions issued by Chambers in 1959 and Abbey Library of London in 1973 (208p. each).

_____. The Penguin book of wines. Harmondsworth and London: Penguin Books, 1965. 297p. G36360

> Reprinted in 1968 and 1971.

SICHEL, Peter M.F. and ALLEN, Judy Lay. Which wine? The wine drinker's buying guide. New York: Harper and Row, 1975. G36370

> Second edition of 242p. published by A.W. Visual Library of New York in 1977.

SICHEL, Peter M.F., ed. The wines of Germany: Frank Schoonmaker's classic. Completely rev. ed. New York: Hastings House, 1980. 223p. Illus. G36380

SIEGEL, Hans. Guide to the wines of Germany. London: Pitman, 1978. 123p. Illus. G36390

> Also published in 1979 by Cornerstone Library of New York.

SILL, Webster H. Grape culture in Pennsylvania. Harrisburg: C.E. Aughinbaugh, printer to the State of Pennsylvania, 1912. G36400

SILVERMAN, Harold I., ed. Pride of the wineries. San Francisco: California Living Books, 1980. 197p. Illus. G36410

SIMARD, Armand. What is cognac brandy? Cognac: Comité International du Commerce, 1933. [8p.] G36420

SIMMONDS, A.F. A Barossa Valley farm. Milton, Australia: Jacaranda Press, 1973. 36p. G36430

> Comments on wine and winemaking.

SIMMONDS, Charles. Alcohol. Its production, properties, chemistry, and industrial applications. London: Macmillan, 1919. 574p. G36440

ANDRÉ L. SIMON (1877-1970)

André L. Simon — bibliophile, gourmet, wine connoisseur, historian and writer — is unrivaled in his contribution to the "art of good living." Born in Paris, he came to London in 1902 as the English agent for the champagne house of Pommery and Greno. A year later, the editor of the *Wine and Spirit Trade Review* commissioned him to write twelve articles on the history of the champagne trade in England. Bitten by the bug of "printer's ink," Simon went on to write over 100 books and pamphlets on wine and food, many of which in his early years were published at his own expense. Simon's knowledge of wine was encylopedic, and his literary style is imaginative, clear, concise and distinctive.

Simon collected wine books all his life, and his personal collection was one of the finest ever assembled by an individual. His love of books is well described by Hugh Johnson in the foreword to the Holland House facsimile reproduction of *Bibliotheca Vinaria*: "His senses of sight and touch were as well developed as his famous sense of taste. Books to him were also and always objects of physical attraction or otherwise. I remember many occasions when he took book after book from his shelves for me to admire their print, their woodcuts or their bindings."

He was one of the founders of The Wine Trade Club, and at thirty-two was elected its first president. He also co-founded the Saintsbury Club (see Saintsbury), a London dining club which still meets biannually.

In 1932, at the age of fifty-five, his life seemed shattered when he was discharged as Pommery and Greno's agent. But his bitterness and vow never to have anything more to do with the wine trade were short-lived. Within months he was on his way to Madeira and upon his return he attempted, unsuccessfully, to revive his adopted country's interest in Madeira wines. Shortly thereafter, he contracted with Constable, publishers, to edit a series of popular books on wine. With the help of his friend, A.J. A. Symons, Simon came upon the idea of forming a wine and food society with Simon responsible for the dinners, tastings and for editing the quarterly journal. The idea quickly proved to be popular and within three weeks of its inception there were 232 members. Today the International Wine and Food Society has 150 chapters throughout the world and approximately 8,000 members.

Simon believed that "a man dies too young if he leaves any wine in his cellar," and in keeping with that philosophy, only two magnums of claret remained in his personal cellar when he died at the age of ninety-three.

SIMON, André L. Alcohol and the human body. London: The Wine Trade Club, 1912. G36460

_____. André Simon's French cook book. Boston: Little, Brown, 1938. 370p. Illus. G36470

> Chapters on the art of good living, menus, recipes, lists of culinary and vinous terms, and an outline of famous European wines.

_____. The art of distillation; a lecture delivered at Vintners' Hall by the Wine Trade Club on Tuesday, the 23rd, April 1912. London: The Wine Trade Club, 1912. 46p. G36480

_____. The art of good living. A contribution to the better understanding of food and drink together with a gastronomic vocabulary and a wine glossary. London: Constable, 1929. G36490

This book is designed to help the reader better understand what constitutes good living by way of good food and good wine. The heart of the book consists of "A Wine Dictionary" and "A Gastronomic Vocabulary." There are descriptions of vintage port, sherry, claret and other wines and of foods from hors d'oeuvres to desserts. From a historical perspective, connoisseurs may find the opening chapter on eating and drinking in the dining cars, hotels and restaurants of England to be of interest.

A deluxe limited edition was also published by Constable. The first American edition was published in 1930 by Alfred Knopf. A second revised edition was published by Knopf in 1935 and by Michael Joseph in 1951.

_____. The art of making wine; a lecture delivered at Vintners' Hall by the Wine Trade Club on Friday, the 22nd, March 1912. London: The Wine Trade Club, 1912. 37p. G36500

_____. Australian wine buyers guide. Sydney: Eclipse Books, 1969. 47p. G36510

Abridged edition of his *The Wines, Vineyards and Vignerons of Australia.*

_____. Basic English fare. London: Gramol Publications, 1945. 104p. Illus. G36520

_____. Bibliotheca bacchia. Tome I. Incunables. London and Paris: Maggs Brothers, 1927. 237p., Tome II. Seizieme Siecle. London: Maggs Brothers, 1932. 255p. G36530

Mr. Simon did not limit his discussions to authors and books on viticulture, the art of winemaking, table manners, drunkenness, decrees and regulations relating to the wine trade, but included medical books, treatises on agriculture and even the works of classical writers such as Plato, Hippocrates, Homer, Horace, etc. from which he extracted the wine interest.

The first volume was limited to 250 numbered copies and is devoted entirely to books in all languages printed in the 15th century (Incunables) and describes 182 items. This volume is illustrated by sixty facsimile reproductions of title pages, woodcuts, etc.

The second volume, which covers the 16th century, was published in 275 numbered copies and describes 723 items. It is illustrated by 114 reproductions of title pages and woodcuts from Simon's own collection of books, not only giving a picture of 16th century life but also of book illustration in France, Italy, Germany and Switzerland. It contains descriptions of some 240 books not mentioned in Vicaire's *Bibliographic Gastronomique.*

Both volumes contain three indexes: an alphabetical index of authors; a chronological index of dates of publication; and a geographical index of the various presses. In French.

_____. Bibliotheca bacchia. Reprint. London: The Holland Press, 1972. 255p. Illus. G36540

This reprint of Simon's two volumes is contained in one volume and is a limited edition of 350 copies.

_____. Bibliotheca gastronomica. A catalogue of books and documents on gastronomy. London: The Wine and Food Society, 1953. 196p. Illus. G36550

This is not a bibliography in the true sense of the word, but a catalog of Mr. Simon's personal library. "A Catalogue of some of the books which have given me considerable pleasure to collect in the course of the past half-century. . . ." There are 1,644 titles, many of which are annotated. The edition was limited to 750 copies. Scarce.

_____. Bibliotheca gastronomica. Reprint. London: The Holland Press, 1978. 196p. Illus. G36560

This is a facsimile reproduction of the original 1953 edition and was also limited to 750 copies.

_____. Bibliotheca vinaria; a bibliography of books and pamphlets dealing with viticulture, wine-making, distillation, the management, sale, taxation, use and abuse of wines and spirits. London: Grant Richards, 1913. 339p. G36570

Simon noted: "In the present Bibliography are included not only all the books which form the library of the Wine Trade Club, but also all those which I know of and which it is hoped to add to the Club collection in due course." Only 180 copies were printed, at Simon's expense. Rare.

_____. Bibliotheca vinaria. Reprint. London: The Holland Press, 1979. 341p. Illus. G36580

A facsimile reproduction of Simon's "Office Copy". One of the original copies was interleaved with blank pages for Simon's use, unnumbered and marked "office copy". Simon used these blank pages to update his collection and to enter other wine books of which he became aware. This edition reproduces Simon's handwritten notes exactly as he penned them and is much more complete than the original 1913 edition. This work was published in a limited edition of 600 hand-numbered copies and is beautifully bound.

_____. The blood of the grape; the wine trade text book. London: Duckworth, 1920. 302p. G36590

The substance of lectures delivered by Mr. Simon at the Wine Trade Club during the winter of 1919-1920. It is a general purpose work covering the wine trade, what wine is, the different kinds of wine, the blending of wine, the care of wine, and wines of France and other countries. Several subsequent editions.

BIBLIOTHECA VINARIA

A BIBLIOGRAPHY OF BOOKS AND PAMPHLETS
DEALING WITH VITICULTURE, WINE-MAKING
DISTILLATION, THE MANAGEMENT, SALE
TAXATION, USE AND ABUSE OF
WINES AND SPIRITS

BY

ANDRÉ L. SIMON

AUTHOR OF "A HISTORY OF THE WINE TRADE IN ENGLAND," ETC.

LONDON
GRANT RICHARDS LTD.

_____. Bottlescrew days. Wine drinking in England during the 18th century. London: Duckworth, 1926. 273p. Illus. G36600

Chronologically this is really Volume IV of the *History of The Wine Trade in England*. In researching this interesting period of English history, Mr. Simon found that its two outstanding features were ". . . the extraordinary drunken habits of rich and poor alike . . . and the considerable influence which the invention of the corkscrew has had upon civilization in general, and table manners in particular." There are also chapters on wine glasses and drinking songs and toasts. An important reference. Published in 1927 by Small, Maynard of Boston.

_____. By request: An autobiography. London: The Wine and Food Society, 1957. 180p. Illus. G36610

Simon reports the main incidents, friendships and activities of his long life. An indispensable book for those interested in Simon, the Wine and Food Society, the Saintsbury Club, etc. It includes an incomplete bibliography of Simon's writings, though prepared by Simon.

_____. The cellar register. Being a bin book wherein wine lovers are conveniently enabled to record their judgment of the wines and spirits they have owned and the details of their purchase and consumption. London: The Wine and Food Society, 1938. G36620

_____. Champagne. New York and London: McGraw-Hill, 1962. 224p. Illus. G36630

_____. Champagne. The elixir of youth. London: Pommery and Greno, 1930. 31p. Illus. G36640

_____. Champagne. With appendices on corks; methods of keeping and serving champagne; vintages; brands, shippers. London: Constable, 1934. 140p. G36650

_____. Claret and Sauternes, classified list of the best hocks and moselles with notes upon German wines. London: Wine and Food Society, 1919. 22p. Illus. G36660

_____. The commonsense of wine. London: Wine and Food Society, 1966. 192p. Illus. G36670

An excellent book for the beginner. Laid out in a question-and-answer format.

_____. Concise encyclopedia of food and wine. 1939. G36680

Also published in 1952 by Bramhall House, New York.

_____. A concise encyclopedia of gastronomy, section VIII, wine. London: The Wine and Food Society, 1939. 178p. G36690

Published in nine sections.

_____. The concise encyclopedia of gastronomy. London: Collins and New York: Bramhall House and Harcourt, Brace, 1952. 827p. Illus. G36700

_____. A dictionary of gastronomy. New York: Farrar, Straus, 1949. 264p. G36710

> Published in London by The Wine and Food Society, 1949. Also a 1970 edition.

_____. A dictionary of wine. London: Cassell, 1935. 266p. Illus. G36720

> Published in New York by Longmans, Green and Co., 1936.

_____. A dictionary of wines, spirits and liqueurs. London: Herbert Jenkins, 1958. 167p. G36730

> German edition published in 1960. Revised editions published in 1961 and 1963.

_____. The different names of wine. Melbourne: 1920. 8p. G36740

> A lecture delivered before the Wine Trade Club, London, on November 11, 1919.

_____. Drink. London: Burke Publishing, 1948. 272p. Illus. G36750

> This is an anthology about drink beginning with Noah's wine *yayim*. The chapters are interlaced with poetry, songs, color reproductions of famous paintings, and photographs of wine glasses. An appendix covers the service of wine, suggested menus and recipes for cocktails, and includes Hilaire Belloc's "An Heroic Poem in Praise of Wine." Subsequent editions including 1953 edition by Horizon Press.

_____. The elixir of youth. Notes on champagne, graves, sauternes, chablis, hock and other white wines, still and sparkling. London: The Wine Trade Club, 1924. G36760

_____. Encyclopedia of wines. New York: Quadrangle Books, 1973. 301p. Illus. G36770

> This was Simon's last work and was published after his death. Contains over 7,000 entries of wines and wine areas.

_____. English fare and French wines; being notes toward the furtherance of the entente cordiale gastronomique. London: Newman Neame, 1955. 76p. Illus. G36780

_____. English wines and cordials. London: Gramol Publications, 1946. 144p. Illus. G36790

> A short history of English wines followed by recipes for homemade "wines" of various types, mead, etc.

_____. Everybody's guide to wines and spirits. London: Charles Skilton, 1966. 194p. Illus. G36800

> This is a modified version of the earlier *Wines and Spirits: The Connoisseur's Handbook*.

_____. Fashions in food and wine. 1968. G36810

_____. Food. London: Burke Publishing, 1949. 272p. Illus. G36820

This is an anthology of stories and poems about food and memorable meals, with attention given to wines. Also published by Horizon Press, New York, in 1953.

_____. Food and drink. London: The Wine Trade Club, 1919. G36830

A part of a series of "educational" booklets written by Simon for the Wine Trade Club Education Committee.

_____. Food and wine; an exhibition of rare printed books. 1961. 51p. G36840

_____. Gazetteer of wines. London: The International Wine and Food Society, 1972. 312p. G36850

_____. German wines. A classified list of the best hocks and moselles with notes upon German wines. London: The Wine and Food Society, c1939. 23p. G36860

_____. The gourmet's week-end book. London: Seeley Service, 1952. 348p. Illus. G36870

_____. Guide to good food and wine; a concise encyclopedia of gastronomy. London: Collins, 1956. 816p. Illus. G36880

Second edition published in 1960 and third edition in 1963.

_____. The history of champagne. London: Ebury Press, 1962. 192p. Illus. G36890

This is exactly the same book as *Champagne* except it lacks the chapter "American Champagne" by Robert J. Misch and four of the appendices pertaining to American usage. Reprinted by Octopus Books in 1971.

_____. The history of the champagne trade in England. London: Wyman, 1905. 193p. G36900

This was the first book written by Simon. It grew out of twelve articles on champagne he was commissioned to write for the *Wine Trade Review*. Rare.

_____. The history of the wine trade in England. Vol. I. London: Wyman, 1906. 387p. G36910

Describes the rise and progress of the wine trade in England from the earliest time to the end of the 14th century. Vol. I sold so poorly that the "prints" of Vols. II and III were drastically reduced. Consequently Vols. II and III are rare, although Vol. I can sometimes be found.

Mr. Simon once remarked that "There is more hard work and original information in these three volumes than in all my other books." All three volumes were printed at Simon's expense. Essential reference works.

_____. The history of the wine trade in England. Vol I. Facsimile reprint. London: The Holland Press, 1964. 387p. G36920

_____. The history of the wine trade in England. Vol. II. London: Wyman, 1907. 339p. Illus. G36930

The progress of the wine trade in England during the 15th and 16th centuries.

_____. The history of the wine trade in England. Vol. II. Facsimile reprint. London: The Holland Press, 1964. 339p. G36940

_____. The history of the wine trade in England. Vol. III. London: Wyman, 1909. 435p. Illus. G36950

The wine trade in England during the 17th century.

_____. The history of the wine trade in England. Vol, III. Facsimile reprint. London: The Holland Press, 1964. 423p. Illus. G36960

_____. How to enjoy wine in the home. London: Newman Neame, 1952. 32p. Illus. G36970

_____. How to make wines and cordials. Dover: 1972. 144p. Illus. G36980

Reprint of the 1946 edition published under the title: *English Wines and Cordials.*

_____. How to serve wine in hotels and restaurants. London: Newman Neame, 1952. 24p. G36990

_____. In praise of good living, an anthology for friends. London: Frederick Muller, 1949. 63p. Illus. G37000

Second edition published in 1952.

_____. In the twilight. London: Michael Joseph, 1969. 182p. G37010

_____. In vino veritas. London: Grant Richards, 1913. 202p. G37020

The first six lectures which Simon delivered at the Vintners' Hall for the Wine Trade Club during the winter months of 1911-12.

_____. The International Wine and Food Society's encyclopedia of wines. London: The Society, 1972. 312p. G37030

_____. Know your wines. London: Coram Publishers, 1956. 116p. Illus. G37040

_____. Let mine be wine: the philosophy of wine. The anatomy of wine. The geography of wine. The choice of wine. The service of wine. London: The Wine and Food Society, 1946. 24p. G37050

_____. A list of the books dealing with wine. n.p., n.d. 10p. G37060

_____. Madeira and its wines. Funchal: Casa Pathe, 1938. 20p. G37070

_____. Madeira and its wines. Funchal: Issued by Madeira Wine Association, 1947. 18p. Illus. G37080

_____. Menus for gourmets. New York: Hearthside Press, 1961. 119p. G37090

_____. My French friend. A farce in one-act. London: Palmer-Sutton, 1912. G37100

Only a small number of copies (about fifty) were printed at Mr. Simon's expense, and sold to raise money for the Wine and Spirit

Trade Benefit Society, where it was produced for the first and only time by the Dramatic Society of the Wine Trade Club. Rare.

_____. The noble grapes and the great wines of France. New York: McGraw-Hill, 1957. 180p. Illus. G37110

The twenty-four color plates by Percy Hennell reproduce the exact size, shape and color of the grapes. Mr. Simon in the introduction states that this was the first time this was accomplished in the book trade.

_____. Notes on the late J. Pierpont Morgan's cellar book, 1906. London: Privately printed by the Author at the Curwen Press, 1944. 37p. G37120

Mr. Simon takes the reader on a tour through the wine cellar of J. Pierpont Morgan, then one of the wealthiest men in America. Simon details the wines in the cellar and compares them to his own wine drinking experiences.

Simon was clearly surprised to discover that of the 10,914 wine bottles in the cellar, there were no young wines. About 8,000 fell into the old, or inferentially, the "over the hill" category, and the other 3,000 bottles had enough age to put them in the mature category.

Morgan's preferences obviously ran to champagne (3,860 bottles) and claret (3,080 bottles), mainly first growths. He had a remarkable collection of old madeiras (1,287 bottles), the oldest 1774 and the youngest 1844. Red burgundies were represented (563 bottles) by Romanée-Conti, Clos de Vougeot, Musigny and a few bottles from the Beaune area. The balance consisted of sherry (878 bottles), Rhine (504 bottles), port (368 bottles), sauternes (153 bottles), Moselle (153 bottles) and sixty-eight bottles of white burgundy. The cellar also included 2,280 bottles of cognacs, whiskies, rum and liqueurs. Rare.

_____. Partners. A guide to the game of wine and food match-making. London: The Wine and Food Society, n.d. 20p. Illus. G37130

_____. Petit dictionnaire de poche francais-anglais, l'usage des sommeliers. The wine butler's French-English Pocket Dictionary. Paris: l'Imprimerie du Griffon, c1929. G37140

_____. Port. London: Constable, 1934. 130p. G37150

The chapter on the Burnay sale shows Simon's skill as a writer, and the character sketch of Arthur Southard is a brillant example of making words come alive.

_____. Record of the feast of the Five Princes Swan Feast, 1934-1935. London: Vintners' Hall, 1935. 26p. G37160

_____. The Saintsbury Club; a scrap book, by "The Cellarer". London: Privately printed for The Saintsbury Club by the Curwen Press, 1943. 83p. G37170

An account by Simon of the founding, history, membership, cellar contents and menus of the Saintsbury Club from 1931 through 1942. Limited to 200 copies. Scarce.

_____. The Star Chamber dinner accounts. London: The Wine and Food Society, 1959. 88p. Illus. G37180

The King's Privy Council, which can be traced to those who counseled William the Conqueror, was appointed by the reigning English monarch. Originally the Council advised the king on matters of state and made the laws for the kingdom. Over time, some of the Lords of the Privy Council, including the Lord Chancellor and the Archbishop of Canterbury, met as a Court for judicial purposes in a large apartment adjacent to the old Palace of Westminster in London. The room they met in was ornamented on the ceiling with gold stars applied over a blue background, and the Court came to be known as the Court of the Star Chamber.

These "Lords of the Star Chamber were a law unto themselves; there was no appeal allowed and no hope left when sentence had been passed by them." Since their procedure did not follow the English common law, great abuses of judicial power occurred. Finally, their zeal in supressing the opponents of Charles I led to the abolition of the Star Chamber by the Long Parliament in 1644.

Since the Lords were "guests" of the sovereign when they met, detailed expense accounts were kept of their expenditures, especially for food and drink. Somehow, André Simon acquired some 250 of the dinner accounts from 1519 to 1639. Of these, he selected fifty from 1567 to 1605, the period covering most of Shakespeare's life, and gives us glimpses of the social life of that time. To those interested in the history of wine and food this comprises an extraordinary account of what the rich ate and drank in Elizabethan times. (These accounts are rendered in modern English.)

In order to make the "Accounts" more intelligible to us, Mr. Simon has added "Commentary on Tudor Food" (forty-one pages) which includes details of the wines they drank and some Tudor recipes that provide insight as to how foods were cooked, prepared and served to the Lords of the Privy Council.

_____. Star Chamber revels (or, the fountayne of justice) a satyre acted on Friday the eleventh day of June, in the yeare 1602, by the lords of the Queene Elizabeth's most honourable council. Peekskill, New York: The Watch Hill Press, 1937. 45p. G37190

In the introduction, Mr. Simon says: "It was the deciphering of those old Star Chamber Accounts that led me to look up some of the cases which the Lords of the Star Chamber had actually 'heard and determined', and then tempted me to try and bring back to life, in the form and language of an Elizabethan play, the Lords of the Star Chamber in court and at dinner." (See commentary following the *Star Chamber Dinner Accounts* above.)

Here on June 11, 1602, the Lords dispatched summary and erratic "justice", often on the basis of hearsay and rumor, which often involved torture and humiliation. Their regard for women (unless one were a countess) was abysmal. Yet their barbarity did not prevent the Court from drinking and dining superlatively.

The Lords, through statements and songs during dinner, reflect the overwhelming favor with which sack, an early form of sherry, was held by the upper classes. No other wine at that time, not even claret, was close. As one remarks, "Sack is the life, soul and spirit of a man; the fire that Prometheus stole, not from love's kitchen, but his wine-cellar to increase the native heat and radical moisture without which we are but drowsy dust, or dead clay. This is Nectar, the very Nepenthe the gods were drunk with; 'tis this that gave Ganymede beauty, Hebe youth, to Jove his heaven and eternity." To anyone who yearns for the "golden past," and thinks it would have been great to have lived in the days of Good Queen Bess, this play, historically accurate, serves sombre notice. This book was entirely handmade, printed on handmade paper ". . . wrested from a reluctant hand press by James Hendrickson, poor wretch, who by the Grace of God might have been otherwise, but not more pleasantly, employed," and limited to 275 copies.

_____. The supply, care and sale of wine: a book of reference for wine merchants. London: Duckworth, 1923. 208p. G37200

_____. Tables of content; leaves from my diary. London: Constable, 1933. 280p. G37210

This is a record of 121 luncheons and dinners where good food and fine wines were enjoyed in the company of appreciative friends. There is an index of hosts and guests, an index of wines and a chronological schedule of vintages.

_____. Vine and its fruit; a lecture delivered at Vintners' Hall by the Wine Trade Club on Monday, 26th, February 1912. London: The Wine Trade Club, 1912. G37220

_____. Vintagewise. A postscript to Saintsbury's notes on a cellar book. London: Michael Joseph, 1945. 174p. G37230

Critical notes on the quality of various wines tasted by the author. Many subsequent editions published.

_____. What about wine? All the Answers. London: Newman Neame, 1953. 56p. G37240

Wood engravings by David Gentleman.

_____. The wine and food menu book. London: Frederick Muller, 1956. 377p. G37250

_____. Wine and the wine trade. London: Pitman, 1921. 110p. Illus. G37260

Deals with the wine trade of England, past and contemporary, and the whole process of wine making from the growing of the grapes and the work in the vineyard to the bottling and selling of wines. A revised second edition of 129p. was published in 1934. In 1947, the Wine Trade Club published a pamphlet of 50p. under the same title. Four lectures delivered to the wine trade students at Vintners' Hall, London, and at Birmingham in autumn, 1946.

_____. Wine and the wine trade in England, retrospect and prospect. 1932. G37270

_____. The wine connoisseur. London: The Wine Trade Club, 1923. 32p. Illus. G37280

_____. The wine connoisseur's catechism. London: The Wine and Food Society, 1934. 40p. G37290

Also published in 1935 by Epicurean Press.

_____. Wine in Shakespeare's days and Shakespeare's plays, read at the four hundred and sixty-third meeting of the Sette of Odd Volumes held at the Savoy Hotel, London, on the 24th day of November, MCMXXXI by André Simon, vintner to the Sette. London: Privately printed by Ye Sette of Odd Volumes and imprinted at the Curwen Press, 1931. 34p. G37300

Simon was a member of Ye Sette of Odd Volumes, a literary dining club of mostly lawyers and writers, and new members were expected to make a literary communication to the Sette called Opusculum. This was Simon's contribution and it was privately printed and issued to all members of the Sette in 1931 and limited to 199 copies. Rare.

_____. Wine in Shakespeare's days and Shakespeare's plays. London: Privately printed for the Author by Curwen Press, 1964. 34p. G37310

Republished on the 400th anniversary of Shakespeare's birth, the title is indicative of this small book's contents. Simon tells us about the living conditions of that era and why the breadwinner stopped by the nearest tavern before going home. The text is imaginatively illustrated with reproductions of paintings, engravings and prints from Shakespeare's days.

_____. A wine primer. London: Michael Joseph and New York: Eriksson-Taplinger, 1946. 152p. Illus. G37320

A text book for beginners on how to buy, keep and serve wine. Many subsequent editions.

_____. Wine that maketh glad the heart of man. Wolverhampton: Louis Connolly, Wine Grower and Shipper, 1930. 32p. Illus. G37330

Various editions.

_____. The wine trade of England; a lecture delivered at Vintners' Hall by the Wine Trade Club, 20th November, 1911. London: The Wine Trade Club, 1911. 63p. G37340

_____. Wines and liqueurs from A to Z. London: Wine and Food Society, 1935. 58p. G37350

Subsequent editions.

_____. Wine and spirits, the connoisseur's textbook. London: Duckworth, 1919. 273p. G37360

This was the first book that Simon did not finance by himself and that was offered for sale to the public by booksellers.

_____. Wines and spirits, the connoisseur's handbook. London: Charles Skilton, 1961. 194p. Illus. G37370

_____. The wines of France. New York: The Wine and Food Society of New York, 1935. 64p. G37380

Subsequent editions in 1937, 1939 (published by the French government) and 1957 as an enlarged and revised edition by the ComitéNational de propagande en faveur du vin.

_____. The wines, vineyards and vignerons of Australia. Melbourne: Lansdowne and London: Paul Hamlyn, 1967. 194p. Illus. G37390

SIMON, André L. and AVERY, Ronald. Talking of wine. London: Pye Records, 1962. G37400

This is a recording of André Simon and Ronald Avery discussing some basic facts and fallacies about wine, and how to use and enjoy it. Though not a book, it is included as a unique piece of Simoniana.

SIMON, André L. and CRAIG, Elizabeth. Madeira wine, cakes and sauce. London: Constable, 1933. 153p. G37410

The book opens in dialogue form:

"What a mess the world's in!"

"It was ever in a mess."

"Not in the good old days."

"They were far worse."

"Nonsense!"

"Listen!"

"Go ahead."

"When bloody Richard was King of England, some five hundred odd years ago, Charles the Mad was King of France, John the Bastard King of Portugal, Mohammed King of Granada, the Emperor Wenceslas had been deposed by the Pope of Rome, and the Pope of Rome deposed by the Pope of Avignon. There was naught else but civil wars, heresies, murders, persecutions, famine and pestilence. So much for your good old days."

"How do you know?"

"I have been looking up all sorts of records and stories of the period in search of informaton about Zarco."

"Never heard of him. Who was Zarco?"

John Goncalves Zarco, born in 1393, was the discoverer of the island of Madeira, "a dank forest full of creeping bugs and buzzing insects, but not a living soul." After forty years "he left a thriving community basking in the sunshine, free from the fear of pests, plague and famine" — an island "covered with fields of sugar cane and vineyards, as well as all sorts of fruit trees."

There are chapters on the sweet wines of madeira, malmsey and vidonia, and on rainwater, Habisham, Victorian madeiras, and the madeira wines of today.

Elizabeth Craig's contribution to the book relates to "Early Morning Malmsey," "How to Give a Madeira Party" and "Madeira in the Kitchen."

SIMON, André L. and HALLGARTEN, S.F. Great wines of Germany and its famed vineyards. New York: McGraw-Hill, 1963. 192p. Illus. G37420

SIMON, André L., comp. A catalogue of some manuscripts and early printed books illustrating "The Art of Good Living" from the collection of André L. Simon. January, 1931, exhibited at the First Edition Club. London: The Pelican Press, 1931. 30p. G37440

In the foreword to the catalogue H. Warner Allen wrote: "In his best qualities, Larensis (who 'took pride in gathering about him many men of culture and entertained them with conversations as well as with the pleasures of the tables') must have been such a man as André Simon, Deipnosophist, Opsodaedalus, Enologist, Gastronomer, Cunning Contriver of Dainty Meals, and Connoisseur. He would have appreciated the idea of an exhibition of rare manuscripts and books illustrating 'The Art of Good Living.' I doubt, however, whether he possessed more than a fraction of Simon's forceful personality, and he was immeasurably inferior in his theoretical and practical knowledge of the artistic principles on which good living is based."

On display were manuscripts from the 12th to the 17th century; the first dated edition of the earliest printed book on cookery. Among other rarities were: the collected writing of Cato, Varro, Columella and Palladius dealing with matters connected with agriculture and viticulture; an interesting and detailed account of how the banquets of the ancients were served; Parma municipal ordinances regulating the sale of food and drink in taverns; a very rare collection of familiar recipes; a rare treatise of the use of wine gaugers, coopers and brokers; a treatise (1536) on the management of wine; an account of the magnificence of Darius' table; a rare booklet (1545) on how to behave at table, etc.

_____. Food and wine. An exhibition of rare printed books assembled and annotated by André L. Simon. London: National Book League, 1961. 60p. G37450

SIMON, André L., ed. The Bolton letters. The letters of an English merchant in Madeira 1695-1714. Vol. I. 1695-1700. London: Werner Laurie, 1928. 192p. G37460

Volume I consists of ninety-eight letters written by William Bolton, a Madeira wine merchant, to his London agent, Robert Heysham. The letters contain many references to wine. Simon published the letters at his own expense but he "sold hardly any copies at all: the bulk of the edition happily, a small one, was pulped and Volume II was never published." For this reason an original copy of Volume I is rare. Photocopies of Volume I are generally available. Simon gave the typescript of the 1701-1714 letters, which had been prepared for Volume II, to Graham Blandy, a member of the Madeira trade. Mr. Blandy privately published Volume II in 1960.

_____. The search after claret. London: Palmer, Sutton, 1912. G37470

A facsimile reproduction of Richard Ames' three rare pamphlets, "Search after Claret," "Farther Search after Claret" and "Last Search after Claret," with some introductory "Notes on Claret." Only fifty numbered copies printed. Rare.

_____. We shall eat and drink again. Hutchinson G37480

(See GOLDING, Louis.)

_____. Wine and food. A gastronomic quarterly. London: Wine and Food Society, 1934-1970. G37490

Published quarterly over a thirty-seven year period by the Wine and Food Society. A complete set consists of 149 journals covering the history of wine and food, book reviews, vintage notes, memorable meals, etc. by most of the then prominent wine and food writers.

_____. The wines of the World Pocket Library. London: The Wine and Food Society, 1950. 15p. each. G37500

1. Champagne, 2. Port, 3. Sherry, 4. South Africa, 5. Claret, 6. Graves and Sauternes, 7. Burgundy, 8. Hocks and Moselles, 9. Brandy, 10. Rum.

These, and the following series of booklets, were written by various authors. Simon was the editor of the series and the author of several of the booklets.

_____. The wines of the World Pocket Library. London: The Wine and Food Society, 1951. 15 pages each. G37510

11. Madeira, 12. Italy, 13. Yugoslavia, 14. Switzerland and Luxembourg, 15. California, 16. Alsace, Arbois and the Loire Valley, 17. The Rhone, Provence, Languedoc and Roussillon.

SIMPLE facts about wines, spirits, ale and stout. New York: Alex D. Shaw, c1934. 64p. G37520

SIMPSON, John. The grape vine, its propagation and culture. London: Routledge, 1883. 104p. Illus. G37530

SIMPSON, Leonard Francis. The handbook of dining or how to dine. London: 1859. G37540

SIMPSON, W. Philosophical discussion of fermentation. London: W. Cooper, 1675. 149p. G37550

SIMSON, Sally. Wine of Good Hope. Saayman and Weber, 1983.

SINGLETON, Vernon L. Phenolic substances in grapes and wine and their significance. New York: Academic Press, 1969. 282p. G37560

SIOLI, P., comp. Historical souvenir of El Dorado County, California, with illustrations and biographical sketches of its prominent men and pioneers. Oakland: By the Author, 1883. 272p. Illus. G37570

> Includes biographical accounts of several vintners and some information on the wine industry.

SITWELL, Sacheveral. Portugal and Madeira. London: Batsford, 1954. 244p. Illus. G37580

> A guide that covers the history, people, customs and their wines and foods.

SLADE, Daniel. The evolution of horticulture in New England. New York: Putnam, 1895. 180p. G37590

> Includes grapes.

SLATE, G.L. and WATSON, J. and EINSET, J. Grape varieties introduced by the New York State Agricultural Experiment Station, 1928-1961. Ithaca, NY: New York State Agricultural Experiment Station, 1962. 48p. G37600

SLATER, Leslie G. The secrets of making wine from fruits and berries. Lilliwaup, WA: Terry Publishing, 1965. 90p. Illus. G37610

SLESSOR, Kenneth. The grapes are growing: the story of Australian wine. Sydney: The Australian Wine Board, 1963. 50p. Illus. G37620

> Revised edition published in 1965.

SMEED, T. The wine merchant's manual. A treatise on the fining, preparation of finings, and general management of wine consumed in this country. London: Smith, Elder, 1845. 81p. G37630

SMITH, Charles W. Pruning fruits and vines. Melbourne: Robertson and Mullens, 1958. 212p. G37640

SMITH, D. Nichol. The Saintsbury centenary oration delivered by Professor D. Nichol Smith at the 27th meeting of the Saintsbury Club, 23 October 1945. London: Privately printed at The Curwen Press for the Saintsbury Club, 1946. 10p. G37650

SMITH, D.S. Outstanding Australian wines I have seen. Sydney: Wine and Food Society of New South Wales, 1953. 18p. G37660

SMITH, George of Kendal. A compleat Body of Distilling . . . containing an exact method of making all the compound cordial-waters . . . consisting of all the directions necessary for learning the distillers art . . . London: 1725. 150p. G37680

_____. A complete body of distilling, explaining the mysteries of that science, in a most easy and familiar manner; containing an exact and accurate method of making all the compound cordial-waters now in use . . . 2nd ed. London: Printed for B. Lintot, 1731. 152p. G37690

_____. A compleat body of distilling, explaining the mysteries of that science, in a most easy and familiar manner; containing an exact and accurate method of making all the compound cordial-waters now in use.

With a particular account of their several virtues. As also a directory consisting of all the instructions necessary for learning the distiller's art; with a computation of the original cost of the several ingredients, and the profits arising in sale. Adapted no less to the use of private families, than of apothecaries and distillers. In two parts. 3rd ed. London: 1738. G37700

There is also a 1766 edition.

_____. The nature of fermentation explained, with the method of opening the body of any grain or vegetable subject, so as to obtain from it a spirituous liquor: exemplified by the process of preparing rum, as 'tis manag'd in the West-Indies. To which is added a collection of several compound cordial waters, with the art of preparing some artificial wines, not hitherto published. London: Printed for B. Lintot, 1729. 56p. G37710

_____. The practical distiller and a treatise on making artificial wines. London: Printed for B. Lintot, 1734. 57p. G37720

SMITH, George S. Seminar on district wines, Sunday, March 10, 1968. Rutherglen, Victoria: Rutherglen Wine Festival, 1968. G37670

SMITH, Joanna. The new English vineyard. London: Sidgwick and Jackson, 1979. 241p. Illus. G37730

The recent interest in England for growing grapes for making wine has created a need for knowing how to do it. This book explains how to plan, plant and harvest a vineyard. Contains a gazetteer of British vineyards and their wines.

SMITH, S. and Sons. 100 years in the good earth: a centenary history of the development of the Yalumba vineyards Angaston, South Australia, 1849-1949. Adelaide: 1950. 37p. Illus. G37740

SMITH, W.B. Bleasdale, 1850-1950; a centenary history of Bleasdale, Langhornes Creek, South Australia. Adelaide: Potts' Bleasdale Vineyards, 1950. 21p. G37750

SMITH, Wallace. Garden of the Sun. Los Angeles: Lymanhouse, 1939. 558p. G37760

Discusses vineyards of the San Joaquin Valley.

SNEESBY, Norman. A vineyard in England. London: Robert Hale, 1977. 223p. Illus. G37770

The story of a family's hardships and joys in replanting its 2.7-acre plum and apple orchard into a vineyard.

SOLIS, Virgil. Drinking cups, ewers, vases . . . London: James Russell, 1862. 23p. G37780

SOMERVILLE, Edith Oenone and MARTIN, Violet Florence. In the vine country. London: Allen, 1893. 237p. Illus. G37800

SONOMA and Mendocino wine tour. St. Helena: Vintage Image, 1979. 69p. Illus. G37810

SOUTH African produce, with special reference to the history, production and export of the wine industry. London: P.B. Burgoyne and Co., 1926. G37820

> P.B. Burgoyne and Co. was the only wine merchant firm in England whose interests related solely to British Empire wines. This firm had started importing and selling Australian wines as early as 1871.

SOUTH African wines, spirits and liqueurs; a handbook on their composition, preparation, care and serving. Stellenbosch: Wine, Spirit and Malt, 1958. 83p. G37830

SOUTH Australia. Royal Commission into the Grape Growing Industry report. Adelaide: Gov't. Print. Off., 1966. 26p. G37840

SOUTH Tyrol: Holidays, fruit, wine. Bolzano, Italy: Provincia Autonoma di Bolzana-Alto Adige, 1982. Illus. G37850

SOUVENIR of the old white horse cellar. The romance of a famous hostelry. London: Hatchett's Piccadilly, n.d. 20p. Illus. G37860

SPANGLER, Andrew M., ed. Both sides of the grape question. Comprising I. "An essay on the culture of the native and exotic grape." By William Saunders. II. "Physiography in its application to grape culture." By F.J. Cope. III "A contribution to the classification of the species and varieties of the grape vine, with hints on culture." By J.M. McMinn. Philadelphia: By the Author and New York: C. M. Saxton, 1860. 96p. Illus. G37870

SPEAIGHT, Robert. The companion guide to Burgundy. London: Collins, 1975. 351p. Illus. G37880

> Discusses the architecture of Burgundy more than its wines, but wine is discussed.

SPEECHLY, William. A treatise on the culture of the vine, exhibiting new and advantageous methods of propogating, cultivating and training that plant, so as to render it abundantly fruitful. Together with new hints on the formation of vineyards in England. York: Printed for the Author by G. Peacock, 1790. 224p. Illus. G37890

> Speechly (1733-1819) was the gardener to the Duke of Portland, to whom the book is dedicated in appreciation of his support and encouragement and use of "his Grace's nobel library." The treatise is divided into four books: book I, *The Vine*; book II, *The Vinery*; book III, *Grafting*; and book IV, *Vineyards*. Edward Hyams in his work *Grapes Under Cloches* refers to a small but admirable body of English writing on the subject of viticulture of which he states: "The best of them all is that of Speechly, already mentioned, a model of the sound, practical, well-written and beautifully printed manual." Speechly's treatise was well received and second and third editions were published in 1805 and 1821. An attempt to determine through the British Library the number of first-edition copies published was unsuccessful because no records survive on the printing firm of G. Peacock. Scarce.

A

TREATISE

ON THE

CULTURE OF THE VINE,

EXHIBITING NEW AND ADVANTAGEOUS METHODS OF

PROPAGATING, CULTIVATING, AND TRAINING

THAT

P   L   A   N   T,

SO AS TO RENDER IT ABUNDANTLY FRUITFUL.

TOGETHER WITH

NEW HINTS ON THE FORMATION

O F

VINEYARDS in ENGLAND.

By WILLIAM SPEECHLY,
GARDENER to the DUKE of PORTLAND.

YORK:
PRINTED FOR THE AUTHOR, BY G. PEACOCK;
AND SOLD BY G. NICOL, BOOKSELLER TO HIS MAJESTY, PALL-MALL;
J. DEBRETT AND J. STOCKDALE, PICCADILLY; AND
E. JEFFERY, NEAR CARLETON-PLACE, LONDON.
MDCCXC.

_____. A treatise on the culture of the vine . . . Together with new hints on the formation of vineyards in England. 2nd ed. London: Longman, 1805. 300p. G37900

_____. A treatise on the culture of the vine . . . a treatise on the culture of the pineapple and the management of the hot-house. 3rd ed. London: Longman, 1821. 363p. G37910

SPENCER, Edward. The flowing bowl. "A treatise on drinks of all kinds and of all periods, interspersed with sundry anecdotes and reminiscences.". London: Grant Richards, 1899. 243p. G37920

> Reprinted in 1925 by Stanley Paul of London.

SPENCER, Herbert. Cognac country: The Hennessy book of a people and their spirit. London: Quiller Press/Christie's Wine Publications, 1983. 150p. Illus. G37930

> Contains 170 color photographs by Fred Mayer. The book chronicles the Charantes region from Neolithic times to present and describes all aspects of cognac production from the vine through distillation and the aging process.

SPINOLA, Oberto. The Martini Museum of the history of wine making. Turin: Martini and Rossi, 38p. Illus. G37940

> A short history of wine making, customs and artifacts. Includes photographs of outstanding museum pieces.

SPOONER, Alden Jermain. The cultivation of American grape vines, and making of wine. Brooklyn: A. Spooner, 1846. 96p. Illus. G37950

> After a short history of the unsuccessful attempts to grow foreign vines, the author describes the origin of and his personal experience with the native Isabella. His vineyard was in Brooklyn, New York, where the Isabella had been cultivated as early as 1816. For half a century this was the grape of choice in the eastern states, eventually giving way to the Concord. Spooner gives a description of other useful native grapes and an informative summary of grape growing in vineyards from Nantucket Island to North Carolina. Second edition published in 1858.

SPRAGUE, W.V. Dr. Sprague's reply to Professor Stuart's letter addressed to him though the American Temperance Intelligencer on August, 1835, relative to his late sermon on the exclusion of wine from the Lord's Supper. Albany: Packard and Van Benthuysen, 1835. 29p. G37960

SPURRIER, Steven. The concise guide to French country wines. London: Collins Willow and New York: Perigee Books, 1982. G37970

SPURRIER, Steven and DOVAZ, Michael. Academie du vin complete wine course. London: Century Publishing and New York: Putnam, 1983. 224p. G37980

> Also published by Christie's Wine Publications.

The SQUIRE'S recipes: in which are described the methods by which Thomas Hoggson, esquire, compounded the twelve most famous toddies that distinguished his hospitality. Sudbury, England: Roger Buck, 1784. G37990

See Hoggson, Thomas.

STAMBOIS, Charles E.M. The great cognac brandies. London: 1933. G37995

STANISLAWSKI, Dan. Landscapes of Bacchus, the vine in Portugal. Austin and London: University of Texas Press, 1970. 210p. Illus. G38000

STEEL, Anthony. The custom of the room or early wine books of Christ's College, Cambridge. Cambridge: W. Heffer, 1949. 123p. Illus. G38010

STEIN, Clem. The joy of home winemaking. New York: Stravon Educational Press, 1973. 96p. Illus. G38020

STEINLAGE, Gerald F. Wines, brewing, distillation. Carthagena, OH: By the Author, 1972. 91p. G38030

STEPHAN, John, M.D. A treatise on the manufacture, imitation, adulteration, and reduction of foreign wines, brandies, gins, rums . . . Philadelphia: By the Author, 1860. 280p. G38040

STERN, Gladys Bronwyn. Bouquet. New York: Knopf, 1927. 263p. Illus. G38060

An account of two couples who made a wine tour of France. A second edition was issued in 1933.

STEVENSON, J., M.D. Advice medical, and economical, relative to the purchase and consumption of tea, coffee and chocolate; wines, and malt liquors: including tests to detect adulteration; also remarks on water, with directions to purify it for domestic use. London: Printed for F.C. Westley, 1830. 204p. G38070

STEVENSON, Robert Louis. Napa Wine. San Francisco: Westwinds Books, 1974. 38p. G38080

In 1880 Robert Louis Stevenson honeymooned in Silverado, an abandoned silver mining camp in the northern part of California's Napa Valley.

The first Napa vineyard had been planted in 1838 by Charles Yount. By 1880 the valley was well planted in vines, and during his stay, Stevenson visited the cellars of Colin McEachran, Jacob Schram (Schramsberg) and the Beringer brothers.

In 1883 Stevenson published an account of his stay in Silverado, "The Silverado Squatters," which appeared in serial form in *The Century Magazine*. Mr. Brian McGinty in his introduction to this volume notes that "Napa Wine" was first printed in the expanded book edition printed in London by Chatto and Windus and by Roberts Brothers in Boston, having been omitted along with three other chapters from the Century serialization.

At that time very little California wine was, knowingly, drunk by Americans. Much of the wine was sent to England and much, according to what a San Francisco wine merchant told Stevenson, was bottled under the names of nonexistent French chateaux.

It is a very brief memoir, approximately ten pages, but it is a significant literary account of the beginning Napa Valley wine industry. Drawing on his travels on the Continent, Stevenson contrasts the beginning California vineyards with the ancient vineyards of Europe, then dead or dying from phylloxera. He deplores the fact that the Californians did not, for economic reasons, age their wines but writes, "the smack of California earth shall linger in the palate of your grandson."

He was prescient enough to forsee their great promise. Despite their own subseqent devastation by phylloxera and the insanity of Prohibition, many California wines are now among the finest on earth.

This edition was limited to 950 copies with historical notes and an introduction by Brian McGinty. The notes by McGinty are invaluable in explaining the many ancient and classical references of Mr. Stevenson. Bound in cloth and boards with decorative papers by Brian Day. Printed by Cranium Press, San Francisco. The same account was published in 1965 by James Beard with an introduction by M.F.K. Fisher and in 1924 by John Henry Nash.

_____. The Silverado Squatters. London: Chatto and Windus and Boston: Roberts Brothers, 1883. 287p. G38090

Several subsequent American editions were published. Chapter three discusses Napa Valley wines.

STIEFF, Frederick Philip. Eat, drink and be merrie in Maryland. New York: Putnam's, 1932. 326p. Illus. G38100

Though primarily a book of recipes, it contains the official accounts of three "entertainments" of General George Washington at the Maryland State House in the 1780's. Great amounts of wine were drunk, especially madeira, but very little "spirits." Mr. Stieff was a journalist with the Baltimore *News Post* and the founder of the Wine and Food Society of Baltimore, Maryland.

STOCKHAM, G.H. Temperance and Prohibition. Oakland: 1888. 131p. G38110

Stresses the importance of the use of wine rather than prohibition.

STOCKLEY, Tom. Winery tours in Oregon, Washington, Idaho and British Columbia. Mercer Island, WA: The Writing Works, 1978. 125p. Illus. G38120

_____. Winery trails of the Pacific Northwest. Mercer Island, WA: The Writing Works, 1977. 64p. Illus. G38130

STOCKTON, John. Victorian bottles, a collectors guide to yesterday's empties. London: David and Charles, 1981. Illus. G38140

STOKES, Alan. Vineyards of north east Victoria. Chiltern, Victoria: Federal Standard, 1970. 25p. G38150

Cover title: "A brief history of the vineyards in the north east of Victoria."

STOLL, Horatio Francis. California's important grape industry. San Francisco: California Grape Grower, 1941. 31p. Illus. G38160

_____. California's viticultural industry must be protected. San Francisco: California Grape Protective Association, 1914. 16p. G38170

_____. The grape districts of California. San Francisco: By the Author, 1931. 47p. Illus. G38180

_____. Wine-wise; a popular handbook on how to correctly judge, keep, serve and enjoy wines. San Francisco: H.S. Crocker Press, 1933. 120p. Illus. G38190

STONE, Frank. Catalog of wine education materials. A listing of wine education aids and resources available to assist the wine industry, the wine merchant and the wine educator. Salt Lake City: The Society of Wine Educators, 1984. G38200

Updated annually.

STONE, Samuel. Liquor buyer's guide. New York: Information, 1970. 170p. G38210

The STONYFELL Vineyards, 1858-1958; being the history of Stonyfell vineyards and a record of the one hundred years of winemaking. Adelaide: Griffin Press, 1958. 25p. G38220

STORM, John. An invitation to wines; an informal guide to the selection, care, and enjoyment of domestic and European wines. New York: Simon and Schuster, 1955. 201p. Illus. G38230

The STORY of champagne. Written by a member of *The Times* advertising staff, after a visit to Messrs. Moet and Chandon's vineyards and establishments at Épernay. London: Wertheimer, Lea, 1905. 32p. G38240

The STORY of Wente wines. Livermore, CA: Wente Bros., 1952. 16p. Illus. G38250

STREET, Julian Leonard. Civilized drinking. *Redbook Magazine*, c1933. 33p. G38260

_____. Paris a la carte. New York: John Lane, 1912. 79p. G38270

_____. Table topics. Edited, and with additions by A.I.M.S. Street. New York: Knopf, 1959. 289p. Illus. G38280

_____. Where Paris dines, with information about restaurants of all kinds, costly and cheap, dignified and gay, known and little known: and how to enjoy them; together with a discussion of French wines and a table of vintages by a distinguished amateur. Garden City, NY: Doubleday, Doran, 1924. 322p. Illus. G38290

Numerous subsequent editions.

_____. Wines, their selection, care and service. New York: Knopf, 1933. 194p. G38300

Numerous subsequent editions.

STREETER, David, comp. Novel California vineyards. Del Sol Press, 1981. Unpaged. G38310

> This is a bibliography of twenty-eight novels framed within a California wine industry setting. Limited to fifty copies.

STRINGER, Carlton. Wines; what to serve, when to serve, how to serve. Scarborough, New York: Canape Parade, 1933. 63p. Illus. G38320

STROM, S. Alice Edith. And so to dine. A brief account of the food and drink of Mr. Pepys, based on his diary. London: Frederick Books, George Allen and Unwin, 1955. 99p. Illus. G38330

> (See also Mendelsohn, Oscar.)

STRONG, W.C. Culture of the grape. Boston: Tilton, 1866. 355p. Illus. G38340

> By the end of the Civil War, cultivation of the grape had become a subject of extraordinary interest and a rapidly growing body of literature in the United States. This well-researched contribution to that body of literature by a Massachusetts vintner, covers all aspects of the cultivation of the grape and the development of grape growing and wine making in the United States and Europe. The author discusses the prices of famous Bordeaux wines and even analyzes the soil of Chateau Margaux.

STUART, Moses. Scriptural view of the wine question in a letter to the Rev. Dr. Nott. New York: Levitt, Trow Publishers, 1848. 64p. G38350

SULLIVAN, Charles. Like modern Edens; winegrowing in Santa Clara Valley and Santa Cruz Mountains - 1798-1981. Cupertino, CA: California History Center, 1982. 198p. Illus. G38360

SUTCLIFFE, Serena. The wine drinker's handbook. New York: Simon and Schuster and London: David and Charles, 1982. 224p. Illus. G38370

SUTCLIFFE, Serena, ed. André Simon's wines of the world. 2nd ed. New York: McGraw-Hill, 1981. 639p. Illus. G38380

> Many changes have taken place since Mr. Simon compiled *Wines of the World* in 1950 and 1951. To update this important work, fourteen wine specialist writers have contributed chapters on France, Germany, Italy, Spain and Portugal, sherry, port, Madeira, North America, including a greatly expanded section on California, South America, Australia, New Zealand, England and South Africa. The material is well-written and researched, especially the chapter on the wines of Germany. Nicely illustrated with fifty-six color plates and twenty-nine maps. A valuable reference.

_____. Great vineyards and winemakers. London: Macdonald, 1982. 256p. Illus. G38390

> The editor singles out sixty-seven vineyards as "great." Wine buffs will take exception to some of the inclusions. There is also a detailed introduction to each wine country, with a history and map. The book is superbly illustrated with color photographs and contains vintage charts for Australia, California, France, Germany and Italy, together with a glossary of terms.

SUTHERLAND, Douglas. Raise your glasses. A light-hearted history of drinking. London: Macdonald, 1969. 200p. Illus. G38400

SUTHERLAND, G. Directions for planting the vine, being part 1 of his South Australian vinegrower's manual. Adelaide: Gov't. Print. Off., 1892. 70p. G38410

_____. The South Australian vinegrower's manual; a practical guide to the art of viticulture in South Australia. Adelaide: Gov't. Print. Off., 1892. 176p. G38420

SUTTON, A. Musings past and present. Sydney: Wine and Food Society of N.S.W., 1957. 13p. G38430

SUTTOR, George. The culture of the grape-vine, and the orange, in Australia and New Zealand: comprising historical notices; instructions for planting and cultivation; accounts from personal observations, of the vineyards of France and the Rhine; and extracts concerning all the most celebrated wines, from the work of M. Jullien. London: Smith, Elder, 1843. 184p. G38440

SUYDAM, James. A treatise on the culture and management of grape vines. Brooklyn, NY: J.A. Gray, Printer, 1856. 71p. G38450

SYMINGTON, J.D. Port wine . . . Oporto: 1954. 20p. G38460

SYMONDS, James Addington. Wine, women and song: medieval Latin students' songs. London: Chatto and Windus, 1884. 183p. G38470

Verses of love and wine mainly from the *Carmina Burana*. Scarce. Third edition of 208p. published in 1907.

SYMONS, William. The practical gager: or, the young gager's assistant. To which are added all the necessary tables for gaging and fixing the utensils of victuallers, common brewers, and distillers. London: Printed for J. Nourse, 1770. 323p. Illus. G38480

Subsequent editions published in 1799, 1803, 1815 and 1819 by Wingrave and Collingwood and in 1821, 1826 and 1838 by Collingwood and Whittaker.

T., A.R. A guide to good wine. 2nd ed. London and Edinburgh: Chambers, 1959. 208p. G38490

TAIT, Geoffrey Murat. The art of appreciating wine. London: Harper, 1931. G38500

_____. Port: from the vine to the glass. London: Harper, 1936. 174p. Illus. G38510

_____. Practical handbook on port wine. London: Harper, 1925. 60p. Illus. G38520

TANNERS wholesale price list. Shrewsbury, England: Tanners Wines Ltd., 1982. 80p. Illus. G38530

Although this is a price list, each country and district is fully annotated with vintage notes, vignettes and maps. Nicely illustrated. Issued annually.

The TAPSTERS downfall and the drunkards joy. Or, a dialogue between *Leather-beard* the Tapster of the Sheaves, and *Ruby-nose*, one of his ancient acquaintance, who hath formerly eaten three stone of rost beefe on a Sunday morning; but now (being debarred of that priviledge) sleights him; and resolves to drinke wine altogether. [London]: MDCXLI [1641]. 6p. Illus. G38540

> A dialogue on the commercial struggle between ale and fortified wine. Leather-beard is a tapster going to ruin, despite his history of providing roast beef and mince pies, plum-cake and cheesecake along with his ale and beer, because of the new licensing laws of "the correcting parliament," which forebade sale of ale on Sundays. "Ruby-nose" has benefited from the breaking of the patent of "the great Grape-sucker that hath the Patent for medium wine . . . at Westminster," and has given up beer for sherry: "I shall not need now to breake two shilling for a quart of sack; Ile drinke no more beere now . . . I sweare by the Baccanalian Fountaine, Ile no more Beere or Ale, it is drinke for the mechanicks; poore and will make a man lowsie, I am resolved never to drinke any thing but Canarie." Leather-beard remonstrates with him, but he holds firm. It closes with Leather-beard's resolution to hire "some five or six of the chiefest Balad-Rimers . . . to make pamphlets and learned Ballads of that great Alderman's (See Abell, Alderman) projects and the end thereof, and how many poore Vintners he broake." Rare.

TARR, Yvonne Young. Super-easy step-by-step winemaking. New York: Vintage Books, 1975. 108p. Illus. G38550

TARTT, Gene, ed. The vineyards almanac and wine gazetteer, 1980. Los Altos, CA: The Vineyard Almanac & Wine Gazeteer, 1979. 96p. Illus. G38560

> Published annually.

TAYLEUR, W.H.T. Home brewing and wine making. Middlesex: Penguin Books, 1973. 336p. Illus. G38580

TAYLOR, Allan. What everybody wants to know about wine. New York: Knopf, 1934. 312p. Illus. G38590

TAYLOR, Ellen M. Madeira: its scenery, and how to see it. London: 1882. 261p. G38600

> Second edition, revised, of 265p. was published in 1889. Includes a discussion of its vines and wines.

TAYLOR, Gennery. Easy to make wine. 2nd ed. New York: Gramercy Publishing, 124p. Illus. G38610

_____. Easymade wine and country drinks. 3rd ed. London: Rightway Books, 1965. 124p. Illus. G38620

TAYLOR, Greyton H. Treasury of wine and wine cookery. New York: Harper and Row, 1963. 278p. Illus. G38630

TAYLOR, Howard. The handbook of wines and liquors. Milwaukee: J.O. Dahl, 1933. 56p. G38640

TAYLOR, James. Tables for the calculation of wine, beer, cider and common bottle glass . . . with the excise duties and drawbacks . . . London: By the Author, 1820. 48p. G38650

TAYLOR, John. Drinke and welcome; or the famous history of the most part of drinks, in use now in the kingdomes of Great Britaine and Ireland, etc. London: Printed by Anne Griffin, 1637. 26p. G38660

TAYLOR, Sally. California wine maps and directory. San Francisco: Sally Taylor and Friends, 1983. 30p. Illus. G38670

>A listing of nearly 500 winery addresses and telephone numbers together with maps and recommendations on places to stay and eat in the ten major wine-growing regions of California.

TAYLOR, Sidney B. Wine, wisdom and whimsy. Portland, OR: Winepress Publishing, 1969. 160p. Illus. G38680

>A compilation of the first eight editions of *The Purple Thumb*, the first magazine in America devoted to wine arts and to home beer and winemaking.

TAYLOR, Walter Stephen. Living wine grapes of the Finger Lakes, an ampelography. Hammondsport, NY: Greyton H. Taylor Wine Museum, 1972. G38690

_____. Wine grape varieties. Hammondsport, NY: Finger Lakes Wine Museum, c1969. Illus. G38695

TAYLOR, Walter Stephen and VINE, Richard P. Home winemaker's handbook. New York: Harper and Row, 1968. 195p. Illus. G38700

TEISER, Ruth and HARROUN, Catherine. Wine making in California. New York: McGraw-Hill, 1982. 239p. Illus. G38710

>The story of wine making in California from the mission fathers through the setbacks of Prohibition and vine diseases to its current international recognition as one of the world's great winegrowing areas. 285 black and white photographs.

TENNENT, Sir James Emerson. Wine, its use and taxation. London: James Madison, 1855. 178p. G38720

TERRINGTON, William. Cooling cups and dainty drinks. A collection of recipes for "cups" and other compounded drinks, and of general information on beverages of all kinds, including wine. London and New York: G. Routledge and Sons, 1869. 223p. G38730

>Wine is discussed in the first half of this book which provides a collection of recipes for the making of beverages of all kinds and combinations.

The VINTNERS' Company. Record of the visit of master and wardens of the ancient mystery of vintners of the city of London to Portugal, March, 1928. [London: The Company, 1928]. 44p. G38740

THERON, Christian J. and NIEHAUS, Charles G. Wine making. 3rd ed. Stellenbosch: Gov't. Print., c1948. 94p. G38750

Practical instructions on the making of wines, their care, diseases, distillation, and analyses.

THIEBAUT DE BERNEAUD, Arsenne. The vine-dresser's theoretical and practical manual, or the art of cultivating the vine: and making wine, brandy and vinegar. New York: P. Canfield, 1829. 158p. Illus. G38760

Translated from the second French edition.

THOLLANDER, Earl. Back roads of California. Menlo Park, CA: Lane Magazine and Book Company, 1971. G38780

THOMAS, Frank A. (pseud). See under Schoonmaker, Frank. G38790

THOMAS, Lately. Delmonico's; a century of splendor. New York: Houghton Mifflin, 1967. G38800

Founded in 1827, by two Swiss brothers in New York City, Delmonico's set the highest standards in wine, food and service until the restaurant's demise in the 1920's by dint of the Volstead Act. Every great American restaurant that followed (e.g. the Astor House) was directly influenced by Delmonico's.

A principle feature of the book is a facsimile reprint of an everyday Delmonico's menu from 1838. It was discovered after years of search. The carte of eleven pages includes prices in shilling and pence. Since New Yorkers knew little French, an English translation is provided. The wine list is stunning for its time. Listed are twenty red bordeaux, including all of what would be classified as first growths in 1855; four white bordeaux, and forty other rhones, burgundies, rhines, champagnes, maderias and sherries. There are only six red burgundies shown but they are first-rate, including Clos Vougeot, Chambertin and Richebourg.

Many great banquets were held at Dominico's including those for Charles Dickens in 1842 and 1868. The incredibly elaborate menus for those occasions are reprinted.

Wine was indispensible with the food served at Dominico's. When Prohibition came, the restaurant could not survive due to the loss of income from wine sales and from loss of patronage caused by the lack of wine. The name survives as a synonym for the very finest in eating and drinking.

THOMAS, Raymond D. Shakespeare's alcoholics and some observations concerning "the subtle blood o' the grape".

White Plains, NY: Alcohol Facts, Inc., c1949. 16p. G38810

Although essentially a temperance pamphlet, it discusses in depth the references to wine in Shakespeare's plays.

THOMAS-STANFORD, Charles. Leaves from a Madeira garden. London and New York: John Lane, 1909. 290p. Illus. G38820

Contains a small but interesting section on the reasons for the downfall of Madeira wines.

THOMPSON, Bob. The pocket encyclopedia of California wines. New York: Simon and Schuster, 1980. 128p. Illus. G38830

>Subsequent editions.

THOMPSON, Bob, ed. California wine. Menlo Park, CA: Lane Magazine and Book, 1973. 224p. Illus. G38840

>Hundreds of photographs, many historic.

_____. California wine country. Menlo Park, CA: Lane Books, 1971. 95p. Illus. G38850

_____. The guide to California's wine country. Menlo, CA: Sunset Books, Lane Publishing, 128p. Illus. G38860

>In addition to the more traditional wine areas, the text provides an interesting chapter about Los Angeles, where wine was first made in California. There is an appendix with instructions on how to read a wine label, a glossary of California wines and wine grapes, a list of red and white varietals and who makes them, the California twenty-point wine-tasting scoring system, and a discussion of the various procedures wine tasters use in attempting to identify wines blind. The book is nicely illustrated with black and white and color photographs by Ted Streshinsky. Slip cover.

THOMPSON, Bob and JOHNSON, Hugh. The California wine book. New York: Morrow, 1976. 320p. Illus. G38910

THOMPSON, Gladys Scott. Life in a noble household, 1641-1700. New York: Knopf, 1937. 407p. Illus. G38870

>An account based upon the household papers of William Russell, fifth Earl and first Duke of Bedford. Chapter X gives details of the Duke's considerable wine cellar and is of interest for not only the types of wines but how they were shipped and stored and for other historical information.

>The earliest purchase was of a cask of claret in 1653, which came with twelve dozen stone bottles packed in a flasket or bottle case, and for which a gross of corks was ordered. The use of corks to stopper wine bottles in place of oiled hemp had been in use from about the turn of the 17th century, and by the middle of the century had become fairly common. However, these early corks were conical in shape and fit loosely in the bottles. The process of maturing wine in the bottle had not yet been developed.

>The largest purchase in 1658 was for sixty-five gallons of canary wine (a sweet wine from the Canary Isles that lays claim to Shakespearean recognition) and, for the first time, glass bottles were ordered. Six years later the steward ordered sixty-two bottles of "Shably". According to André Simon, this is the first record of chablis in an English wine account. Sillery, a still champagne, was purchased in casks for the first time in 1664 and, thereafter, appeared regularly in the household accounts.

>In 1684 port made its first appearance and seven years later white port was ordered. Other purchases included brandy, burgundy and red wines from Navarre and Provence in southern France. Al-

though yearly wine costs increased as a result of ever-increasing custom duties, the Earl's continuing purchases were proof that wine had a high priority in the life of this noble family.

THOMPSON, Vance. Drink and be sober. New York: Moffat, Yard, 1915. 231p. G38880

THOMPSON, William. A practical treatise on the cultivation of the grape vine. Edinburgh and London: William Blackwood, 1862. G38890

> The first edition was published in 1862. It was immediately popular and by the time of publication of the eighth edition in March of 1875, 10,000 copies had been sold. In 1879 when the ninth edition was published, the full effects of *Phylloxera vastatrix* were being felt in the world's vineyards. The author's suggested solution was that all the affected vines, and a margin of healthy ones around the affected vines, be destroyed and the land replanted with wheat and other crops "til the roots of the vines will have died and the insects with them, when the land could be replanted with vines. . . . Nothing short of this will meet the case." Fortunately, for the wine lover, a less drastic solution was found in American rootstock.

_____. A practical treatise on the cultivation of the grape vine. 3rd ed. Edinburgh and London: William Blackwood, 74p. Illus. G38900

THOMSON, Thomas. Brewing and distillation. With practical instructions for brewing porter and ales according to the English and Scottish methods, by William Stewart. Edinburgh: A. and C. Black, 1849. 324p. G38920

THORNE, E. The heresy of teetotalism in the light of scripture, science and legislation. London: Simpkin, 1903. 331p. G38930

THORPE, William Arnold. English and Irish glass. London: Medici Society, 1927. 35p. Illus. G38940

> Some wine connoisseurs consider the wine glass — its shape, color and quality — almost as important as the wine. The value of the book is threefold. It instructs the would-be collector on how to start collecting rare glasses; it provides a learned historical sketch of this craft, and contains beautifully reproduced illustrations in color and monochrome. Thorpe was in the Department of Ceramics of the Victoria and Albert Museum and this work was obviously a labor of love.

_____. A history of English and Irish glass [with a volume of plates]. 2 vols. London: Medici Society, 1929. Illus. G38950

THORPY, Frank. New Zealand wine guide. Auckland: Hamlyn, 1976. G38960

_____. Wine in New Zealand. Auckland: Collins Bros., 1971. 199p. Illus. G38970

> Revised and enlarged edition, 1983, Penguin Books.

THUDICHUM, John Louis William. The aesthetical use of wine and its use upon health . . . London: International Health Exhibition, 1884. 23p. G38980

Covers Doctor Thudichum's lectures on this subject at the International Health Exhibition in 1884 and his message was clear: "Ay! Good wine is a cure for melancholy! and if there were more good wine in the world there would be less melancholy in it. All factors which provide happiness, promote health. And as wine promotes happiness it promotes health. But it does so on the condition that it be aesthetically used, i.e., in accordance with the dictates of feeling, reason, and sciences."

_____. Alcoholic drinks. London: W. Clowes, 1884. 70p. G38990

_____. On wines, their production, treatment and use. Six lectures. London: Royal Society for Encouragement of Arts, Manufactures and Commerce, printed by W. Trounce, 1873. 43p. Illus. G39000

_____. Report of the chemical analysis of the wines of the Pure Wine Association Limited. London: 1871. 16p. G39010

THUDICHUM, John Louis William and DUPRE, A. A treatise on wines: their origin, nature, and varieties, with practical directions for viticulture and vinification. Abridged ed. London and New York: George Bell, 1894. 387p. Illus. G39020

André Simon in commenting on this edition noted: "Most of the scientific data contained in the 1872 edition have been omitted, but the majority of the errors have been retained. It lacks the thoroughness of the earlier work. . . ." Also a New York printing.

_____. A treatise on the origin, nature, and varieties of wine: being a complete manual of viticulture and oenology. London and New York: Macmillan, 1872. 760p. G39030

In discussing the origin and physiology of vines, the authors refer to geological evidence that proves that in lignite, taken from a mine at Salzhausen, in Hesse-Darmstadt, north of the Main River, there were fossil impressions of leaves of the vine and grape seeds. It has been estimated that the geological formation of those impressions is at least a hundred thousand years old.

TIGNEY, Frederick. Wine roads of France. London: Charles Letts, 1977. 85p. Illus. G39040

TIGNEY, Nancy. Wine roads of Italy. London: Charles Letts, 1977. 96p. Illus. G39050

TIMBRELL, Tilly. The winemaker's dining book: week by week menus for winemakers. Andover, England: Amateur Winemaker, 1972. 238p. Illus. G39060

TIMOTHY, Brother. The Christian Brothers as winemakers. 1974. 142p. G39065

See California Wine Oral History Series.

TITTERTON, W.R. Drinking songs and other songs. London: Cecil Palmer, 1928. 64p. Illus. G39070

Edition limited to 100 copies.

A TOAST to your health; a brochure of unusual features. Sydney: Produced by O.L. Ziegler, n.d. G39080

TOD, H.M. Vine-growing in England. London: Chatto and Windus, 1911. 113p. G39090

TODD, F. Dundas. Little red guide to home brewed wines. Victoria, BC: Victoria Printing and Publishing, 1922. 32p. G39100

TODD, William John. A handbook of wine; how to buy, serve, store, and drink it. London: Jonathan Cape, 1922. 103p. Illus. G39110

_____. Port: how to buy, serve, store and drink it. London: Jonathan Cape, 1926. 95p. Illus. G39120

TOLLEYS of Hope Valley and their South Australian wines. Hope Valley, S.A.: Douglas A. Tolley Pty., 1973. Unpaged. G39130

TOMES, Robert. The champagne country. London: Routledge and New York: Hurd and Houghton, 1867. 231p. G39140

> An account of the Champagne country by an American who lived in Reims for eighteen months during the mid-19th century. Although the vineyards, champagne houses and personalities are discussed, the author makes some incisive observations about the crudeness, insensibility and impoliteness exhibited by Reims' upper-class citizenry. He also provides an account of how champagne was made and the incredible breakage of bottles (one champagne house in 1746 had only 120 bottles survive out of 6,000). An interesting personal account.

TONTA, Geoff. The butler's guide to the making of wines, beers, and liquors in a gentleman's cellar. Auckland, New Zealand: Wineglass Pub., 1977. 96p. G39150

TOPOLOS, Michael and DOPSON, Betty. California wineries: Napa Valley, Vol. 1. St. Helena, CA: Vintage Image, 1975. 193p. Illus. G39160

> The book has two sections. The first explores the history of the Napa Valley, and the second is a study of its wineries. The first section is illustrated with old photographs obtained from museums and private collections, many of which were previously unpublished. The second section is illustrated with fifty-four full-page line plates by the artist Sebastian Titus. The foreword is by Andre Tchelistcheff. The first publication was a limited edition of 2,000 copies. (For Vol 2, see Latimer, Patricia.)

_____. Napa Valley wine tour. St. Helena, CA: Vintage Image, 1978. 189p. Illus. G39170

TORBERT, Harold C. The complete wine and food cookbook. New York: Galahad Books, 1970. 386p. Illus. G39180

TORBERT, Harold and TORBERT, Frances. The book of wine. Los Angeles: Nash Publishing, 1972. 401p. G39190

TORRES, Miguel A. The vine and wines of Spain. Barcelona: 1982. 197p. Illus. G39200

Torres, Miguel A. and READ, Jan. The wines and vineyards of Spain. San Francisco: The Wine Appreciation Guild, 1984. 200p. Illus. G39205

TOVEY, Charles. Alcohol versus teetotalism. London: Longman, Green, Longman, Roberts and Green, 1863. G39210

> Although Tovey takes the side of alcohol, this is not a brief for over-indulgence. The concluding chapter sparkles with such names as Pliny, Horace, Homer, Plutarch, Chaucer, Ben Jonson, Burke, Franklin and Pitt as well as other ancient and modern sages who favored a "cheerful" glass.

_____. British and foreign spirits: their history, manufacture, properties, etc. London: Whittaker, 1864. 376p. G39220

> As a young boy Tovey operated a still, and his first employment was connected with working the stills of a large rectifying distillery. Thus he acquired a lifelong acquaintance with various kinds of spirits. The book is divided into chapters under the following headings: distillation, gin, hollands, geneva, whisky, brandy, rum, punch, liqueurs and cordials.

_____. Champagne: its history, manufacture, properties . . . with some remarks upon wine and wine merchants. London: Hotten, 1870. 140p. Illus. G39230

> More of a personal account of the author's visit to Champagne than a detailed history. It is written in an unpretentious style, and is enlivened with anecdotes and opinions.

_____. A potpourri of wine words, e.g. ancient wines and poetry, Bacchanalian lyrics, past and present drinking habits, wine anecdotes, the origin of wine terms . . . G39240

> Unable to verify.

_____. Wine and wine countries: a record and manual for wine merchants and wine consumers. London: Hamilton, Adams, 1862. 365p. G39250

> The author quotes extensively from Barry, Henderson, Busby, Redding, Mulder and others and he combines these wine sources with his own knowledge of the subject. The blend makes for interesting reading, with discussions ranging from early English vineyards to the wines and vineyards of the world. Tovey also strikes out against the adulterators of wines. His love of claret is best expressed through his recommendation (morning joggers are you listening?) that "those who take exercise before breakfast . . . would find one-third or half a bottle of light Medoc diluted with water far more invigorating than warm tea or coffee."

_____. Wine and wine countries: a record and manual for wine merchants and wine consumers. 2nd ed. London: Whittaker, 1877. 519p. Illus. G39260

_____. Wine revelations. London: Whittaker, 1880. 82p. G39270

> Second edition, 1883.

_____. Wit, wisdom and morals distilled from Bacchus. London: Whittaker, 1878. 295p. G39280

TOYE Nina and ADAIR, A.H. Drinks long and short. London: Heinemann, 1925. 67p. G39290

TRACY, S.M. Grape growing in the South. Washington: United States Agriculture Department Farmers' Bulletin 118, 1900. 32p. G39300

A TREATISE on the cultivation of the grape in vineyards. By a member of the Cincinnati Horticultural Society. Cincinnati: Wright, Ferris, 1850. 48p. Illus. G39310

TREBER, Grace Jane. Directory, department store-wine shops and wine stores in major U.S. cities. New York: International Wine Society, 1976. 135p. G39330

_____. World wine almanac and wine atlas - complete wine buying guide and catalogue of wine labels. New York and Paris: International Wine Society, 1976. 289p. Illus. G39340

TREGONNING, Barbara. Fruits of the vine. Melbourne: Australian Dried Fruits Association, c1955. Illus. G39350

TREMLETT, Rex. Homemade wine. London: Transworld, 1967. 125p. Illus. G39360

TRESISE, Charles E. Tavern treasures. Dorset, England: Blandford Press, 1983. 176p. Illus. G39380

> Although essentially a book about pub collectibles, it contains information on corkscrews, decanters, wine labels, wine case ends and other wine accessories.

TREUE, Wilhelm. The Deinhard story. London and Coblenz: 1969. G39390

> Unable to verify.

TRITTON, Suzanne Mabel. Amateur wine making; an introduction and complete guide to wine, cider, perry, mead and beer making, and to the cultivation of the vine. London: Faber and Faber, 1957. 239p. Illus. G39410

> Several subsequent editions.

_____. Grape growing and wine-making from grapes and other fruits. Almondsbury: Grey Owl Research Laboratories, 1951. 32p. Illus. G39420

_____. Grape growing and wine making including the vintner's calendar. Almondsbury: Grey Owl Research Laboratories, 1949. 32p. Illus. G39430

_____. Successful wine and beer making. Rev. ed. Almondsbury: Grey Owl Laboratories, 1960. 65p. G39440

_____. Trittons' guide to better wine and beer making for beginners. London: Faber and Faber, 1965. 157p. Illus. G39450

> Second edition in 1969.

_____. Wine making from pulps, fruits, juices and concentrates. Rev. ed. Almondsbury: Grey Owl Laboratories, 1963. 22p. G39460

TRUMAN, Benjamin Cummings. See how it sparkles. Los Angeles: G. Rice and Sons, 1896. 63p. G39470

   Reprinted in 1973, 67p. with a foreword by Roy Brady.

TRYON, J.H. A Practical treatise on grape culture, with instructions how to prune and train the vine on the horizontal-arm system. Willoughby, OH: 1885. 22p. Illus. G39480

   Also an 1887 edition.

TRYON, Thomas. A new art of brewing beer, ale and other sorts of liquors, so as to render them more healthful to the body, and agreeable to nature. Together with easie experiments for making excellent drinks with apples, currants, goosberries, cherries, herbs, seeds, and hay . . . London: Printed for Tho. Salusbury, 1690. 142p. G39490

   Second and third editions published in 1691.

_____. The way to get wealth; or an easie way to make wine of gooseberries . . . equal to that of France . . . the true art of distilling of Brandy . . . II. A help to discourse, giving an account of trade of all countries . . . III. A book of knowledge for all persons . . . London: Printed for G. Conyers, c1702. 96p. G39500

   A second enlarged edition was published in 1706; a third edition of 120p., n.d.

TUDOR, Dean. Wine, beer and spirits. Littleton, CO: Libraries Unlimited, 1975. 196p. G39510

TUDOR, Emma. October dawn. A short and practical treatise on the manufacture of home made wines from the native grapes of New England. Cambridge: Riverside Press, 1926. 63p. G39520

TUOR, Conrad. Wine and food handbook. London: Hodder and Stoughton, 1977. 255p. G39530

TURNBULL, Grace H. Fruit of the vine as seen by many witnesses of all times. 3rd ed. Baltimore: By the Author, 1952. 178p. Illus. G39540

   Cover title: A symposium of social drinking.

TURNER, Ann and TURNER, Paul. Home wine making step-by-step. London: Foulsham, 1982. G39550

TURNER, Anthony and BROWN, Christopher. Burgundy. Its wines, food, architecture and history. London: Batsford, 1977. 208p. Illus. G39560

TURNER, Bernard Charles Arthur. Behind the wine list. London: Mills and Boon, 1968. 124p. Illus. G39570

_____. Better winemaking and brewing for beginners. London: Pelham Books, 1971. 127p. Illus. G39580

   Second edition of 133p. in 1972; and a third edition of 158p. published in 1973.

—————. The Boots book of home wine making. London: Published for Boots the Chemists by Wolfe Publishing, 1971. 160p. Illus. G39590

—————. The compleat home winemaker and brewer. London: Mitchell Beazley, 1976. 160p. Illus. G39600

> Covers the history and theory of wine-making. Includes a calendar giving a month by month guide to the types of fruit and vegetables available for wine making.

—————. Easy guide to home-made wine. London: Mills and Boon, 1968. 89p. Illus. G39610

—————. Enjoy your own wine. A beginners guide to enjoying wine at home. London: Mills and Boon, 1959. 93p. G39620

—————. Fruit wine. London: Mills and Boon, 1973. 95p. G39630

—————. Growing your own wine. London: Pelham Books, 1977. 96p. Illus. G39640

—————. Home made wines and beers. London: Park Lane Press, 1979. 80p. Illus. G39650

—————. Improve your winemaking. London: Pelham Books, 1964. 143p. G39660

> Second edition of 143p. by Taplinger Publishing of New York in 1967.

—————. The Pan book of wine making. London: Pan Books, 1975. 173p. Illus. G39670

—————. A practical guide to winemaking. London: Hutchinson, 1966. 144p. Illus. G39680

—————. Recipes for home-made wine, mead and beer. London: Mills and Boon, 1968. 105p. Illus. G39690

—————. The winemaker's encyclopedia. London and Boston: Faber and Faber, 1979. 208p. G39700

—————. The winemaker's companion: a handbook for those who make wine at home. London: Mills and Boon, 1975. 221p. Illus. G39710

—————. Winemaking and brewing. Rev. ed. London: Pelham Books, 1976. 133p. Illus. G39720

TURNER, Bernard Charles Arthur and ROYCROFT, Edwin Arthur. The AB-Z of winemaking. London: Pelham Books, c1966. 203p. Illus. G39740

TURNER, William. A new boke of the natures and properties of all wines that are commonly used here in England, with a confutation of an errour of some men, that holde, that Rhennish and other small white wines ought not to be drunken of them that either haue, or are in daunger of the stone . . . London: William Seres, 1568. 95p. G39750

> This was the first complete book in English on the subject of wine. William Turner was by education and training an ideal candidate to write this book. He was educated at Cambridge and later ac-

A new Boke

of the natures and pro-
perties of all Wines that
are commonlye vsed here in
England, with a confutation of an
errour of some men, that holde, that
Rhennish and other small white wines
ought not to be drunken of them that either
haue, or are in daunger of the stone,
the reuine, and diuers other
diseases, made by Wil=
liam Turner, Doc=
tor of Phi=
sicke.

Wherunto is annexed the booke of the natures
and vertues of Triacles, newly corrected and set foorth againe by
the sayde William
Turner.

Imprinted at London,
by William Seres.
Anno. 1 5 6 8.

quired a medical degree. He also became well-known as a botanist and scientist. As such, Turner should have been interested in how wine was made but does not discuss wine making methods or grape varietals.

The physician in Turner seems to have gotten the upper hand and his treatise on wine is mainly concerned with warning his contemporaries away from too great of an indulgence in the sweet and strong wines of the Mediterranean region, and a defense of the white Rhine wines and their medicinal benefits.

André Simon stated that "Among the 16th century books there is none that I value more than William Turner's *A new Boke of Wines.*" Simon describes the circumstances surrounding his acquisition of this book in December of 1919: "Hugh Cecil Lea, who owned the *Wine and Spirit Trade Review*, came to see us. We had but lately moved from Wimbledon to the flat in Westminster where we still live, with a great many more books than we had then. There was a loud double knock at the door, and a registered letter to be signed for. It was not a letter but a small book, and I was absolutely thrilled to find that it was a perfect copy, from the Huth Sale, of William Turner's *A new Boke of the natures and properties of all wines that are commonly used here in England*, 1568. This is the first book in English to deal exclusively with wine, and the fact that all the wines mentioned by Turner, and no others, figure in one or the other of Shakespeare's plays is strong evidence that it was used by Shakespeare as his reference book on wines. Be that as it may, Turner's little book is a most desirable possession for any collector, and I had long been hoping that one day I might get a copy. And now the day had come. But the bill had also come, and it could not have come at a more unfortunate time, for the move to London had been a great expense. Hugh Cecil Lea evidently caught sight of my worried face, and coming over to me took from my hand both the little book and the bill with it. He looked at them both, folded the bill, put it in his pocket, and gave me back the book: 'This is my Christmas present to you', he said quite definitely. 'Forget about that bit of paper in my pocket; it's mine.' A gift indeed!"

According to Simon there are only eight known copies in existence: ". . . three imperfect ones in the British Museum, one imperfect copy in the Library of Congress, U.S.A., one in the Bodleian, one at Wadham College, Oxford, one in the Library of Sir Gerald Templer, and our copy, a perfect copy, which is from the Huth Collection." Simon's copy, from the property of Mrs. J. D. Simon, was auctioned at Sotheby's on May 18, 1981 and sold for 3,500 pounds. The well-known British book dealer, Bernard Quarich, was the successful bidder on behalf of an undisclosed buyer. Considering the price of the pound in relation to the dollar, the fact that the buyer had to pay Sotheby's a 10% commission, and probably a 10% commission to Quarich, the cost was about $8,000.00. This is not a large sum when you consider that *A Book of Wines* is rarer than the Gutenberg Bible - there being fifty-two known copies of the Gutenberg Bible.

_____. A book of wines, by William Turner, together with a modern English version of the text by the editors and a general introduction by Sanford V. Larkey . . . and an oenological note by Philip M. Wagner. New York: Scholars' Facsimiles and Reprints, 1941. 79p. G39760

Fortunately, a facsimile reprint is available with a modern English text. However, this facsimile is scarce and a collector's item in its own right.

TWIGHT, Edmund Henry. The food value of wine. New York: American Wine Press, 1937. 8p. G39770

_____. New methods of grafting and budding vines. Berkeley: 1892. 13p. Illus. G39780

Reprinted in 1902.

_____. Resistant vines and their hybrids. Sacramento: 1903. 13p. Illus. G39790

TYSON, Bruce T. Australian varietal wines. Sydney: McWilliams, 11p. G39800

UNGER, E.R.H. What is wine? A chemical investigation into the properties of wine, its adulteration, and effects on the system. Manchester: A. Heywood, c1865. 15p. G39810

UNITED NATIONS. Industrial Development Organizations. Information sources on the beer and wine industry. New York: United Nations, 1977. 81p. G39820

UNITED STATES DEPARTMENT OF AGRICULTURE: Report of the Commissioner of Patents for the year 1857. G39830

Included in a number of Department of Agriculture yearly reports (issued with various titles) are numerous reports from various areas in the country which contain some succinct accounts by knowledgeable observers. In this year, Major John Le Conte of Philadelphia describes American grape vines of the Atlantic States, and G.C. Swallow describes grape culture in Missouri.

UNITED STATES DEPARTMENT OF AGRICULTURE: Report of the Commissioner of Patents for the year 1858. G39840

Includes articles on "Grape and Wine Culture in Calfornia" by A.W. M'Kee of San Francisco, "Grapes and Wine of Los Angeles" by Matthew Keller of Los Angeles, "Culture and Management of the Zante Current Grape" by S.B. Parsons of New York and "Cultivation of Grapes in New England" by R.H. Phelps.

UNITED STATES DEPARTMENT OF AGRICULTURE: Report of the Commissioner of Patents for the year 1860. G39850

Includes much material on grapes and wine making, including articles by S.J. Parker, M.D. of Ithaca, NY, a translation of Dr. Ludwig Gall, Daniel Goodloe's history of wine making, etc.

UNITED STATES DEPARTMENT OF AGRICULTURE: Report of the Commissioner of Patents for the year 1861. G39860

> Includes articles on Kelley's Island, Ohio; grapes of North America; grape culture and wine making; grape culture of native and foreign varieties; and mildew by William Saunders.

UNITED STATES FOREIGN AND DOMESTIC COMMERCE BUREAU. Foreign markets for wine and other grape products. Washington: Trade information bulletin no. 835, 1936. 50p. G39870

V. (pseud). The vine and wine making in Victoria, by "V" and "Beberrao". Melbourne: Wilson and Mackinnon, 1861. 64p. G39880

VACHELL, Horace Annesley. The best of England. London: Faber and Faber, 1930. 271p. G39890

> A book about things the author feels Englishmen most love: hunting; shooting; fishing; racing; polo; cricket; soccer; tennis; rugby; golf; and wine and food. Mr. Vachell, through his friendship with André Simon, acquired a considerable knowledge of wine, and the chapter entitled "Food and Wine" describes some of his more memorable wine experiences. Mr. Vachell was a well-known and successful novelist. Also published by Alfred A. Knopf.

VALAER, Peter J. Blackberry, other berry and fruit wines, their methods of production and analysis. Washington: Treasury Dept., 1950. 53p. G39900

_____. Wines of the world. New York: Abelard Press, 1950. 576p. G39910

VALCHUIS, Robert F. and HENAULT, Diane L. The wines of New England. Boston: Wine Institute of New England, 1980. 44p. Illus. G39920

VALENTE-PERFEITO, J.C. Let's talk about port. Porto: Instituto do Vinho do Porto, 1948. 100p. Illus. G39930

VAN BUREN, J. The Scuppernong grape: its history and mode of cultivation, with a short treatise on the manufacture of wine from it. 2nd ed., rev. and enl. Memphis: Goodwyn and Co., 1871. 60p. Illus. G39940

VAN RENSSELAER, Stephen. Early American flasks and bottles. Southampton, New York: Cracker Barrel Press, 1921. 109p. Illus. G39950

VAN VOORST, John. Drinking cups and their customs. 2nd ed. London: 1869. G39960

> Unable to verify.

VANCE, Louis James. The one best drink - wine and some facts about American wines. New York: American Wine Growers Association, 1937. 20p. G39970

VANDOR, Paul E. History of Fresno County, California, with biographical sketches. Los Angeles: Historic Record Co., 1919. Illus. G39980

> Two volumes. Contains discussions of grape growing and wine making.

VAROUNIS, Georges. An introduction to French wines and spirits. Los Angeles: Franco-American Wine Co., 1933. 68p. Illus. G40000

VENGE, Per. Easy lessons in imported wines. Los Angeles: 1959. 28p. Illus. G40010

> Second edition in 1961; third edition in 1964.

VERDAD, Don Pedro (pseud). From vineyard to decanter, a book about sherry. London: Edward Stanford, 1876. 121p. G40020

VERDIER, Paul. History of wine; how and when to drink it. San Francisco: City of Paris, 1933. 42p. Illus. G40030

> Contains information on Prohibition and the "big future" as seen by a wine retailer. Second edition in 1935.

VERONELLI, Luigi. The wines of Italy. Rome: Canesi Editore, 1950. 326p. Illus. G40040

> Contains fifty pages of tipped-in Italian wine labels.

VERSFELD, Marthinus. Wine and wisdom - four reflections. Cape Town: Tafelberg Publishers, 1978. 82p. Illus. G40050

> The publisher invited a philosopher, an educator, a clergyman and a physician to give their views on the uses and place of wine in a modern, civilized society. The four essays "Wine and Wisdom," "Good Wine Needs No Bush," "A Sermon of Sorts," and "Your Health is Wine" are supplemented by thirty-nine black and white photographs by Chris Jansen.

VESPRE, Francois S. Dissertation on growth of vines in England. London: 1786. 69p. G40060

VIALA, Pierre and RAVAZ, L. American vines: their adaptation, culture, grafting and propagation. Translated abridgement of the 2nd French ed. by W. Percy Wilkinson and J. Gassies. Melbourne: F.W. Niven, 1899. 88p. G40070

_____. American vines: their adaptation culture, grafting and propagation. San Francisco: Freygang-Leary, 1903. 299p. Illus. G40080

> An important work by two French viticulturists on how to defeat phylloxera in California.

_____. American vines: their adaptation, culture, grafting and propagation. Translation of the 2nd French ed. by Raymond Dubois and W. Percy Wilkinson. Melbourne: Robert S. Brain, 1901. 297p. Illus. G40090

VICTORIA AND ALBERT MUSEUM. Bottle-tickets. London: H.M.S.O., 1958. [31]p. Illus. G40100

> Bottle tickets is another expression for decanter labels. See Penzer, Norman Mosley.

VIDOUDEZ, Michael. The great wines of the world. New York: Crescent Books, 1982. 96p. Illus. G40110

This book is beautifully illustrated with more than 200 color photographs. It also contains text covering most of the wines of the world.

VILLA MAIOR, Julio Maximo de Oliveira Pimentel, Visconde de. The viniculture of claret; a treatise on the making, maturing, and keeping of claret wines. San Francisco: Payot, Upham, 1884. 148p. G40120

VILLANIS, P. Theoretical and practical notes upon wine-making, and the treatment of wines, especially applied to Australian wines. Adelaide: Webb, Vardon and Pritchard, 1884. 106p. G40130

_____. Wine making and the treatment of wines exclusively applied to Australian wines. Adelaide: Webb, Vardon and Pritchard, 1884. G40140

Unable to verify.

VILMORIN, Louis de. Cognac. Paris: Remy Martin, 1962. 38p. Illus. G40150

VINE, G. Homemade wines. How to make and how to keep them. London: Groomsbridge and Sons, n.d. 48p. G40170

VINE, Richard P. Commercial winemaking, processing and controls. Westport, CT: Avi Publishing, 1981. 493p. Illus. G40180

The VINEYARD: being a treatise showing I. The method of planting . . . cultivating and dressing of vines . . . II. proper directions for . . . making . . . and curing all defects in the wine, III. An easy . . . method of . . . raising . . . compound fruit . . . IV. New experiments grafting . . . V. The best manners of raising . . . compound fruit . . . Being the observations made by a gentlemen in his travels. London: Printed for W. Mears, 1727. 192p. Illus. G40200

A second edition published in 1732.

VINTAGEWISE. A preview of this year's great California wines complete with winemakers' cellar notes. St. Helena, CA: Vintage Image, 1980. 206p. Illus. G40210

The VINTNER's, brewer's, spirit merchant's and licensed victualler's guide: containing the history, theory and practice of manufacturing wines . . . Numerous important hints on cellaring . . . Selections from the excise laws . . . By a practical man . . . 2nd ed. London: Wetton, 1826. 372p. G40220

This was a popular guide. A third edition was published in 1828, a fourth edition in 1829, and an abridged edition in 1838.

The VINTNERS' company. Some account of the ward of Vintry and Vintners' Company. By W.H. Overal . . . The merriments of the Company. By J.G. Nichols . . . Biographical notes by some eminent members. By Thos. Melbourn . . . From the transactions of the London and Middlesex Archaeological Society. London: c1870. 89p. G40230

VIRGINIA Dare Vineyards. Incredible. Isn't it? Penn Yan, NY: Virginia Dare Vineyards, 1928. Unpaged. Illus. G40240

This is a very ingenious advertising brochure of Virginia Dare Vineyards, Bluff Point, Lake Keuka near Penn Yan, New York for an imaginative product, i.e., instant wine. The brochure begins with descriptive illustrations and text: "There are some things a fellow simply can't believe. The stuff that will grow hair on a billiard ball, for instance. Or something that will reduce your weight forty pounds in a week. Or a keg of grapes which you add some water, pronounce the magic word "Abracadabra" and get a finished champagne." The brochure goes on to note that "it is our problem to advertise - not hair growers or fat reducers - but grapes to which you add water and pronounce the magic word 'Abracadabra.' We cannot tell less than the truth." The brochure offers an absolute money-back guarantee to anyone who is dissatisfied with the champagne that results in six to eight weeks. The Virginia Dare Vineyards sold only concentrated grapes for the production of claret, burgundy, sparkling burgundy, rhine, sauternes and chablis. The brochure cautions the reader "not to confuse Virginia Dare with the 'kickless d-alcoholized' champagnes now on the market." This was a clever scheme to circumvent the Prohibition laws.

Three years later the Vino Brick Company in California refined this idea and marketed concentrated grapes in the form of "wine bricks" which sold like "hot cakes" all over the East Coast. The purchaser was advised to eat the bricks but under no circumstances should the bricks be placed in water because ". . . this will result in a delicious wine." When the government in August, 1931, seized several thousand of the wine bricks, it was reported that the well-known gangster, Al Capone, opened negotiations with the Vino Brick Company to become their exclusive sales agent in the Eastern states. The government's injunction was lifted and sales on Fifth Avenue in New York City and throughout the East Coast resumed.

The originator of the "wine brick" may have gotten inspiration for this marketing scheme from the Bible. The use and sale of condensed wine or "raisin cakes" was well known in Biblical (see 2 Samuel VI, 19 and Hosea III, 1) and ancient times (see Younger, William).

VISPRE, Francois Saverio. A dissertation on the growth of wine in England; to serve as an introduction to a treatise on the method of cultivating vineyards in a country from which they seem at present entirely eradicated; and making from them good substantial wine. London and Bath: R. Cruttwell, 1786. 69p. G40250

VITICULTURE of the Cape Colony. London: Edward Stanford, 1893. 25p. G40260

VITUCCI, Gino. Overseas study tour to observe and study wine grape growing and wine industry in Europe and USA. Canberra: 1976. 16p. Illus. G40270

VIZETELLY, Ernest Alfred and VIZETELLY, Arthur. The wines of France, with a chapter on cognac and table waters. London: Witherby, 1908. 176p. Illus. G40280

HENRY VIZETELLY (1820-1894)

Henry Vizetelly, journalist and publisher, was born to "printers ink"; both his grandfather and father had been printers. Vizetelly's first serious exposure to wine came in 1869 when he was commissioned by the *Pall Mall Gazette* to write a series of articles on the French vintage. (See commentary *Glances Back Through Seventy Years.*)

Vizetelly, living in Paris when the Franco-Prusssian war broke out, was captured and only narrowly escaped execution. Following the war he took up residence outside of Paris and "resumed my studies of the more famous wines of the world and every succeeding autumn for the next half dozen years I visited scores of celebrated vineyards in Champange, the center and south of France, along the Rhine and Moselle and in the Palatinate." Vizetelly's knowledge of wine earned him appointments as a wine juror at the Vienna and Paris exhibitions.

After the death of his second wife, Vizetelly returned to England, resumed publishing and introduced hundreds of books translated from foreign authors. His publications of the works of M. Zola resulted in his imprisonment and his "financial ruin."

VIZETELLY, Henry. Facts about champagne and other sparkling wines, collected during numerous visits to the Champagne and other viticultural districts of France, and the principal remaining wine-producing countries of Europe. London: Ward, Lock, 1879. 235p. Illus. G40290

> In addition to champagne, the author discusses the sparkling wines of Saumur, Sauternes, Burgundy, the Jura, southern France, Germany, Austro-Hungary, Switzerland, Italy, Spain, Russia, and the United States, including New York State and California. Sparkling sauternes was the creation of E. Norman and Co. whose headquarters were in Charente Valley. We are told that Sauternes' "transformation into a sparkling wine has been very successfully accomplished." Samples of a sparkling Barsac were submitted to the Paris Exhibition of 1878.

> This was the precursor of Vizetelly's more famous work *A History of Champagne with Notes on the Other Sparkling Wines of France.* There are 112 illustrations from original sketches.

_____. Facts about champagne collected during numerous visits to the champagne district. London: Vizetelly and Co., 1890. 159p. Illus. G40295

_____. Facts about port and madeira, with notices of the wines vintaged around Lisbon and the wines of Tenerife. London: Ward, Lock and New York: Scribner and Welford, 1880. 211p. Illus. G40300

> In the autumn of 1877 Vizetelly, accompanied by his son, Ernest, visited Portugal, Madeira and Tenerife in the Canary Islands. Before describing his visit to the port wine country, Vizetelly tells us about the wines of Bucellas, Carcavellos and Termo, all from the immediate vicinity of Lisbon. These wines were popular in the 18th century and were imported and served by Thomas Jefferson. Vizetelly's account of port sets out its history and the way in which it was made and provides vivid descriptions of the region and the people.

HISTORY OF CHAMPAGNE

WITH NOTES ON

OTHER SPARKLING WINES.

PART I.

I. EARLY RENOWN OF THE CHAMPAGNE WINES.

The Vine in Gaul—Domitian's edict to uproot it—Plantation of Vineyards under Probus—Early Vineyards of the Champagne —Ravages by the Northern tribes repulsed for a time by the Consul Jovinus—St. Remi and the baptism of Clovis— St. Remi's Vineyards—Simultaneous progress of Christianity and the cultivation of the Vine—The Vine a favourite subject of ornament in the Churches of the Champagne—The culture of the Vine interrupted, only to be renewed with increased ardour—Early distinction between 'Vins de la Rivière' and 'Vins de la Montagne'—A Prelate's counsel respecting the proper Wine to drink—The Champagne desolated by War—Pope Urban II. a former canon of Reims Cathedral—His partiality for the Wine of Ay—Bequests of Vineyards to religious establishments—Critical ecclesi-astical topers—The Wine of the Champagne causes poets to sing and rejoice—'La Bataille des Vins'—Wines of Auviller and Espernai le Bacheler.

ALTHOUGH the date of the introduction of the vine into France is lost in the mists of antiquity, and though the wines of Marseilles, Narbonne, and Vienne were celebrated by Roman writers prior to the Christian era, many centuries elapsed before a vintage was gathered within the limits of the ancient province of Champagne. Whilst the vine and olive throve in the sunny soil of the Narbonnese Gaul, the frigid climate of the as yet uncultivated North forbade the production of either wine or oil.[1] The 'forest of the Marne,' now renowned for the vintage it yields, was then indeed a dark and gloomy wood, the haunt of the wolf and wild boar, the stag and the auroch; and the tall barbarians of Gallia Comata, who manned the walls of Reims on the approach of Cæsar, were fain to quaff defiance to the Roman power in mead and ale.[2] Though Reims became under the Roman dominion one of the capitals of Belgic Gaul, and acquired an importance to which numerous relics in the shape of temples, triumphal arches, baths, arenas, military roads, &c., amply testify; and though the Gauls were especially

[1] Diodorus.   [2] Livy.

B

This is a well-written and interesting account of these wine areas. The author's journeys are illustrated with 100 engravings from original sketches by his son or from original photographs. A valuable reference.

_____. Facts about sherry, gleaned in the vineyards and bodegas of the Jerez, Seville, Moguer and Montilla districts during the autumn of 1875. London: Ward, Lock and Tyler, 1876. 108p. Illus. G40310

This is a first-hand account of Vizetelly's three-month visit to the sherry districts of southern Spain. His initial reports were published in the *Pall Mall Gazette* and were subsequently revised and expanded into this book. This is an interesting book not only because it tells us about sherry, but because of what it tells us about the people, their customs, and their problems. We are told how the vineyards are patrolled by armed guards; the kidnapping for ransom of wealthy vintners; the seductive movements of a gypsy dance; the shooting of prisoners under the pretense of an attempt to escape, and the taste of the wines. A worthwhile book for reading or for reference. Illustrated with sixteen full-page engravings and numerous sketches.

_____. Glances back through seventy years: autobiographical and other reminiscences. 2 Vols. London: Kegan Paul, Trench, Trubner, 1893. 431/432p. G40320

The second volume of Vizetelly's autobiography tells us of his first visit to the wine country in the autumn of 1869. Accompanied by his wife and eldest son, Vizetelly landed in Paulliac ". . . the commune which produces two of the finest wines in the world, Chateau Lafite and Chateau Latour, and three other wines only a shade inferior, namely, Brane-Mouton [Mouton-Rothschild], Pichon-Longueville, and Pichon-Longueville-Lalande: a circumstance which those who are not connoisseurs in wine will properly appreciate when I explain that it is like a picture gallery possessing the two best works of Raffaelle ever painted, and three of Titian's grandest."

He visited Chateau Lafite, Latour, LaRose [now Gruaud-Larose], Cos d'Estournel, Margaux, Haut-Brion and Yquem. At Cos d'Estournel his wife was not allowed into the press-house because the owner held the superstition that "if any woman entered the *cuverie* while the wine was being made it would cause the generous liquor to turn."

At Chateau d'Yquem he describes the annual party that was held when the vintage ended: "[A] fete called *Accabailles*- a Gascon term signifying the finish - was held when all the people who had taken part in the work were entertained at a substantial dinner at which Chateaux d'Yquem, not new or inferior wine, flowed as freely as water. As soon as the feast was over . . . the hugh press-house being lighted up . . . dancing commenced."

From Bordeaux, Vizetelly traveled on to Hermitage, Beaujolais, Macon, Meursault and the Cote d'Or. He observed that the famous

Burgundy wines were made in the "old-fashioned manner of three centuries ago." At Chambertin, he looked in the press-house "where I saw the same ponderous old press at work which used to crush the grapes that produced the favorite wine of the first Napolean. . . ."

_____. A history of champagne with notes on the other sparkling wines of France. London: Vizetelly and Co., and New York: Scribner and Welford, 1882. 263p. Illus. G40330

A remarkable work that traces the history of Champagne and its wine over 1,800 years. But even Vizetelly, for all his research and devotion to champagne, could not answer the perennial question: "Who invented sparkling champagne?"

Vizetelly records many instances of the tendency of the old wines of certain growths of the Marne to effervescence, and quotes from Baccius, the learned physician to Pope Sixtus V, to the effect that in the 16th century there were wines "which bubble out of the glass, and which flatter the smell as much as the taste."

He candidly admits that, despite "minute and painstaking researches," he could not determine when sparkling champagne made its first appearance, and that ". . . it seems most probable that the tendency to effervesce became even more marked in the strong-bodied gray and 'partridge eye' wines, first made from red grapes about 1670, than in the yellowish wines previously produced." Vizetelly was inclined, like many other authorities, to ignore these earlier claims, and to give credit to the Benedictine, Dom Pérignon, for his unrivaled work on behalf of champagne. Whatever may have been accomplished before him is not comparable with what he achieved, not only to the wine itself, i.e., the blending of wines from different vineyards, but in obtaining a perfectly white wine from black grapes (previously gray in color), in perfecting the froth, but also in regard to the development of its corks and glasses. For these reasons, most of the wine lovers of the world are willing to accept Dom Pérignon as the originator of champagne as we know it.

This is Vizetelly's best-known work. It is a revised and considerably expanded version of *Facts About Champagne and Other Sparkling Wines*. The text is strikingly illustrated with 350 engravings, including numerous illustrations from ancient manuscripts and 200 original sketches made under the author's supervision.

_____. A history of champagne with notes on the other sparkling wines of France. Facsimile of 1882 edition. London: Andrew Low Fine Wines Ltd., 1980. 267p. Illus. G40340

A quality fascimile reprint published by the wine merchant, Andrew Low of Suffolk, England. Limited to 500 copies.

_____. How champagne was first discovered and how the wine is now produced; with an account of a visit to the establishment of Messrs. Moet and Chandon, at Epernay, and various recipes for making champagne cup. London: Ward, Lock, 1879. 68p. G40350

Republished by Vizetelly and Co. in 1883 of 73p. and 1890 of 90p., illustrated.

_____. The wines of the world characterized and classed: with some particulars respecting the beers of Europe. London: Ward, Lock and Tyler, 1875. 202p. G40360

VOEGELE, Marguerite C. and WOOLLEY, Grace H. Drink dictionary. New York: Ahrens Publishing, c1961. 192p. Illus. G40370

WAGENYOORD, James. The Doubleday wine companion. Garden City, NY: Doubleday, 1983. 176p. G40395

_____. The wine book. New York: Quick Fox, 1980. 120p. Illus. G40390

PHILIP M. WAGNER (1904)

Philip Wagner is best known for introducing and popularizing French hybrid vines in the Eastern United States. Hybrid vines are genetic crosses between the classic wine grapes of Europe (Vitis vinifera) and certain American species. The object was to combine the wine quality of the European vine with the vigor, hardiness and disease resistance of the American vine. These hybrids were the basis for a new winegrowing industry in areas east of the Rockies, where the classic European species had not succeeded. To carry out his work with these hybrid vines, Wagner and his wife, Jocelyn, established the Boordy Nursery in Maryland. The Boordy Vineyard Winery was a normal outgrowth of the nursery.

The purpose of the winery was to demonstrate that the availability of hybrids makes winegrowing commercially feasible in many parts of this country where grapes had never been grown and wine never made before. The purpose of the nursery was to provide a source for these new grape varieties, then otherwise unavailable in this country. From 1938 to 1943, Wagner was editor of the *Baltimore Evening Sun* and then became editor of the *Baltimore Sun* and remained so until his retirement in 1964.

WAGNER, Philip M. American wines and how to make them. New York: Knopf, 1933. 295p. Illus. G40410

Explains how to make good wine at home. The process is described as "almost as simple as boiling an egg." Second, revised edition of 367p. published in 1936. At the time of its publication in 1933, it was the only English-language book in print on wine making from grapes. Several revised editions.

_____. American wines and wine making. New York: Knopf, 1956. 264p. Illus. G40420

This is a rewritten version of *American Wines and How to Make Them*. It contains references to French hybrid wines. The eighth printing of the fifth edition was published in 1975.

_____. Grapes into wine; a guide to winemaking in America. New York: Knopf, 1976. G40430

The paperback edition of this book is in its seventh printing.

_____. Wine grapes; their selection, cultivation and enjoyment. New York: Harcourt, Brace, 1937. 298p. Illus. G40440

Contains practical material on the varieties of wine grapes best suited to various parts of America, with chapters on vine propagating, vine pruning and training, disease prevention and grape growing districts.

_____. A wine-grower's guide; containing chapters on the past and future of wine-growing in America, the management of a vineyard, and the choice of suitable wine-grape varieties. New York: Knopf, 1945. 230p. G40450

> Subseqent revised edition in 1965 called *A Wine-grower's Guide: An Interesting and Informative Book for the Amateur Viticulturist on the Cultivation of Wine Grapes*. Also reissued under this title in 1972, 224p. and in 1982.

WALCH, G., comp. Glass of champagne: the story of the king of wines with a description of its preparation, mode of storage, and distribution, as carried out by Messrs. Krug and Company. Melbourne: M'Carron, Bird, 1885. 47p. G40490

WALDO, Myra. The pleasures of wine. New York: Gramercy Publishing, 1963. 190p. G40500

WALKER, A. The unfermented wine question. Edinburgh: E and S Livingstone, 1912. 15p. G40510

WALKER, G.J. Prospects for wine grape production in the Shire of Kaniva. Kaniva, Australia: c1971. 201p. G40520

WALKER, Henry. 1001 questions and answers about wine. Secaucus, NJ: Lyle Stuart, 1976. 254p. G40530

WALKER, James (of Leith). Hints to consumers of wine: on the abuses which enhance the price of that article. Edinburgh: Peter Hill, 1802. 57p. G40540

WALLACE, E. The game of wine. New York: Harper and Row, 1977. 381p. Illus. G40550

WALLS, Bill. Southern vineyards sketchbook. Adelaide: Rigby, 1976. 63p. Illus. G40560

WALTER, Frederick. Wine and wine making. Compliment of Fred Walter, with the hope that light, dry wines may be more appreciated. Norfolk, VA: Whitson Press, 1938. 8p. G40570

WARD, Ebenezer. The vineyards and orchards of South Australia. Adelaide: The Advertiser, 1862. 78p. G40580

> Reprinted from a series of articles written by Ward expressly for the *South Australian Advertiser and Weekly Chronicle*. A limited edition of 750 copies was reprinted in 1979.

WARD, H.W. Book of the grape, together with a chapter on the decorative value of the vine by the editor. London and New York: J. Lane, 1901. 97p. Illus. G40590

> Subsequent edition in 1925.

WARD, Jack. The complete book of vine growing in the British Isles. London: Faber and Faber, 1983. 192p. Illus. G40595

_____. Merrydown - wine of Sussex. Merrydown Wine Company, 1966. 19p. Illus. G40600

Preface by André L. Simon.

WARD, Ned (Edward). The delights of the bottle: or, the compleat vintner. With the humours of bubble upstarts. Stingy wranglers. Dinner spungers. Jill tiplers. Beef beggars. Cook teasers. Pan soppers. Plate twirlers. Table whitlers. Drawer biters. Spoon pinchers. And other tavern tormentors. A merry poem. To which is added a South Sea song upon the late bubbles. By the author of the Cavalcade. London: Printed by W. Downing, 1720. 56p. G40610

Third edition of 61p. was printed for Sam Briscoe of London in 1721.

WARNER, Charles K. The winegrowers of France and the Government since 1875. New York: Columbia University Press, 1960. 303p. G40620

Subsequent edition of 303p. was published by the Greenwood Press of Westport, CT in 1975.

WARNER, Ferdinando. A full and plain account of the gout . . . 2nd ed. London: Cadell, 1768. 306p. G40630

Wine receives its share of the blame.

A WARNING piece to all drunkards and health-drinkers: faithfully collected from the works of English and foreign learned authors of good esteeme, Mr. Samuel Ward and Mr. Samuel Clark, and others. With above one hundred and twenty sad and dreadful examples of God's severe judgements upon notorious drunkards. Twelve of the chiefest are graved in copper-plates, to deterr others from like provoking sins, and healths with a huzza . . . London: Printed for the Author, and are to be sold by Langley Curtis, 1682. G40640

Rare.

WARRE, James. Past, present and possible future state of the wine trade . . . London: J. Hatchard, 1823. 102p. G40650

Second edition of 125p., including supplementary notes, was issued in 1824 under a slightly modified title.

WASHBURNE, George R. and BRONNER, Stanley, eds. Beverages de luxe. Louisville: The Wine and Spirit Bulletin, 1911. 98p. G40660

WASON, Betty. Giving a cheese and wine tasting party. New York: Grosset and Dunlap, c1975. 144p. Illus. G40670

WASSERMAN, Sheldon and WASSERMAN, Pauline. Guide to fortified wines. Morganville, NJ: Marlborough Press, 1983. 210p. Illus. G40680

Discusses all the major fortified wines together with a comprehensive list of port vintages.

_____. Sparkling wine. Piscataway, NJ: New Century Publishers, 1984. 288p. Illus. G40685

_____. White wines of the world. New York: Stein and Day, 1978. 236p. G40690

_____. The wines of the Cotes du Rhone. New York: Stein and Day, 1977. 230p. Illus. G40700

_____. The wines of Italy. New York: Stein and Day, 1976. 277p. Illus. G40710

WASSERMANN, Adeline, comp. The Schenley Library bibliography. New York: Schenley Distillers Corporation, 1946. 98p. G40720

WATERS, I. The wine trade of the Port of Chepstow. Chepstow, Australia: Chepstow Society, 1967. Unpaged. G40730

WATERSON, M.J. The U.K. market for beers, wines and spirits 1977 to 1985. London: Staniland Hall, 1978. 55p. Illus. G40740

WATKINS, Derek. Wine and beer making. London: David and Charles, 1978. 128p. Illus. G40750

WATKINS, Michael. Wining and dining in East Anglia. Ipswich: East Anglian Magazine, 1969. 128p. Illus. G40760

WATNEY, Bernard M. and BABBIDGE, Homer D. Corkscrews for collectors. London: Philip Wilson Publishers, 1981. 198p. Illus. G40770

> The authors are co-founders of the "International Correspondence of Corkscrew Addicts," which is limited to fifty members. This work traces the history of corkscrews, their developments in design and mechanical principles. Also published by The Wine Appreciation Guild.

WATSON, Rowland. Merry gentlemen, a Bacchanalian scrapbook. London: T. Werner Laurie, 1951. 240p. Illus. G40780

> "Being a curious diverting and instructive miscellany of the bacchanalian arts and sports, with notes, quotes and comments; the whole having been gathered together for your especial entertainment."

WATT, Alexander. Bordeaux and its wine. Paris: Ministre des Travaux, Publics, 1957. 20p. Illus. G40790

WAUGH, Alec. In praise of wine and certain noble spirits. London: Cassell and New York: William Sloane, 1959. 304p. Illus. G40800

_____. Merchants of wine; being a centenary account of the fortunes of the House of Gilbey. London: Cassell, 1957. 136p. Illus. G40810

_____. Wines and spirits from the Time-Life Books Series "Foods of the World.". Alexandria, VA: Time-Life Books, 1969. 208p. Illus. G40820

WAUGH, Evelyn. Wine in peace and war. London: Saccone and Speed, 1947. 77p. Illus. G40830

An account of the London wine merchants, Saccone and Speed. The illustrations are by Rex Whistler. Scarce.

HARRY WAUGH (1904)

Mr. Waugh's lifelong employment in the wine trade began in 1934 with a position as a clerk with a London wine merchant. After the war, he went to work for Harvey's of Bristol and became their principal buyer of clarets and burgundies. Through talent and hard work, he eventually became a director at Harvey's. Since 1966 he has been a consultant, wine writer and a director of Chateau Latour. He is considered to have one of the best palates in the wine trade and is well known for having responded to the question, "Have you ever mistaken a burgundy for a bordeaux, Mr. Waugh?" by saying: "Not since lunch." Waugh was the first English wine writer to recognize and acknowledge the emergence of California wines. He is one of the co-founders of the London Zinfandel Club and a wine consultant for Les Amis du Vin, the Ritz Hotels of London, Queen Elizabeth II, and others. Among his pupils he lists Michael Broadbent, Collin Fenton, Robin Don and the late Martin Bamford.

WAUGH, Harry. Bacchus on the wing: a wine merchant's travelogue. London: Wine and Spirit Publications, 1966. 203p. Illus. G40850

_____. The changing face of wine. London: Wine and Spirit Publications, 1968. 109p. G40860

Second edition published in 1969 and third edition published in 1970.

_____. Diary of a winetaster; on recent tastings of California and French wines. New York: Quadrangle Press, 1972. 228p. Illus. G40870

Records two years of visits and tastings in French and California vineyards.

_____. Harry Waugh's wine diary, volume six. London: Christie's, 1975. 109p. Illus. G40880

_____. Harry Waugh's wine diary, volume seven. London: Christie's, 1976. 132p. G40890

_____. Harry Waugh's wine diary, volume eight. London: Christie's, 1978. 164p. Illus. G40900

_____. Harry Waugh's wine diary, volume nine. London: Christie's, 1981. 205p. Illus. G40910

_____. Pick of the bunch. London: Wine and Spirit Publications, 1970. 238p. Illus. G40920

_____. The treasures of Bordeaux. Washington, DC: Les Amis du Vin, c1980. Illus. G40930

Limited edition of 1,000 copies.

_____. Winetaster's choice; the years of hysteria, tastings of French, Californian and German wines. New York: Quadrangle, 1974. 209p. G40940

A compendium of wines tasted by the author in France, Germany and the United States during 1971 and 1972. Like his other books, this is a collection of his tasting notes from dinners and tastings.

WAVERMAN, Luey. The penny pincher's wine guide. 1983. 224p. G40950

Reviews more than 500 domestic and foreign wines available in Canada and priced at less than $8.00.

WEAVER, Robert. Grape growing. New York: John Wiley, 1976. 371p. Illus. G40960

WEBB, A. Dinsmoor, ed. Chemistry of winemaking; a symposium . . . April, 1973. Washington, DC: American Chemical Society, 1974. G40970

WEBBER, Alexander. Wine. A series of notes on this valuable product . . . London: Edwin T. Oliver, 1889. 185p. G40980

WEBSTER, T. and PARKES, Mrs. American family encyclopedia of useful knowledge, or book of 7223 recipes and facts: a whole library of subjects useful to every individual. New York: J.C. Derby, 1854. 1,238p. Illus. G40990

Chapter IV (pp. 605-656) covers nearly every aspect of wine. Subjects addressed are: making wine; foreign wines; domestic wines; recipes for making wines; management of the wine cellar; adulteration of wine, and coopering.

WECHSBERG, Joseph. Blue trout and black truffles: the peregrinations of an epicure. New York: Knopf, 1953. 288p. G41000

Mr. Wechsberg was a noted epicure who contributed frequently to *The New Yorker, Holiday*, and *Gourmet* magazines. Though this is not a wine book as such, it does contain chapters on visits to Chateau Lafite-Rothschild and Chateau d'Yquem. He also comments on the wine cellars of a number of France's great three-star restaurants, memorable meals and the wines accompanying them.

At Lafite-Rothschild, he quotes the *regisseur* (manager) as saying, while they shared a bottle of the 1924, "Montaigne, as Mayor of Bordeaux, always took a few bottles along to Paris when he went there to get a loan for the city of Bordeaux. 'I have more faith in the eloquence of our wine than in that of my tongue to move the hearts of those gentlemen in the Louvre,' he would say. How right he was!"

WEINBERG, Florence M. The wine and the will: Rabelais's Bacchic Christianity. Detroit: Wayne State University Press, 1972. 188p. Illus. G41010

WEINHOLD, Rudolph. Vivat Bacchus: a history of wine and its viticulture. Germany: Editions Stauffacher, 1976. Illus. G41020

WEINMANN, J. Manual of the industry of sparkling wines; description of the chemical and practical processes customarily used in Champagne. Translated by Charles A. Wetmore. Piedmont, CA: 1917. 105p. G41030

WEKEY. Sigismund. The land, importance of its culture to the prosperity of Victoria with special reference to the cultivation of the vine. Melbourne: James G. Blundell, 1854. 45p. G41040

WELBY, Thomas Earle. The cellar key. London: Gollancz, 1933. 160p. G41050

_____. The dinner knell, elegy in an English dining-room. London: Methuen, 1932. 203p. G41060

WELD, Charles Richard. Notes on Burgundy. London: Longmans, 1869. 244p. G41070

WELLS, David A. The book of agriculture or, the annual of agricultural progress and discovery for 1855 and 1856. Philadelphia: Childs and Peterson, 1856. 400p. G41080

WELLS, Guy. An intoxicating hobby: the ABC of home-made sugar wines. New York: Comet Press Books, 1959. 38p. Illus. G41090

WELLS, Syd. Fine wines from the desert. New York: Quartet Books, 1980. 134p. Illus. G41100

WENTE, Ernest A. Wine making in the Livermore Valley. 1971. 97p. G41105

See California Wine Oral History Series.

WEST, William. Wine and spirit adulterators unmasked in a treatise setting forth the manner employed and the various ingredients which constitute the adulterations and impositions effected with the different wines and spirits . . . also showing the method by which the notice of the excise is evaded. London: 1827. 128p. G41110

_____. Wine and spirit adulterators unmasked in a treatise setting forth the manner employed and the various ingredients which constitute the adulterations and impositions effected with the different wines and spirits . . . also showing the method by which the notice of the excise is evaded. To which is annexed a brief exposition of the deleterious nature of British brandy, and of the gross frauds which are practised therewith . . . By one of the old school. 3rd ed. London: Robins, 1829. 216p. G41120

WESTLAND, Pamela. A taste of the country. London: Hamish Hamilton, 1974. 167p. Illus. G41130

Contains a chapter on wine-making.

WESTNEY, R. The wine and spirit dealer's and consumer's vade-mecum . . . Edinburgh: 1810. G41140

Unable to verify.

_____. The wine and spirit dealer's and consumer's vade-mecum . . . New ed. London: Sold by Lackington, 1817. 162p. G41150

WESTON, J.M. Wine from where the mistral blows. London: Wine and Spirit Publications, 1981. 85p. Illus. G41160

Deals with the wines of Languedoc-Roussillon and exported under the labels of Minervois, Corbieres, Cotes du Roussillon, Blanquette de Limoux and Fitou. Thomas Jefferson, in retirement, became aware of these wines and imported them to Monticello in cask. His favorites were Claret de Bergasses from Languedoc, Limoux and Ledenon - all red wines.

WETMORE, Charles A. Ampelography of California. A discussion of vines now known in the state, together with comments on their adaptability to certain locations and uses. San Francisco: Merchant Publishing Company, 1884. 22p. G41170

_____. How to raise the price of grapes, and an analysis of the sweet wine law. Sacramento, CA: A.J. Johnston, 1891. 15p. G41180

_____. Propagation of the vine . . . San Francisco: 1880. 25p. G41190

_____. The rational use of wines in health and disease. San Francisco: W.A. Woodward Printers, 1905. 17p. G41200

_____. Treatise on wine production. Sacramento, CA: A.J. Johnston, 1894. 92p. G41210

WHAT, how and where champagne is made. Buffalo: Seaver's Steam Printing Establishment, 1856. G41220

Unable to verify.

WHEATLEY and Sons. Old masters: catalog of old brandies and a few great wines. London: 1930. G41230

This catalog was produced to advertise a collection of exceptionally fine old cognacs. For each cognac, Dennis Wheatley, later known for his novels, wrote a brief historical essay on its period of origin. The illustrations are from original engravings. Limited edition of 1,500 copies.

WHEATLEY, Dennis Yates. At the sign of the flagon of gold. London: Wheatley and Sons, 1930. 14p. Illus. G41240

There are thirteen illustrations made from original engravings that were for many years in the possession of the Tsar of Russia. At the time of publication, the engravings were part of the collection of the author. The engravings are by Jan Van Eyck, Johann Schwartz, Albrecht Durer, Hans Holbein, etc. Limited edition of 1,500 copies.

_____. Drink and ink, the memoirs of Dennis Wheatley. London: G41250

Chronicles Wheatley's years as a wine merchant and his subsequent meteoric rise as a best-selling novelist. This is an account of a young wine merchant who not only sold wine but used it to seduce a succession of young ladies.

_____. 1749-1949: the seven ages of Justerini's. London: Riddle Books, 1949. 85p. Illus. G41260

WHITAKER, Alma. Bacchus behave! The lost art of polite drinking. New York: Frederick A. Stokes, 1933. 140p. G41270

WHITAKER, Tobias. The tree of humane life, or, the blood of the grape. Proving the possibilitie of maintaining humane life from infancy to extreme old age without any sicknesse by the use of wine. London: Printed by I.D. for H.O., 1638. 73p. G41280

WHITE House wine cellar. New Standard Wine Company, c1905. G41290

A prospectus with many illustrations showing vineyards around Keuka Lake. A strong recommendation is made for drinking New York champagne.

WHITE, Anthony G. Architecture of wineries: a selected bibliography. Monticello, IL: Vance Bibliographies, c1982. G41300

WHITE, E.K. Winemaking for beginners. Adelaide: Rigby, 1974. 64p. G41310

WHITE, Francesca. Cheers - a spirited guide to liquors and liqueurs. London: Paddington Press, 1977. G41320

WHITE, O.E.D. A guide and directory to Australian wine. Melbourne: Lansdowne, 1972. 238p. Illus. G41330

WHITEBROOK, William. Art and mystery of brewing and receipts for English wines, laid open to every family. 3rd ed. London: By the Author, 1822. 16p. G41340

WHITEHEAD, Jessup. Steward's handbook and guide to party cartering. Chicago: By the Author, 1889. 464p. G41350

Many subsequent editions.

WHITINGTON, E. South Australian vintage 1903. Adelaide: W.K. Thomas, 1903. 74p. Illus. G41360

WHITMORE, Orin Beriah, Rev. Bible wines vs. the saloon keeper's Bible; a study of the two-wine theory of the Scriptures and an arraignment of the argument for Biblical sanction of the use of intoxicants. Seattle: Press of the Alaska Printing, 1911. 115p. G41370

WHITMORE, William Wolryche. The wine duties. London: Longman, Brown, Green and Longsman, 1853. 33p. G41380

WHITWORTH, Eric W. Wine labels. London: Cassell, 1966. 63p. Illus. G41390

WICKS, K. Wine and wine-making. London: Macdonald, 1979. 96p. Illus. G41400

WIDMER'S WINE CELLARS, INC. The promise of Widmer wines. Naples, NY: 1964. Unpaged. Illus. G41410

_____. Wine artistry. The story of Widmer's. Naples, NY: n.d. Unpaged. Illus. G41420

WIJK, Olof, ed. Eat at pleasure, drink by measure. London: Constable, 1970. 192p. Illus. G41430

WILDMAN, Frederick J. A few wine notes. New York: M. Barrows, 1960. 32p. Illus. G41440

WILDMAN, Frederick S., Jr. A wine tour of France. 4th ed. New York: Wm. Morrow, 1972. 335p. Illus. G41450

A travel guide of French vineyards, restaurants and inns and containing much about wine. Recommended reading for those planning a wine tour of France. Prior and subsequent editions.

WILE, Julius, ed. Frank Schoonmaker's encyclopedia of wine. Rev. 7th ed. New York: Hastings House, 1978. 473p. G41460

Contains significant revisions of Schoonmaker's editions. See Schoomaker, Frank.

WILEY, Harvey Washington. American wines at Paris exposition of 1900. Washington: Gov't. Print. Off., 1903. 40p. G41470

_____. Beverages and their adulteration . . . Philadelphia: Blakiston, 1919. 421p. Illus. G41480

WILKINSON, William Percy. An examination of the wines retailed in Victoria. Melbourne: Australasian Association for the Advancement of Science, 1901. 12p. G41490

_____. The nomenclature of Australian wines in relation to historical commercial usage of European wine names, international conventions for the protection of industrial property, and recent European commercial treaties. Melbourne: Thomas Urquhart, 1919. 54p. G41500

WILLIAMS, C.D. A simple guide to Andalusia. William and Humbert, 1926. Illus. G41520

Andalusia is the southern most province of Spain. The guide describes the principal cities and their points of interest, and the sherry wines of Jerez-de-la-Frontera.

WILLIAMS, D.M. The wine merchant's book of recipes. Glasgow: William Gilmour, n.d. 108p. G41530

WILLIAMS, Edward. Virginia's discovery of silke-wormes, with their benefit. And the implanting of mulberry trees. Also addressing and keeping of vines, for the rich trade of making wines there . . . London: Printed by T.H. for J. Stephenson, 1650. 75p. Illus. G41540

WILLIAMS, Fleetwood. Observations on the state of the wine trade, occasioned by the perusal of a pamphlet on the same subject by Mr. Warre. 2nd ed. London: 1824. 23p. G41550

WILLIAMS, H.I. 3 bottle bar. New York: M.S. Mill, 1943. 64p. Illus. G41560

WILLIAMS, Howard. Home made wine and beer. The manufacture of wines and liquors without the aid of distillation. The art of distilling and rectifying spirituous liquors and alcohol. Home made beers. Cider and fruit brandies. Chicago: Charles T. Powner, 1944. 190p. G41570

WILLIAMS, J.L. The manufacture of flor sherry. Adelaide: 1943. G41580

Unable to verify.

WILLIAMSON, Darcy. Wild wines. Bend, OR: Maverick Publications, c1980. G41590

WILLIAMSON, G.C. An old monastic cellar book. London: By the Author, [192?]. 5p. Illus. G41600

At the request of André Simon, Mr. Williamson interpreted an old [c1375] manual book of the cellarer of the Estates of the Monastery of Polling, near Weilheim, in Upper Bavaria. The author concludes that the book "constitutes a document of great historic value concerning monastic life, monastery rentals, the cultivation of wine, and the districts in Bavaria in which there were then productive vineyards."

_____. Shakespeare's wine book, i.e. William Turner's new boke of nature and properties of wine. London: By the Author, 1923. 20p. G41610

Mr. Williamson contends that Shakespeare used Turner's book as his reference book on wines. (See Turner, William).

WILSON, Iris. William Wolfskill, 1798-1866: frontier trapper to California ranchero. Glendale, CA: A.H. Clark, 1965. 268p. Illus. G41620

This work on Wolfskill, one of California's earliest wine producers, contains information on the growth of California's wine industry from the 1840's to the 1860's.

WILSON, Rev. A.M. The wines of the Bible; an examination and refutation of the unfermented wine theory. London: Hamilton, Adams, 1877. 380p. G41630

Roman Catholic doctrine, and that of the Eastern Orthodox Church, have always held that through the miracle of transubstantiation the bread and wine of Communion become the body and blood of Christ. Even prior to the Reformation this doctrine was a source of conflict. Many viewed Communion as being purely symbolic, or claimed that consubstantiation occurred, which is the mystical union of the believer with Christ and other believers.

It has been apparently accepted by all that the wine used in Communion (or the Lord's Supper in many Protestant faiths) was wine, i.e. fermented grape juice. However, in time, this issue also became a source of controversy. It is not known exactly when the attack on the use of wine in Communion began, but it was especially heavy in the 19th century in England and the U.S. Many Protestant denominations had strong anti-alcohol sentiments and could not accept that Christ would drink alcohol. Many ingenious theories were spun in an attempt to prove that Christ drank unfermented grape juice and to explain what actually occurred when he performed the miracle of changing the water into wine.

Reverend Wilson challenges the unfermented-wine theories. In the preface, he says, "Having been a teetotaler for more than thirty years, my personal habits, associations and sympathies have all been in favor of the unfermented theory, but the facts encountered in the present investigation have constrained me, reluctantly, to conclude that so far as the wines of the ancients are concerned, unfermented wine is a myth." He then proceeds to give his arguments against the use of unfermented wine in Biblical times. In doing so, he effectively repudiates the most "scholarly" of the unfermented-wine theories.

WILSON, Robert Forest. How to wine and dine in Paris. Indianapolis: Bobbs, Merrill, 1930. 122p. G41640

WINE. Alexandria, VA: Time-Life Books, 1983. 176p. Illus. G41650

WINE ADVISORY BOARD

The Wine Advisory Board was created by the California legislature in 1938 and operated under the jurisdiction of the California Director of Agriculture. The board consisted of industry members and had as its main purpose the promotion of California wines. Its operating funds were collected through assessments on every gallon of California wine that was sent into trade channels. Many of its promotional pamphlets and brochures were published through the California Wine Institute. The Board was later disbanded.

The following publications were published by the Wine Advisory Board.

WINE ADVISORY BOARD. Adventures in wine cookery. San Francisco: 1965. 128p. Illus. G41670

_____. California wine cookery and drinks. San Francisco: 1967. 24p. Illus. G41680

_____. California's wine wonderland; a guide to touring California's historic grape an wine districts. San Francisco: 1962. 32p. Illus. G41690

_____. Epicurean recipes of California winemakers. San Francisco: 1969. 94p. Illus. G41700

_____. Favorite recipes of California winemakers. San Francisco: 1963. 128p. G41710

_____. Gourmet wine cooking. The easy way. San Francisco: 1968. 128p. Illus. G41720

_____. Hostess book of favorite wine recipes. n.p., n.d. 29p. G41740

_____. Little wine cellar all your own. San Francisco: n.d. 15p. Illus. G41750

_____. Magic in your glass. An introduction to wine.. San Francisco: Prepared by Wine Institute, 1966. 24p. Illus. G41760

_____. Uses of wine in medical practice (a summary). 3rd ed. San Francisco: 1960. 47p. Illus. G41770

_____. The wine cook boo'k. Fifty-four home tested recipes for making good food taste better. San Francisco: n.d. [1955]. 31p. Illus. G41780

_____. Wine cookery, the easy way. San Francisco: Prepared by Wine Institute, 1966. 24p. G41790

_____. Wines and wines serving. San Francisco: n.d. 28p. Illus. G41810

WINE album. Adapted from *Monseigneur Le Vin*, Paris 1927. Text by Louis Forest. Illustrations by Charles Martin. New York: Metropolitan Museum of Art and Coward, McCann and Geoghegan, 1982. 79p. Illus. G41820

Monseigneur le Vin was not a single volume, but a series of five color illustrated monographs issued between 1924 and 1927 by Etablissements Nicolas, the largest of all French wine retailers. The first volume deals with wines from Biblical times to present; the second describes the wines of Bordeaux; the third is devoted to the wines of Burgundy; the fourth enumerates the other wines of France with descriptions of the regions producing them; the final volume (the volume reproduced herein) covers the wine cellar, decanting, adapting the wine to the menu, how to drink wine, a dissertation on wine glasses, with eight tipped in plates illustrating the correct kind of wine glasses. The text in this version of the fifth volume has been translated from French to English but does not contain the eight tipped-in plates.

The art deco line and color illustrations by Charles Martin (a then prominent illustrator, designer of sets and costumes for the theatre and ballets, fashions, furniture, etc.) have been nicely reproduced and some additional line drawings added that were taken from a four-page advertising insert.

The original fifth book of the *Monseigneur le Vin* series was titled, *L'Art de Boire*, and 32,000 copies were printed by Draeger Freres Press on French vellum paper.

The success of *Monseignuer le Vin*, inspired Nicolas to launch *Les Liste Des Grands Vins*. These catalogs were published annually from 1928 through 1973 except for 1937, the war and immediate postwar years, 1940 through 1948, 1952, 1968, and 1972. The *raison d'etre* of these superb publications was promotional and each catalog contains a list of Nicolas wines and prices and was mailed to favored customers. The catalogs are color illustrated by many of France's best artists, including Kees Van Dongen, Leon Gischia, Jean Hugo, André Marchand, Roland Oudot, Bernard Buffet. The early production of the catalogs was under the supervision of A.M. Cassandre (considered by many to have been the greatest poster artist and typographer of his time) and are excellent examples of the French graphic arts.

In addition to the catalogs, Nicolas commissioned and published several special publications: three folio sized folders of art by Paul Iribe: *Blanc et Rouge* (1930), *Rose et Noir* (1931), and *Bleu, Blanc, Rouge* (1932) and in 1936 *Mon Docteur le Vin* illustrated with nineteen beautiful large black and white and color drawings by Raoul Dufy, typography by A.M. Cassandre and superbly reproduced by Draeger Freres. In commenoration of Nicolas' 150th birthday in 1972, *Le Genie de Vin* was published with thirteen color illustrations by André Derain that had been commissioned in 1948.

WINE AND FOOD SOCIETY OF SOUTHERN CALIFORNIA. Fifty distinguished California wines, selected by the Wine and Food Society of Los Angeles, with a foreword by Maynard McFie. Los Angeles: Ward Ritchie Press, 1941. 23p. Illus. G41830

WINE AND FOOD SOCIETY, London. Lest we forget. Cellar book. London: n.d. 63p. G41840

_____. The Wine and Food Society's library catalogue no. 1. English and American books. 16th thru 20th century. London: 1946. 92p. G41850

WINE AND FOOD SOCIETY, Pittwater. The first twenty years, history of the Wine and Food Society of Pittwater, researched and compiled by the members. Pittwater, Australia: 1976. G41860

WINE AND FOOD SOCIETY, San Francisco. Biennial vintage tour 1967. San Francisco: Wine and Food Society, 1967. Unpaged. G41870

_____. 1946 vintage tour of the San Francisco and Los Angeles branches of the Wine and Food Society to Napa and Sonoma Counties. San Francisco: Grabhorn Press, 1946. 12p. Illus. G41880

_____. 1955 vintage tour of the San Francisco and Los Angeles Wine and Food Societies, September 24-25. San Francisco: Grabhorn Press, 1955. 18p. G41890

_____. A Tasting of California red table wines. San Francisco: Wine and Food Society, 1952. [22p.] G41900

_____. The vintage tour 1950. Napa and Sonoma Valleys. San Francisco: The Wine and Food Society, 1950. 20p. G41910

_____. The vintage tour 1952. Santa Clara and Livermore Valleys. San Francisco: The Wine and Food Society, 1952. 23p. G41920

_____. The vintage tour 1957, Sacramento-Livermore and Santa Clara Valleys. San Francisco: Grabhorn Press, 1957. 14p. G41930

_____. The vintage tour 1959. San Francisco: The Wine and Food Society, 1959. 18p. G41940

_____. Vintage tour of the Los Angeles and San Francisco branches of the Wine and Food Society, September 25th and 26th, 1948. San Francisco: Grabhorn Press, 1948. 25p. G41950

> Contains information on the early work at the University of California College of Agriculture at Davis and on early wine producers.

_____. The Wine and Food Society of San Francisco and the Italian Commercial Attache present a tasting of Italian white, rose and red wines and a display of vermouths, aperitifs, bitters, sparkling wines and liqueurs, Thursday, September 6, 1956. San Francisco: 1956. [20p.] G41960

_____. The Wine and Food Society of San Francisco and the Society of Medical Friends of Wine present a tasting of California white and rose wines, Thursday, June 26, 1958. San Francisco: 1958. [16p.] G41970

_____. The Wine and Food Society of San Francisco presents a tasting of California white, rose and red sparkling wines. San Francisco: Wine and Food Society, 1958. 14p. G41980

WINE and Spirit Trade Review trade directory. London: William Reed, 1967. 389p. Illus. G42020

WINE and the artist. New York: Dover and London: Constable, 1979. 135p. Illus. G42030

> Contains 104 of the prints and drawings contained in the Christian Brothers' collection in the Wine Museum of San Francisco. It is a delightful anthology of pictures about winemaking and wine drinking in mythology and religion—and its place in celebration and humor.

WINE and wisdom, or the tipling philosophers. A lyrick poem. To which are subjoin'd, the most remarkable memories of the following ancients . . . Socrates . . . Plato . . . Epicurus . . . Copernicus. London: 1710. 40p. G42050

WINE—AUSTRALIA; a guide to Australian wine. Written and compiled by the Australian Wine Board. Melbourne: Nelson, 1968. 94p. Illus. G42060

The WINE-BIBBER's temperance society. Boston: Lee and Shephard, 1877. 76p. G42070

WINE butler. Official organ of the Guild of Sommeliers. London: 1955. G42100

WINE cellar album; a personal record of purchases and usage of wine for your greater enjoyment of nature's unique beverage. San Francisco: Fortune House, c1970. G42110

WINE diary 1982. Stellenbosch: Cape Wine Academy, 1982. G42120

The WINE-DRINKER'S manual. London: Marsh, 1830. 296p. G42140

> A well-written account of the best known vineyards and the different processes of winemaking. Chiefly derived from the works of Jullien, Henderson, M'Culloch and other experts of the day.

WINE for profit; knowing, selling Australian wine. Adelaide: Australian Wine Board, 1968. 128p. Illus. G42150

The WINE graffiti book, compiled by "The 4 Muscateers." London: Quiller Press, 1982. Unpaged. Illus. G42160

WINE INSTITUTE

The Wine Institute is a non profit association of California wineries that represents its members in industry-wide matters. Membership in the association is voluntary and currently includes 474 wineries representing over 95% of the wineries of California. Income to operate the Wine Institute comes from dues, with individual wineries paying in ratio to their production volume.

Although policy of the Institute is directed by a board of directors, the day-to-day operations are carried out by a full-time staff. John de Luca is president, and its main office is at 165 Post Street, San Francisco, California. The following were published by the Wine Institute of California.

WINE INSTITUTE. Advertising summary. Wine laws, regulations and inter-
pretations, revised to April 11, 1952. San Francisco: 1952. 38p. G42190

_____. Analysis of foreign markets relating to legal and important re-
quirements and restrictions. San Francisco: 1962. [58]p. G42200

_____. Annual wine industry statistical survey ... 12th, 1948. San
Francisco: G42210

  Issued in three parts each year with tables and graphs.

_____. Before the U.S. Tariff Commission and the Committee for Reci-
procity Information. Brief of the Wine Institute in opposition to the
proposal to reduce the duties on wine and brandies made from grapes
... San Francisco: 1960. 16p. G42220

_____. By-laws (as amended March 4, 1948). San Francisco: n.d. 15p.
G42230

_____. The California wine industry. San Francisco: 1948. [4]p. G42240

_____. California wine type specifications ... San Francisco: 1948. 8p.
G42250

  Recommended as a desirable guide to California wine and brandy
  types for guidance of judges at state fairs. Prepared by the Technical Advisory Committee of the Wine Institute.

_____. California's wine wonderland; a guide to touring California's his-
toric grape and wine districts. 200th anniversary, California wine,
1769-1969. San Francisco: 1968. 30p. G42260

  Numerous subsequent editions.

_____. Definitions of terms for wine salesmen. San Francisco: 194?.
G42270

_____. Dictionary of California wine types. San Francisco: n.d. [8]p.
G42280

_____. Grapes and vines; their varieties and qualities. San Francisco:
n.d. 11p. G42290

_____. Grapes and wine and why they are so essential to the agri-
cultural prosperity of Alameda County. San Francisco: 1946, 1947. [4]p.
G42300

_____. Grapes and wine ... of Alameda County. San Francisco: 1948.
[4]p. G42310

_____. Grapes and wine, keystone of agriculture in Alameda County.
San Francisco: 1948. [4]p. G42320

_____. Grapes and wine, keystone of agriculture in Contra Costa
County. San Francisco: 1948. [4]p. G42330

_____. Grapes and wine, keystone of agriculture in Fresno County. San
Francisco: 1948. [4]p. G42340

_____. Grapes and wine, keystone of agriculture in Kern County. San
Francisco: 1948. [4]p. G42350

_____. Grapes and wine, keystone of agriculture in Kings County. San Francisco: 1948. [4]p. G42360

_____. Grapes and wine, keystone of agriculture in Madera County. San Francisco: 1948. [4]p. G42370

_____. Grapes and wine, keystone of agriculture in Mendocino County. San Francisco: 1948. [4]p. G42380

_____. Grapes and wine, keystone of agriculture in Napa County. San Francisco: 1948. [4]p. G42390

_____. Grapes and wine, keystone of agriculture in Riverside County. San Francisco: 1948. [4]p. G42400

_____. Grapes and wine, keystone of agriculture in San Benito County. San Francisco: 1948. [4]p. G42410

_____. Grapes and wine, keystone of agriculture in San Joaquin County. San Francisco: 1948. [4]p. G42420

_____. Grapes and wine, keystone of agriculture in Santa Clara County. San Francisco: 1948. [4]p. G42430

_____. Grapes and wine, keystone of agriculture in Sonoma County. San Francisco: 1948. [4]p. G42440

_____. Grapes and wine, keystone of agriculture in Southern San Joaquin Valley. San Francisco: 1948. [4]p. G42450

_____. Grapes and wine, keystone of agriculture in Stanislaus County. San Francisco: 1948. [4]p. G42460

_____. Grapes and wine, keystone of agriculture in Tulare County. San Francisco: 1948. [4]p. G42470

_____. Guide maps to California wineries. Prepared for Wine Advisory Board by Wine Institute. San Francisco: 1946-48. 83p. G42480

_____. A guide to wines; California wine land of America. San Francisco: 1958. 32p. Illus. G42490

_____. Home wine cellars. San Francisco: 16p. Illus. G42500

_____. Hot wine drinks. San Francisco: n.d. [4]p. G42510
Ten tested recipes.

_____. Imports of wines into the United States, by principal countries of origin, and total, by years, 1956-1961, inclusive. San Francisco: 1962. 30p. G42520

_____. 1946 wine consumer survey. Prepared for Wine Advisory Board by Wine Institute and J. Walter Thompson Company, August 1946. Cover-title.. San Francisco: 1946. 33p. G42530
Results of 4,000 taste tests.

_____. Selective bibliography of wine . . . San Francisco: 1942. 34p. G42540
A 1944 edition of 40p. and was revised in 1947, 39p.

_____. The story of wine and its uses; a non-technical guide to wine, including wine types, how wine is grown, wine quality, the history of wine, the industry today and a glossary of wine terms. San Francisco: 1963. 49p. Illus. G42550

_____. Thirtieth annual wine industry statistical survey. II. Wine Institute Bulletin 1380, 14p. April 19, 1966; III.

Wine Institute Bulletin 1384, 34p. May 20, 1966. San Francisco: 1966. G42580

>   Published annually.

_____. Wine and health as food . . . in therapy. San Francisco: n.d. 13p. G42590

>   Nine editions.

_____. Wine handbook series, practical, non-technical handbooks on wines and wine-selling. San Francisco: 1943. 4 Vols.Illus. G42600

_____. Wine in American life. San Francisco: Weiss Print., 1970. 59p. G42610

>   A one-day symposium sponsored by the Wine Institute, held in New York.

_____. Wine markets of the United States; survey of state and local prohibition areas, January 1, 1947 . . . Comp. for Wine Advisory Board by Wine Institute. San Francisco: 1947. 48p. G42620

_____. Wine tasting party. San Francisco: 1966. 24p. Illus. G42630

_____. Wines and winemaking; types and techniques. San Francisco: n.d. 21p. G42650

WINE museum of San Francisco. The Christian Brothers Collection. San Francisco: 16p. Illus. G42660

WINE of California. Atchison, Topeka and Santa Fe Railway Company, 1937. [33p.]Illus. G42670

WINE service procedures. Boston: Cashners Books International, 1976. 132p. Illus. G42690

WINE, 1788-1939 — Compiled in the interest of the Australian Wine Industry. Adelaide: Australian Wine Board, 1939. G42700

WINE talk; a symposium. Canberra: Acton Press, 1979. 176p. Illus. G42710

WINE tasting in California. A free weekend. Los Angeles-San Francisco: Camaro Publishing, 1977. 187p. Illus. G42720

WINE TRADE CLUB. The art of wine-making. A lecture delivered at Vintners' Hall, by the Wine Trade Club on Friday, the 22nd March, 1912. London: Crutched Friars, E.C., Palmer Sutton, 1912. 37p. G42740

_____. The vineyards of the world. London: Wyman, 1912. 54p. G42750

_____. Wine and the wine trade; five lectures. London: Wine and Spirit Publications, 1947-50. G42760

>   Vol. 1, 1947, 55p.; vol. 2, 1948, 63p.; vol. 3, 1950, 52p.; vol. 4, 1950, 55p.

_____. Wine Trade Club library: catalogue of books. London: The Club, 1930. 17p. G42770

WINE trade loan exhibition catalog of drinking vessels, also books and documents . . . London: Wine Trade Club, 1933. 92p. Illus. G42780

> This exhibition was sponsored by the Wine Trade Club of London to provide exhibits illustrating the history of the wine trade in England. Aside from a small section of Greek and Roman antiquities, the exhibits were English and covered such items as ancient tapestry, manuscripts, books, drawings, engravings, pottery, drinking horns, cups, wine tasters, funnels, jugs, bowls, silver decanter labels, decanters, drinking glasses, etc. The catalog also includes 135 pages of black and white photographs of the exhibits. The quality of the catalog is perhaps best described in a letter found in one of the catalogs written on Boodle's (an exclusive London private club) stationery: "My Dear Horace: I have been for 1½ hours at the show. The light is too bad to read the documents. The exhibits are good — the catalog is so good that unless you are set on going I doubt if it is worth the time." The books exhibited were compiled by André Simon.

WINE vaults vindicated; remarks from the partial and arbitrary conduct of magistrates with respect to publicans licences . . . with a refutation of the cruel and unjust aspersions cast upon the retailers of wines and spirits . . . London: Hughes, Ludgate-Hill, 1816. 90p. G42790

WINE, what is it? London: Foster and Ingle, 1856. G42800

WINERIES of New South Wales and Northern Victoria. Sydney: Department of Tourism, 1978. Illus. G42820

WINES and Vines yearbook of the wine industry. San Francisco: 1949. 154p. Illus. G42830

> An annual publication of *Wines and Vines* magazine. The 1940-41 edition was the first issue.

WINES, beers and party drinks. London: Macdonal Education for WI Books, 1979. 101p. G42850

WINES, spirits and ales for all occasions. London: County Associations, c1954. 64p. G42860

WINES; what they are, where they come from, how they are made. London: 1952. 24p. G42880

> Reprinted in 1961.

WINE'S whys and wherefores. London: De Tassigny and Gauthier, 1951. 24p. G42890

WINES, Frederic H. and KOREN, John. The liquor problem in its legislative aspects. Boston and New York: Houghton, Mifflin, 1897. 342p. G42900

> Second edition of 425p. published in 1898.

WINKLER, Albert Julius. General viticulture. Berkeley and Los Angeles: University of California Press, 1962. 633p. Illus. G42910

> Considered by some as the definitive book on grape growing.

WINKLER, Albert Julius. Viticultural research at University of California, Davis. 1973. 144p. G42915

> See California Wine Oral History Series.

_____. General viticulture by A.J. Winkler, J.A. Cook, W.M. Kliewer, L.A. Lider. Rev. and enlarged ed. Berkeley and Los Angeles: University of California Press, 1974. G42920

WINROTH, Jon. Wine as you like it. Neuilly-sur-Seine: Int. Herald Tribune, 1981. G42930

WINSTON, Basil J. and FIRESTONE, Ross. Getting into wine. New York: Bantam Books, 1975. 236p. G42940

WISE, Dorothy. Homemade country wines. London: Hamlyn, 1978. 50p. G42950

WISLEY Handbook. Grapes indoors and out. London: The Royal Horticultural Society, 1979. 95p. Illus. G42960

WISTER, Owen. Watch your thirst. A dry opera in three acts. New York: 1923. Illus. G42970

> The setting is Mount Olympus; the cast, Jupiter, Bacchus, Venus and the rest, with Ganymede playing the bootlegger. Gods, men and wine are threatened by Prohibition, but Vice triumphs in the end. Limited edition of 1,000 copies.

WOBBER, Florence. Ballads of the wine mad town. San Francisco: By the Author, 1916. 98p. Illus. G42980

WOELFEL, Barry. Through a glass, darkly. Thirteen tales of wine and crime. Beaufort Books, 1984. G42985

WOOD, Morrison. More recipes with a jug of wine. 9th ed. New York: Farrar, Straus and Cudahy, 1965. 400p. G42990

_____. Through Europe with a jug of wine. New York: Farrar, Straus and Cudahy, 1964. 302p. G43000

_____. With a jug of wine. New York: Farrar, Straus and Cudahy, 1949. 379p. G43010

_____. With a jug of wine. London: Frederick Muller, 1958. 288p. G43020

WOODBURN, Elizabeth. United States alcoholic beverage and grape collection. Hopewell, NJ: By the Author, c1981. 24p. Illus. G43030

> Mrs. Woodburn for many years was a prominent book dealer specializing in horticulture and wine books. She assembled a collection of early American books on viticulture and viniculture that is now housed in the Virginia State Library, Richmond, Virginia.

WOODIN, G.B. All you need to know about wine. Mt. Vernon, NY: The Peter Pauper Press, 1969. 62p. Illus. G43040

WOODLEY WINES. Centenary of Woodley Wines. Glen Osmond, South Australia: 1956. 9p. G43050

WOODWARD, G.M. Elements of Bacchus, or toasts and sentiments given by distinguished characters. London: 1792. G43060

Unable to verify.

WOODWARD, George E. and WOODWARD, F.W. Woodward's graperies and horticultural buildings. New York: By the Authors, 1865. 139p. Illus. G43070

Interesting engravings of mid-Victorian buildings.

WOON, Basil. The big and little wines of France. Vol. 1. London: Wine and Spirit Publications, 1972. 204p. Illus. G43090

A compilation of articles first published in *Wine* magazine as a series of reports from the lesser-known wine districts. Also contains a pronunciation guide titled "The Language of Wine."

_____. The big and little wines of France. Vol. 2. London: Wine and Spirit Publications, 1976. 253p. Illus. G43100

This volume and its predecessor are unusual in that they deal more with the little wines than with the great ones.

WORLIDGE, John. Dictionarium rusticum (gentlemen's companion). London: S. Speed, 1669. 278p. G43120

_____. Vinetum Britannicum or a treatise of cider, and other wines and drinks extracted from fruits growing in this Kingdom. With the method of propagating all sorts of Vinous Fruit Trees. And a description of the New-Invented Ingenio or Mill, for the more expeditious making of Cider. And also the right way of making Metheglin and Birch-wine. To which is added A Discourse teaching the best way of improving Bees. London: Printed by J.C. for Thomas Dring, 1676. 186p. G43130

Second edition, 1678; third edition of 236p., 1691.

The WORSHIPFUL Company of Vintners. Copies of charters . . . London: By the Company, c1900. 67p. G43140

WORTH, W.I. The compleat distillers, or the whole art of distillation practially stated, and adorned with the new modes of working now in use. 2nd ed. London: Printed for J. Taylor, 1705. G43150

Unable to verify.

WORTH, William Y., M.D. A new art of making wines, brandy, and other spirits, complient to the late act of Parliament, concerning distillation . . . Wherein is laid down full and effectual directions, for the making of wholesome and medicinal wines; as also a true and facile way to bring low wines into proof spirits . . . Lastly . . . a general treatise concerning the original and nature of diseases, together with their cure by spagirick medicines. London: Printed for T. Salusbury, 1691. 153p. G43160

_____. The Britannian magazine: or, a new art of making above twenty sorts of English wines . . . More pleasant and agreeable to the English constitution than those of France. With the way of making brandy and other spirits; as likewise how to make artificial clarets, Rhenish . . . 3rd ed. London: Printed for N. Bodington, c1700. 133p. G43170

WORTHINGTON, Richard. An invitation to inhabitants of England to manufacture wines from fruits of their own country. Worcester: Crosby and Co., 1812. 39p. G43180

WRIGHT, Helen Saunders. Judging home-made wine and beer. Andover, England: n.p. G43190

_____. Old-time recipes for home made wines, cordials and liqueurs from fruits, flowers, vegetables, and shrubs. Boston: D. Estes, 1909. 156p. Illus. G43200

> Subsequent editions in 1919 and 1922.

WRIGHT, John. An essay on wines, especially on port wine . . . London: Printed for J. Barker, 1795. 68p. G43210

WRIGHT, Richardson Little. The bed-book of eating and drinking. New York and Philadelphia: Lippincott, 1943. 320p. Illus. G43220

WYNDHAM, Guy Richard C. Port; from grape to glass. London: Wine and Spirit Publications, 1947. 66p. Illus. G43230

_____. Sherry; from grape to glass. London: Wine and Spirit Publications, 1949. 66p. Illus. G43240

WYNN, Allan. The fortunes of Samuel Wynn. Winemaker, humanist, Zionist. Melbourne: Cassell, 1968. 236p. Illus. G43250

YAPP, Robin and YAPP, Judith. Vineyards and vignerons. Dorset, England: Yapp Bros., 1979. 125p. Illus. G43260

> The Yapps import Loire and Rhone wines. Covers the wines favored by the authors. Charcoal drawings by Charles Mozley.

YEADON, Anne and YEADON, David. Wine tasting in California. Los Angeles and San Francisco: Camaro Publishing, 1973. 187p. G43270

YORKE-DAVIES, Nathaniel Edward. Wine and health. How to enjoy both. London: Chatto and Windus, 1909. 103p. G43280

YOUMANS, Edward Livingston. Alcohol and the constitution of man . . . New York: Fowlers and Wells, 1853. 127p. Illus. G43290

YOUNG, Alan. Australian wines and wineries. Cammeray, Australia: Horowitz Grahame Books, 1983. 200p. Illus. G43300

> 1984 edition published by The Wine Appreciation Guild.

YOUNG, Alexander Bell Filson. New leaves. London: Martin Secker, 1915. 276p. G43310

> This volume is composed of a number of essays on various subjects. Two essays that will appeal to the wine lover are entitled "Thirst" and "The Neglect of Wine." "Thirst" deals with the treatment of food and drink in literature and makes the point that many authors who have treated the subject never really understood drink.
>
> "The Neglect of Wine" bemoans the "colossal ignorance" of Englanders on wines and places the blame for this on the English butler, the wine merchant and the family physician. As for the family doctor the author has these good words of advice: "To the

majority of physicians wine is simply wine, a medium for the administration of alcohol in mild doses. The differences in medicinal values between, let us say, a Chateau Margaux 1890 and a Romanée or Chambertin 1904, is a mystery to them; although the alternative and curative properties of the Bordeaux and the toning and vitalising effects of the Burgundy are so different as to be almost opposite in their physiological effects. . . . And one of these days some physician will make a fortune who, instead of studying fashionable drugs, which in his heart he despises, turns his attention to the curative and hygenic properties of different wines; who orders his happy patients perhaps a goblet of Chateau Yquem, or, peradventure, a couple of glasses of Old Tokay - one when the sun is at the meridian, and one when he is at his setting."

YOUNG, E.B. What inducements can we offer to vinegrowing? Adelaide: Burden and Bonython, Advertiser Office, 1892. 12p. G43320

YOUNG, Mathew. Tables of the weight of spirits . . . London: 1830. 15p. G43330

YOUNG, Noel and MACINTOSH, Graham. Wine verities, a portfolio of letterpress prints. Santa Barbara, CA: Capricorn Press, 1971. Unpaged. Illus. G43340

> Eight letterpress bottle illustrations with wine quotes packed around, in and forming wine bottle shapes. Edition limited to 250 copies. Scarce.

YOUNG, Thomas. The epicure: or a treatise on the essence of anchovies, the age and quality of foreign wines, British wines and brandy . . . making cyder and perry . . . [and a] new method of rearing poultry . . . London: Harding, 1815. 88p. G43350

YOUNGER, William. Gods, men and wine. London and Cleveland: Wine and Food Society in Association with World Publishing, 1966. 516p. Illus. G43360

> This book is, as James Laver says in the Foreword, an astounding piece of erudition. Published under the aegis of the Wine and Food Society, it is a profound and successful effort to provide us with a detailed overview of the history of wine based upon all available records, including the major findings of recent archaeological research. It is the most complete and scholarly history of wine and the vine in the English language. Ranging from prehistoric times to the late Victorian era, it covers all aspects of wine from its early use by the gods of mythology to ancient and modern practices of adulteration.
>
> The book opens with a magnificient description of a modern port vintage on the River Douro. The reason for beginning there is that, "The vintage of the modern Douro brings one closer than any other to the feeling of antiquity. It thus reflects into the modern world an outline picture of ancient wine-making. That the flavour of antiquity should happen here in this river valley is an accident, since the Douro is the latest of the great European vineyards."

Following this chapter we are in the shadows of the vine's ancient past and begin a fascinating vinous journey through time. We follow the trail of the vine over the centuries and through various empires. We travel ancient trade routes and participate in the findings of scholars and archaeologists. And since wine in the Western world involved all aspects of man - art, religion, science, war, agriculture - it is not surprising that a reading of the book provides a general history of Western man, especially man of the Middle Ages. Food, weather, customs, living conditions, even the costs of production, are discussed. In effect we are provided with a course in the humanities, filtered through the leaves of the vine.

The book, designed by George Rainbird, is an elegant volume with sixteen full-page color plates and hundreds of black and white photographs of ancient wine scenes and artifacts. Most of the footnotes are set in a wide margin to the right of the text, providing an aesthetically pleasing page. There are eight important appendices - e.g., Wine of Ancient Egypt, Greece and Rome, Measures and Money of Ancient Greece, Medieval wines, and a chapter on "Drinking in America" by John Hutchinson is included.

Mr. Younger, who as a professional writer, wrote both poetry and successful mystery novels, imbues his text with a sense of the excitement and mystery of wine. It is unfortunate that we will see no more books from Mr. Younger, for he died in 1961 at the age of forty-three. In fact, he didn't live to see this extraordinary book through the press. It was completed by his wife, Elizabeth, and a staff of able assistants.

YOXALL, Harry W. The enjoyment of wine. Michael Joseph, 1972. 199p. G43370

Subsequent edition in 1974 by Drake of New York.

_____. The wines of Burgundy. London: The International Wine and Food Society and New York: Stein and Day, 1968. 191p. Illus. G43380

Subsequent editions.

_____. Women and wine. The Saintbury Oration, Privately printed, 1954. 9p. G43390

ZAMARINI, Guido. Tested formulary for perfumes, cosmetics, soaps, liquors, wines and syrups. Mexico City: 1937. 525p. G43400

ZAMORANO choice: selections from the Zamorano Club's Hoja Volante, 1934-1966. Los Angeles: Zamorano Club, 1966. G43410

Seven articles about wine were written by Charles K. Adams, André L. Simon, Phil Townsend Hanna, Marcus Crahan, and Will Clary. Limited to 300 copies. Scarce.

ZANELLI, Leo. Beer and winemaking illustrated dictionary. London: Kaye and Ward, 1979. 121p. Illus. G43420

_____. Home winemaking from A to Z. London: Kaye and Ward, 1971. 135p. G43430

First American edition of 135p. was published in 1972 by A.S. Barnes.

ZAUNER, Phyllis. Wine country: the Sonoma and Napa Valleys. Zanel Publications, 1983. Illus. G43440

ZIEGLER, O.L. Vines and orchards of the garden state: South Australia's fruit growing industry. Adelaide: Mail Newspapers, 1928. 271p. Illus. G43450

ZINFANDEL selections. 20 award winning Zinfandels with winemaker's comments and tasting notes. St. Helena, CA: Colonna, Caldewey, Farrell: designers. Distributed by Vintage Image, 1979. Unpaged. Illus. G43460

ZUPAN, Walter. Viennese heurigen handbook. Austria: Rhein-Donau-Verlag Wien, 1959. 63p. Illus. G43470

In English.

Part
2

Chronological Index

YEAR   CHRONOLOGICAL INDEX

YEAR   CHRONOLOGICAL INDEX

YEAR   CHRONOLOGICAL INDEX

YEAR CHRONOLOGICAL INDEX

YEAR   CHRONOLOGICAL INDEX

YEAR   CHRONOLOGICAL INDEX

YEAR   CHRONOLOGICAL INDEX

YEAR   CHRONOLOGICAL INDEX

YEAR   CHRONOLOGICAL INDEX

YEAR CHRONOLOGICAL INDEX

YEAR CHRONOLOGICAL INDEX

YEAR   CHRONOLOGICAL INDEX

YEAR   CHRONOLOGICAL INDEX

YEAR   CHRONOLOGICAL INDEX

YEAR CHRONOLOGICAL INDEX

YEAR CHRONOLOGICAL INDEX

Part
3

Short-Title Index

SHORT – TITLE INDEX

SHORT – TITLE INDEX

SHORT – TITLE INDEX

SHORT – TITLE INDEX

SHORT – TITLE INDEX

SHORT – TITLE INDEX

SHORT – TITLE INDEX

SHORT – TITLE INDEX

SHORT – TITLE INDEX

SHORT – TITLE INDEX

SHORT – TITLE INDEX

SHORT – TITLE INDEX

SHORT – TITLE INDEX

SHORT – TITLE INDEX

SHORT – TITLE INDEX

SHORT – TITLE INDEX

SHORT – TITLE INDEX

SHORT – TITLE INDEX

SHORT – TITLE INDEX

SHORT – TITLE INDEX

SHORT – TITLE INDEX

SHORT – TITLE INDEX

SHORT – TITLE INDEX

SHORT – TITLE INDEX

SHORT – TITLE INDEX

SHORT – TITLE INDEX

SHORT – TITLE INDEX

SHORT – TITLE INDEX

SHORT – TITLE INDEX

SHORT – TITLE INDEX

SHORT – TITLE INDEX

SHORT – TITLE INDEX

SHORT – TITLE INDEX

SHORT – TITLE INDEX

SHORT – TITLE INDEX

SHORT – TITLE INDEX

SHORT – TITLE INDEX

SHORT – TITLE INDEX

SHORT – TITLE INDEX

SHORT – TITLE INDEX

SHORT – TITLE INDEX

SHORT – TITLE INDEX

SHORT – TITLE INDEX

SHORT – TITLE INDEX

SHORT – TITLE INDEX

SHORT – TITLE INDEX

SHORT – TITLE INDEX

SHORT – TITLE INDEX

SHORT – TITLE INDEX

SHORT – TITLE INDEX

SHORT – TITLE INDEX

SHORT – TITLE INDEX

SHORT – TITLE INDEX

SHORT – TITLE INDEX

SHORT – TITLE INDEX

SHORT – TITLE INDEX

SHORT – TITLE INDEX

SHORT – TITLE INDEX

SHORT – TITLE INDEX

SHORT – TITLE INDEX

SHORT – TITLE INDEX

SHORT – TITLE INDEX

SHORT – TITLE INDEX

SHORT – TITLE INDEX

SHORT – TITLE INDEX

SHORT – TITLE INDEX

SHORT – TITLE INDEX

SHORT – TITLE INDEX